Decade of Betrayal

DATE DUE

Decade of Betrayal

Mexican Repatriation in the 1930s

Revised Edition

FRANCISCO E. BALDERRAMA
AND RAYMOND RODRÍGUEZ

UNIVERSITY OF NEW MEXICO PRESS ■ ALBUQUERQUE

PRINTED IN THE UNITED STATES OF AMERICA
11 10 09 08 07   2 3 4 5 6

LIBRARY OF CONGRESS CATALOGING-IN-PUBLICATION DATA

Balderrama, Francisco E.
   Decade of betrayal : Mexican repatriation in the 1930s /
Francisco E. Balderrama and Raymond Rodríguez.— Rev. ed.
        p. cm.
   Includes bibliographical references and index.
   ISBN-13: 978-0-8263-3973-7 (pbk. : alk. paper)
   ISBN-10: 0-8263-3973-5 (pbk. : alk. paper)
1. Mexican Americans—History—20th century.
2. Mexican Americans—Economic conditions.
3. Depressions—1929—United States.
4. Return migration—Mexico—History—20th century.
5. Mexicans—United States—Economic conditions.
6. Mexican Americans—Employment—History—20th century.
7. Mexicans—Employment—United States—History—20th century.
8. Mexico—Economic conditions—1918–
I. Rodriguez, Raymond, 1926– II. Title.
   E184.M5B35 2006
   323.1168'7207309043—dc22

                          2005024861

Book design and type composition by Kathleen Sparkes
Text in this book is set in Utopia 9.5/14
Display type is Officina

Cover art by Nora Mendoza

■ ■

To our beloved families and heirs,
without whose inspiration and support
it would have been impossible to complete this work.
And to the memory of those whose lives were
affected by the ordeal of repatriation

■ ■

Contents

Acknowledgments

Our sincere appreciation goes to the Ford Foundation and the National Endowment for the Humanities, whose generous grants made this research and project feasible. We also wish to acknowledge the Secretaría de Relaciones Exteriores in permitting us to utilize its Archivo in Mexico City and the U.S. National Archives for their generous help and cooperation in making documents available. And *mil gracias* to repatriation survivors who shared their tragic and illuminating experiences.

A migrant family of Mexicans on the road with tire trouble, February 1936. Photograph by Dorothea Lange, courtesy of the Library of Congress, FSA Project.

Introduction
Saludos

For all Americans, the decade of the 1930s was one filled with frustration and disenchantment. The very tenets of our democratic/capitalistic system came under close scrutiny and vociferous criticism. Some critics diagnosed the system's condition as terminal and predicted its imminent demise. Fed by record unemployment, rampant hunger, and a dulling omnipresent sense of despair, the dire predictions seemed on the verge of becoming realities.

Americans, reeling from the economic disorientation of the depression, sought a convenient scapegoat. They found it in the Mexican community. In a frenzy of anti-Mexican hysteria, wholesale punitive measures were proposed and undertaken by government officials at the federal, state, and local levels. Laws were passed depriving Mexicans of jobs in the public and private sectors. Immigration and deportation laws were enacted to restrict emigration and hasten the departure of those already here. Contributing to the brutalizing experience were the mass deportation roundups and repatriation drives. Violence and "scare-head" tactics were utilized to get rid of the burdensome and unwanted horde. An incessant cry of "get rid of the Mexicans" swept the country.

Although the Mexican community was especially hard hit by the depression and endured incredible suffering, discrimination, and maltreatment, *barrio* residents did not lose hope. With unwavering determination, they withstood the onslaught unleashed against them. In their efforts to survive, a cadre of grassroots organizations developed. However, the lack of resources seriously impeded their efforts to combat the ever-worsening crisis. Nonetheless, the groups made a valiant attempt to assist *colonia* residents as well as Mexicans who decided to leave the United States or were being repatriated. In many instances, those unable to eke out a living, but too proud to accept charity or to apply for welfare, opted to return to Mexico.

For thousands of indigents, the option of returning to Mexico presented what appeared to be a viable alternative to a life and an economy gone sour. Visions and promises of a better life and the push/pull effect of the border convinced many depression-weary families to return to *la madre patria*, Mexico. The bewildered repatriates were victims of a tragedy that they did not understand and which defied all logic. Many believed the depression was merely a scheme to get rid of them and to ship them back to Mexico. This belief was reinforced by the fact that other ethnic groups were not being hassled and repatriated.

Across the nation, colonias and barrios literally disappeared as families lost the struggle to survive. The oft-repeated phrase *"el diablo nos está llevando,"* "things are going to hell," seemed to aptly sum up the situation. A gnawing, fatalistic sense of apprehension prevailed as families remaining behind tried to hang on to the last vestiges of a normal life. There was little the beleaguered communities could do but wait for the depression to end and for the anti-Mexican hysteria to subside.

Many Americans sincerely believed that getting rid of the Mexicans would create a host of new jobs. According to the zealots, alleviating the unemployment situation would automatically end the depression. Succumbing to vocal outcries, employers laid off their Mexican workers. A few employers regretted their action and helped their former workers return to Mexico. Travel arrangements and transportation costs were often shared by local charity organizations and county relief agencies. Welfare officials cynically calculated how much money they could save by getting rid of the unemployed Mexicans. Some businessmen, growers, and church groups felt compelled to protest against the callous, often illegal methods used in expelling the Mexicans. The Spanish-language press on both sides of the border vociferously protested the harsh treatment accorded their compatriots. They resented the fact that no other racial or ethnic group was subjected to as much abuse as the Mexican community.

The Mexican government, although still struggling to recover from the effects of the 1910 Revolution and its aftermath, endeavored to assist returning Nationals and their American-born children. A series of programs and concessions including suspension of import duties, reduced transportation costs, subsidized colonization ventures, and guaranteed loans were implemented. However, the unceasing stream of refugees strained the nation's resources and created a backlash among local residents.

The difficulties encountered in attempting to adjust to two conflicting cultures exacerbated the situation. Adults found that the family and friends they had left behind were now total strangers. The Mexico they remembered no longer existed. For American-born children, trying to adjust to life in Mexico proved to be a very traumatic experience. Their turmoil would not end until they returned to the land of their birth. But the deep-seated scars of rejection by both cultures would remain imbedded in their lives forever.

In recounting the tragic experiences and suffering endured by the Mexican community caught in the throes of the depression, deportation, and repatriation, *Decade of Betrayal* explores the most crucial and significant series of events ever to befall a group of immigrants and their children. It delineates the resultant consequences on both sides of the border, from the American and Mexican perspectives. However, its uniqueness lies in emphasizing the calamitous experiences of the individuals who underwent the ordeal of betrayal, adjustment, and shame. In doing so, it adds to the studies conducted by economist Paul Taylor, anthropologist Manuel Gamio, and sociologist Emory Bogardus during the 1930s. These eminent scholars initiated a new era in the field of American and Mexican historiography by focusing on the role of Mexicans in the United States.

Other researchers did not focus on the Mexican repatriations until the 1970s, with the emergence of the study of Chicano history. Abraham Hoffman's *Unwanted Mexican Americans* emphasized repatriation policy primarily as it was carried out in Los Angeles. Mercedes Carreras de Velasco's *Los Mexicanos que devolvió la crisis* outlined the Mexican government's orientation toward repatriation.[1] Additional depression studies have appeared in the 1980s and 1990s. Significant works have focused on the role of the urban center of San Antonio, Texas; industrial workers in the

Midwest area of Detroit; and the exploitation of women in the canneries of southern California.[2]

More recently, significant studies have appeared contributing to our understanding of repatriation. Repatriation has been explored as a leading factor among others in two respective investigations of the depression. George Sánchez's *Becoming Mexican American* regarded the repatriations in Los Angeles as an influence on the formation of the ethnic and cultural identity of Mexican Americans. In *Mexican Workers and the American Dream*, Camille Guerin-Gonzales studied the American dream, with its promise of opportunity, and how it became a justification for exploitation, including repatriation of rural Mexicanos in California. In *El valle del Río Bravo Tamaulipas, en la década de 1930*, Mexican scholar Fernando Saúl Alanis Enciso also has uncovered new information and presented important findings regarding the policies of President Lázaro Cárdenas and its impact on the repatriation of Mexicans. These works substantiate the impact and significance of repatriation on the Mexican population.[3]

Decade of Betrayal provides the first comprehensive treatment of the repatriation movement in the United States and Mexico. The work chronicles the treatment of the Mexican community by American and Mexican authorities during the decade of the Great Depression. The emphasis is on relating the story rather than exploring sociological theories. *Decade of Betrayal* is a social history rather than historical sociology. The narrative is based largely upon archival materials and oral interviews in order to present a comprehensive view of the Mexican experience during the decade.

The work makes an important contribution to the field of Mexican American and Chicano studies. It adds significantly to the limited number of works dealing with Mexicans and Mexican Americans during the decade of the Great Depression. Consequently, it should be of interest not only to scholars or students of Mexican American history, but also to individuals interested in ethnic or race relations and their effect on society and governmental policy.

In telling this tragic story, a sincere effort has been made to enable readers to understand and appreciate the full extent of the calamity. The courage and perseverance of Mexican Nationals, Mexican Americans, and their children, as exemplified in this volume, should serve as an inspiration not only for their heirs, but for all who share and continue to believe in the American dream. Inexplicable as it may seem, it was that dream that nurtured and sustained many of the repatriates during their banishment and exile in Mexico. The hope and desire to someday return to the land of their birth aided and abetted them when tearful despair seemed to be their only destiny. This was especially true among teenagers who longed to return to their native land. In some instances, many years passed before the dream became a reality. For those who had arrived in Mexico as very young children or as mature adults, there was no reason to return; often there was nothing to go back to. For those who desired to return, the lure of steady jobs and good wages during the World War II era provided added incentive for coming home and fulfilling their dream. A number of young men returned in time to render military service to their country and most did so willingly despite the treatment that had been accorded them and their families.

Repatriates who returned to the United States were so busy assimilating, working, and raising families, that they did not have time, or cared to dwell on the fate that had befallen them in their youth. Few of them ever discussed the ordeal with their children. Bits and pieces of conversation were overheard from time to time but most of their offspring had to wait until the advent of Chicano Studies classes before becoming fully aware of the extent of the deportation and repatriation terror unleashed against the Mexican community during the Great Depression. An interest and burgeoning curiosity led their children and grandchildren to explore the ordeal and to emulate the indomitable spirit exemplified by their elders.

Their quest has been invigorated, in part, by legislative hearings, a lawsuit, and the resulting media coverage. A topic that had been essentially ignored, even in history texts, was suddenly accorded a degree of attention that surpassed anything ever conceived. There is talk of demanding a formal apology, a fiscal remuneration and inclusion of the topic of repatriation in the educational curriculum. The belief and hope is that by creating public awareness, hysteria will not be allowed to overcome an innate sense of decency and fair play, to the detriment of some other unpopular or suspect minority group. A nation that ceases to be governed by law and justice places itself in dire peril.

A truckload of Mexican migrants returning to their homes in the Rio Grande Valley from Mississippi where they had been picking cotton in October 1939. Photograph by Russell Lee, courtesy of the Library of Congress, FSA Project.

Immigration
Al Norte

Voy a los Estados Unidos	*I'm going to the United States*
Para ganar la vida	*To earn a living*
Adiós, mi tierra querida	*Good-bye my beloved country*
Te llevo en mi corazón	*I carry you in my heart*
—"Corrido del Inmigrante"	—"Ballad of the Immigrant"

Changing one's place of residence in the eternal quest for a better life is a common historical phenomenon. The wave of expatriates continues unabated to the present time.[1] The ebb and flow of migration has always resulted in increased tension and apprehension. This has been especially true when immigration involved significant numbers of newcomers or outsiders. Differences in class, language, religion, culture, and race or ethnicity have traditionally tended to estrange new arrivals from the established or native residents. These diverse factors have fostered divisiveness and exerted a negative influence even in modern times. There were many critical factors that determined an immigrant's role and place in their newly adopted society.

Mexicans emigrating to the United States during the early decades of the twentieth century encountered the same problems and challenges as former immigrants. They found that their adjustment to American society was profoundly influenced by such factors as social class, culture, language, religion, and ethnicity. Seemingly, no immigrant group has escaped the stigma attached to their particular nationality or place of origin. All new-comers must "pay their dues" before being accepted or assimilated by their adopted country. By a sheer stroke of fate, massive immigration from Mexico coincided with the end of massive European immigration.

Traditionally, it has been the lure of steady employment and wages surpassing what they could earn at home that has enticed Mexicans to come to America. Not many of them made the trek north with the intention of becoming permanent residents or of seeking U.S. citizenship. They came *por sólo un poquito tiempo* (for only a little while). Most of them intended to return home after they had accumulated a financial nest egg. The passage of time and acculturation to "Yankee ways" dimmed or subverted their original intent. For them, the border was merely an inconvenience. Prior to 1924, traffic moved easily in both directions almost at will and facilitated field hands returning home after the harvest season.

Although Mexicans are often regarded or treated as recent arrivals, they are actually part of a well-established community in the United States. Mexicans have resided in the Southwest—especially in the states of California, Arizona, New Mexico, and Texas—since the halcyon days of the missions and the ranchos of storied folklore. However, the number of Mexican Nationals increased dramatically when immigrants began pouring into the area after the turn of the century. "The large numbers of Mexicans . . . arriving daily to Los Angeles," observed Mexican Consul Guillermo Andrade, "is truly notable."[2] In 1908, economist Victor S. Clark echoed Andrade's observation. In a report to the U.S. Labor Department, he noted that an increasing number of Mexicans were living outside of the Southwest.[3] This dispersement continued to grow over the years. By the 1920s Mexicans could be found harvesting sugar beets in Minnesota, laying railroad tracks in Kansas, packing meat in Chicago, mining coal in Oklahoma, assembling cars in Detroit, canning fish in Alaska, and sharecropping in Louisiana.

Adventurous immigrant families and single men fanned out across the United States from border to border and sea to sea. Among them were Genaro Torres and three companions who worked their way along the gulf states and eventually settled in Portsmouth, Virginia in 1916. There, the town's only Spanish-speaking family befriended them. Torres, formerly a major in Francisco Villa's army, finally felt safe and secure. He had been captured at the battle of Agua Prieta, across the border from Douglas, Arizona, and sentenced to death by the *Federales*, but had escaped. Fearing for his life and safety, he obtained a "safe-conduct pass" to leave Mexico.[4] Like many other immigrants, he had no intention of remaining permanently in the United States. He planned to return to Mexico as soon as it was opportune or safe to do so.

In Portsmouth, Torres got a job in a shoe repair shop and learned the cobbler's trade. Like many married men, once established he sent for his wife, who was waiting for him in the city of Guanajuato with their three young children. Before joining the *Villistas*, Torres had been the mayordomo of a local *hacienda*. Due to his influential connections, his wife, Wenceslada, affectionately known as Vence, was able to obtain a letter guaranteeing her safe passage to the border. This enabled Vence to join her husband Genaro without any serious incident, even during the chaos of the Mexican Revolution.[5]

The massive flow of Mexicans to the United States grew dramatically during and after the 1910 Mexican Revolution. The increase was reflected in the official statistics of the United States Immigration and Naturalization Service as well as in reports of Mexico's Secretaría de Relaciones Exteriores (SRE), the Department of Foreign Relations. While the two governments varied in their reporting procedures, the assessments by both indicated that at least half a million Mexicans entered the United States legally between 1899 and 1928.[6] United States census takers in 1930 calculated that approximately 1,422,533 Mexican Nationals and Mexican Americans lived in the United States.[7] Knowledgeable historians and demographers have concluded that by 1930 more than 10 percent of Mexico's entire population was residing in the United States.

The preceding statistics were undeniable evidence that Mexicans were the largest new immigrant group in the United States. These quantitative figures provided misleading undercounts. Research indicates that in all probability more than a million Mexicans entered the United States before the advent of the Great Depression. These revised estimates have taken into account those who entered without proper documentation. These undocumented migrants, as is the case even today, feared detection and avoided government surveys and census takers.[8] Even though a precise count was impossible, Mexican emigration was truly phenomenal and ranks as one of the great mass movements in history. The onset of immigration drastically transformed the nature and character of the Spanish-speaking population in the American Southwest. It also added extensively to the growth of Mexican colonias and enclaves in other parts of the United States. Except for the state of New Mexico, where the offspring of the settlers who came during the Spanish/Mexican era remained a majority, in other areas the new immigrants quickly outnumbered the original Spanish or Mexican residents.

Mexican immigrants were usually associated with unskilled, backbreaking jobs and marginal or menial occupations. The Dillingham Commission Report, an early immigration study, noted that "the members of this race have always been the hewers of wood and drawers of water."[9] The caste-like employment pattern that developed was a very effective way of denying Mexican Nationals as well as native-born U.S. Mexicans the opportunity to attain better or higher-paying jobs. Even though some Mexicans had the requisite skills, training, or experience qualifying them for skilled positions, they were restricted to *pico y pala*, or pick and shovel work. The prevailing discrimination encountered in seeking meaningful employment was readily attested to by many early immigrants. Merchant Eduardo Negrete and optometrist Dr. Reynaldo Carreón recalled the prejudicial treatment accorded them by American society when attempting to market their goods and services.[10]

In spite of being relegated to unskilled, poor-paying jobs, Mexicans continued to trek north. During the early part of the century, crossing over into the United States was relatively easy. Immigrants Ramón Curiel from Jalisco, Pablo Alcántara from Durango, and Jesús Casárez from Michoacán all recalled that their entry into the United States consisted merely of walking or wading across the border. Others, such as Juan Rodríguez, avoided the inconvenience of wading the river by paying a penny to walk across a small footbridge spanning the Rio Grande.[11] These and numerous other testimonies confirm the fact that there were few legal barriers imposed on Mexican immigration during the early decades of the twentieth century. It should be noted that Congress did not impose the eight-dollar head tax or require Mexican Nationals to pass a literacy test until 1917.[12] While many immigration laws were passed during this early period, their enforcement was usually extremely lax.

There were seldom more than sixty Bureau of Immigration agents stationed along the entire length of the U.S.–Mexican border at any one time. This was ludicrous, to say the least, for the International Boundary between the two countries stretches from the Pacific Ocean to the Gulf of Mexico. This is a distance of nearly two thousand miles and spans the states of California, Arizona, New Mexico, and Texas. In 1924, Congress, recognizing the growing traffic along the border, belatedly established the U.S. Border Patrol with a complement of 450 agents. This limited force was responsible for patrolling both the Mexican and Canadian borders. The primary impetus for creating the new agency was to stop the smuggling of Asians and Europeans into the United States. Those aliens, rather than the Mexicans, were perceived as a threat to the integrity of America's northern and southern borders. Although deterring Mexican immigration was not the main concern of the bill, the new legislation did establish regulations that could be applied to immigrants from Mexico.[13]

However, the Border Patrol and the Immigration Service exercised their extensive police powers selectively. This was done in order to serve the needs of influential growers and industrialists. Regulations were loosely enforced when Mexican workers were needed to harvest crops or increase production in the mines or on the assembly lines. Conversely, the strict letter of the law was applied when Mexican labor exceeded the seasonal demand. Then, deportation raids at the work sites, usually before payday, became common occurrences. The raids were sometimes conducted at the request of unscrupulous employers. The Border Patrol and the Immigration Service were often assisted in their roundups by local police and sheriff's deputies.[14] It is therefore not surprising that Mexican communities viewed local law-enforcement agencies with fear, enmity, and distrust.

Although the United States government did not consider the Mexicans a serious immigration threat during the early twentieth century, neither were they greeted or welcomed with open arms. Mexicans were often accorded rude treatment, even when following official procedures and seeking legal entry. Immigration officials consistently displayed disdain and obnoxious behavior toward Mexican Nationals. Immigrants were repeatedly forced to wait long, tedious hours before being serviced. It was not unusual for them to wait patiently all day long only to be told that they must return again the following day and endure the same arduous procedure. During the process, all immigrants, men, women, and children, were herded into crowded, examination pens. As many as five hundred to six hundred persons were detained there for endless hours without benefit of drinking fountains or toilet facilities. Mexican immigrants viewed the mass public baths and clothing disinfections as indignities.[15]

The immigrants resolutely endured these degrading procedures because they had no other choice. America provided their only hope for a better life.

Parents sought gainful employment for themselves and educational opportunities for their children. Neither of these was deemed readily available in their native land. A variety of socioeconomic and political factors combined to generate and foster the compelling necessity to leave the land of their birth. For Mexicans, a major factor contributing to their plight was the scarcity of good farmland. Early twentieth-century Mexico was an agriculturally oriented nation. Over 90 percent of the people lived on farms, ranches, or in rural villages. Yet, despite long, arduous backbreaking work, even in the best of times, its agrarian population barely eked out a living. Each year, fewer and fewer farmers were able to support themselves by tilling the increasingly marginal land. The amount of good farmland barely equaled that found in the combined states of Iowa and Nebraska.

Sparse rainfall also made agriculture a difficult and precarious undertaking. Only about 12 percent of Mexico receives adequate and timely rainfall. This is particularly critical in the Central Plateau, where the majority of the Mexican population has traditionally resided. Only 10 percent of the Central Plateau is suitable for the production of foodstuffs. This region includes the states of México, Guanajuato, San Luis Potosí, Querétaro, Hidalgo, Jalisco, and Aguascalientes. This area contributed more than two-thirds of Mexico's immigrants to the United States.[16] Compounding the situation was Mexico's dramatic increase in population. Demographers have estimated that Mexico mushroomed from approximately nine million people in 1876 to over fifteen million inhabitants in 1910.[17]

Coincidentally, this period encompassed the dictatorship of Porfirio Díaz. Under his reign, Mexico experienced an expanding land monopoly controlled by a few rich agriculturalists, commonly referred to as *hacendados*. These individuals were often foreign or absentee landowners living in Mexico City, the United States, or Europe. Aided by favorable government legislation and a sympathetic legal system, these land barons acquired massive tracts of Mexico's national domain as well as control of *ejidos*, lands formerly farmed collectively.[18] This avaricious accumulation of land resulted in over five million families losing their small farms or plots of land. In 1910, the agricultural population of Jalisco, Michoacán, and Guanajuato was at a record high of approximately 2,537,625 persons. Nonetheless, only 3.2 percent of the rural heads of households owned any property.[19]

The disparity between the increase in population and the loss of land and homesteads made life in the countryside extremely austere for countless *campesinos,* or farm workers. These two factors created a large, landless labor force that could be readily exploited. Wages for rural peasants never rose above fifteen cents per day from 1876 to 1910, the span of the *Porfiriato* dictatorship. Whereas wages remained low, the costs of basic commodities and food increased significantly. The price of corn, the staple of the poor working class, rose by more than 50 percent from 1877 to 1903.[20] Such a momentous increase in this vital mainstay of the campesino's diet was due to a shift in agricultural priorities.

A booming international market for sugar, coffee, henequen, cotton, and cattle meant greater profits. This financial windfall convinced large landowners to shift to ranching and the cultivation of export crops. Predictably, less land was allocated to the planting of crops required for sustaining the *peones'* meager diet. Visitors to the Porfirian countryside often encountered campesinos who were barely able to subsist on a near-starvation diet of corn tortillas, beans, and a few vegetables. Hunger and malnutrition were accepted facts of life. Reports of actual starvation in the Mexican countryside were not uncommon.

Accolades were heaped on Porfirio Díaz's administration for creating a stable government and a profitable commercial environment. This achievement was attributed to the *pax porfiriato*, the first prolonged era of peace and order in Mexico since the overthrow of Spanish rule. An equally critical factor was the extensive increase of foreign investments. Given what amounted to carte blanche by the government, foreign investors took the lead in developing the lucrative oil and railroad industries. Foreigners were also the chief proponents in reviving the mining and textiles industries, which once had been thriving enterprises but had been allowed to languish and stagnate.

This overpowering foreign influence gave rise to the popular refrain, "Mexico, mother of foreigners and stepmother of Mexicans." The statement probably best summarized the pro-foreign policies and practices of the Porfiriato regime. In reality, along with foreign entrepreneurs, a small, elite native bourgeoisie developed. It believed fervently in the sanctity of the free-market concept of supply and demand. However, the vast majority of Mexicans did not share in nor benefit from the nation's economic growth. To the contrary, low wages and a declining standard of living further eroded the miserable lot of the average campesino. Thus, many of them, in their relentless search for survival, were forced to leave their rural *pueblos* and mountain villages in the hope of earning a decent living elsewhere. A few were fortunate enough to find gainful employment in the revitalized mining and textiles industries or in the new oil exploration and railroad-building enterprises. A campesino could earn fifty cents a day working on the railroad, or *el traque*.[21] It was a skill many of them would later find useful in the United States.

By Mexican standards, wages were significantly higher in the northern part of the country. In comparison to other regions, the frontier borderlands traditionally provided better employment opportunities. This was apparent even during the turn of the century. Miners who earned twenty-five cents a day in the Central Plateau could earn three times as much in the quarries of the northern border states.[22] In spite of the rigorous climate and harsh conditions, the lure of a living wage was too tempting to resist. Once in northern Mexico, the substantially higher wages and steady work to be had on the American side of the border acted as an irresistible magnet. Campesinos simply crossed the *línea,* or international boundary. According to Lucas Lucio, José B. Solórzano, and Enrique Vásquez, these aspects were irresistible factors in influencing their personal decision to emigrate to the United States.[23]

Although pressing economic need was the overwhelming force compelling Mexicans to cross the Río Bravo del Norte, some immigrants were also victims of the political turmoil sweeping the country. The Revolution of 1910, the first social revolution of the twentieth century, began as a crusade against the tyrannical and corrupt dictatorship of Porfirio Díaz, but it soon developed into a bitter civil war to determine which revolutionary faction would rule Mexico. The Revolution shook the very foundations of Mexico's rigid society. It is frequently cited as a major factor in inducing Mexicans to emigrate. Yet contrary to this popular belief, immigration figures during the war-torn period from 1910 to 1920 were lower than for either the ante- or postbellum years.[24] The ensuing land-tenure issue was more effective in driving people out of Mexico than the war's lethal bullets or its wanton destruction had been.

The Revolution and its bitter aftermath created a situation that gave the United States an aura of a safe haven. The refugees included not only poor campesinos but also *gente decente,* or people of stature. Among the latter was Adolfo de la Huerta, a major political figure who had served as interim president in 1920. After leading an unsuccessful rebellion against President

Alvaro Obregón in 1923, de la Huerta, like many of his disillusioned compatriots, fled to the United States.

Many Catholics seeking sanctuary from the religious upheaval and persecution that followed the Revolution also fled the country. Since gaining its independence from Spain, the central government's relationship with the Catholic Church can best be characterized as tenuous. Nevertheless, a *modus vivendi* had been worked out between the two entities during the Díaz dictatorship. However, the Revolution disrupted the government's precarious relationship with the Roman Catholic Church. Apart from the government, the Church with its vast wealth was the nation's second major institution. Its position was unquestionable since approximately 50 percent of the land was owned or controlled by the Church.

Open confrontation between the Church and the revolutionary government flared when Archbishop Primate José Mora y del Río, the Church's leading spokesman, publicly opposed implementation of the 1917 Constitution. Church leadership viewed the Constitution as a charter for the secularization of Mexico because it espoused the socialist principles and ideals of the Revolution. The revolutionary document sanctioned what the Church considered were radical changes in areas that had traditionally been within its domain. The Church's primary objection was the secularization of public education. It was not prepared to cede control over the minds and morals of the young to a government espousing socialistic ideas.

In essence, the gauntlet had been thrown down and the Church could either submit or defy the government, by force if necessary. The leaders of the holy crusade managed to mobilize and field armies against the revolutionary infidels. Marching under the banner of "*Viva Cristo Rey*!" "Long, live Christ the King!," some twenty-five thousand Catholics fought the government's armies from 1926 to 1929. The battle cry of "Viva Cristo Rey" christened this insurrection as the Cristero War or the Cristero Revolt. The government's ruthless suppression of the rebellion precipitated enormous destruction of property and loss of life. Due to the vast amount of destruction in the El Bajío region, the area accounted for over 50 percent of the immigrants fleeing Mexico during the height of the revolt in 1926 and 1927.[25] Resident expatriates, among them Catholic lay leaders José David Orozco and Julio C. Guerrero, welcomed their banished compatriots.[26]

The Cristero Revolt affected families on both sides of the border. Among those adversely affected by the Cristero Revolt were Genero Torres and his family, who had earlier settled in Portsmouth, Virginia. In 1924, the family decided it was safe to return to *la madre patria* (motherland) and made their way from Virginia to El Paso. "There, we learned that the Cristero Revolt was brewing," recalled Dan Torres, who had been born while the family lived in Virginia.[27] "Since we were Methodists, we did not believe it would be safe for us to continue our journey. Since we had relatives in California, it seemed a good time to visit them. My dad eventually opened his own shoe repair shop and earned his living as a cobbler."[28]

Although the revolutionary government prided itself on overthrowing the dictatorship of Porfirio Díaz and crushing the religious revolt, it was not able to cope with the emigration problem. Emigration actually increased after the 1910 Revolution, much to the chagrin and embarrassment of the new ruling junta. Part of the exodus was due to circumstances beyond the new government's control. A decade of war had claimed one-tenth of Mexico's population and its economy was in ruins. The Cristero Revolt and de la Huerta's insurrection made a bad situation worse. As a result, the government was saddled with financial and social obligations that it was not in a position to resolve.

Plagued with a myriad of domestic problems, the question of emigration was assigned a low priority as the nation struggled to survive. Despite its internal problems and chaotic state, the revolutionary government did attempt to provide some degree of protection for citizens emigrating to the United States. It endeavored to do so via the provisions in Article 123 of the 1917 Constitution. Article 123 stipulated that Mexican immigrants must have a valid, signed contract indicating hours, wages, and conditions of employment. By 1920 the government had designed a model contract to facilitate implementation of the stated requirements. Unfortunately, this administrative gesture was doomed to failure because the contract proved to be legally unenforceable. Effective implementation required the cooperation of the American government, but it was not forthcoming. The proposed contract, therefore, could not be relied upon to produce any benefits.

In truth, both nations benefited by ignoring Article 123's protective constraints. Like the Porfiristas, the revolutionary government recognized that emigration served as an important safety valve for relieving political and economic pressures at home. Each campesino who left lessened the burden on the nation's faltering economy. It also meant one less malcontent demanding economic change and political reform. A recurring benefit to the local economy was the fact that Nationals in the United States regularly sent money home to their families. This financial largesse helped to relieve economic pressure on the government.

Especially effective in attracting Mexican workers to the United States was the presence of American economic interests in Mexico. American businesses played key roles, particularly in the major industries of mining, ranching, and railroads prevalent in northern Mexico. Investor William Cornell Green operated mines in Cananea, mining magnate Solomon R. Guggenheim built smelters in Monterrey, and mogul William Randolph Hearst owned ranches in Chihuahua.[29] American companies conducting business in Mexico frequently transported Mexican employees across the border to American plants and facilities. A classic example was Anaconda Copper, which relocated Mexican employees as early as 1908 from northern Sonora to southern Arizona.[30]

Railroad companies and agricultural bureaus followed the example of Anaconda Copper. Other companies preferred obtaining Mexican labor through the use of free-lance labor contractors known as *contratistas* or *enganchistas*. Enganchistas, representing major American firms, were common in the border cities by the end of the first decade of the twentieth century.[31] A recruitment handbill distributed by the Ford Motor Company enticed José Santos Herrada and other Mexicans to leave San Antonio, Texas and to relocate in Detroit, Michigan. The lure of steady work and earning five dollars a day as promised in the handbill was impossible to resist.[32] In addition to recruiting workers in the border states, enganchistas frequently crossed the border, going as far south as the Central Plateau in a relentless search for Mexican labor. Although the hiring of Mexicans to work in the United States was in clear violation of the contract labor law of 1885, seldom did the contratista's flagrant disregard of the law lead to criminal charges, convictions, or substantial fines. J. O. White Driggs, of Idaho, for example, frequently advertised for Mexican workers to harvest peas and consistently failed to pay wages. According to numerous complaints received by the Mexican Embassy, he was over $5,000 in arrears.[33] Recovery of lost wages was virtually impossible and unscrupulous employers defaulted workers with impunity. Often, they were abetted by law enforcement officials.

The enormous profits to be made from the illicit traffic were too tempting and made the risk worthwhile. Additional profits were drawn from fees garnisheed from the wages of the workers. Excessive profiteering was generated by charging the workmen exorbitant prices for transportation and sustenance.[34] Among the more notorious cases of ill treatment by enganchistas was the virtual imprisonment of Mexican laborers on ships from San Francisco and Seattle bound for the salmon canneries in Alaska. Money paid in advance enticed Mexican workers to sign contracts to work in Alaska. Contracts were written only in English and were usually incomprehensible to most Mexican workers. The contracts required cannery workers to follow all orders given by the foreman: to work all day, seven days a week, and to eat only Chinese food. The employees were also required to waive all rights to request higher wages or better working conditions.[35] As early as 1917, the Mexican embassy complained to the American State Department upon learning of Mexican workers being shanghaied to Alaska. Even though the State Department requested action from both the Department of Labor and Department of Commerce, the Mexican embassy reported that "nothing tangible has been obtained." This violation of human rights continued unabated. In 1931, fourteen years later, Mexico City's *El Universal Gráfico* headlined "5,000 Mexicans living as virtual slaves in Alaska." The newspaper claimed that "thousands of Mexicans were stranded in California without work," and were willing to sign up for jobs in the canneries.[36]

The contratistas were a vital factor in providing the workers needed for the spectacular economic growth taking place in the southwestern states of California, Arizona, New Mexico, and Texas. Mexican labor was needed to produce the raw materials and foodstuffs required by the burgeoning industrialization in the Northeast. The number of Mexican workers in the United States increased significantly. The need for cheap labor coincided with the restriction of immigration from Asia and Europe. Beginning in the 1880s, exclusionary laws denied entry to Asian immigrants, particularly to the Chinese and Japanese. Massive European immigration was severely curtailed by the outbreak of World War I. Fear of Bolshevism and disillusionment with postwar Europe resulted in the enactment of immigration quota laws in 1917, 1921, and 1924.[37]

Afraid that the emerging immigration quotas would severely restrict their accessibility to Mexican workers, growers and ranchers took their case to Congress. Agriculturists clamored for the right to import the Mexican workers needed by corporate agriculture and large-scale ranching. Massive reclamation and irrigation projects had been undertaken with the passage of the Newlands Reclamation Act in 1902. These projects made possible the extensive irrigation required for planting melons in the Imperial Valley of California, citrus crops in the Rio Grande Valley of Texas, and cotton in the Salt River Valley of Arizona. The sudden extensive development made a cheap source of labor necessary. Growers pleaded for the admission of Mexican workers because "nothing else was available."[38]

Profitable farming depended on a skilled and readily available labor force. Agricultural production, particularly during the critical harvest season, entailed a labor-intensive process employing vast numbers of agricultural workers. Even more workers were required with the advent of refrigerated railroad cars and improved methods of preserving and packaging vegetables. Perishable, but highly profitable, exotic fruits and vegetables could now be shipped to the heavily populated eastern cities. Farmers and ranchers first doubled and then tripled production as markets grew and profits soared.

Agricultural expansion stimulated extensive railroad construction in the Southwest. By 1909 there were six railroad companies servicing the region. They employed more than six thousand Mexicans to lay track and to maintain the right-of-way. Working on el traque provided ready employment and a relatively easy transition for many Mexicans. Many of those who laid track in Mexico before migrating north found employment on American railroads. Working on the various railroad lines contributed significantly toward establishing a Mexican presence beyond the Pacific Southwest. As a result of their jobs, Nationals traveled to the Pacific Northwest, the Midwest, the Northeast, and virtually every other region of the country. Slowly, around each rail terminus, new enclaves developed. A classic example was Chicago, with a population of approximately twenty-five thousand Mexicans. In Chicago, in addition to working for the railroad, Mexicans secured employment in meat-packing plants, in machine shops, in steel mills, and on the assembly lines. In 1928, the Mexican Consulate in Chicago reported that Mexicans were obtaining better jobs and estimated that "more than four hundred young Mexicans" were employed as clerks and semiskilled workmen by Stewart Electric, International Harvester, Victor X-Ray, and Western Electric. Better-paying jobs in similar industries were also available to Mexicans in Omaha, Gary, Pittsburgh, Detroit, and other major cities of the Midwest and Eastern seaboard.[39]

Only the sugar-beet industry rivaled the railroads in serving as a powerful catalyst in establishing Mexican communities where none had ever existed before. The presence of Mexicans outside of the American Southwest, especially in the Midwest and the mountain states, astonished American society. "How in the world did they [the Mexicans] get way up here; when and why did they come?"[40] The preceding comment was how the International Institute of the Young Women's Christian Association (YWCA) began its report on Mexicans in St. Paul, Minnesota. In investigating the Mexicans, as part of its mandate to assist immigrants and ethnic groups in adjusting to American society, the International Institute concluded that prejudice and lack of education were the two outstanding problems faced by Mexican immigrants. The YWCA study was surprised to discover that there were some 1,459 Mexicans living in St. Paul, Minnesota and observed that many of them were former employees of members of the Sugar Beet Growers Association.[41]

The important relationship between the Mexican and the sugar-beet growers began when the Dingley Tariff Act of 1897 placed a high tax on foreign sugar. This tariff made domestic production of sugar highly profitable, and the sugar beet industry boomed. The industry expanded dramatically from producing 793,000 tons of sugar in 1899 to 3,902,000 tons in 1909 and 7 million tons in 1929.[42] According to a 1933 estimate, the Mexican beet-worker population totaled "55,000, one-third more than in the late 1920s."[43] The *betabelero*, the Mexican sugar-beet worker, became the primary source of labor. They replaced the Poles, Russians, and others who had labored in the fields before the 1929 immigration quota law went into effect.

Mining also experienced an unprecedented boom. As in agriculture and manufacturing, mining required a readily available and cheap labor force. Mexicans filled this need perfectly. They usually worked longer shifts and did the most perilous jobs in the bowels of the earth without proper safeguards, lighting, or ventilation. In spite of this, they were paid only half of what white miners earned. The mines were situated in isolated company towns, and workers were strictly segregated. No fraternization or interaction between Mexican and Anglo miners was permitted. Among the worst offenders was the Phelps-Dodge Company. On one occasion when workers rioted demanding better housing, pay, and working conditions, the protesters were hauled hundreds of miles into the desert and abandoned. No water, food, or means of transportation were provided. It was a severe object lesson for others who might hold similar ideas.[44]

Given the significant contributions made by Mexican workers, when

Congress considered applying immigration quotas to Mexico in 1928, growers and ranchers objected strenuously. Among them was Fred H. Bixby, a
prominent Southwest rancher with some 100,000 acres in California and
250,000 acres in Arizona. In an impassioned plea, Mr. Bixby stated: "We
have no Chinamen, we have no Japs. The Hindu is worthless, the Filipino is
nothing, and the white man will not do the work."[45] Similar protests were
heard from Texas to Alaska and from California to New York. Opposition to
restricting immigration was voiced not only by ranchers and farmers, but
by industrialists and mine owners as well.

Efforts to restrict Mexican immigration peaked when potent anti-
immigration bills were introduced by East Texas Congressman John O. Box
and Georgia Senator William J. Harris. Ostensibly, the measures sought to
limit immigration from the Western Hemisphere. But opponents believed
the true intent was to curb immigration from Mexico. Box and Harris represented cotton-growing areas. Their constituents wanted to reduce or
eliminate competition from cotton growers in the Southwest who were
employing Mexican labor.[46]

The proposed immigration-quota bills reflected the fears of many
politicians, community leaders, and civic organizations. These groups often
labeled Mexican Nationals as "the most undesirable people to come under
the flag."[47] Newspapers in Mexico and Spanish-language newspapers in the
United States launched a vigorous campaign disparaging the United States
for its racist attitudes and calling for the defeat of the proposed legislation.

Eventual defeat of the Harris/Box bills, however, was due primarily to
international repercussions rather than to their perceived racial overtones.
One of the key deterrents was that if restrictions were applied to Mexico and
the rest of the hemisphere, they must also be applied to America's northern
neighbor, Canada. Additionally, restricting immigration from Mexico and
South America would generate extremely negative publicity and ill will. The
U.S. government was anxious to maintain positive relations in the region
because they were perceived as beneficial to American business interests.
An increasing amount of raw materials from Latin America was being
imported to sustain the United States' industrial and commercial empire at
home and abroad.

Although the Harris/Box bills were defeated, the ensuing debate clearly
revealed America's attitude toward Mexican immigrants and the perception
of their role or status in American society. Opponents claimed that Mexicans

were mentally, physically, and culturally deficient and classified them as sub-standard human beings. University of California noted biologist and eugenist Dr. S. J. Holmes lent his professional reputation and gave credence to the debate by declaring that Mexicans were "below par physically, and in intellectual capacity."[48] It was a common view shared by academicians in major universities, ranging from Berkeley to Harvard. Pseudo-biological arguments were employed to illustrate or to prove the alleged inferiority of all Mexicans. They were depicted as being indolent and amoral, with a proclivity toward criminal behavior.[49] Conversely, proponents of immigration claimed, just as vociferously, that Mexicans were honest, hard workers and ideally suited to perform hard physical labor under the most adverse working conditions.

Among those praising Mexican immigrant labor was Charles C. Teague, president of the California Fruit Growers Exchange. He declared, "Mexican casual labor fills the requirements of the California farm as no other labor has done in the past." Teague expressed his admiration for the Mexican worker's ability to withstand "the high temperatures of the Imperial and San Joaquin Valleys."[50] The Santa Paula citrus grower also pointed out that white laborers refused to do farmwork because they were constitutionally (physically) unsuited to perform it. On the other hand, he concluded that Mexican workers were well adapted to field conditions.

Charles Teague was not alone in his praise. The seemingly natural ability and reputation of Mexicans as extraordinary farm workers was frequently stressed in testimony before congressional committees. C. V. Maddus, an official of the Great Western Sugar Company, also gave Mexicans high marks. He praised them for being a "God-fearing, family-loving, law-abiding set of people."[51] According to other employers, Mexicans were credited with the virtues of being "docile, patient, usually orderly in camp, [and] fairly intelligent under competent [meaning Anglo] supervision."[52] But the key factor for American agriculturalists and industrialists was the Mexicans' "willingness to work for low wages."[53] In reality, of course, they had no other choice.

The virtues of Mexican immigrant labor became a litany recited by industrialists as well as by agriculturalists. Bethlehem Steel President Eugene G. Grace expressed high regard for Mexican workers' willingness "to work hard and return to their homeland when need for them has passed."[54] Despite their praise of the Mexican workers' character and traits, employers joined Mr. Grace in assuring Congress that the Mexicans were here only on a temporary basis. California grower S. Parker Frieselle vowed before the

House Committee on Immigration and Naturalization that the civilization of California would never be built on a Mexican foundation.[55]

Echoing a similar sentiment, Texas Congressman John Nance Garner asserted that Mexicans had a "homing pigeon" instinct that assured their return to Mexico. Community leaders and civic groups viewed their anticipated departure as beneficial since Mexicans were considered socially and culturally inferior and therefore unsuitable for American citizenship. Some individuals cited climate as a deterring factor. Mexicans, it was averred, could not survive the cold weather of the Midwest, the Eastern seaboard, or the Pacific Northwest. Therefore, the rationale went, they would never settle permanently in the United States. This meant that Mexican Nationals could be exploited with impunity and discarded when their services were no longer required.[56]

The views of Eugene G. Grace, S. Parker Frieselle, and John Nance Garner were shared by Dr. George P. Clements, in charge of agricultural affairs for the Los Angeles Chamber of Commerce. Clements was an avowed advocate of unrestricted importation of Mexican farm workers. He advised growers and ranchers that they should treat the Mexican well "until his term of employment is over, then return him to his home."[57] Clements based his advice not on humane compassion, but on the grounds that fair treatment guaranteed farmers and growers a constant supply of dependable labor. A day laborer summarized the adverse attitude of employers toward their Mexican workers with the sage observation: "You want us as long as we are strong and well and able to do five dollars [worth of] work for three dollars; when we get sick and we can't work [then] we get nothing but kicks."[58]

Lack of understanding or appreciation of the Mexican immigrants' vital economic role was a result of how they were perceived by the Anglo community. They were viewed primarily as an exploitable labor force imported to perform seasonal tasks. As such, they were considered as temporary rather than permanent residents. Ironically, this view was prevalent even in the Mexican community. Most Mexicans regarded themselves as being here *por sólo un poquito tiempo* (for only a little while). Many of them actually came with the hope or intent of acquiring a little nest egg and then returning to Mexico to live out their remaining years in modest comfort. The unintended length of their stay was attested to by the number and progressive ages of children born while their Mexican parents were in the United States.[59] Even those who had been in the United States for a long time held on to their dream despite the fact that as the years passed their hopes faded. This attitude was a very distinctive feature or characteristic of Mexican immigration. For Mexican immigrants, the mother country was always just next door.

This was especially true in the Southwest, where the proximity of the border constantly beckoned loyal sons and daughters. The umbilical cord did not have to be severed. It provided them with a sense of security and well-being. This was important, for rampant discrimination convinced them that regardless of their status, to the Anglo community they "would always be Mexicans." Laborer Emilio Martínez and merchant Francisco Balderrama Terrazas shared this view despite being longtime residents.[60] Mexicanos, therefore, preferred to retain their Mexican citizenship. Naturalization statistics underscored this fact. Applications for American citizenship were substantially below those of other immigrant groups. In 1910, 1920, and 1930, the Census Bureau reported that only 5 to 13 percent of the Mexican Nationals were American citizens. The percentages for European-born nationalities was 45 percent to 49 percent in the same period. During the Great Depression only about 2 percent of Mexican Nationals applied for citizenship.[61] Proud of their cultural heritage, Mexican Nationals saw no reason to pledge allegiance to a nation that viewed all Mexicans as second-class citizens. In actuality, family allegiance superseded all other ties or bonds in the Mexican community.

Al Norte
DOCUMENTS

■ ■

"Do They Go Back" Charles C. Teague
Source "A Statement on Mexican Immigration,"
Saturday Evening Post *200, 10 March 1928.*

A STATEMENT ON MEXICAN IMMIGRATION
By Charles C. Teague

Do They Go Back?

Though it is true that the itinerant Mexican laborers who would be
chiefly affected by the projected exclusion measure are not of this
class, they are so far from being undesirables that the Southwest would
experience great difficulty in getting along without them. Most of the
great development work of this area has been accomplished and is
maintained by Mexican labor. The great industries of the Southwest—
agricultural, horticultural, viticultural, mining, stock raising and so
on—are to a very large extent dependent upon the Mexican labor which
this law would bar out. This region's railways were built and their
roadways are maintained by Mexicans.

If, as it is claimed, the city of Los Angeles is devoting much of its
charitable funds to Mexican relief, it is probable that the funds are not
as carefully handled as they should be, as it is a significant fact that
El Paso, with a Mexican population of from 60 to 70 per cent, devoted but
6 per cent of its charitable budget to Mexican relief in 1926. Los Angeles'
Mexican population, as stated above, is but 5 per cent of the total.

Dr. George P. Clements, manager of the agricultural department
of the Los Angeles Chamber of Commerce and a close student of the
Mexican both in Mexico and California, says that misguided and
unconsidered charity makes a habitual indigent of the Mexican.
As long as he is "being taken care of by the Government"—the Mexican's
primitive conception of food-and-clothes dole—he need not work.
He won't work, consequently.

Congressman John N. Garner, of Texas in a statement before the House Committee on Immigration, in 1926, said: "My observation is, living right there on the border, or within fifty miles of it, that 80 per cent of the Mexicans that come over for temporary work go back."

Observations by California farm advisers, labor agents and large employers of Mexican casual labor confirm this statement.

There is little evidence anywhere in rural California of a Mexican disposition to acquire land and make permanent settlement. There is no large body of Mexicans on the soil as citizens and landholders such as the solid units of Europeans in the Northern Middle West.

There are around 136,000 farmers in California. Of these, 100,000 have holdings under 100 acres; 83,000, farm tracts under forty acres. With these small farmers their project is one-man affair until harvesting period is reached, then they need ten, twenty or fifty hired hands to get their crop off and into market. Fluid, casual labor is for them a factor determining profits or ruin. Specialized agriculture has reached its greatest development in California. The more specialized our agriculture has become, the greater has grown the need for a fluid labor supply to handle the cropping.

Mexican casual labor fills the requirements of the California farm as no other labor has done in the past. The Mexican withstands the high temperatures of the Imperial and San Joaquin valleys. He is adapted to field conditions. He moves from one locality to another as the rotation of the seasonal crops progresses. He does heavy field work-particularly in the so-called "stoop crops" and "knee crops" of vegetable and cantaloupe production- which white labor refuses to do and is constitutionally unsuited to perform.

W. E. Goodspeed, superintendent of the California Orchard Company in the Salinas Valley, says: "Our peak harvest demands run from 400 to 500 employees as against a normal labor demand of from 75 to 100. We have tried out every form of transient labor except the Negro, with the result that we have found it necessary to confine our surplus as nearly as possible to Mexicans." This statement is typical of growers' experience on both large and small properties. Farm advisers, labor agencies and ranch managers in the San Joaquin Valley, in the citrus and walnut districts south of Tehachapi and the irrigated districts of the Coachella and Imperial valleys agree that at present Mexican casual labor constitutes between 70 and 80 per cent of the total of that class.

California agriculture is not wedded to Mexican labor because it is cheap labor. According to statistics of the United States Department of Agriculture, California paid the highest farm wage—ninety dollars— in the country in 1926. Where white labor is available it works with Mexican and at the same wage. According to the same statistics the average United States farm wage is fifty dollars.

It is increasingly demonstrated that in certain production areas, notably in the growing cotton acreages of the San Joaquin Valley, white casual labor refuses to work at these jobs. Of 2000 whites from Oklahoma who came to the San Joaquin cotton areas two years ago, less than 2 per cent finished the season.

If, as some claim, there is some social problem connected with the immigration of Mexicans, those who are proposing the closing of the door to them will bring to the Southwestern states a much more serious one by forcing agriculturists to bring in Porto Rican negroes or Filipinos which they certainly will do as a matter of self-preservation before they will let the industries perish and certainly no one can maintain that either of the races mentioned would be as desirables as the Mexican. A large percentage of the Mexicans return to Mexico after the harvests are over. The most of the balance are alien and could be deported should any serious problems arise. On the other hand, if either of the other races mentioned are brought here in numbers they would have to be supported through the periods when there is no work to do.

A step is being taken in the mitigation of any problems that arise from concentration cities, in the first of a projected chain of cooperative farm- labor bureaus—the Agricultural Labor Bureau of the San Joaquin Valley— designed to facilitate the constant distribution of the farm-labor stream.

California agriculture is convinced that a sudden shutting off of the only reservoir of dependable farm labor left to it—Mexico—would create a disastrous labor vacuum entailing ruinous bidding as between section and section, and all growers in competition with industry and the rail- roads, with results reflected in higher freight rates, a sharp rise in the pro- cess of all farm products and disturbance in the field of rural finance.

It, therefore, is united in asking that Congress shall not pass restric- tive measures on Mexican immigration until, through congressional committees or presidential commission, that body can possess itself of all facts involved in the problem.

DOCUMENTS

■ ■

"THE HORRIBLE HELL OF ALASKA" ALFONSO FABILA
Source: Alfonso Fabila, El Problema de la Emigración de
Obreros y Campesinos Mexicanos. *(México D.F.: Talleres
Gráficos de la Nación, 1929), 24–27.*

The Horrible Hell of Alaska

When the Mexican laborer starts to lose faith in finding work, he
gradually steers himself to San Francisco, where he roams the wharf,
famished as a rabid dog fighting over a scrap of bread. His days are dark
and frightening visions haunt his nights, exaggerated by hunger and the
pained memory of his distant children, more starved than he.

Protestant churches open their temple doors. Putrid shelters
where hundreds of miserable men sleep in overcrowded revulsion.
Job hunting in all of California, they have ended up in San Francisco.
They are the predestined.

In the morning, the church feeds them, then thrusts them out to
the street as if pouring out its sickening misery.

The jobless Mexicans continue to roam.

Pedro García told me the following narrative, which I transcribed
without adding a single comment:

"A large man of wiry hair approached me at a time that I felt a
desperation greater than at death's beckoning. I was worth nothing.
I was a total failure!"

"Listen"—he told me—"don't be sad. Now you have no work, but
I know of an embarkation leaving tonight heading towards Alaska. What
do you say if we leave together? We get five dollars a day. Take courage!
There's nothing to spend it on, no women, no wine. Save your cents in a
knot for the family and return prosperous in three month's time. Enough
to return to Mexico. I say you'll make a profit! Animal furs bring in lots of
money. Do you dare? Worse is to die from doing nothing. Salmon fishing
is the best bargain. Will you join us? We are many Mexicans. Twenty from
Sonora, ten from Nuevo Laredo, thirty from central Mexico, and loads
from Jalisco. Come on! You lose nothing by risking!"

The man who speaks is Mexican. Though born in California, he
still shows indigenous features; yet, three generations ago he sold
himself to Jewish merchants, exploiters of lives.

"I took off to Alaska. I have no words, sir, to describe the tortures. A nameless winter and unequalled deprivations stole the last hopes of returning to my family.

"Four years did I spend there. Four years that seemed eternal. The five dollars were no lie, but when we got paid at the end of the week, hunger had forced me to spend them. A pair of flannel pants thick enough to prevent the snow from soaking through cost a week's worth and the animals I hunted were not enough to obtain a fur coat. Still, I needed it. My limbs stiffened into knots preventing all freedom of movement in my hands. The ice destroyed them. As to fire—to sleep in a heated log cabin was costly!

"The sea! What endless ocean and its salty air that had sickened my breath! Night brought terrifying solitude. Wine? There was wine. The lungs asked for the warmth and drinking it was indispensable. Love? Not a single woman's caress to forget bitterness for an instant. The beastly flesh raged viciously so that the native woman, with her flattened face and goose walk appeared to be the only salvation.

"I knew a story about a colleague told by those who had stayed from the year before. They found him with a woman and the jury forced him to remain on the island. They gave him a rifle and a cabin to live in. They had a son. He remembered that three children awaited him at their mother's lap in a hut in San Miguel de Allende, and one night, when the dark shadows deepened, he took his boat and lost himself amidst the monstrous ice floes of the frozen sea.

"The tale of my fellow countryman who preferred suicide to an existence next to a stupid woman who had given him a son and the spectacle of her ugliness, obsessed me and I preferred the anguish of my youth tortured by desire over a union that would also lead me to suicide.

"God opened a good path for me. I possessed a strong will. I drank nothing but hot coffee and herbal tea, enduring six months as if under forced labor until I had earned enough to bring me back home. One man saved out of a hundred that perish! Francisco Torres also came with me, but in what consumptive state! Shattered!"

They say that Bishop Hanna of San Francisco declared before the press that Mexicans are a burden for the church and other charitable societies. Men, crazed and tubercular constantly need to be repatriated on the county's behalf. Does this pious man not realize that the very deeds of the United States are the cause of such burgeoning expense so suffered by his Holy Institution?

Can you expect not to thrust to Sea the crazed and tubercular if that is the cruel pay of suffering?

Some return from Alaska. Not all die there. They return blind and rheumatic for the rest of their lives, with hands useless, shriveled as if in a gesture of perpetual anguish. Hands that long hours with the fishnets went numb from cold and chests that, worn-out from coughing lost all strength. Perhaps they will cross the Rio Grande and seek the humble nook where a poor old woman awaits her missing son. Will such head, done in, die in the lap of the woman who birthed him? Such is the only hope and final smile upon the face of the shipwrecked man who died in a sea of illusion!

Adventures! Fortunes! All a lie! Alaska is the hell that extinguishes faith and quickens curses to the lips. Curses against the foreign exploiters and against one's own, who in turn abandon out of ignorance the legions of men whose arms are wanted by Mexican fertile soil.

■ ■

VISIT TO SUGAR BEET FIELDS, DETROIT CONSUL YGNACIO BATISTA TO SECRETARY OF FOREIGN RELATIONS, 20 AUGUST 1930.
Source: Mexico City, Archivo de la Secretaría de Relaciones Exteriores,IV-76–49.

[seal of Mexican consulate]
Consulate of Mexico   Re: Inspection of [sugar] beet fields.
                                 Detroit, Michigan, August 20, 1930.

Honorable Secretary of State.—México, D.F.
In conformance with the authorization which your Authority was so kind as to grant me through our Consulate General in New York, Friday the 15th instant, at six o'clock in the morning, I left this city to begin my tour of inspection through the sugar-beet fields, heeding the invitation which the Michigan Sugar Company had extended in this regard. The results of my observations during this trip are the following report, which I hereby offer to you.

The tour occupied last Friday, Saturday, and Sunday, that is the 15th, 16th, and 17th of the present month, and the person who accompanied me was Mr. Lucío Ramírez, of Mexican nationality, who for a number of years offered his services, in various capacities, to the above-mentioned company at its plant in Alma, Mich., and who, at the present time, carries out the functions of Contracting Agent of the company in Detroit, employed in contracting workers from Mexico and other countries.

In Gratiot, Saginaw, Lapier, Clinton, and Tuscola counties is located the most important nucleus of plantations of the afore-mentioned enterprise, in which it has established five sugar plants, in the following towns: Caro, Sebewaing, Bay City, Saginaw, and Alma. I visited the plantations and the plants, speaking at length with the administrators of the latter, to whom I suggested the appropriateness of dealing through the Consulate with whatever difficulties might arise with the Mexican workers, offering them amicable mediation, which they accepted, agreeing that many of the aforesaid difficulties develop and become ever more arduous to resolve due to the ignorance of our countrymen with respect to the language of this country.

In this interchange of impressions with the administrators regarding the situation of our countrymen in the fields of their respective jurisdictions, in general they expressed very favorable opinions as to the character and energetic work of our countrymen, and they explained in detail the manner in which are carried out the different operations of sowing, thinning, weeding, and harvest of the beets, and we discussed, finally, the reason for which a number of difficulties have presented themselves with respect to our compatriots, especially with respect to the dimensions of the plots they work, since these dimensions serve as the basis for their daily wages.

In each of the counties to which I have referred, I visited a number of Mexican families, and I was able to note that they are actually living in conditions that, while not the best that might be desired, are at least much better than the conditions of the Mexican families residing in Detroit, given that the latter, because of the critical condition of the economy of the state, which has resulted in the loss of their jobs for the great majority of the settlement, find themselves passing through a very difficult period, and their living conditions are, quite possibly, even miserable.

The company sets aside for its workers, in the fields, free housing; these houses are generally of wood, and are in very good condition, although many of them are in need of repairs, which it has not been possible to carry out, as it was explained, the considerable losses which the Michigan Sugar Company has suffered recently having prevented this; I was able to see to it during my visit, nevertheless, that the respective administrators attend immediately to the complaints which several of our countrymen presented to me regarding the lack of window panes or fire screens or chimneys, etc., which were immediately taken care of for them.

That which has most adversely affected our workers in the beet fields is the drought experienced in this region and in all of the North Central area of the United States during the present season; for, in addition to working in the beet fields, in years past they had the opportunity to work at sowing and harvesting wheat, beans, cucumbers, and corn, and the crops of the three last-mentioned products have been severely damaged this year by the aforementioned drought. Nonetheless, several families have managed to find work of this kind, which offers them a daily profit of $2.00 per ten-hour workday, and in which almost the whole family is employed, thus encountering a considerable alleviation of the economic situation in which they find themselves.

I received only five complaints, during my tour, regarding difficulties with the dimensions and tasks assigned to the Mexicans, which were favorably resolved with respect to the interests of the latter, by means of mediation by the undersigned.

In addition to the plants that I have mentioned, there are three others, but in these the Mexican families are a minority, so that 750 families from our country work in the five aforementioned, forming approximately 40 percent of the total number of workers in the company, the remaining 60 percent being composed of Germans, Poles, Belgians, Dutch, and Russians.

I was also in the general offices of the Columbia Sugar Company in Bay City, with the object of meeting the upper management and negotiating with them with regards to the complaint on the part of three of our countrymen working in their plantations in Mount Pleasant; they heard with courtesy the aforesaid complaint, also arising from questions as to dimensions, and offered to make suitable amends to our compatriots.

In sum, the number of families which I visited in the counties

I toured amounted to sixty-four, in total, having heard and transmitted to the administrators all their complaints and difficulties, and having obtained in this effort the most successful outcome possible, for I sincerely believe that this trip will serve to ensure that in the future the complaints of our workers will receive due attention from the managers of the aforementioned enterprise, who offered to collaborate with the undersigned, in the spirit of justice, in the resolution of all the problems of our compatriots.

I believe it only just to point out as an important piece of information that in spite of the fact that the sugar companies of the state of Michigan have been suffering considerable losses in recent years, because of the low price which their product commands in the marketplace, in general they fulfill their promises to our compatriots and manage to satisfy them; although it is certain that this results in benefit to themselves, since they understand very well that the employment of Mexican braceros is indispensable for the harvest of their crops.

Another of the matters which was presented to me as a real problem during my tour, and one which is very difficult to resolve, is the fact that, according to the complaints of our countrymen, this year a very limited assignment was given them, awarding them a very limited expanse of ground to work; this, let me repeat, would be very difficult to resolve, since due to the present excess work force, arising from the enormous number of people who find themselves unemployed, the crops were sown simultaneously in the various regions, and it has been necessary to carry out the work almost at the same time, eliminating in this way the recourse of past years, which consisted in finishing one task and beginning another additional one in a different field.

Although the harvests of corn, cucumbers, and beans, I repeat, were severely adversely affected by the drought, it appears that the harvest of sugar beets, which are in very good condition, will be one of the best of the last five years, for which in that respect our compatriots will obtain a good profit at harvest time.

In general the conditions under which our farm laborer works in the fields which I visited are as follows: the wage which is paid for hilling and thinning is $10.00 per acre; for weeding (generally two weedings are needed per season), $3.00; and for the harvest, $10.00 per acre. All tasks involved in the production of sugar beets are paid, then, per acre of land worked. When they receive extra work—in the aforementioned crops of corn, beans, etc.—they are paid per ten-hour workday, at the rate of $2.00 per day, or $.25 per hour.

I was able to ascertain, in addition, that the difficulties which present themselves with respect to dimensions are due in almost all cases to the impossible situation in which our compatriots find themselves, lacking the instruments or the requisite knowledge with which to corroborate the aforesaid dimensions, it being the case moreover that almost all of them take into account the total extent of the ground, while the company's agronomists only and exclusively take into account the cultivated area, measuring it in acres of 43,560 square feet.

In concluding this brief summary of the conditions and problems of the Mexicans employed in the sugar-beet fields of the state, it remains only for me to express my certainty that in the future, with the knowledge which I have acquired of the aforesaid problems, and the good relations of amity which I have managed to establish with the upper management of the sugar enterprises, the efforts in defense of the interests of our afore-mentioned compatriots which this office might undertake will be more effective, and the complaints which might be received from them more easily resolvable, in a just and equitable manner.

I cannot conclude without expressing to your Authority the sincere gratitude which all the Mexicans demonstrated toward our government, upon learning the object of my visit, and the interest which they demon-strated upon my speaking to them of the works which the revolutionary government itself is carrying out for the well-being of our country, many of them indicating themselves disposed to return to the country, as soon as they might assemble a sum in order to dedicate themselves, there, to farming, applying the knowledge of modern methods of cultivation which they have acquired during their stay in this country.

Informing you of the results of my trip, which the solid support of your Authority has made possible, let me reiterate my gratitude to you and the assurance of my very distinguished consideration.

EFFECTIVE SUFFRAGE. NO REELECTION.

Consul,

[signature]

cc: The Mexican Embassy in Washington and
The consulate General in New York.

The Francisco Balderrama Terrazas family store in Los Angeles, c. 1936. Courtesy of Enrique Balderrama.

The Family
La Vida

Cuando pienso en mi famila	*When I think of my family*
Ganas me dan de llorar	*It makes me want to weep*
Que si la crisis se	*Because if the depression is*
Alarga	*Prolonged*
A donde iremos a dar	*Where shall we end up*
—"Los Desocupados," Corrido	—"The Unemployed," Ballad

The family is the most universal feature of human existence. It is the basis of all societies and cultures. Modern industrialization and urbanization unleashed important changes that impacted not only the workplace but the home environment. The loss of cottage industries and the passing of a stable family farm life were seen as threats to the vitality and continuity of the family unit. Yet these adverse forces have not prevailed. The family, often in a modified form, retains its unique role as society's fundamental socioeconomic unit. Survival of the family can be attributed to the fact that it is not merely a societal entity. It is a living process, providing sustenance, socialization, and acculturation to its members. No individual escapes having his or her identity nurtured within some type of family context.

In the Mexican culture of the 1930s, both the nuclear and the extended families played very significant roles. The nuclear or parental family transmitted to its offspring values, attitudes, practices, and mores of acceptable conduct. Interaction with the extended family served to define and reinforce rules and norms governing social etiquette, moral deference, and familial hierarchies. This cultural legacy was exemplified by customs and traditions that often superseded legal edicts or decrees. Behavior patterns and interpretive language infused the acculturation process with nuances, sentiments, and a spirituality to which outsiders are not privy. A natural reaction among all groups, therefore, was to distrust those who were perceived as being "different." Quite naturally, when Mexicans emigrated to the United States they gravitated to established barrios and colonias in which they had friends or family in an attempt to preserve their identity and to cope with a strange environment.[1]

Initially, societal and cultural bonds with Mexico were stressed, but with the passage of time, the family's orientation began to change. New modes and attitudes were gradually adopted and accepted as part of the culture. Eventually, baseball and hot dogs vied with soccer and tacos. Although the changes produced cultural clashes, the family remained a link to the past and a step forward into the future. It embodied not only acculturation and change, but continuity and stability as well. This would stand it in good stead, for during the Great Depression the strength and self-reliance of the family was sorely tested.

The preeminence of the family among Mexicans was readily apparent. Emigrating to the United States was a family affair. Commonly, heads of households came first in order to acquire a job, find a place to live, and save money to enable their families to join them. This group of men constituted the *solos*, married men who had come to the United States by themselves. There were also the *solteros*, or bachelors, who fully expected to return and marry the girl back home. V. F. Garza, after living in East Chicago, Indiana, returned to his native Chihuahua to marry his sweetheart Anna.[2] However, solteros often met and married local Mexican women or occasionally even a *gringa* or *güera*, an American girl.[3] Prior to being reunited with their families, getting married, or returning home, solos and solteros often boarded with relatives or friends. Few households did not have a younger brother, uncle, cousin, or brother-in-law living with them.

The significance of the Mexican family was clearly noted in Consular Service *nacimientos* (birth records). Consular regulations stipulated that all children born abroad of Mexican parentage should be registered at the nearest consulate within six months. This was required in order to establish and protect their rights under their eligibility for dual citizenship. However, the regulation was seldom observed. The few parents who complied usually registered all of their children at the same time. Since most consular offices were located in major cities, families in rural or farming communities were at a decided disadvantage. As a result, a majority of the children were never registered. In most cases, parents registered their children only if required to do so when seeking some form of consular assistance.

An examination of consulate records concerning place of birth reveals distinct patterns among Mexican families. Older children were generally born in Mexico or at some point near the border. Younger siblings were born while the family chopped cotton in Texas, picked fruit in California, or harvested beets in Colorado. Others were born while their fathers worked on the assembly lines in Detroit, boned beef in Chicago, or labored in the coal mines of Pennsylvania. The presence of children and the growth of families were important reasons influencing Mexicans to settle in a particular locale and to seek steady work rather than seasonal employment. Both factors added significantly to the stability of the family unit.[4]

The unique role of the Mexican family was evident from the very beginning of the immigration experience. Family ties served as an important link in the emigration chain stretching from deep within Mexico to cities throughout the United States and Alaska. In truth, one could travel the length and breadth of North America without ever being far removed from the protective cloak of *la familia*, the extended family. Due to this situation, failure to master the English language seldom proved to be a serious handicap. Mexican immigrants had an invisible network informally maintained by *las comadres*, women bound together by friendship or family ties, who somehow managed to keep in touch with relatives and friends on both sides of the border. Few things happened "here" today that were not known "there" tomorrow.[5]

Fortunately, geography favored Mexican immigrants. Most of them lived and worked within close proximity to the U.S.–Mexican border. Furthermore, following the Revolution, Mexican and American railroads provided economical transportation for Mexican families emigrating to the United States or returning to Mexico. This contributed immensely to preserving family solidarity. When the Dillingham Commission surveyed Mexican railroad workers in 1911, it discovered that they were accompanied by their families more often than any other group of workers.[6]

Working on the railroad often meant actually living on el traque. Señorita Cruz Sánchez kept house for her older brother while he toiled on a crew maintaining tracks stretching from the Southwest states of Arizona and New Mexico to the Midwest belt of Kansas and Illinois. Cruz made a home out of the railroad boxcars assigned as living quarters near the roundhouse where the trains were serviced. The antiquated boxcars consisted only of a bedroom and a kitchen, with furnishings limited to a stove and sink. Any amenities such as cabinets and windows were built by the workers themselves. Emanuel Gómez of Silvis, Illinois remembered his father hoisting him into a cradle hanging from the ceiling of the boxcar his family lived in. The family and other Mexicans lived in the railroad yard of the Rock Island Lines. Not all railroad employees lived in boxcars. Señorita Sánchez recalled that Anglo foremen "never lived in the section houses but had nice homes."[7]

In spite of adverse conditions, news of *el oro y el moro* (the gold and the glory) of El Norte (the United States) was spread by family members and friends who had lived and worked in the United States. Tales were often embellished by a vivid imagination and stories improved in the retelling. Friends and relatives in Mexico listened in wide-eyed amazement to yarns about life in *"Los Estados Unidos."* Negative aspects were usually glossed over or conveniently forgotten. Tales of steady work and good wages lured both men and women north. Women were especially enticed by visions of modern conveniences. The availability of indoor plumbing, gas and electricity, and well-stocked stores seemed too good to be true. Awed listeners resolved to go north and see for themselves, enjoy the good life, and earn *mucho dinero* (a lot of money).[8]

The question of whether or not to emigrate was a family matter and was usually settled only after the pros and cons had been thoroughly discussed in both the immediate and extended family. A key factor influencing the decision to emigrate was whether there were relatives or close friends that the new arrivals could rely upon for help. In Mexican families, there always seemed to be room for *uno más* (one more). Both the Raya clan in East Los Angeles and the Martínez family from Bucareli, Durango, had younger siblings who arrived to join older brothers and sisters. On many occasions after a separation of several years, wives were reunited with husbands often with children the fathers had never seen. A typical example was the Juan Rodríguez family. His wife, Juanita, and her six-year-old daughter, Rosa, joined him after a separation of several years. Coincidentally, mother and daughter arrived in Los Angeles from El Paso in 1918, on the eve of the sixteenth of September, Mexico's Independence Day.[9] Accounts of such reunions are endless.

Anthropologist Robert R. Alvarez, Jr. noted the significance of family ties while tracing the migration of Mexicans from Baja California to the border regions of Southern California. Alvarez's research and analysis during an extended period of time revealed the power and vigor of the family. Rather than diminishing in scope, the family actually grew in stature and strength. Family solidarity increased and experienced a new maturation.[10] This occurred rather naturally because, in order to survive, members had to depend upon one another. The concept of rugged individualism, so revered in American literature, was the antithesis of the Mexican experience. In Mexican society, who and what a person is is determined by family status and affiliation.

Due to its dominant presence during the depression, the family emerged as a focal point of study and attention among social workers, educators, and sociologists. Based on their research and observations, the family was held responsible for the failure to amass material wealth; it was viewed as a serious obstacle to the acculturation of the children; and parents were accused of not caring about providing basic support services for their youngsters. No aspect of Mexican family life escaped scrutiny and comment. Newspapers and journals had a field day in trumpeting the charges and accusations that were seldom verified but were accepted at face value. Mexican families were accused of harboring ignoble, un-American sentiments and characteristics. Slothfulness, shiftlessness, and lack of ambition were traits frequently attributed to the Mexican culture. Helen Walker, a Southern Californian naturalization teacher, noted piously, "The Mexican peon dislikes work. Work is work, joy is joy. . . . There is no such thing as the joy of working at difficult tasks."[11] No matter how hard Mexicans worked or how successful they were, they confronted discrimination and prejudice throughout American society. Restaurants and theaters frequently barred Mexicans. Kansas resident Lorenza Lujano recalled being told she "had no right to drink it [a soda] in the store or sit at the fountain."[12] Forced to go outside, she threw her coke away in disgust and anger. In California Gloria Moraga remembered that because of her "fair complexion, an usher led her away from the section of the theater designated for the Mexicans and Indians."[13] In Des Moines, Iowa, John Ortega's family was allowed to sit on the main floor of the theater due to their light complexion. The Mexicans and Negroes forced to sit in the balcony would throw popcorn, peanuts, and candy wrappers, down on them to show their displeasure and resentment. Connie Pérez recalled that in Arizona where her father was a mining engineer, she was the only Mexican allowed to attend school with the white children due to her fair complexion. Albino Piñeda still has a sign from a Wyoming restaurant stating: "No Dogs, Negroes or Mexicans."[14]

Apparently, no matter how inane the charges were, it was "open season" on the Mexican family. It became fashionable to associate negative traits with the so-called pathological nature of the Mexican character. Sociologist Emory Bogardus observed, "They [the Mexicans] live so largely in the present that time has no particular meaning to them."[15] It is baffling how a trained sociologist came to such an erroneous conclusion. This absurd type of statement was usually followed by allegations that Mexicans were incapable of deferring instant self-gratification, and that they were spendthrifts and child-like in their desires. Professor Bogardus and his colleagues should have conferred with bankers in Los Angeles and Chicago about their Mexican customers and their sizable savings accounts. Dr. Bogardus did attempt to be more realistic than many of his contemporaries. He ascribed behavioral patterns to societal factors rather than merely citing the common racist explanations, then in vogue, of genetic or biological deficiencies.

The same kinds of absurd charges were made in relation to education. In El Paso, Texas, schoolteachers blamed the family "for the perpetuation of ignorance and immorality" among Mexican students.[16] In making such charges, critics ignored the discriminatory practices prevalent in education. In rural areas, Mexican students frequently had to walk miles to reach the often segregated school site. Ignacio Guerrero, recalled that on school days they "had to walk four miles; [because] they didn't pick Mexicans up on the bus."[17] The school bus was reserved for Anglo students. When the white students drove by in the bus they would taunt and tease the Mexican students plodding along the dusty roads. At school, students attended crowded classrooms. Antonia Medina remembered that at her rural school in Michigan all the Mexican students, from kindergarten to 12th grade were in the same classroom with a single teacher. In Long Beach, California Mexican children attending Bryant School were placed in the Americanization Room taught by a teacher without a college degree, until they mastered the English language.[18] In addition, the students' ability to communicate with each other was severely limited because Spanish was commonly prohibited both in the classroom and on the playground. Anyone caught speaking Spanish was severely punished. "Violators" at a Texas school "were relegated to sit by a fencepost, an area known as a breeding place for snakes and other pests."[19] Even though schools often limited the aspirations of Mexican children, it was amazing that Mexican children "often proved very good students if allowed to go to school" according to American Consul Stewart E. McMillan in Piedras Negras.[20]

Too often their education and training was geared to prepare them to perform unskilled manual tasks. The authoritarian principal of a segregated school decreed: "The girls will have more extensive sewing, knitting, crocheting, drawn work, rug weaving, [and] care of the sick. With the aid of a nursery, they will learn the care of little children. The boys will be given more advanced agriculture and shop work of various kinds."[21] Even in non-segregated schools, counselors traditionally assigned Mexican students to shop or vocational-type classes. One individual recalled that in high school, he was assigned to shop classes three periods a day. When a period was deducted for physical education and one for lunch, that left two periods a day for academic subjects. Discouraged, he finally dropped out of school.[22] With Mexican children being deliberately programmed for failure, is it any wonder that educational achievement eluded them? Yet, rather than accept any responsibility or admit fault, the educational system preferred to blame the family for the students' lack of academic success.

In many instances, the Mexican family depicted by social workers was based on stereotypical misconceptions. According to the typical scenario: The husband was portrayed as domineering and wielded unassailable authority. Conversely, the wife was viewed as the docile spouse whose undying devotion to her family bordered on sainthood. Such disparate images defined the perception of Mexican men and women for many Americans. In actuality, there were many obvious parallels between Mexican and American families. Family unity, respect for parents, religious beliefs, a strong work ethic, a law-abiding attitude, and a sense of loyalty, duty, and honor were values shared by both cultures. Unfortunately, few efforts were made to understand the personal psyche, cultural values, or material concepts of the Mexican people. Researchers ignored the dynamism and rich variations in Mexican family life. Disregard of such critical aspects produced a contrived or distorted image. Yet their conclusions became the basis for the sociological explanations popularly pandered and accepted during much of the twentieth century.

As is readily apparent from the literature of the period, the accepted pathological view of the Mexican family ignored or misrepresented the historical context of Mexican life in the United States. Little is said about the determination displayed by Mexicans in combating school segregation, their courage in battling for labor rights, or their resourcefulness in surviving in the midst of the Great Depression. Instead, the portrayal of the Mexican family as a dysfunctional unit served to deflect challenges and criticism of the American ethos of equality and justice. Americans hung tenaciously to the belief that a lack of personal effort and academic orientation were the only obstacles to success. Therefore, if an individual did not succeed, it was due to innate character deficiencies. This rationale absolved society of any blame or responsibility. The exponents completely disregarded the fact that insidious discrimination plagued Mexican children at every turn.

In spite of the low esteem in which it was held by American society, the persistence, strength, and indomitable spirit of the Mexican family were conspicuous in both nuclear and extended households. Their influence and dominance was readily apparent by the close contact that family groups maintained with each other on both sides of the border. This strong relationship was characteristically found in all colonias. Only places of origin rivaled the family in determining where Mexican immigrants would settle in the United States. Reinforcing this perception, one researcher found that most families in Argentine, Kansas, were from Tangancicuaro, a small agricultural village in the state of Michoacán. The "Tangas" had been migrating regularly between Tangancicuaro, Michoacán, and Argentine, Kansas, since the turn of the century. Apparently, that was when the first Tangas were recruited to work on the railroad. Tangas who settled in Argentine, Kansas, not only shared the same birthplace but were commonly members of the same clan or related family group.[23]

Not all Mexican immigrants followed relatives or close friends to the same location in the United States. Nor did all of them reside with family or kinfolk. This was especially true for many solos and solteros. During its formative years, the Mexican community in Chicago was comprised primarily of single or married men living alone. Husbands were often forced to leave wives and families behind, either in Mexico or in the Southwest, until they found a job and a place to live.[24] Due to the large number of lonely men, Mexican communities in Chicago, Detroit, Gary, and other cities in the Midwest were plagued by seamy bars and pool halls. The Mexican community of Indiana

Harbor, Indiana had some twenty-nine pool halls, the largest number of any business catering to the Mexicanos. The same situation prevailed in other cities with an abundance of single men. In Los Angeles, clusters of cheap bars could be found along north Main Street in Sonora Town, as it was commonly known.[25] Pool halls and saloons provided a modicum of social life and assuaged the loneliness resulting from being separated from family and loved ones.

One sad consequence was that hard-earned wages were often squandered or gambled away in one night of revelry. In spite of the many temptations, however, Mexican anthropologist Manuel Gamio, American economist Paul S. Taylor, and other scholars found that the overwhelming majority of solos and solteros regularly sent money home to their families. Money orders were usually dispatched before getting caught up in *la parranda*, a weekend of merrymaking. Occasionally, as men traveled alone in their quest to earn a living and their hopes of returning to Mexico dimmed, new legitimate or illicit families were established. Even then, many men continued to send money home. Rarely were wives and children or parents or siblings callously abandoned. The practice of sending money home to loved ones was so ingrained in the conscience, that it continued even during the chaos and disorder brought about by the 1910 Revolution. Although the Mexican postal service was unable to guarantee delivery, money orders were religiously purchased and posted.

In the United States, private postal-service companies were formed to take advantage of the lucrative business. Among the most successful was the Los Angeles Mercantile Company. The company had agents in all U.S. cities with a Mexican population large enough to warrant its services. It had major offices in Los Angeles, San Antonio, Kansas City, and El Paso. In addition to transmitting funds safely, a wide variety of articles could be shipped to representatives stationed in over two hundred towns in Mexico. Los Angeles Mercantile and similar postal companies served as effective avenues of communication between the Mexican heartland and the growing number of Mexican communities north of the border.[26]

Employers quickly recognized the importance of families among Mexican migrant workers and successfully exploited this feature for generating maximum profits. The Mexican family became the preferred work unit for agricultural contractors in literally every state in the Union. In the sugar-beet industry, entire families were contracted to thin, top, and harvest beets from

California to places as far east as Minnesota and Michigan. When hiring, it was common practice to give preference to families with children over six years of age so they too could work in the fields. In 1935, a federal-government study on child labor revealed that Mexican families constituted over 65 percent of the sugar-beet workers in the Midwest and Rocky Mountain states.[27] In most instances, due to low wages, parents had no choice but to take their children into the fields in order to earn enough to make ends meet. Labor contractors made certain that wages remained slightly above the subsistence level, thus providing an incentive for workers, and their families, to return the following year.

Getting families to return was important because most other ethnic groups would not work in the beet fields. It was a dirty, miserable job that gave real meaning to the term "backbreaking" labor. The work was done with two "instruments of horror" designed by the devil, according to one worker. One was the infamous "short hoe," which had a handle twelve to eighteen inches long. A regular long-handled hoe could have been used, but it was considered harmful to the plants. With the short hoe, there was less margin for error. However, the modified hoe required the user to work in a bent-over position or crawl along the dusty rows of beets for ten or twelve hours a day. At the end of the shift, it was nearly impossible to stand up straight. For young bodies, it eventually meant assuming a partially stooped position and suffering painful backaches for life. The other tool, more correctly called a weapon, resembled a razor-sharp machete with a mean, semi-curved, three inch hook riveted on the end. Working at breakneck speed to pick up the beet with the hook and slice off the top in one deft motion was dangerous work. It was rare to meet a *betabelero* (beet worker) who had not lost a finger or did not bear the scars of his trade.

As terrible as conditions were for adults, they were even worse for the children. Yet, although they suffered their share of injuries and abuse, they still made an attempt to enjoy their stunted youth. There seemed to be an inner, undefined desire to savor however briefly the moments of their fleeting childhood. A former sugar-beet worker in Chicago recalled that during lulls in the work schedule the children somehow found the energy to play. "They made up games with the rows of beets; they took turns minding the baby, who sat like a king upon a mat in the middle of the field, or they chased rabbits or caught grasshoppers," he recounted wistfully.[28] Many of the children would never learn to read or write. Their interrupted schooling seldom exceeded the sixth grade. By then, they were considered old enough to do a regular day's work.

To mask the exploitation of child labor, attempts were made to picture Mexican families as working in an idyllic setting. Helen S. Walker, an Americanization teacher, attempted to portray a picturesque scene of work in an orchard: "the children pick, the uncles and aunts pick, the mother and sisters pick, while the father and big brothers shake the trees."[29] From her description, it could be perceived as a pleasant afternoon outing. However, Flavio Valenciana did not have any happy memories of picking walnuts, olives, or strawberries in his youth. He recalled that "sleeping on the ground, cooking in an open fire, and washing without running water was...uncomfortable and depressing."[30]

In California, where higher wages and somewhat better working conditions attracted more Mexicans than in any other state, the family remained the preferred work unit. As the harvest season approached, it was not uncommon to find families camped at the edge of groves and fields for weeks at a time. Hoping to be among the first hired, they waited patiently for the *pisca*, the fruit-picking season, to begin. In order to be available when the whim of nature and the agriculturalists demanded their services, migrant workers provided their own transportation and makeshift shelter. During the height of the fruit-picking season, they scurried from one labor camp to another, seeking work. As one observer commented: "Entire families move up and down the valleys of California...only to suffer repeated disillusionment."[31]

Like their cousins in the beet fields, migrant children suffered the most as the family struggled vainly to eke out a living. Callous employers saw them not as children, but merely as one more pawn to be exploited. When working "piecework," everyone had to pitch in, in order for the family to survive. The life of the migrant family was a brutal existence devoid of luxury and filled with endless days of grueling, backbreaking toil. During the harvest season, there were no Sundays and holidays or even rest periods or coffee breaks. Clumps of bushes served as convenient latrines. Working and living conditions in the migrant camps defied description. Growers seldom provided any hot water, restrooms, showers, or even enclosed shelters where workers could rest their weary bodies. An eyewitness lamented the tragic plight of a young woman with two little babies forced to live out in the open, exposed to the elements, with only the corner of an old toolshed available for cooking purposes.[32]

As a consequence of the horrendous working conditions, the lack of even the most rudimentary sanitation and housing facilities, and prolonged malnutrition, Mexican families suffered from a variety of serious illnesses and an inordinately high death rate. One of the most dreaded scourges afflicting the Mexican community was tuberculosis, the great pestilence of the period. The dreaded disease reached epidemic proportions in the Mexican community. As early as 1929, Mexicans accounted for 21.2 percent, or 98, of the 461 cases of tuberculosis recorded that year in Los Angeles County, but they made up only 10 percent of the local population.[33] By 1933, the number of Mexican cases had grown substantially. Los Angeles County reported that Mexican cases constituted 30.5 percent or 459 cases out of a total of 1,505 tubercular patients. The death rate among Mexican infants in Los Angeles was also exceedingly high. Methodist Minister Bromley G. Oxnam reported that the infant-mortality rate among Mexican children was three times greater than for the general population. Oxnam's findings were later confirmed in a study conducted by the Child Welfare Division of the Los Angeles Health Department.[34]

San Antonio, the city with the second-largest number of Mexican residents in the United States, had the highest ratio of tuberculin cases in North American cities with a population over 100,000. Mexicans constituted a significant portion of those cases, and their death rate was three times higher than it was for blacks and four times higher than for Anglos.[35] In San Antonio, the death rate among Mexican children under two years of age was 300 percent higher than for children in the Anglo community.[36]

The preceding statistics underscore the anguish, despair, and heartache that tuberculosis posed for the Mexican community. The highly contagious virus thrived in the squalid, overcrowded living conditions endured by the Mexican population. Nearly every family in the colonia had members or relatives who were *tísicos* (tuberculars). The actual number of those afflicted was undoubtedly higher, but in the barrios many incipient cases went unreported or undetected. Part of the problem was fear, especially among children, of "being sent away." Treatment for "consumption," as tuberculosis was commonly called, usually involved isolating patients in county sanitariums. In the closely knit Mexican family, prolonged separation kindled deep-seated fears and feelings of anxiety. When one was ill and needed loving care, one relied on family, not on strangers. There was also the persistent and haunting belief or fear that no one went to a hospital or sanitarium unless there was no hope of recovery. People went there to die! For many Mexican families, visits to the sanitarium became routine weekend outings.

Dora Raya, a former tubercular patient, vividly recalled the recurring feelings of homesickness and despair she experienced while interned at Los Angeles County's Olive View Sanitarium. Although separation from family and friends was a very trying and painful experience, the greatest tragedy was the loss of a loved one. *El delgadito*, the invisible one, claimed many lives. Emilia Castañeda de Valenciana tearfully recalled learning of her mother's untimely death due to consumption. She received the heart-rending news on a day that should have been a joyous occasion for her, her first holy communion.[37] Death of a beloved family member was a terrible tragedy, but the most devastating ordeal was the loss of a child. This wrenching experience was frequently endured by Mexican families.

The loyal support of friends and neighbors formed the invisible fabric that made it possible for Mexicans not only to endure repeated deaths in the family, but also to survive the ordeal of the depression. Knowing they were not alone helped to buoy spirits and to maintain the resolve not to give in to adversity. Thus, in the face of the nation's worst economic crisis, most Mexicans remained hopeful in spite of ample reason to despair. They lived and celebrated each day with reverence and gusto. Their passion for life was apparent in how free time was frequently spent. Sing-alongs, enlivened by old ballads and *corridos*, were an important source of diversion and enjoyment. Parents spent time in telling children *dichos* or *refranes*, which were designed, like Aesop's fables, to teach or impart moral themes and values. *Leyendas*, stories and legends from Old Mexico, were great favorites and were often repeated. *Chistes*, jokes and riddles, were also popular modes of passing time. In the evening, migrant farm children listened, enthralled, as parents who had spent a lifetime under the open sky regaled them with stories about nature and the heavens.[38]

Nearly every household had a hand-wound Victrola on which a few scratchy records were played until they were worn out. For families with radios, one recurring problem was that children wanted to listen to their favorite American programs while their elders preferred to listen to Spanish-language programs. Occasionally, by adroitly stretching the budget, a family could take in a movie. Children usually opted for movies made in Hollywood, while their parents favored Spanish-language films made in

Mexico. Older teenagers were often, albeit reluctantly, given permission to attend the movie of their choice. Parents were certain that English dialogue was not the only interest drawing their teenagers to the local theater. Mothers were reluctant to allow their teenage daughters to attend movies unless accompanied by a relative or a younger brother or sister. A nickel bag of candy, which could last through a double feature, assured the younger sibling's silence.[39]

The rivalry between Spanish and English transcended the spheres of recreation and entertainment. Although Spanish remained the dominant or preferred language among most parents, English rapidly made heavy inroads. In many cases, a real dichotomy or dualism developed. The diversified media was an omnipresent means of acculturation. Consequently, Mexican families in the United States reflected not only the Mexican past but also the American present. Most Mexican youngsters grew up with their feet planted firmly in both cultures.[40]

A very common and unobtrusive way of nurturing Mexican folkways occurred via the dinner table. Mealtime was very important, for it drew the family together and provided an opportunity for them to relax and share news of the day's activities. Although, traditionally, children were to be seen and not heard, during dinner they too were free to join in if there was a lull in the conversation. Courtesy dictated that adults speak first, and woe to any child who interrupted them. Everyone thus learned what was happening in the colonia and beyond as adults chatted and exchanged information. News from relatives in the United States or Mexico was always a welcome aspect of the conversation. High on the list was news of who had been deported or repatriated, who had gotten a job or been laid off. Also discussed was who was getting married and who was having another baby. Juicy tidbits not fit for tender ears would be glossed over and reserved for discussion after the children had gone out to play. In the growing dusk, hide-and-seek or tag were favorite pastimes.

Even though food was scarce and tended to assume a certain monotony, housewives prided themselves in making simple meals as nutritious and tasty as possible. In most families, certain rituals were followed in the preparation of many food items. Tortillas, whether corn or flour, had to be made by hand and cooked on a *comal*, a cast-iron grill. Beans had to simmer all day on top of the stove in an *olla*, an earthen pot. Among the purists, the olla could not be used for any other purpose. *Antojitos y platitos*, special delicacies, were lovingly prepared whenever the lean food budget permitted it. The ubiquitous beans and tortillas were often supplemented with a variety of tasty soups made of rice, lentils, *fideo* (vermicelli), vegetables, or whatever else was available. Spicy salsa or fresh chilies were commonly used to season the simple cuisine to suit the Mexican palate. Meat, although inexpensive, was normally served only on special family occasions. Milk, when available, was reserved for the very young. Neighbors and relatives often shared food in potluck fashion. Equally as welcome as the food was the warm camaraderie and good humor that accompanied the shared meal.[41]

Religion and their spiritual faith was an important source of solace and comfort for the Mexican family. The vast majority of the Mexicans, perhaps 98 percent, considered themselves nominally, if erratic, Catholics. In spite of the fact that certain Protestant sects, particularly fundamentalists and evangelical groups, were constantly proselytizing, they made minimal inroads. The faithful remained steadfast in their beliefs.[42] Even though the status of the Catholic Church and the role of religion were heatedly debated in Mexico's postrevolutionary government, the masses remained fiercely loyal to the church. As attested to by the Cristero Revolt in 1926, they were even willing to die to preserve the Holy Faith. Regardless of official tirades and formal government decrees, the people understood one vital and overpowering truth: Only the Church could save your soul and assure you everlasting life. In addition to eventual salvation, the Church provided welcome refuge and a serene haven for the downtrodden.

Lacking the material resources to withstand the onslaught of the Great Depression, Mexicans instinctively turned to the Mother Church. The Church not only consecrated the spiritual life of the faithful, but their secular life as well. Sacred rites for the family included baptism, first Holy Communion, confirmation, marriage, and eventually last rites. In addition, going to confession, doing penance, praying the rosary, offering novenas, and saying the stations of the cross were acts of reverence and contrition sanctioned by the Church. Through these mystic rituals, religious traditions were passed from one generation to the next.[43] Mothers played a critical role in this endeavor. Bringing the children up in the Holy Faith was considered to be a sacred trust.

Even if mothers worked outside the home, it was a mother's duty to see that the children were *bien educados* (well educated). Being well educated had nothing to do with formal schooling. Primary concern was with social deportment. This was an integral part of a code of conduct commonly referred to as *la cortesía Mexicana*, or courtesy coupled with manners and good breeding. The foremost manifestation of a child being bien educado was treating elders with courtesy and respect. Even if one came from the poorest family in the colonia, one was expected to adhere to the code of conduct. Since rude behavior reflected adversely on the family, punishment was severe and swift.

A great deal of time and attention was devoted to rearing children properly. Children were perceived as being a blessing, *un bien de Dios* (a gift from God). With their innocent cries of glee and natural exuberance, they provided one of the few real pleasures enjoyed by parents during this bleak and dreary era. Vera Godoy happily remembered that her mother "still had time to play with us," even though she was busy keeping house and making handicrafts in order to augment the family income.[44] The large number of children in Mexican families also taxed Mexican mothers. Frances Dominguez occasionally worked as a bit player in Hollywood, but she could not pursue an acting career because she had to "concentrate her efforts on raising ten boys."[45] Parents regularly did without in order to stretch the family income and assure that children's needs would be met. The children always came first, regardless of how poor the family might be. For a loving mother, no sacrifice was too great if undertaken for the sake of her child. In recounting the long hours she spent scrounging for food, Teresa García Coronado of Tucson, Arizona, vowed she would do it all over again because "that which I did for my children gave me no shame."[46]

Apart from raising the children, one of the most critical jobs confronting Mexican women was stretching the sparse household budget. They had to make every penny count. Many adults whose childhood encompassed the depression recalled that it was Mamá who parceled out the money to pay the rent, buy groceries, and purchase school clothes as well as a myriad of incidentals. Vera Godoy remembered how her mother "took care of the money, largely because her father had no time to make decisions. . . . He was either working or looking for work."[47] Jesusita Solís spoke for most housewives when she stated that in her family "we were accustomed to my handling the household budget." Housewives handled money with great skill and frugality. They were often accused of skinning the buffalo before spending the nickel. Somehow, they managed to save *unos centavitos* (saving a little money) for a rainy day or for an occasional treat for the children.[48]

Faced with continued loss of income as the depression worsened, many wives were forced to devise ways of supplementing the family budget. Dora Raya and Irma Amparano recalled their mothers working as domestics for *los ricos*, affluent whites.[49] An enterprising mother in Detroit packed lunches for single men in her neighborhood who still had jobs in the local factories. In Los Angeles, Rafaela Ruiz de Balderrama prepared hot lunches for Mexicans who worked next door at an egg-packing plant or at a nearby laundry. Her initiative helped the struggling family to keep their little "mom-and-pop" grocery store going.[50] Some women, especially those who were the sole head of their household, were forced to take in boarders. There were a growing number of such households because husbands had been deported and the family was forced to fend for itself. In some cases, wives and children had been abandoned by fathers unable to bear the shame of not being able to support them.[51]

Beset by their own problems, amazingly, women still found time to help others. Informal groups commonly referred to as *comadres*, consisting of family or close personal friends, pooled and shared what little they possessed to help truly destitute families survive the crisis. They were never too busy to lend a helping hand, to share a pinch of this or that, or quietly make *un prestecito* (a small loan) when needed. Many families survived the depression due to the kindness and generosity of relatives and neighbors. In nearly every colonia, *damas*, women who were members of the small middle or professional class, organized to help *los pobrecitos* (the less fortunate). In San Antonio, led by Father Carmelo Tranchese, pastor of Our Lady of Guadalupe Church, the damas, although numerically small, became a veritable army. The devout women organized the Catholic Relief Association. They fed the hungry, clothed the needy, sheltered the homeless, and ministered to the ill.[52] The association was one of many groups that sprang into existence not only in San Antonio, but in nearly every colonia where an attempt was made to help the needy.

"La Beneficencia Mexicana" was another aid society established by the women of San Antonio. Although it was headed by an all-male board of trustees, the Beneficencia was managed by a female board of directors. They organized the charitable clinic to provide medical care for pregnant women living in the colonia, on the west side of the city. Expectant mothers were eligible to receive prenatal care after paying a minimal fee of twenty-five cents for their initial visit. All subsequent visits, consultations, or examinations were free.[53] This was a very progressive approach, for during the 1930s many Mexican children were still born at home with a *partera* (midwife) in attendance. In such cases, much of the prenatal care was based on the advice of mothers, close friends, or the local *curandera*, or healer, who often doubled as the midwife. In the colonia, there were heated, emotional debates as to whether the "clinic" or the "home" approach was best. Among the more traditional and modest women, the latter practice was accepted as the natural method of having children. As in the case of tuberculosis or other illnesses, there was a reluctance to entrust one's health to outsiders.

The damas in San Antonio may appear to have been more aggressive in organizing and rendering assistance to the colonia, but in reality, women everywhere proved to be the mainstays of their respective colonias during the Great Depression. This belies the image, then in vogue, of Mexican women as docile and subservient. A young woman from Gary, Indiana, in recalling her strong-willed mother and grandmother, observed that researchers did not understand the nuances of behavior that prevailed in the Mexican culture. When strangers were present, a wife generally deferred to her husband and let him speak for the family. However, once alone, there was no hesitation in letting him know exactly how she felt about any situation.[54] Children understood who really "wore the pants" in the family. The equivalent expression in the Mexican community is *fajarse las naguas*. A mother's strong will and quiet determination made her a force to be reckoned with, both within the family and in the colonia, when she and her comadres joined forces.

Even before the advent of the depression, women were already active in the affairs of the colonia. In 1926, a group known as "La Sociedad de Madres Mexicanas" was organized in Los Angeles to help finance the legal defense of compatriots facing civil or criminal charges. They often held fund raisers in local theaters in order to raise the necessary funds.[55] *Las Madres* or *Madrecitas*, as they were affectionately known, focused their attention on the nondescript cases ignored by everyone else. Las Madrecitas regularly visited city and county jails to provide toiletries and sundry articles to needy prisoners. They also provided vital contacts between inmates and relatives who were unable to visit the prison. Since very few Mexican families had telephones, the Madrecitas often delivered messages or letters to aggrieved families. Furthermore, Las Madres assisted the prisoners' families in coping with the incarceration or pending deportation of a loved one.

Awareness generated by the efforts of the Madrecitas even benefited celebrated cases, such as that of Juan Reyna in Los Angeles. According to published accounts, Reyna was driving in downtown Los Angeles when his car went out of control and struck a parked car. The car, as luck would have it, was a police car. Reyna was arrested amid shouts of "you dirty Mexican" and "you filthy Mexican." While being escorted to the police station by three officers, Reyna managed to disarm one of the detectives. He then shot and killed one officer and wounded another before being subdued. During his trial, Reyna expressed no regret or remorse for his action. Rather, he declared that he wished he had killed all three officers for having called him "a dirty and filthy Mexican."[56] The Madrecitas, with the assistance of other organizations, urged Mexicanos to support Reyna. The colonia press published vivid details of his arrest, the sensational trial, his mysterious death in prison, and his elaborate funeral.

Corridos immortalized Juan Reyna for knowing "how to defend your dignity, and even risk your life, to honor your nationality."[57] Local residents Alejandro Castro and Eduardo Negrete vividly remember the Madrecitas' crusade to save Reyna as well as the numerous monetary contributions made in his behalf by residents in the Southland's colonias.[58] Even the poorest people contributed their few pennies. The extensive donations were attributed to the colonia's awareness of the widespread prejudice and discrimination exhibited by police toward residents in barrios throughout the country. Consequently, Reyna's claim of verbal abuse was readily accepted as factual. It was similar to incidents that could be recounted by nearly every Mexican in the United States.[59]

While a relatively small number of individuals required assistance from the Madrecitas, thousands of poor families regularly sought help from "La Cruz Azul Mexicana." This agency, the equivalent of the American Red Cross, was controlled and operated entirely by women. Chapters were established in every major colonia in an effort to respond to the needs of an increasingly destitute population. The range of programs and activities of Cruz Azul chapters across the country was truly impressive. They ran the gamut from raising funds, helping disaster victims, dispensing medical supplies, and assisting indigent repatriates to counseling compatriots. The Los Angeles chapter, led by Elena de la Llata, a prominent colonia and civic leader, gained international prominence. On one occasion, a fund raiser for the chapter was held in Mexico City to assist it in aiding underprivileged children in Los Angeles.[60] Financial constraints limited the material assistance that the Cruz Azul was able to provide, but its presence and the moral support provided by the dedicated women inspired hope and confidence.

In addition to their demanding domestic roles, women also worked as breadwinners outside the home. Some toiled alongside their husbands in dusty fields under a scorching sun, while others labored in stinking canneries amid clouds of steam, or slaved in sweltering sweatshops in the garment industry. Female wage earners included wives, single mothers, and young women. Work was seldom sought for personal financial gain. Regardless of their marital status, the vast majority of women worked in order to help the family survive. A typical example was Concha Hernández, a widow with three children, Cruz, Elena, and Samuel. She tried her hand at making all kinds of handicrafts that she peddled around town. A jovial person in spite of her adversity, she often joked "A todo le tirro y a nada le pego"—I shoot at everything and hit nothing.[61] Her meager earnings often meant the difference between eating or going hungry.

Even though economic necessity was the primary reason for Mexican women entering the labor market, oral interviews indicate that most single women looked forward to working before getting married. A job gave them not merely a feeling of self-reliance, but a sense of freedom and independence. The workplace also enabled young eligible women to expand their circle of friends, and they often met and married relatives or friends of their coworkers. Esperanza Gallardo volunteered that she was "very happy" working in a foundry as a molder for nearly two years. In addition to "giving my money to the family," she was able to avoid close parental supervision. "My mother was very strict, [I had] no friends and [was] not allowed to go out . . . besides church there was nothing else."[62] Gallardo's situation was a rather typical case. Mothers traditionally doubled their vigilance when their daughters reached marriageable age.

Whether married or single, women were a critical source of labor for many industries. Fruit and vegetable canneries were among those that recognized and prized their skills. "Mexican women are desirable and more efficient than white women. They are accustomed to working with fruit," one employer stated.[63] While the canning industry might extol the dexterity of the women workers, such praise did little to improve the dreadful working conditions found in the fruit and vegetable– or fish-canning plants. Mexican women were traditionally assigned to the most dangerous operations. The women frequently suffered cuts and burns as they sliced the hot steaming vegetables or filleted the fish at breakneck speed. Anglo women were also employed in the canneries, but they were usually assigned to cleaner and less-hazardous duties. In spite of the fact that Mexican women were given the dirtiest and most demanding tasks, their wages were substantially less than those received by Anglo women.[64] Furthermore, as in every other industry, sexual harassment by male supervisors was a commonplace occurrence.

Exploitation of female workers was not limited to the canneries. One of the worst offenders then, as now, was the garment industry. Its sweatshop conditions have been portrayed and chronicled in countless stories and films. A survey of Los Angeles manufacturers in 1933 revealed that over 40 percent of all women employed in the garment industry earned less than five dollars per week after working ten hours or more a day, six days a week. This was considerably lower than the fifteen to sixteen dollars per week recommended as minimum scale by President Franklin D. Roosevelt's Re-Employment Agreement and the state of California.[65] Low wages forced women to take piecework home in a vain attempt to earn enough to support their families. After putting in a strenuous 10-hour day, weary and bleary-eyed women, after finishing their household tasks and putting the children to bed, continued stitching, hemming, and sewing buttons on garments. When working with delicate fabrics, the fine and precise stitching required had to be done by hand. It did not take long for eyesight to be permanently damaged.

An endless supply of desperate workers eager for jobs resulted in extremely low wages in all industries. Some Mexican workers were not paid wages but in kind. A common practice in Southern California and elsewhere was to allow unemployed Mexican families "to clean the fields and buy the produce at reduced rate," after the harvest was over. This forced young children ten years of age or younger to work in the fields with their parents. Eight-year-old Josefina Chávez helped her mother pick cotton or other crops in season.[66] Most families were forced to pool their meager earnings in order to survive. Vera Godoy, Esperanza Gallardo, Dora Raya, and Irma Amparano attributed the survival of their respective families to working and pulling together.[67] Sometimes family members had to travel great distances to find work. Esperanza Gallardo recalled accompanying her brother when he went to Monterey, California, to work in a fish cannery.[68] Parents feared for the health and safety of their offspring. To assuage their fears, mothers insisted that sons, but especially daughters, board with relatives or close friends whenever possible. However, since they were expected to pay room and board in order not to become a burden, precious little money was left to be sent back to their own families. Many doubted whether the sacrifice and the prolonged separation that such an arrangement entailed were worth the trouble.

Some disgruntled individuals sought easier and more profitable means of survival, which sometimes led to involvement in illegal or questionable activities. Bootlegging of liquor prior to the repeal of Prohibition was a source of badly needed income. In every city in the nation where large enclaves or colonias were located, suppliers catered to the lucrative Mexican trade. Homemade wine and beer enjoyed a ready market as men sought to drown or momentarily forget their sorrows.[69] Another illicit endeavor was prostitution. Driven by hunger, some young women were forced into a life of shame in order to feed themselves and their families. When the pecan industry collapsed in San Antonio, a Salvation Army worker observed sadly: "They [young girls] come down . . . evenings to work, and take their earnings back to their parents. Sometimes their parents don't know where they go."[70] Hunger pains superseded pangs of pride, even if parents surmised the source of the tainted money.

Lack of jobs, less than subsistence wages, and deterioration of living conditions were bound to evoke illegal or amoral behavior, even among normally law-abiding men and women. In New Orleans, for instance, the police arrested Transito Velázquez for creating a public disturbance. The police reported that a group of "Mexicans had not worked for about thirty days were causing considerable trouble." They were in a desperate situation after "their household effects were attached" for nonpayment of their grocery bills.[71] But the same set of circumstances aroused the determination of others not to let poverty rob them of their dignity and self-respect. Leaders of both sexes urged the rank and file in the colonias to continue their quest for honest employment, decent salaries, and better working conditions. Unfortunately, a common tactic utilized by the establishment to discredit advocates of reform was to label them as Marxists or communist agitators, thus providing an excuse for deporting unwanted Mexican immigrants.

La Vida
DOCUMENTS

■ ■

LIVING ON AN AMERICAN FARM. ANGELINA AYALA.
Source: Interview with Angelina Ayala. Courtesy of Angelina Ayala.

We lived on a small truckfarm and raised produce for the local markets. But due to the depression, eking out a bare living had become virtually impossible. My father would get up early in the morning, long before dawn in order to do some irrigating before getting ready to take the produce to the local farmers' market in the hope of finding a buyer.

There were six children in the family and we all pitched in and tried to do whatever we could to help out with the chores. Those of us old enough to work in the fields picking corn, tomatoes, string beans, or squash were expected to do our share since there was no money to pay for hired help. . . . Occasionally, Dad did get friends or neighbors to give a hand in an emergency. They were usually paid in produce.

We also had goats, chickens, ducks, and pigs to look after. We had lost our cow so we got milk from a neighbor who lived a couple of miles away. It was my job to make the daily morning trek, rain or shine to get the milk. We also drank a lot of goat's milk in the steaming cups of hot chocolate Mom would make for our breakfast. Like most farmers, we bought food in bulk. Flour was brought in one hundred pounds, several sacks at a time. The sacks could then be used for dish towels or other purposes. . . . A hundred pound sack of pinto beans would last a long time. . . . Without a refrigerator, all cooking had to be done on the spot. With six kids, leftovers were no problem. Mom was a great cook and had a real talent for making soups of all kinds, but she could not bake. If her biscuits were not eaten immediately, they became hard as rocks.

Although we did not have much, Mom was very picky about what she would let us eat. The hot chocolate was made from pieces of raw chocolate. *Té de limón* (lemon tea) was another morning drink, made from freshly picked leaves grown in her garden. We were never allowed to drink coffee. She believed it would hamper our ability to learn English.

On hot summer days, Kool-Aid or pop were usually unaffordable, although sometimes we would trade produce to a vendor who occasionally came by the farm. We looked forward to that. However, Mom preferred to make us *agua fresca* (a sweet drink) she made by combining fresh fruits and vegetables. No artificial sweeteners were used. It was a real treat.

Living on a small, isolated farm meant we were usually left to invent ways of entertaining ourselves. By today's standards our existence was rather bleak. We had no electricity, indoor plumbing, or running water. Having no radio, we relied on a victrola for our musical entertainment. The records were played until they grew old and scratchy. Games of tag, hide and seek, baseball, and similar sports were organized when time permitted after all the chores were done. Reading by a lone kerosene lamp around the kitchen table was a common pastime. The kitchen served many purposes since it was the only place that had heat, due to the large wood-burning stove. It was kitchen, dining room, living room, and recreation room. A huge table with benches on both sides dominated the floor space.

Yes, things were hard for our family during the depression but Mom somehow kept up our spirits. Each night the family would gather in the kitchen, kneel on the bare wooden floor, join hands and pray together.... Due to our poor circumstances, there was talk about returning to Mexico. However, Mom and I went to talk to the local priest to determine if we could be forced to leave, that is to be repatriated. He advised us that since five of the six children were born here and were American citizens by birth, we could not be forced to leave. Many of our friends did leave looking for a better life. Mom prayed for a better day so we stayed. Some of those who left, later came back. Dad was in favor of going but Mom, a headstrong woman, refused. When the farm petered out we moved to the city and continued our struggle to survive. For us, like so many other people, World War II changed everything.

■ ■

PETITION TO MEXICAN PRESIDENT. EUGENIO MORALES MEZA OF
BROOKLYN, NEW YORK TO THE PRESIDENT OF MEXICO, 23 APRIL 1932.
*Source: Mexico City, Archivo de la Secretaría de
Relaciones Exteriores, IV-350–40.*

SER-April 23, 1932.

I am a twenty-year-old youth who has lived in this country since the age
of ten. I have completed elementary and high school and am currently
attending evening classes at City College in New York with the intention
of pursuing a career in civil engineering. My scores have been satisfactory,
as I can demonstrate, and my attendance records confirm my assiduous-
ness in class.

Due to the recent situation, my father who is out of work, finds it
impossible to help me continue my studies. I too, despite my own efforts,
have not been able to find a job that grants me what I need.

In view of this, and out of my ambitiousness to continue studying,
I have resolved to direct myself to you, Mr. President. If possible, would
you kindly request the consulate supply me with the necessary resources
for me to relocate to the capital where I could continue my studies?

I will gladly furnish the consulate with my school transcripts and
necessary references in order to prove my good will.

Crossing the International Bridge between Juárez, Mexico, and El Paso, Texas, in May 1937. Photograph by Dorothea Lange, courtesy of the Library of Congress, FSA Project.

Deportation
Adiós, Migra

Después de ser explotados	*After being exploited*
En estas tierras del Norte	*In these lands of the north*
Ahora son arrojados	*Now they are being thrown out*
Por no tener pasaporte	*For not having a passport*
—"La Crisis Actual," Corrido	—"The Present Crisis," Ballad

In what was later to become the United States of America, the first deportation case took place in 1639. The Pilgrim settlers at Plymouth Rock authorized the removal of "pauper aliens" from their midst.[1] Virginia and other British colonies followed suit. Their actions should not be considered unusual. Exile, deportation, banishment, excommunication, and inquisitions all have one thing in common: They are legal, bona fide ways of getting rid of unruly, unpopular, or unwanted elements in any given society. The right of banishment of foreigners remains an acceptable or legitimate right of a sovereign government.

In the United States, during the 1930s, there were twenty-six basic reasons or charges commonly utilized for deportation purposes. Among them were the following offenses: suffering from epilepsy, engaging in prostitution, being physically unable to work, and not being self-supporting. Minors could be deported for entering without being accompanied by their parents. In addition, there were the usual charges of entering the country illegally, being a person of poor moral turpitude, being convicted of a crime, becoming a public charge, advocating the overthrow of the government, or being a carrier of contagious diseases.[2]

The most common cause of deportation was for entering or being in the country illegally. The vast majority of all Mexicans were deported for that particular reason.[3] Once apprehended, illegal aliens had two courses of action available to them. First, they could ask for a hearing in the hope of finding a sympathetic immigration officer. This was especially true for individuals who had fled Mexico because of civil war, religious persecution or military insurrection. Hopefully, the Immigration and Naturalization Service (INS) official could be convinced that being returned home would place the detainee in a life-threatening situation. In very rare instances, political asylum might be granted after a review of the situation. Although the law provided the above safeguard, immigration officials seldom informed illegal aliens of their rights. Since immigration authorities commonly served as accusers, judges, and juries, they had a vested interest in not volunteering any information. Wholesale violations of basic human rights were a common occurrence.[4] Generally, this could be done with impunity because Mexican immigrants were ignorant of the law and seldom had the opportunity to file complaints about their treatment.

In most cases, Mexicans in the United States illegally were readily persuaded to exercise their second option: "voluntarily" returning to their own country. This practice was so prevalent that many consuls felt obligated to condemn the process. In exasperation, the consul in Phoenix, Arizona, lodged a protest with his immediate superior, the Consul General in El Paso, about the arbitrary deportation of Mexican Nationals.[5] In reality, it was not difficult to convince Nationals that returning home voluntarily was the best choice available to them. The reason was quite simple: If individuals asked for a formal hearing and were denied entry, they were automatically barred from ever being eligible to reenter the United States. On the other hand, if they agreed to voluntary deportation, no arrest warrant was issued and no legal record or judicial transcript of the incident was kept. The deportees were free to reenter the U.S. legally at some future date. As remote as this possibility might be, it offered a flicker of hope. The proximity of the border also afforded Mexicans an opportunity to try again—either legally or *de contrabando* (illegally). On the other hand, some Mexican Nationals were tempted to "voluntarily" return to Mexico because trials were not always speedy.

Visiting the Del Rio jail on June 2, 1931, Mexican Consul Lisandro Peña, for example, found six Mexican Nationals who had been held since March for violating the Immigration Act of 1929. "Since they are unable to provide bail," Consul Lisandro reported to the Mexican Consul General in San Antonio, "they must remain in jail until October when court is held."[6] The Mexican Consul General was successful in arranging for a more timely trial. On July 25th, a special session of the District Court was convened in San Antonio and ordered the deportation of fifty Mexicans, seventeen from Del Rio, three from Laredo, and thirty from San Antonio.

Another situation that often resulted in deportation proceedings involved Mexican Nationals who were accused of committing a crime. The possibility of avoiding trial and perhaps a lengthy jail term presented a strong lure to accept deportation. Most Mexicans were unable to afford a lawyer; consequently, they stood little chance of winning their case even if they were innocent of the charges against them. Caught in the maze of the American legal and judicial system, befuddled suspects usually chose what appeared to be the easiest way out of their dilemma. Their confusion was compounded because of the language barrier. Although some courts did employ Spanish-speaking interpreters, there were seldom any interpreters available during the initial critical questioning or pretrial period.[7] In some instances, the judicial proceedings amounted to little more than a kangaroo-court trial.

In order to reduce incarceration costs, Mexican prisoners were often offered reprieves and could have their jail sentences commuted if they agreed to deportation. The Los Angeles County Jail estimated that it cost approximately $1.00 a day to keep Mexicans incarcerated. It reported that during the fiscal year 1932–1933, 2,452 males and 100 females were booked. This caused a drain on the county's limited funds.[8] Deportation was therefore utilized as an effective way to reduce prison costs. The procedure was also utilized by state and federal prison officials. That was the reason for the shipping of ninety prisoners from the McNeil Federal Penitentiary in the state of Washington to Mexico.[9] In another instance, Hilario Valdez, who was serving a life sentence in the Oklahoma State Penitentiary, had his sentence commuted, was released and deported.[10] However, given the status of most Mexican prisons, the majority of the prisoners preferred to serve their time in American jails. There was also the question of extradition-treaty arrangements with Mexico. Although a *quid pro quo* situation prevailed, Mexico was not particularly pleased about receiving individuals convicted of having broken an American law. Consul Rafael de la Colina complained that since Nationals were being dismissed en masse to create jobs for Americans, some compatriots had no other choice but to turn to a life of crime in order to survive. He bemoaned the fact that judges ignored the extenuating circumstances and imposed the most severe sentences possible.[11] Also, violations of American laws or sociomores did not always square with Mexican laws or accepted modes of behavior. In Mexico, especially in the rural areas, many disagreements, particularly if they were "affairs of honor," were still settled *mano a mano* (man to man).

Deportation proceedings were also implemented against Mexicans when the American government initiated action to expel persons who were deemed to be undesirable. This procedure consisted of issuing an arrest warrant citing the alleged violation and entailed conducting semi-judicial hearings. In most instances, the Immigration and Naturalization Service inspectors conducted the hearings. The hearings, although official in nature, tended to be conducted in a rather informal manner and lacked the safeguards associated with a court of law. The immigration inspector acted as interpreter, accuser, judge, and jury. An alien with a limited knowledge of American quasi-legal procedures and hampered by a lack of English was at a decided disadvantage. The fate of the accused depended on the personal whim of the immigration officer. Traditionally, agents did not allow detainees to confer with a lawyer until after they had obtained a signed statement from the accused. The information was then used to obtain an arrest warrant and/or a deportation order. In many instances, the arrest warrant was issued *after* rather than prior to the interrogation proceedings.

At the conclusion of the hearing, the INS inspectors sent their recommendations to the Secretary of Labor in Washington, D.C., who was responsible for overseeing the Immigration Service. There, a panel of five to ten members reviewed each case. Due to the backlog of cases during the 1930s, two additional review panels were created. As a rule, the panels supported or upheld the hearing officer's recommendation. In most cases, the decision of the review board was final. As a final safeguard, an individual could appeal the INS verdict and ask for a court trial. An appellant had the option of being represented by an attorney, if he could afford one. Court costs and other factors severely limited the number of Nationals who could avail themselves of this opportunity for redress.

As the deportation system was then structured, wherein the immigration agents exercised almost total control of the process, deportation procedures were made to order for wholesale violations of basic human rights. Mass raids and arrests were often conducted without benefit of warrants. Individuals were often held incommunicado and not allowed to see anyone. Without the opportunity to post bail, deportees languished in jail until the next deportation train was formed.[12] These procedures were the norm, rather than the exception, during the 1930s. With the advent of the depression and abetted by the hue and cry to "get rid of the Mexicans," the situation grew worse as the Immigration Service swung into action. No stone was left unturned or tactic untried as it ran roughshod over the Mexican community. The federally appointed Wickersham Commission, chaired by the distinguished Reuben Oppenheimer, stated in its 1932 report: "The apprehension and examination of supposed aliens are often characterized by methods [which are] unconstitutional, tyrannic, and oppressive." Perhaps the most important recommendation of the commission was "that some legislative discretion be given to prevent cases of unnecessary hardship and suffering to an alien's family."[13] Many colonia residents including, José Díaz and Emilio Flores, vividly remember the terror and fear created by the raids.[14] However, the INS denied any and all charges of misconduct.

The intensity of the Immigration Service's efforts in Mexican barrios and colonias is attested to by the Service's own statistics. During the period from 1930 to 1939, Mexicans constituted 46.3 percent of all the people deported from the United States. Yet, Mexicans comprised less than 1 percent of the total U.S. population.[15] The massive deportation dragnet struck terror in Mexican communities across the nation. Since the Immigration Service was housed within the Department of Labor, it might be surmised that the Service had a vested interest in getting rid of as many Mexicans as possible. The deportation of more Mexicans meant more jobs for "real Americans." In a telegram to Colonel Arthur M. Woods, U.S. Government Coordinator of Unemployment Relief, C. P. Visel, spokesman for Los Angeles Citizens Committee for Coordination of Unemployment Relief, stated: "We note press notices this morning. Four hundred thousand deportable aliens U.S. Estimate 5 percent in this district. We can pick them all up through police and sheriff channels. Local U.S. Department of Immigration personnel not sufficient to handle. You advise please as to method of getting rid. We need their jobs for needy citizens."[16]

Many individuals and organizations energetically supported the Immigration Service's patriotic endeavors. Among them was the AFL, the American Federation of Labor. Its members were led to believe that getting rid of the Mexicans would open up jobs for deserving Americans. Organized labor resented the fact that Mexicans worked for lower wages. The fact that they did so out of necessity rather than through choice made no difference to labor spokesmen. Conveniently overlooked was the fact that union labor was demanding ten dollars a day or more while Mexicans could be hired for half as much.[17] Mexican workers were also bitterly resented because they were preferred by employers over Anglo workers. The reason for the preference was that Mexicans were loyal, worked harder, and did better work.[18] To get rid of the unwanted competition, the AFL pressured the Immigration Department to interrogate Mexicans wherever they found them. According to one witness, "For a time officers of the Department would arrest Mexicans by the truckload; they would drive up in front of a store or poolroom and fill the truck, take them to the Department for questioning and . . . thousands of them have been deported."[19] At times in communities close to the border, apprehended individuals would simply be rushed to the border and dumped.

Also supporting mass deportation were a variety of patriotic groups and organizations. Two of the most outspoken were the Veterans of Foreign Wars and the American Legion. In East Chicago, Indiana, for instance, some 3,000 persons were shipped to Mexico in a program organized by the American Legion with guards assigned to ride the trains to maintain law and order. They chose to forget or ignore the fact that Mexican Nationals and Mexican Americans such as José Santos Herrada, had served alongside them in the trenches in France during World War I.[20] In addition, the National Club of America for Americans urged all loyal Americans to join in demanding that the government get rid of all Mexicans by deporting them. The group also demanded that the United States close its borders and end all immigration from Latin America.[21] Also fanning the flames of anti-alienism were influential newspapers and magazines. Among the most vociferous were the Hearst newspaper chain and the *Saturday Evening Post* magazine.[22] In the Midwest, the *Chicago Tribune* repeatedly called for the elimination of the alien horde. The biased articles appealed to the public's base fears and added to the hue and cry to get rid of the Mexicans.

Responding to the *vox populi*, Congress considered a series of bills designed to facilitate deportation. Among the most drastic actions was H.R.

4768 by Congressman Sam Hobbs of Alabama. The bill called for the establishment of concentration camps for all aliens ordered deported and who were not out of the country within sixty days. There was also H.R. Bill 3472, which sought to remove all limitation regarding the deportation of aliens who became public charges.[23]

Such individuals would be deported at government expense and would never be eligible to reenter the United States. Also introduced was H.R. Bill 5921, which would have drastically changed the provisions of existing deportation laws. It provided that: any alien convicted of a crime involving moral turpitude and sentenced to a year or more in jail could be deported upon the completion of his jail term, when paroled, or even if pardoned. Carrying a concealed deadly weapon would constitute a case of moral turpitude, and a prison term and heavy fine would be imposed on violators of this provision. Any immigrant admitted under a quota system could be deported if the person did not declare their intent within a year of becoming an American citizen or failed to fulfill the necessary requirements toward becoming naturalized. The bill gave broad discretionary powers to immigration officials to issue warrants of arrest and to detain suspected deportable aliens.[24]

Astutely sniffing the political winds and responding to the growing public groundswell against Mexicans, Congressman Martin Dies of Texas introduced legislation designed to facilitate deportation efforts. His half-dozen bills represented about a quarter of the legislation clamoring for more effective deportation proceedings. In one of his bills, Congressman Dies proposed deporting the six million aliens reportedly residing in the United States. In support of his racist views, Congressman Dies authored an article entitled "The Immigration Crisis," which was published in the *Saturday Evening Post,* April 20, 1935. In the article, Dies stressed that no unemployment problem would exist if the twenty million immigrants admitted since 1880 had been denied entry. The article served no useful purpose other than to pander to the racial fears and prejudices of an already overwrought public.

To implement the proposed deportation provisions more effectively, it was proposed that the Immigration Service be transferred from the Department of Labor to the Justice Department.[25] Although the Immigration Service was eventually transferred, this did not enhance either the efficiency or the reputation of one of the most severely criticized agencies in the federal government. The *Los Angeles Times* criticized the Immigration Service's methods and called for an investigation of Walter Carr, director of the Immigration Service in Los Angeles, and his reprehensible raids. After conducting its own investigation, the Los Angeles County Bar Association issued a critical report entitled the "Lawless Enforcement of the Law." In its report, the Bar Association condemned the agency's procedures and the wholesale violation of basic human rights.[26] Most observers and critics agreed with the criticism. Nevertheless, once again, the INS denied all allegations of wrongdoing.

Numerous complaints were continually leveled against the tactics utilized by the immigration agents in carrying out raids and roundups, commonly known as *levas* or *razzias* in the colonias. All Mexicans, whether legal or illegal, looked alike to immigration officials. In street sweeps throughout the nation's major cities, people who "looked Mexican" found themselves at risk of being picked up and taken into custody. To act first and ask questions later seemed to be the policy of the Immigration Service. Arrests were often made without warrants or even probable cause. In Southern California, radio announcer José David Orozco and community leader Dr. José Díaz recalled "women crying in the streets when not finding their husbands," after deportation sweeps had occurred.[27]

Deportation sweeps also were conducted at the Mexican border where Mexican Nationals, legal residents of the United States were often denied entry when returning to the United States. On February 2, 1931, at the height of the Hoover administration deportation roundups, custom officers stopped Mrs. Angela Hernández de Sánchez as she was returning from a week-long trip visiting relatives in Carrizal, Chihuahua. She had never encountered any difficulties when crossing the border on previous visits to Mexico. However, this time she was arrested and detained. Proof of residence was demanded and medical tests for venereal diseases were ordered. There was no reason or justification for this action. Mrs. Sánchez had been a continuous resident of the United States since 1916 and therefore, under current immigration law, not subject to deportation. Furthermore, two of her children were born in the United States. With the assistance of the National Catholic Welfare Conference, Sánchez provided evidence of residence as well as a negative blood test for venereal disease. However, in spite of the evidence, the Department of Labor ordered her and her children deported.[28]

In its zealous quest to increase its body count, the Immigration Service focused its efforts where the largest concentrations of Mexicans were found. Deportation figures wove a sinister web across the United States. Between August 1933 and May 1934, New York, Boston, Detroit, Chicago, Pittsburgh, St Louis, New Orleans, Kansas City, Denver, Oklahoma City, and Salt Lake City contributed 326 Mexican Nationals to the deportation dragnet.[29] In order to improve the body count, Colorado Governor Edwing C. Johnson threatened "to call the National Guard to round up foreigners and expel them from the state."[30] Any city in the Southwest could be picked at random, and it would be difficult to find one in which Mexicans had not been summarily picked up and subjected to illegal search and seizure and deportation, based on nothing more than racial profiling, a procedure that was patently illegal. In six California cities, including San Francisco, Los Angeles, and San Diego, 549 Mexicans were deported during the period cited above.[31]

Since Southern California supposedly contained 5 percent of the nation's deportable aliens, it became the focal point of the deportation frenzy.[32] Raids assumed the logistics of full-scale paramilitary operations. Federal officials, county deputy sheriffs, and city police cooperated in local roundups in order to assure maximum success. Scare tactics, rumors, and propaganda were adroitly used in creating a climate of fear. No one knows how many Mexicans left the country one step ahead of the Immigration Service's talons. Typical of the INS's tactics were the raids conducted in San Fernando and Pacoima, communities adjacent to Los Angeles. Immigration agents, without benefit of search warrants, went door to door demanding that Mexican residents produce verification of legal residency. Those unable to do so were summarily arrested and taken to jail.[33] The San Fernando raid incensed the Mexican community because it took place on Ash Wednesday, a holy day of great significance for Catholics.

The San Fernando raid was vividly described in Spanish to *La Opinión* by María Luna, who witnessed the entire episode. The following excerpts paraphrase a substantive portion of her comments, which were delivered in an excited and agitated manner: "It [the raid] was for us the day of judgment. The *marciales*, deputy sheriffs, arrived in late afternoon when the men were returning home from working in the lemon groves. They started arresting people and holding them in the *rebote*, fronton. The deputies

rode around the neighborhood with their sirens wailing and advising people to surrender themselves to the authorities. They barricaded all the exits
to the colonia so that no one could escape. Some men showed up at the
ball court with their suitcases so they could at least have a change of
clothes en route. There were so many arrestees, the fronton was not large
enough to hold all the prisoners. We the women cried, the children
screamed, others ran hither and yon with the deputies in hot pursuit
yelling at them that their time had come and to surrender."[34]

Los Angeles became a classic case or example of the resolute Immigration Service in action. No secret was made of the forthcoming immigration raids scheduled to take place there. In fact, the prospective raids
were widely publicized as a "scare-head" tactic that, hopefully, would
encourage illegal as well as legitimate residents to leave. On January 29,
1931, the Spanish-language daily *La Opinión* published an extensive article warning its readers about the forthcoming roundups. To emphasize
the seriousness of the situation, it cited similar stories that had appeared
in the *Los Angeles Times* and the Los Angeles Illustrated *Daily News*, on
the day before.

Rumors of impending *levas* (raids) swept through the Mexican colonia.
No one knew what to believe or what to expect. Those who feared the worst
were scared into leaving town of their own volition. Others chose to assume
a low profile and avoided going out unless absolutely necessary. Women
waited until nightfall to do their shopping and children were kept out of
school. The situation was so tense that Mexican Consul Rafael de la Colina
attempted to reassure his compatriots that legal residents had nothing to
fear. Those here illegally, he assured them, would be accorded full protection under the laws governing immigration and deportation. It was even
suggested that illegals should voluntarily surrender to the immigration
authorities, thus making sweeps unnecessary. De la Colina dutifully
informed the Mexican Consul General in San Francisco, Mexico's ambassador in Washington, D.C., and Secretaría de Relaciones Exteriores in
Mexico City about the impending raid. For their information, he enclosed
a copy of *La Opinión* that contained the full text of his remarks to the
Mexican population.[35]

In his dispatch, Consul de la Colina lamented the dire conditions
Mexican Nationals under his jurisdiction were forced to endure. Trapped in
a vicious cycle, Mexicans easily became deportation victims. Consul de la

Colina advised his government that unless the economic situation improved or several thousand Nationals were repatriated or transported to other areas where jobs were available, grave consequences would result. De la Colina reported that in an attempt to avoid problems, he would be meeting during the next two weeks with local city and county officials to discuss the various aspects and alternatives pertaining to the heart-rending situation. As soon as the talks were concluded, he promised to inform his superiors of any agreements that might be made.[36]

Perhaps the most celebrated razzia was the infamous La Placita raid, which occurred on February 26, 1931. Immigration agents under the direction of Walter E. Carr, local superintendant of the Immigration Service, began to gather in Los Angeles. Agents from surrounding counties and cities were requested to assist in the massive effort. They came from San Diego and San Francisco and even from as far away as Nogales, Arizona. Los Angeles Chief of Police R. E. Stackel and County Sheriff William Traeger pledged their support and cooperation to Mr. Carr. It took ten days for the agents to assemble and develop a coordinated plan with local authorities to carry out the raid.

The Placita site was chosen for its maximum psychological impact in the INS's war of nerves against the Mexican community. Approximately four hundred Mexicans found themselves taking their afternoon respite in the sunny park, unaware of the danger that awaited them. Suddenly, at exactly three o'clock the appearance of a large contingent of uniformed and plain-clothes officers shattered the serenity. They were led by a half-dozen immigration agents dressed in olive-drab uniforms. The police immediately posted two officers at each entrance to La Placita to prevent anyone from escaping. The suddenness of the action caught people completely by surprise. A sense of panic swept through the crowd. This type of raid was different from those conducted in business places, where suspected illegals were apprehended individually. A wholesale raid in a public park was something new.

Individuals were lined up and asked to show their passports or other evidence of legal entry and residency. Those not able to produce adequate documentation were detained for further questioning. Some individuals had difficulty in proving that they were in the country legally. What was or was not acceptable proof of legal entry or residency was entirely up to the whim of the interrogating officers. Among those detained for further questioning were about thirty Mexicans, five Chinese, and a Japanese National.[37]

Bystanders who tried to interfere in behalf of detained suspects ran the risk of being subjected to questioning and close scrutiny. That was the experience of Moisés González, who inadvertently stumbled upon the scene. González had his *papeles* (legal papers) with him, which proved that he had resided in the United States continually since entering via El Paso, Texas, in 1923. However, the immigration agent merely pocketed González's papers and shunted him aside to wait with the other suspects. According to eyewitnesses, all attempts to get the agent to relent proved futile.[38] When Vice Consuls Ricardo Hill and Joel Quiñones learned of the raid, they rushed to the scene. The two consulate representatives made an energetic attempt to assist their beleaguered countrymen. However, immigration agents were in no mood to brook interference from anyone. The Vice Consuls were accorded rude and discourteous treatment until their diplomatic identity was established.

Although the raid and the interrogation process lasted only an hour and fifteen minutes, word of the La Placita raid spread through the colonia like a mesquite brushfire. While Vice Consul Hill remained at La Placita, Vice Consul Joel Quiñones went to Walter E. Carr's office to protest the actions of the immigration agents. The immigration chief denied having any knowledge of the event and referred Consul Quiñones to Mr. W. F. Watkins, who was in charge of organizing and carrying out the raid. Mr. Watkins professed that the raids were not aimed at the Mexican people. As proof, he cited the fact that three Orientals and two Europeans had also been apprehended.[39] Assurances were given to Quiñones that even if individuals had been detained, they would be released and no deportation proceedings would be instituted against them if they could prove legal entry.

Raids like the one at La Placita represented the culmination of Secretary of Labor William N. Doak's efforts to transform the Immigration Service. Prior to Doak's appointment, the Immigration Service had languished in comfortable obscurity. That is understandable because until the mid-1920s, when the Border Patrol was established, immigration and deportation matters received only minimal attention. But suddenly, in 1928, the department's dormant status changed dramatically.

Upon assuming office, Secretary Doak instigated a personal vendetta to get rid of the Mexicans. He added his officious voice to calls for ridding the nation of the enemy in our midst. Doak's motivation was purely political, for he was acting under President Herbert Hoover's orders to create a diversion to counteract organized labor's hostile attitude toward his administration. Hoover publicly offered Doak his unqualified support and endorsed the addition of "245 more agents to assist in the deportation of 500,000 foreigners."[40] In instituting an effective deportation program, President Hoover might have been harming his personal financial interests for he was the owner of a ranch in California where reputedly Mexican workers were employed. Nonetheless, anxious to do Hoover's bidding, Doak concocted a figure of 400,000 illegal immigrants eligible to be deported immediately. Deportation meant jobs for real Americans. That endeavor, reasoned Doak, certainly ought to please organized labor, especially the AFL. With the enthusiasm characteristic of all patriotic zealots, Doak launched his massive alien manhunt.[41]

A stringent deportation campaign was launched in Texas amid violent physical threats against Mexicans. In San Angelo, for example, the city was warned that "raids on all Mexicans" were going to be made by vigilante "unemployed groups" calling for immediate movement "south with Mexicans."[42] Reportedly, hundreds of residents were deported daily, and during 1929, more than 17,600 Mexicans were deported from the Rio Grande Valley, alone.[43] A Mexican American educator in Texas chronicled the experience of a Rio Grande Valley family whose mother and father were caught in an immigration raid and deported. The four young children, a boy and three girls, were left to fend for themselves. The son, much to his regret, was forced to drop out of school and get a job in order to support his three younger sisters. He wanted his sisters to continue their education, even though he could no longer attend school. Finding it extremely difficult to survive on their brother's earnings, the children were forced to rejoin their parents in Mexico. Deportation arrangements were made by the Immigration Bureau.[44] However, there were vocal protests against the Immigration Bureau's Texas deportation campaign. The Valley Chamber of Commerce in Harlingen not only protested the federal government's deportation campaign but also organized a meeting attended by hundreds of Mexicans, to assist them in legalizing their residency in the United States.[45] They were considered a valuable economic asset to the region.

Secretary Doak's efforts produced outstanding results. In the first nine months of 1931, more people were deported than entered the United States. In August of that year, over fifteen hundred aliens were deported. September

provided an even more lucrative body count—seventeen hundred deportees were shipped home.[46] Anxious to curry greater favor with organized
labor as well as with the business community, Doak concocted the brilliant
idea of monitoring strikes involving foreigners. Strike leaders and picketers
would be arrested, charged with being illegal aliens or engaging in illegal
activities, and thus be subject to arbitrary deportation. That was the fate
of Esteban Torres's father who was deported to Mexico when Esteban was
only three years old. The future U.S. Congressman never saw his Dad
again. This insidious scheme assumed the proportions of national policy
and became a widely implemented tactic. In California and elsewhere,
many agrarian strikes were broken up by arresting and deporting leaders
who were of Mexican origin.[47]

In addition to deporting strike leaders and labor organizers, ferreting
out and deporting alleged subversives became a favorite tactic of the INS
agents. Dissidents and social reformers were labeled as communists or rad-
icals. Such a designation readily assured public approval and support for
arresting and deporting the unpatriotic ingrates. A victim of this technique
involved folk singer and radio idol Pedro J. González, who utilized his popular morning radio program, "Los Madrugadores," (early risers) to agitate
for just treatment of his compatriots. González's pleas for justice and
humane treatment eventually spelled his doom. He was denounced as a
rabble rouser and agitator. In order to silence him, he was framed on a rape
charge, convicted, sentenced to San Quentin, and later deported, despite
the fact that the young woman later recanted her story and admitted she
lied under coercion by the Los Angeles Police Department. González eventually returned to the United States and settled in the border community of
Chula Vista near San Diego where he died.[48]

Not everyone applauded Doak's roughshod methods. One of his sever-
est critics was the Wickersham Commission. The commission conducted
a thorough review of the deportation situation and issued a report
denouncing the Immigration Service's methods. This infuriated Secretary
of Labor Doak because he believed raiding homes, workplaces, churches,
dancehalls, and similar sites was entirely appropriate. When questioned
about raiding the Finnish dance hall in New York, for example, Doak
exclaimed "We struck pay dirt, didn't we?" And demanded arrogantly,
"where the hell do you expect we are going to get these fellows."[49]
However, his staff and the White House urged Doak to tone down his

remarks and to desist from baiting the commission or the news media. While they succeeded in muzzling him, Doak remained adamant about zealously carrying out his self-righteous deportation policy. In a manner characteristic of the Immigration Service, Doak denied all allegations of illegal procedures, abuses, and misconduct by his agents. All protests fell on deaf ears as the Immigration Service pandered to the public weal.

The indiscriminate sweeps and arrests created havoc in colonias across the nation. The National Catholic Welfare Conference estimated that in El Paso alone over six hundred new welfare cases would be added to the relief rolls during the year as a result of families losing their bread-winners.[50] Some individuals questioned the sheer folly of the entire deportation operation in terms of the fiscal cost incurred. One study indicated that if 1,200 aliens were deported, they would leave behind 1,478 dependents who would be eligible for public welfare. The study also reported that it would cost the government $90,000 to deport the individuals and $147,000 yearly to provide for their families indefinitely or until the children reached legal age. The report also projected that approximately 80 percent of those deported would be eligible to obtain non-quota preference for reentry due to the fact that they had wives, children, or other relatives who were citizens or legal residents.[51]

The deportation efforts and methods of the Immigration Service were often chaotic. There were occasions when the Immigration Service jailed individuals for supposedly giving false information. One such case involved a Mexican family who testified that they paid a $20.00 fee for crossing the border in 1920, and had an employer who had known them since 1920. Unfortunately, since he had died, he was unable to verify their story and the family was incarcerated. The Mexican Consul in San Antonio, however, thought the reason they were jailed was due to a misunderstanding in the "way the questions were asked and the timid nature of our humble classes."[52] Since many aliens did not have papers or led a transient life, it was difficult to determine whether individuals were actually Mexican Nationals or not. Mexican consuls were sometimes called upon to verify claims of Mexican citizenship. Form No. 180, provided by Secretaría de Relaciones Exteriores, was customarily used for that purpose. It ascertained the bearer's name, age, nationality, parentage, identified physical particulars and whether accompanied by children.[53] Charges were often made that the forms were being forged or the information falsified by unscrupulous individuals from Central or South America. Their intent was to be sent to Mexico rather than being deported back to their native countries. The proximity of Mexico made it easier for them to attempt to reenter the United States at a later date.

Much to the dismay and chagrin of the Immigration Service, aliens who could prove they had resided in the U.S. continually for the past five years could not be summarily or arbitrarily deported. Such individuals could be deported only for cause. The *Chicago Evening Post* published a story stating that Secretary of Labor Doak had notified Senator Watson of Indiana that there were few Mexican Nationals in East Chicago, Indiana, or in Gary who could be deported. Secretary Doak explained that only those in the country illegally or those who had arrived within the past three years and had applied for welfare were subject to deportation. One of the reasons for the scarcity of possible deportees was the fact that the Mexican population in the area had dwindled to a mere one thousand people. In spite of this, according to the article, Secretary Doak informed Senator Watson: "While we are not able to effect the wholesale removal of the Mexican aliens from East Chicago and Gary, you may be assured that everything possible will be done to facilitate action on any individual case that may be discovered from time to time."[54]

The number of Mexicans actually residing in the enclaves of Gary and East Chicago, Indiana, or elsewhere was open to conjecture. Faced with a population caught in a high state of flux, even Mexican consuls had difficulty in keeping track of compatriots in their respective districts. The lack of cooperation by American authorities was the number one problem. Although consuls were supposed to be notified whenever Nationals were deported, that requirement was often ignored. Consuls usually learned of the deportation proceedings after the fact. In some instances, this occurred because consulates were located in major cities, often more than a hundred miles away. The consul in Phoenix complained to his superiors that in many instances, by the time postal notification was received, deportees were on their way to or might already have arrived in Mexico.[55]

Notifying the consuls was especially critical when Nationals asked for a formal deportation hearing. Repeated requests by the consuls to be informed of such proceedings were routinely ignored. Whenever the consuls lodged a protest, the Immigration Service promised faithfully that it would endeavor to notify them before any substantive action was taken.

However, consuls were usually informed after individuals had been interrogated and their folders sent to Washington, D.C. for final review. According to one consular official, "When the consuls intervene, the sworn judgment has been made before witnesses about the truth of the statements therein, and it is difficult to deny the statement even when it contains statements that lack verification, and they [compatriots] are thus deported."[56] Even if the deportation file contained contradictions or obvious errors, once it had been sworn to and filed there was precious little that consuls could do to intervene and remedy the situation.[57] In an attempt to prevent such shoddy practices, consuls were instructed not to expedite deportation papers until they had been afforded an opportunity to ascertain the background of each deportee.[58]

Another ongoing point of contention that aggravated the situation and outraged the consuls was the rude treatment routinely accorded Mexican Nationals. A constant stream of complaints inundated consular offices across the length and breadth of the United States. Reports and complaints of harassment, beatings, heavy-handed tactics, and verbal abuse surfaced repeatedly. Racial prejudice was evinced by the open hostility of some U.S. immigration officials. Juan E. Anchado, Mexican consul in Dallas, Texas felt compelled to request SRE to use its influence to get three immigration agents transferred, hopefully, to the Canadian border. The three agents, identified only as Miliken, Wilmoth, and Harris, were accused of using their official capacity to conduct personal vendettas against Mexicans.[59] The Mexican Consul General in Dallas, Luis Lupián, notified SRE that seeking the removal of agents Miliken, Wilmoth, and Harris would serve no useful purpose. The charges of harassment and brutality against the three immigration agents would be extremely difficult to prove.[60] Since many of the Mexican Nationals were *analfabetos* (illiterates) they had virtually no understanding of immigration and deportation laws.

Consuls also objected to the fact that once a Mexican National was taken into custody, the individual could see a lawyer only at the discretion of the immigration official. Since deportation hearings were not considered formal judicial or criminal proceedings, it was not deemed necessary to permit deportees to be represented by legal counsel. Consequently, in most cases, permission was not granted. The excuse given was that lawyers simply aggravated the situation. According to INS Director Walter Carr, lawyers fed upon the hope and misery of the deportees and charged exorbitant fees for their services. Therefore, it was his solemn duty, Carr contended, to protect gullible deportees against unethical exploitation. However, in instances when lawyers were involved, the results usually favored the deportees. It could therefore be reasonably surmised that the Immigration Service had an ulterior and self-serving motive in denying defense lawyers access to potential clients.[61] As a rule, a lawyer could be present only if a decision of the review panel in Washington, D.C., was appealed and a court appearance was granted. In essence, the system was made to order for disregarding the legal rights of deportees and railroading them out of the country.

An increasing sense of outrage at the treatment accorded their compatriots began to ferment throughout the Mexican community even prior to the infamous La Placita raid. The Mexican press had a field day in condemning the United States for its punitive actions. The negative reaction on both sides of the border was especially strong regarding deportation and the burgeoning repatriation efforts especially in Los Angeles County. On January 31, 1931, a lengthy meeting was held regarding how to deal with the dire situation. Attending the meeting were Consul Rafael de la Colina; W. H. Holland, county welfare director; G. S. Strait, county traffic division manager; Dr. George P. Clements, Chamber of Commerce secretary of agriculture; and Walter E. Carr, director of immigration for Southern California.[62] Mr. Carr assured Consul de la Colina that his office took every precaution to ascertain that only those who had violated the law and were here illegally would be deported. He decried the stories and rumors that his office was determined to deport all Mexicans found within his jurisdiction. Carr also assured de la Colina that, under the immigration laws then in effect, mass deportation raids and arrests were not permissible.[63] Such assurances did little to alleviate the apprehension of Mexican residents.

Regardless of Carr's assurances, in the aftermath of the Placita raid, the situation in the colonias in Los Angeles and Southern California rapidly deteriorated as did relations with Mexico. To combat the rumors and stories that were gaining credence in Mexico as well as in the United States, it was decided that the president of the Chamber of Commerce, John A. H. Kerr, should prepare a statement that would be issued to the press and radio media in English and Spanish. A personal letter would also be addressed to the president of the Mexican republic, assuring him and the people of Mexico of the high regard in which they were held by their American neighbors. The release stated in part: "We have always found our fellow citizens of Mexican origin in the main people of high ideals and a peace loving, respectable citizenry." The release continued: "We assume it is unnecessary to call to the attention of our Mexican friends to the fact that they should in no wise be influenced in leaving this section because of idle rumors that the people of Los Angeles do not entertain for them the most cordial friendship or that the Government of the United States is embarked upon any wholesale deportation plan aimed principally at our Mexican people."[64]

Viewed on both sides of the border as the leading advocates of punitive action against Mexicans, Los Angeles civic leaders felt compelled to initiate a conciliatory movement. They believed steps should be taken to diffuse the impact of what might be perceived as rampant racism. It was an image Los Angeles could ill afford during the crucial period prior to hosting the Olympic Games in 1932. The Los Angeles Chamber of Commerce and the Automobile Club of Southern California decided to conduct their own diplomatic exchange by sending Carlos Ariza to meet with their counterparts in Mexico. Ariza assured his hosts that the people of Los Angeles bore Mexicans no ill will. On the contrary, Mexico and its people were held in the highest regard.[65]

However, the public utterances and professions of friendship did not represent the true picture of the low esteem in which Mexican immigrants were held even by those who ruthlessly exploited them. In a private memo written by Dr. George P. Clements to one of his colleagues in the Chamber of Commerce, he stated candidly: "I think that I thoroughly understand the Mexican people and particularly the type of Mexican whom for years we have solicited from Mexico. We have been very careful to demand a sandalled Mexican. . . ."[66] In essence, this callous attitude represented the true feelings that the establishment harbored toward the Mexican people.

Kerr's press release and Ariza's trip failed to allay the fears of the colonia or to satisfy either the Mexican government or the press. It was proposed that in retaliation Mexico should deport seven thousand Americans doing business in Mexico and confiscate their property. It was also proposed that all Americans in Mexico be forced to register and pay a ten dollar fee.[67] There was also the cry to boycott American-made goods and to impose restrictive tariffs. Since Mexico constituted one of the United States' best customers, any cutback in exports would certainly hurt the struggling American economy. Businessmen expressed concern over the employment of Canadian engineers rather than Americans in building the International

Highway. Canadian funding was also being utilized in building the project.[68] For American banks, this meant the loss of desperately needed business. Based on these aspects, it is logical to conclude that subtle pressures
were brought to bear on Director of Immigration Walter Carr to desist from
antagonizing the Mexican community at home and abroad by curtailing
mass deportation raids. The fact that none occurred after 1931 bears out the
logic of this contention.

After the advent of the New Deal administration of Franklin D. Roosevelt,
deportation procedures assumed a more humane aspect. The worst of the
deportation terror abated for a number of reasons. Immigration to the
United States decreased dramatically from previous years. From 1925 to 1929,
2,474,500 immigrants entered the country, whereas from 1930 to 1934, only
1,216,396 entries were recorded.[69] Most of them were legal immigrants admitted under quota to join families already in the United States. The lack of
employment opportunities discouraged many would-be illegal aliens from
entering the country. There was also a reluctance to deport a family member, especially a breadwinner, if the entire family suffered as a result. This
prevented dependent family members from becoming public charges. This
did not mean the end of the deportation terror, but after 1934 the number
of Mexicans being deported fell dramatically by approximately 50 percent.[70]
Even though the INS's efforts had produced limited results, despite all
the furor only 50,000 persons were deported, they created the impression
that welfare and related costs were greatly reduced as a result of its deportation efforts.

Adiós, Migra
DOCUMENTS

■ ■

ANTI-ALIEN ORDINANCE PROPOSAL AND MEMBERSHIP
APPLICATION. NATIONAL CLUB OF AMERICA FOR AMERICANS TO
LOS ANGELES COUNTY BOARD OF SUPERVISORS, SAN DIEGO,
CALIFORNIA, 18 AUGUST 1938.
Source: Los Angeles County Decimal File.

THE NATIONAL CLUB OF
AMERICA FOR AMERICANS, INC.
UNDER THE LAWS OF CALIFORNIA

NON SECTARIAN AND NON PARTISAN

OUR MOTTO

RETAIN AMERICA FOR AMERICAN CITIZENS

OUR INSPIRATION, THE 91ST. PSALM

ADDRESS ALL MAIL TO P.O. BOX 750

SAN DIEGO, CALIFORNIA

Board of Supervisors of
Los Angeles County,
Los Angeles, California.

Honorable Sirs:
In behalf of the National Club of America for Americans Inc., I am
enclosing copies of two proposed ordinances for the consideration
of your honorable body.

The one ordinance calls for prohibiting the granting of labor permits
to any unnaturalized alien to work in Los Angeles County unless no
American citizen is available for the work. The other ordinance calls for
prohibiting any Labor Union or Labor Organization from either electing
or appointing any unnaturalized alien to represent them in any labor
dispute in Los Angeles County. Let the aliens or their friends attack the
Constitutionality of these ordinances and they will find that American

Citizens can also legislate to protect the welfare of their citizens just the same as other Countries have and are doing today for their citizens.

The following suggestions will help you to see that the Board of Supervisors of Los Angeles County have the legal right to pass these ordinances.

REASONABLE INTERPRETATION:

The Constitution must be given a reasonable interpretation, according to the import of it's [sic] terms, and not differently from it's [sic] obvious or necessarily implied sense.

Let us assume that the Board of Supervisor of Los Angeles County wrote the tenth, eleventh, and fourteenth Amendments, to the Federal Constitution also wrote Article 1, Section 3, of the Constitution of California, then let us have faith that they being American Citizens, were practical, were considered sane and possessed a high conception of the patriotic responsibilities for the future welfare of American Citizens when they wrote these laws.

ANY AMERICAN CITIZEN SUBSCRIBING TO THE FOLLOWING PLEDGE IS WELCOME TO JOIN THIS ORGANIZATION.

1. I pledge my first allegiance to God and my country.
2. I pledge to carry into public life the teachings of what is right and wrong as taught by Jesus Christ.
3. I pledge to support and uphold the Constitution and the laws of our country at all times.
4. I pledge to see that our Constitution is enforced in keeping separate the duties of legislative, executive, and judicial branches of our government.
5. I pledge to work for such legislation as may be needed to reduce the cost of expenditures in Local, County, State, and the Federal Government, by doing away with all useless bureaus and overlapping public offices.
6. I pledge to work for an amendment to our National Constitution prohibiting the issuing by any Local, County, State, or the Federal Government of tax-exempt bonds.
7. I shall oppose the United States' entering into entangling alliances with any foreign country in any shape or form.

8. I will study all public questions in order that I may properly perform my duties as an American Citizen.

9. I will serve on jury duty if called, and will testify in court against any violation of our laws if necessary, in order that justice may be done and the laws of our country be upheld.

10. I will work to keep our banking system free from control or undue influence from the international bankers whether they be American or of some foreign country.

11. I believe in the idea of social security for American citizens at the least expense to the public taxpayers, and to secure it without public expense if possible.

12. We recognize the legal and moral right of every nation to legislate to protect and safeguard the welfare of their citizens at all times, and we reserve the same rights to the Forty Eight States and our Federal Government.

13. I favor closing the doors on immigration from all countries for ten years to any one seeking to enter America to find employment or to enter business in competition with American citizens.

14. I favor a federal registration of both American citizens and aliens as a safeguard in time of war and to stop the illegal entry of aliens of all kinds, including criminals and racketeers.

15. I favor stopping the un-American and un-Godlike policy of paying any one to not raise or produce anything at the expense of the tax-payers.

16. I will use my influence to retain America for American citizens, by buying American made goods and farm products in preference to those from foreign countries, and will employ American citizens in preference to aliens.

17. I will vote at all elections, placing my honest convictions above party regularity; and will support for public office only those who are known to stand for civic and moral righteousness and who believe in upholding American laws, American ideals, American customs, and the United States form of government, as well as recognizing that all public offices should be run in the interest of all American citizens at the least expense to the taxpayers.

18. I shall uphold the freedom of speech, the press, and radio, so as to protect the liberties and freedom of American citizens.

DOCUMENTS

19. I shall oppose government by federal bureaus.
20. I shall oppose any attempt at regimentation of the American people.
21. I shall see that the American Indians receive their full rights as American citizens.
22. I shall endeavor to promote a better understanding and closer friendship between American citizens and the citizens of all countries, especially our two neighbors Canada and Mexico.
23. I shall oppose any attempt by congress or any other legislative body to appropriate any of the taxpayers' money to give jobs or work to aliens or to carry aliens on permanent welfare relief.
24. I shall oppose the cancelling or reduction of any of the World War Debts due the United States and will vote to retire from public office any public official who advocates anything else but collecting those debts in full.

■ ■

PRESS RELEASE. J. A. H. KERR, PRESIDENT OF THE
LOS ANGELES CHAMBER OF COMMERCE, 7 MAY 1931.
Source: University of California Los Angeles,
Special Collections Clements Collection, Box 80, Bundle 15.

Because of the friendly and cordial relationship which has always existed between Los Angeles and our southern neighbor, the great Republic of Mexico, the Los Angeles Chamber of Commerce desires to express to our Mexican people its warm appreciation of the fact that this community has been privileged to be designated as the largest city in Mexican population outside of the Republic.

We have always found our fellow citizens of Mexican origin in the main people of high ideals and a peace loving, respectable citizenry.

While we regret that a considerable number of our Mexican people are returning to their home land, we appreciate the patriotic motives which prompt this move and concur in their belief that in the fine present-day progress of their Nation they may well look forward to increasing prosperity for themselves individually and collectively.

We assume it unnecessary to call the attention of our Mexican friends to the fact that they should in no wise be influenced in leaving this section because of idle rumors that the people of Los Angeles do not entertain for them the most cordial friendship or that the Government of the United States is embarked upon any wholesale deportation plan aimed principally at our Mexican people.

The U.S. Immigration officials have repeatedly stated that no alien legally in the United States has any cause for anxiety concerning the activities of the Bureau of Immigration; that Immigration officials are concerned only with persons who are illegally in the United States. Therefore, all those who have come into this country legally not only are permitted to stay here but are welcome and have full protection of the laws of this country.

To the Republic of Mexico, to its people, to its Government officials and to our own Mexican people we extend our cordial cooperation and best wishes.

By order of the Board of Directors
of the Los Angeles Chamber of Commerce
J. A. H. Kerr, President
May 7–1931.

*[handwritten: Release to all media to placate
M. community in L.A. due to deportation activity!]*

Migratory Mexican field worker's home on the edge of a frozen pea field. Imperial Valley, California, March 1937. Photograph by Dorothea Lange, courtesy of the Library of Congress, FSA Project.

Welfare
El Condado

En las puertas del condado	*At the County Welfare Office*
Se ven de todas naciones	*Are seen people of all nations*
Algunos con sus hijitos	*Some with their little ones*
Pidiendo sus provisiones	*Begging for food*
—"El Paisano Repatriado"	—"The Repatriated Countryman"

I n 1929 the world suddenly found itself engulfed in economic flames. In the United States, millions of bewildered, jobless men and women found themselves in demeaning circumstances that none of them had ever foreseen. Some were reduced to rummaging in garbage cans for edible scraps. Others sold apples on street corners or collected old newspapers, rags, and scrap metal to be sold to junk dealers. Those too proud to stand in soup lines rode the rails in a never-ending quest for work. In the richest nation in the world, children went to bed with only gruel in their bellies. The good times of the "Roaring Twenties" had ground to a screeching halt.

As the depression grew worse, state and local governments with large foreign populations scurried to pass laws restricting employment to native-born or naturalized citizens. Colorado Governor Edwing C. Johnson led the crusade in limiting "the possibilities of employment . . . for only native sons."[1] Other states followed suit. The impact was particularly devastating for Mexicans. In the Medina family, the father lost his landscaping job at the University of Arizona because of "a new law requiring all public employees to be American citizens."[2] Employers who violated the law faced a five hundred dollar fine or a prison term of six months. Although the law was seldom enforced, employers used it as a convenient excuse for not hiring Mexicans. If contractors hired nonresidents, they had to justify the reason for doing so or they would not be paid. This edict wreaked havoc with Mexicans who had been loyal employees for many years. It also made it difficult for any Mexican, whether American citizens or foreign born, to get hired.[3]

Mexican colonias and barrios struggled to survive as the combined tide of prejudice and unemployment engulfed them. The economic riptide eroded the colonias' fragile socioeconomic moorings and carried them into treacherous waters. The Alvarado family in Texas "lost everything even their house and furniture." After moving several times, they finally settled in a house with "outdoor toilet facilities and an old wood burning stove."[4] As husbands lost their jobs, wives stepped into the breech and launched a valiant last ditch effort in the family's struggle to survive. Every conceivable effort was made to make ends meet and keep the family together. Mexican families who had always taken pride in paying their own way found themselves driven to the brink of despair. When all else failed and hope faded, they swallowed their pride and joined the hordes at the county welfare agency's windows. Being forced to seek welfare assistance was a traumatic experience that Mexican families would not soon forget. The anguish, pain, and shame would haunt them for years. Proud men found themselves stripped of their role as providers and protectors.[5]

Eventually, even the federal government got into the act by requiring that all firms supplying it with goods and services hire only U.S. citizens. In North Tarrytown, New York, General Motors discharged all alien employees in order not to lose its federal contracts.[6] Nearly every major employer or contractor followed suit. When the New Deal went into effect, employment on WPA (Works Progress Administration) projects was also denied to aliens unless they were World War I veterans. Veteran José Santos Herrada, a Mexican National, and his family survived by working on WPA construction projects in Michigan. The money he earned permitted Herrada to support his repatriated children living with his mother in Mexico and also to pay for their return to Detroit.[7] Many Mexican Americans also found the WPA assistance program critically important. The relief program furnished Concepción Alvarado Escobedo and her sisters with clothing, food, and other amenities.[8] Exceptions also were made for spouses of American citizens and veterans who had served in the military forces of the United States. Also exempted were individuals who had served in the armed forces of nations allied with the United States during World War I. Aliens exempted from making a formal declaration of intent by the Immigration, Naturalization and Repatriation laws were not affected by the decree.[9]

In an ironic twist of bureaucratic inaneness, in order to receive federal relief assistance American citizens had to agree to accept employment on federally funded work projects. At the same time, the federal government decreed that welfare allotments should be increased by 30 percent for those "for whom no Civil Work projects are available . . . or who, because of nationality, cannot take part on Civil Works projects."[10] As a result, in some cases, the allotments received by aliens were larger than those of citizens forced to work for their welfare checks. The inequity of the situation riled many aid recipients, taxpayers, and lawmakers. It helped to fan the flames of the anti-alien feelings sweeping the country. Thus, Mexicans found themselves victims of a situation not of their own making. Given a choice, they would have preferred to be allowed to work for their largesse.

Like other unemployed young men, Pablo Segura was thankful for the $30.00 a month he received from working for the WPA in the CCC, Civil Conservation Corps program. "Twenty-five of it" went to the family, Segura remembered, which left him with only "$5.00 a month."[11] It was not enough to cover his personal needs, but it helped his family to survive.

However, the opportunity to find work eluded Mexicans, as employers everywhere not only acceded to government restrictions but heeded the hue and cry of patriotic groups and organizations to save all jobs for "real Americans." Since few of the Mexican immigrants bothered to apply for citizenship, the refusal to hire foreigners was devastating. The prestigious *New York Times* reported in 1937 that "two million of the two and a half million Mexicans in the United States were out of work."[12] Unemployment among Mexicans ranged from 15 percent to as high as 85 percent. The wide variance was influenced by the season of the year, locale, type of employment, available labor force, and the legal restrictions against hiring noncitizens. As factories and shops closed down, the work schedule in some plants was reduced to one or two days per week. As a result, wages and earnings plummeted. In cities like Chicago, Detroit, Milwaukee, Buffalo, Gary, Indiana, and New York, over 30 percent of all compatriots were out of work. In colonias across the country, employment dropped by an average of 50 percent.[13]

Even agricultural employment proved to be precarious. As prices fell, so did wages. Wages for farm workers dropped to fifteen dollars or less for a sixty-hour workweek. In diverse places like Idaho and Montana, Nebraska and Iowa, and Minnesota and Michigan, the rate for working sugar beets fell from twenty-eight dollars to ten dollars an acre.[14] At that wage, the dirty, backbreaking work did not provide a workman's family with a decent livelihood. Unemployment, coupled with fear of the dreaded northern winters, drove many compatriots to abandon long-inhabited domiciles. In the Chicago area, more than 25 percent of the Mexican populace either returned to Mexico or headed for the Southwest, seeking a warmer climate if not greener pastures. Eventually, the estimated 25,000 population fell to less than 5,000.[15]

Adding to the precarious situation facing Mexican farm workers were the refugees fleeing the Midwest Dust Bowl. The fierce competition for the few scarce farm jobs grew worse. Migrant fruit pickers were especially hard hit, but the impact of the new jobless horde was felt throughout the labor market. Southern California and the Great Central Valley became popular destinations for those homeless knights-errant. It is estimated that more than 350,000 Dust Bowl refugees made their way west. The negative impact on the area was so severe that the Los Angeles County Board of Supervisors adopted a resolution citing the ominous threat to wages and acceptable standards of living. The resolution urged employers to give hiring preference to local farmhands instead.[16] However, knowing the language and customs, plus their willingness to work for starvation wages, gave the "Okies" a decided advantage over Mexican workers. Mexican workers resented the intruders, and outbreaks of violence between the two competing groups were not uncommon.

Another group eroding the labor status of Mexican workers in Southern California were the Filipinos. Usually devoid of any family and living in groups, Filipino men could afford to work for lower wages. In Orange County, the Comisión Honorífica Mexicana attempted to convince the La Habra Citrus Association to hire resident Mexicans rather than the newcomers. Aggravating the situation was the attention that lonely Filipino men paid to young Mexican girls. Viewed by many as "happy-go-lucky," they enjoyed needling Mexican fellow workers by addressing them as *cuñado* (brother-in-law). Mexicans harbored strong feelings of resentment toward the Filipinos as a result of the dual threat they posed.[17]

Unemployment and hunger go hand in hand, and colonias everywhere felt the sharp pain of deprivation. Comités de Beneficencia, Comisiones Honorificas, Brigadas de la Cruz Azul, and other groups attempted to stem the tide of human suffering. However, their resources were extremely limited. Few of them survived for any length of time and even fewer enjoyed any measure of success. Some agencies and groups solicited help from the Mexican government. The position of SRE (Secretaría de Relaciones Exteriores) was to deny such requests except in extreme cases. The national treasury simply could not respond to the myriad requests from groups pleading for assistance.[18] Typical of the requests was a letter signed by thirty-seven heads of families in Rockdale, Illinois, and forwarded to the Mexican consul in Chicago. Written in Spanish, the letter implored the consul to act in their behalf "before they died of hunger, cold or were forced by hunger to resort to a life of crime and dishonor for a piece of bread for their wives and children."[19] As a last resort, they asked for help in returning to Mexico. The letter eloquently expressed the fears and desires of destitute Mexicans in colonias in every sector of the land. Many of them deemed it desirable, perhaps as a way of saving face, to return home rather than accept charity and bring shame upon their families.

As local bootstrap efforts in the colonias failed, Mexicans reluctantly began to queue up at county welfare offices. The decision to apply for welfare was not an easy one. This final indignity was submitted to only after all efforts to find work had failed. Meager savings were stretched to the absolute limit and all available resources were exhausted before succumbing to the despised dole. Watching their children steadily growing more emaciated was a pitiful and heart wrenching sight for parents. It haunted them to see once healthy and happy children steadily losing weight and succumbing to disease as malnutrition wracked their frail bodies. In desperation, many parents felt they had no other recourse but to apply for public assistance. Applying for welfare was made bearable because applicants truly believed that relief was a temporary measure. The economy of the richest nation on earth was bound to turn around soon. No one envisioned a decade of misery and suffering, such a likelihood was simply incomprehensible. The Gamez family from Indiana Harbor, Indiana, remembered the stigma of being on relief: "Being on relief was awful. You could tell, by the way children were dressed, which families were on relief and which were not. Our clothes gave it away! They were of good material and well-made. The trouble was they were all from the same cloth and made from the same pattern."[20]

In California, Los Angeles County experienced a sudden surge in requests for welfare assistance. In 1931, county welfare rolls escalated from thirty-five hundred individuals to thirty-five thousand families. Nothing of this magnitude had ever occurred before. The county Department of Charities was not sure how to proceed. It suffered from a lack of leadership due to a succession of superintendents of charities.[21] It fell upon Rex Thomson, an engineer and administrator by profession rather than a trained social worker, to step into the breach and keep the county's relief program afloat. Previously, Mr. Thomson had been acting in a consulting capacity to the Board of Supervisors. Impressed by his candor and administrative ability, the Board implored him to take over the burgeoning welfare department. As a result, Thomson found himself managing a department that encompassed three-fourths of the county's employees and spent 75 percent of the budget. Due to Thomson's efficiency, the department became a model for welfare agencies across the country. When the New Deal Democrats came to power in 1933, much of the federal welfare plan was based on the Los Angeles model.[22]

Literally overnight, in spite of his limited experience, Rex Thomson became a self-styled expert on welfare and repatriation. His advice and counsel were sought at home and abroad. He made numerous trips to Mexico. Thomson attributed his success to the fact that, as an engineer, he saw people as pieces or cogs of a machine. It was his job to put them in the right place and in the right order so the machine could function properly. A tribute to his acumen and ability was the efficient—some would claim ruthless—manner in which the welfare department handled the monumental task thrust upon it. Thomson had precious little tolerance for inept bureaucrats. Incensed by the ineptitude of subordinates, he complained bitterly to the chairman of the County Board of Supervisors about the caliber of county workers. The chairman responded cogently that if the employees were not inept, he, Rex Thomson, would not be their leader. A chagrined Thomson went back to the department and continued to provide aggressive leadership.[23]

Rex Thomson's assertiveness was imperative due to the increased demand for welfare services. During 1933–34, the worst period of the depression, some 126,000 families, of which 10 percent were Mexicans, were on the dole in Los Angeles County. This constituted over 600,000 individuals. The number of recipients escalated drastically from the figures reported at the end of 1931. By the end of 1934, according to official estimates sixty thousand heads of families had sought help. A bond issue of five million dollars plus a 600,000-dollar contribution from the Community Chest agency had been spent. Yet the amount fell far short of what was needed to meet local welfare needs. Anglo families received a basic grant of thirty dollars a month, but Mexicans received only twenty dollars. The fact that Mexican families tended to be larger was conveniently ignored in determining the amount of the allotments. The justification for the lesser sum was that Mexican families had a lower standard of living and could get along on a cheaper diet.[24] Obviously, the smaller amount created its own self-fulfilling prophecy. Beans, tortillas, soup, and gruel became part of a bland, repetitive diet in Mexican households.

Among the nation's major cities, Los Angeles had the largest number of Mexicans receiving relief. The reason was simple. There were more Mexicans living there than were to be found anywhere else. But in spite of the severe crisis, most Mexican families chose not to demean themselves by asking for public aid. Therefore, contrary to the widely held belief that most Mexicans were on welfare during the depression, such was not the case. As a rule, they constituted 10 percent or less of the total number of families on county aid. "Only 38 percent of those so-called Mexican cases," Los Angeles County reported, "are aliens, the balance being cases of Mexican descent who are American citizens."[25] Moreover, the vast majority of Mexican families receiving charity were established residents of Los Angeles County. Some 62.7 percent had lived in the county for ten years or more while 31 percent had lived there all their life. Receiving charity was a new and revolting experience for these families. As a result, some 49.1 percent were on relief for less than a year and only 43 percent were on relief for one to five years. Clearly living on welfare was not an acceptable way of life for indigent Mexicans.[26] That was the case in Los Angeles, Detroit, and elsewhere.

That was not only the case in Los Angeles, it was a pattern commonly found throughout the country. In Cleveland, Ohio, for example, a total of 100,000 needy families received welfare during the 1932–34 period, but only a small percentage of the recipients were Mexicans. Contrary to the double standard utilized in allocating welfare aid in Los Angeles, in Cleveland all families received a food allowance of four dollars a week. In Illinois, out of a total of 819,038 individuals receiving unemployment relief, 85.1 percent were white. Of the remainder, 14.1 percent were Negroes and less than 0.8 percent were Mexicans or others.[27] Most of the welfare recipients resided in Cook County, which encompassed the city of Chicago. Some twenty-five thousand Mexicans normally resided in the city and its immediate environs. *Excélsior* in Mexico City reported that there were twenty-one thousand Mexicans without work in Chicago. The total was augmented by workers who had come to the city from outlying areas in the vain hope of finding employment. To prevent the growing number of indigents from becoming a problem or a burden, arrangements were made to ship most of them to Mexico. According to the newspaper, the majority of the repatriates from the Chicago area were to be sent directly to Mexico City. They would not be permitted to settle in towns or villages en route to the capital. *Excélsior* reported that repatriates from Detroit and Dearborn, Michigan, as well as from Ohio, would also be arriving in the capital very soon.[28] The number of repatriates increased as automobile assembly lines, steel mills, and other factories laid off more of their Mexican workers. This was the case in Indiana Harbor's Mexican community of some 6,000 people in the City of East Chicago, Indiana. Due to layoffs, "Fully half of the Mexican population was dependent on charitable assistance" and faced severe repatriation pressures.[29] The combination of unemployment, hunger, and the bitter cold presented a dreaded specter to Mexican enclaves in eastern cities.

Los Angeles, Cleveland, and Chicago were not alone in trying to cope with an ever-increasing number of welfare cases. Detroit, Philadelphia, New York, Atlanta, New Orleans, and San Antonio were among cities reeling under the staggering costs of trying to provide a safety net for the indigents in their midst. Available resources simply proved to be inadequate for the task. Cleveland faced a deficit of seven million dollars in meeting its basic relief needs. Chicago desperately needed an additional nine million dollars to cover expenses. Philadelphia estimated it needed fifteen million dollars more to meet its obligations. New York City's welfare appropriation of five million dollars provided aid to less than 7 percent of its needy inhabitants.[30] It was estimated that there were fifteen hundred Mexicans among the jobless New Yorkers who needed assistance.[31] In San Antonio, Texas, 2,000 Mexican workers found themselves in dire straits. More than 475 had been laid off from their city jobs.[32] They joined the growing ranks of their compatriots around the country who had been dismissed in order to comply with the edict forbidding hiring Mexican Nationals and other aliens on public projects.

When applying for welfare in Texas, Mexicans were often subjected to discrimination. Among the complaints lodged by the Consul General in San Antonio with the Mexican embassy in Washington, D.C., was the charge that some welfare authorities were demanding that Mexicans who were legal residents present their naturalization papers or proof of citizenship in order to qualify for public assistance. If they did not have papers, they were instructed to take steps to obtain American citizenship. Since some of the welfare funds involved federal monies, the U.S. State Department was asked to intervene and instruct Texas welfare officials to end the discriminatory practice.[33] Despite the protests, Texas authorities continued to employ their biased tactics. Welfare payments in Texas averaged only $7.08 a month per family. Texas was not alone in its frugality. Other states also offered niggardly assistance. On a monthly basis, Oklahoma provided $4.96 and Arkansas offered $4.86 per family. California offered what must have seemed like a princely sum by comparison, $31.35 a month.[34] If broken down on a per-capita basis, relief costs for U.S. cities from January 1931 to September 1931 averaged $6.59 for Detroit, $3.40 for Los Angeles, $2.41 for Chicago, and $1.69 for Minneapolis. Other expenditures ranged from $0.79 for Denver, $0.53 for Kansas City, $0.49 for Dallas, $0.29 for El Paso, $0.34 for Houston, and $0.15 for San Antonio.[35]

It is, therefore, not surprising that California became a mecca for those down and out on their luck. More unemployed transients were attracted to the Golden State than to any other state in the Union. In the month of September 1936, more than 14,000 people entered the state. In 1937, nearly 105,000 migrants crossed the border into California.[36] It is estimated that between 1933 and 1939, a total of 957,000 people migrated to California. Of this number, approximately 300,000 eventually received some form of state or federal aid. State authorities estimated that nearly thirteen million dollars, exclusive of administrative costs, was expended on their behalf.[37] In self-defense, California instituted a residency requirement of one year before an applicant could be eligible for public assistance. In an attempt to stem the influx, the Los Angeles chief of police arbitrarily established an outpost on the Arizona/California border to prevent indigents from entering the state. The action was a clear violation of the law and patently illegal.[38] Even if families did not receive aid or financial assistance, California's mild climate made camping out or sleeping in a run-down jalopy easier to bear. Approximately 97 percent of those entering the state and seeking welfare were Americans unable to cope with their destitute plight.

Nevertheless, labor unions, veterans' organizations, taxpayers' associations, and patriotic groups joined the chorus of protest against spending public funds to assist aliens. One of the most vocal groups was the National Club of America for Americans, Inc. However, the National Club of America for Americans request "to prohibit appropriation of public money for feeding, caring for or giving jobs to aliens" was beyond the jurisdiction of county boards. "It is beyond the power of your board to adopt ordinances," the Los Angeles County legal counsel advised the supervisors, "to distinguish between aliens and citizens." The legal counsel also pointed out that the California State Legislature had stipulated in the Welfare and Institutions Code 2500 that relief was "to relieve and support all incompetent, poor, indigent persons and those incapacitated by age, disease, or accident."[39] There was no authority to deny aid on the basis of citizenship. Nevertheless, the National Club of America for Americans, headquartered in San Diego, painstakingly tracked the cost of providing aid to Mexicans in California. Its survey concluded that, during a seventeen-month period, the state had spent $2,899,546 and Los Angeles County $3,885,314 on welfare. This amounted to a grand total of $6,784,860, exclusive of administrative costs. Armed with this information, the club demanded that boards of supervisors in all California counties maintain precise records regarding the cost of alien relief. The information would then be shared among the counties and the public via the media. This would enable interested parties to exert pressure on county boards, the state legislature, and Congress to deny assistance to aliens whenever the issue came up for a vote in their respective chambers.[40] The National Club of America for Americans received widespread support for its aggressive stance in behalf of welfare reform.

Responding to public pressure, the Los Angeles County Board of Supervisors ruled that potential recipients of county aid must present a certificate verifying their legal entry into the country or provide proof of citizenship. The Board was attempting to follow the example of New York City that required aliens to submit a certificate of arrival. By enforcing the requirement, the city had pared 16,000 people from its welfare rolls.[41] The enforcement of this requirement in Los Angeles led to a variety of vexing problems.

Many Mexicans had arrived in the United States long before formal entry restrictions were enforced. Others, especially those with a transient lifestyle, had lost their passports or legal papers. Some had no way of verifying one year of continuous residency in the county. Complicating matters was the fact that there were many different ways of evading the welfare paper trail. The system simply could not cope with the varied problems that arose. In one instance, the mother of five children was apprehended for having entered the U.S. illegally and was summarily deported. However, since the children were American citizens, they could not be forced to leave the country. The county, therefore, incurred the expense of having to hire a housekeeper to look after the children until such time as they could be reunited with their mother.[42]

Mexicans comprised less than 10 percent of the relief recipients across the country even though media hype and officials pronouncements made it appear as if the vast majority of those on welfare were either Mexicans or of Mexican extraction. Typical of the inflammatory statements were the comments attributed to H. M. Blaine, member of the Los Angeles County Board of Supervisors. While on a visit to Mexico City, Mr. Blaine allegedly remarked that the majority of the Mexicans in the Los Angeles colonia were either on relief or were public charges.[43] Those blatant accusations from a public official infuriated the Mexican press. It took national umbrage at what was considered to be an insult to Mexico's honor. Due to his remarks and the outrage they evoked, it was rumored that Supervisor Blaine had to be smuggled out of Mexico because American authorities feared for his personal safety.

Reacting to Supervisor H. M. Blaine's inopportune remarks, *El Universal Gráfico*, a leading capital daily, headlined a story entitled "Ungrateful Attitude toward Mexicans Who Have Worked in the United States." The article claimed that Mexican workers contributed more than 200 million dollars a year to California's agricultural prosperity. Their labor had enriched the agriculture barons while workers were paid starvation wages. Now they were being callously shipped out of the country or denied desperately needed assistance. The newspaper challenged the official report that only 12,000 Mexicans had been repatriated. In actuality, it alleged, 49,000 people had been shipped to Mexico from Los Angeles, San Bernardino, and Orange Counties. The newspaper also stated that of the 100,000 people on welfare in Los Angeles, only 10,000 were Mexicans. The article claimed, in self-righteous indignation, that all the recipients were American-born. It proudly asserted that no Mexican Nationals were on relief.[44]

Regardless of the actual facts, allegations kept the anti-Mexican sentiment inflamed throughout the nation during the decade. Local, state, and national officials were incessantly bombarded with letters and petitions. Individuals and organizations demanded that immediate action be taken to curtail the employment of Mexicans. They also wanted them removed from the relief rolls and shipped back to Mexico, where they believed all Mexicans belonged. Typical of the requests was a handwritten letter from L. Clark to President Franklin D. Roosevelt. Mr. Clark stated in part: "Our towns are over run with the Mexican population. They breed like rats, live in huts, mostly are dependent on day labor. Thus they run heavily on charity both medical and food supplies."[45] Clark then repeated the stereotyped charges of the "great menace" posed by the Mexicans unless steps were taken to ship them home. Regretfully, Clark's racist tirade represented the thinking of many well-meaning Americans.

One of the factors that triggered substantial opposition toward the relief programs was the loss of cheap, dependable farm labor. Seeking livable wages, farm laborers migrated to the cities. However, most of them were unable to find work and some gravitated to the relief rolls. According to agricultural employers, once farmhands had experienced the ease of living on welfare, it became virtually impossible to get them back on the farm.[46] Employers' fears were borne out by the fact that despite the high rate of unemployment, a shortage of pickers developed in the San Joaquin Valley. Relief authorities in the surrounding counties tried to induce welfare recipients to apply for the jobs by promising them gasoline and food rations for the journey.[47] However, there were few takers willing to undergo the hardships that farm work entailed.

Consequently, despite the combined efforts of employers and welfare authorities to recruit farm workers, the results were abysmal. The situation was serious and getting worse. As crops ripened, the need for workers grew more urgent. The tactic decided upon was to remove all farmhands from the relief rolls in counties located within the San Joaquin Valley.[48] The state Emergency Relief Administration was asked to cooperate in the venture. Within a week, five hundred workers were declared ineligible for welfare aid and terminated. However, the state Employment Bureau reported that only seventy-five former welfare recipients had shown up on local farms, seeking work.[49] Many welfare critics saw this result as proof positive that being on the dole ruined a person's work ethic and self-esteem. Others criticized the fact that people on relief got as much money or perhaps more than they could earn as farm workers.[50]

Among those complaining about the loss of Mexican farm workers was Dr. George P. Clements, secretary of agriculture for the Los Angeles Chamber of Commerce. In a letter to W. Frank Persons, director of Employment Service, U.S. Department of Labor, Clements stated: "The Mexican, however, even under the most harassing conditions such as housing commissions, sanitation laws, religious funk, and commercial thievery, filled every requirement for agriculture and rough industry even to the loss of his health, his morals, his earnings, and his attitude toward life." Understandably, Dr. Clements lamented, "When the sob sisters of America, particularly those in California, could not get rid of the Mexican in any other way, the Filipino was brought in to displace him, [and Filipinos are] the most worthless, unscrupulous, shiftless, diseased, semi-barbarian that has ever come to our shores . . . even [worse than] the negro [sic]." Clements also voiced his candid opinion regarding other racial groups: "there are only three races in the world whom civilization has not touched—the Scotch, the Indian (and the Mexican is an Indian), and the Irish."[51] Such views by a respected representative of the Chamber of Commerce were obviously not intended for public consumption.

Dr. Clements was not alone in deploring the sudden dearth of dependable, experienced field hands to handle California's exotic fruits and vegetables. Relief authorities were repeatedly implored to desist from repatriating indigent Mexicans until after the crops had been harvested. Cotton growers in Arizona and Texas, like their counterparts in the Central Valley, could not lure city people to harvest their crops. Anglo workers eschewed picking cotton at the prevailing rate per pound. They knew that even if they were deleted from the relief rolls temporarily, they could always get reinstated.[52]

Around the country, Mexicans became the victims of a series of cruel dilemmas. They lost their jobs as a result of laws enacted to prevent them from being hired on public projects. Farm jobs declined due to less acreage being planted. Due to competition from "los Okies," they suffered from a drop in wages. The private sector succumbed to demands that it hire only "real Americans." Also affecting their situation were requirements that denied them access to welfare programs. Those that did get aid ran the risk of being deported or repatriated. In Pennsylvania, for example, Secretary of Welfare E. Arthur Sweeny proposed deporting aliens who had become public charges as a result of being hospitalized. He estimated that 1,359 patients, many of them mentally ill, could be shipped home. The savings to taxpayers would amount to $422,000 annually. Mr. Sweeny also believed that nearly two thousand additional patients could be persuaded to leave "voluntarily." In the hope of augmenting these figures, he ordered a thorough investigation of the status of all aliens receiving any form of public assistance.[53] Other states and counties also attempted to get rid of as many ailing aliens as possible in order to conserve welfare funds.

In Detroit, the Department of Public Assistance conducted an especially aggressive repatriation campaign. A special Mexican Bureau was established in the local colonia to promote repatriation. The Mexican Bureau often denied direct relief funds to Mexicans. Instead, they were given meal tickets and forced to eat at cafeterias where they had to endure public humiliation. As elsewhere, Detroit social workers did not limit their activities only to Mexican Nationals, but included Mexican Americans. "Although Mr. M. had citizenship," and was therefore a legal resident, the case worker "demanded that he repatriate himself in view of the dependency of his family." Another social worker determined that repatriation was best for "Mary Lou (age fifteen), born in Wayne, Michigan," even though she "did not wish to return to Mexico."[54] This callous, heartless attitude made a tragic situation even worse.

Occasionally, among the tragic wreckage of human lives, a bizarrely humorous event brought a chuckle to newspaper readers or radio listeners. In Chicago, an alien appeared in court and complained that he needed a size-42 pair of pants rather than the size-36 given him by the local relief agency. Judge Thomas Green saw red and exclaimed: "You have a lot of nerve. After being in this country nineteen years without becoming a citizen and after living on relief for five years, you kick about it. If you don't like this country—or the pants—get out!"[55] The judge then proceeded to fine the distraught welfare recipient two hundred dollars on charges of disorderly conduct. On a more serious but similar note, Federal Judge John A. Peters in Portland, Maine, admonished fifty-one new candidates for U.S. citizenship to "avoid the alphabetical relief agencies as you would the plague. This country is no place for drones or any leisure classes. People supported by the government are simply eating off their fellow-citizens," he asserted. He exhorted them to be "workers" in their adopted country.[56] Judge Peters's salient remarks represented a prevailing view in society at the time that accepting welfare was in essence "un-American."[57]

Reeling from the loss of jobs and denial of welfare, residents in colonias everywhere began to organize in order to demand and protect their rights. The mood regarding applying for or accepting welfare began to change. There was a growing feeling that they had earned it through the sweat of their brow. Their work had contributed significantly to the vast wealth the nation had amassed. Thus, it was only fair that they should be eligible to receive assistance along with others who were temporarily down on their luck. As the depression worsened, seeking relief lost a great deal of its stigma among Mexicans. How could it be a disgrace, since nearly 85 percent of the people on welfare were Americans—white Anglo-Saxons. That simple fact was very reassuring to the Mexican population. It served as proof that Anglos, for all their vaunted pretense of superiority, were not able to cope with the depression any better than, and in some cases not as well as, those they commonly disdained as "dumb Mexicans." Actually, Mexicans disparagingly believed that Anglos would starve to death in the midst of plenty.

In order to qualify for welfare assistance, the question of U.S. citizenship at first appeared to be a major stumbling block for Mexican Nationals. However, it ceased to be an insurmountable obstacle. Barrio leaders pointed out that while the parents might not be American citizens, most of their children certainly met that criteria. Therefore, the children were entitled to aid the same as everyone else. There was also the growing conviction that Mexicans merited aid more than some other groups, especially recent European arrivals. Many Mexicans could not understand why citizenship status had suddenly assumed such overriding importance. It had never been a factor before, either in getting work or for those who had served in the military during World War I. Mexican immigrants had served their adopted country well. Now it was the nation's obligation to respond in kind. Unfortunately, Americans did not see the situation in the same light.

Mexicans were forced to fight an uphill battle to obtain what they perceived to be rightfully due them. Dallas, Texas, became one of the hotbeds of activity as colonias united to seek their rights. There, the Trade Unity League and Unemployed Councils staged a series of indoctrination meetings. The object was to make people aware of their rights and the recourses available in order to achieve them. At a meeting held in Fair Park on February 25, 1931, organizers disclosed a list of immediate demands. First and foremost was a demand for gainful employment or compensation equivalent to a living wage. That was followed by a demand for immediate aid for those who were unemployed and for destitute farm workers. No one was to be evicted for failure to pay their rent. Utilities were to be provided free of charge to the poor and the unemployed.[58]

In Los Angeles, in the hope of avoiding similar demonstrations as well as keeping Mexicans off the welfare rolls, a variety of alternative projects were proposed. The local Mexican Chamber of Commerce created a committee to look into the feasibility of establishing a Mexican Labor Bureau. The intent was to develop a central labor clearinghouse that workers and employers could utilize to their mutual advantage. It would deal primarily with local agriculturalists who needed assurance that a dependable labor pool would be available to meet their seasonal or ongoing needs. The cooperation of the Chamber of Commerce was sought in promoting the endeavor. Ramón C. Armendariz, a member of the Mexican organizing committee, was designated to serve as the liaison between the two Chambers.[59] Cost of operating the labor bureau was estimated at about thirty thousand dollars a year. In an effort to make the operation self-supporting, it was suggested that members pay a monthly fee. Individuals gainfully employed would be charged one dollar, those working only part-time would pay fifty cents. Anyone working less than seven days per month would be exempt from membership fees.[60]

The concept of having a captive workforce and reducing relief expenditures was carried a step further by the Los Angeles Chamber of Commerce. It proposed setting up Mexican villages in rural areas, where the workers could be housed and readily looked after. This plan was not prompted by any benign attitude or sense of moral responsibility. Rather, it was meant to keep the Mexicans from being exposed to a life of ease by living on relief in the cities. As one Chamber of Commerce interdepartmental memo stated: "By the time the new deal [*sic*] and the more abundant life get through with these Mexicans, agriculture is not going to get any satisfactory labor supplies from the big cities and the sooner they [the growers] realize this, the sooner they will get command of their own situation."[61] To make the proposed plan attractive to Mexican workers, it was suggested that they be guaranteed a certain number of work days during the year. This was viewed as a strong inducement for workers to remain in the area and to be available whenever needed. The assurance of a job would enable them to satisfy their basic needs, and it would keep them off the welfare rolls.

An alternative proposal was to establish Mexican villages as adjuncts to the local missions. Possible sites included Missions San Fernando, San Gabriel, and San Juan Capistrano. In the villages, Mexicans would be trained to perform cultural rituals and to produce a variety of handicrafts. Both activities could become virtual gold mines for the out-of-work participants. The arrangement was also viewed as an opportunity to counter the negative way in which Mexicans were normally perceived in Southern California. Hopefully, an enhanced image of the Mexican would be projected to the public. In essence, they would be quaint, living dioramas.[62] One local sage observed that Mission San Juan Capistrano was famed for the yearly return of the swallows, but that in this instance the Mexicans would be the real pigeons. Like so many other "pie in the sky" schemes proposed during the depression, this one also died on the drawing board. In a unique attempt to keep citrus workers in the San Gabriel Valley away from cities and off welfare, a WPA survey group proposed building one thousand houses for Mexicans employed in the orchards. The WPA planners designed a model unit of 500 square feet with two bedrooms, 9' x 11' each; a kitchen, 10' x 11' and a living room, 11' x 14.' All houses had the added luxury of screened windows and doors. The proposed project was halted when local residents complained that the houses were "too good for Mexicans."[63] It was also feared that the housing project would set a bad precedent and force employers to provide adequate housing for their farm workers.

As inept as the schemes may appear, they represented efforts to conceal critical social issues. Civic leaders and local businessmen were willing to consider any scheme that might work. The mission village was merely a variation of a favorite theme in Southern California. Located three miles north of Claremont was the Padua Hills theater/restaurant center. Mexican musicians, artists, and youths were hired to sing, play music, and serve food to the tourists.[64] The relaxed, carefree ambiance captured the flavor and created the mood of dining in old Mexico. Rural Padua Hills had its urban counterpart in downtown Los Angeles's Olvera Street with its curio shops and picturesque restaurants. The Olvera Street merchants commissioned the famous artist David Alfaro Siqueiros to paint the America Tropical mural. But his portrayal of the Americas was deemed too controversial and bad for business.[65]

All groups and agencies acted in what they deemed to be their own best interests. A case in point was the stance taken by the AFL (American Federation of Labor) when it was asked to speak up in behalf of Mexican workers who were being laid off throughout the land. The union replied that with three million of its own members unemployed and many others facing reduction in working hours, it was in no position to offer any help to Mexican workers. The Mexican press correctly pointed out that the labor union's rationale rang hollow since it had never endeavored to help Mexican workers. Even when there was no economic crisis, the AFL had turned a deaf ear to pleas for help from Mexican workers who were facing starvation.[66] In truth, rather than a sympathetic friend, the union was an earnest foe.[67] Lack of support by organized labor simply compounded the magnitude of the problems faced by Mexicans striving to avoid going on relief.

In spite of the odds against them and the failure of plans designed to aid them, Mexicans continued their efforts to escape the dole. However, they were not always successful. Data for Los Angeles County can be viewed as representative of their situation throughout the nation. According to the federal census of 1930, Mexicans comprised 175,601 or 7.95 percent of the county's 2,208,000 population. An investigation of 64,403 unemployment cases in 1933 revealed that 6,970 cases involved Mexicans or Mexican Americans. Their combined total accounted for 10.8 percent of those unemployed. A detailed examination of 11,717 welfare cases found that 5.4 percent of the total number were Mexican Americans born in the United States and 9.0 percent were citizens of Mexico.[68]

During 1933, the number of Mexican aliens added to relief rolls throughout the country increased significantly. The reason for the increase was attributable directly to the federal government. In the face of rising costs for local, state, and national welfare programs, taxpayers hounded their elected representatives for fiscal relief. In response to repeated requests by states and counties for federal funding, the government agreed to assist them with the financial burden imposed by escalating welfare costs. However, to qualify for federal assistance, state and county governments were forbidden to make any distinction or to show any preference between citizens and noncitizens. Both groups were deemed eligible to receive direct state or county aid. Since the federal government provided 35 percent of the welfare funds, primarily through local civil works programs, participating agencies had no choice but to comply with the directive.[69]

Earl E. Jensen, superintendent of charities for the county of Los Angeles, mirrored the sentiments of welfare departments across the land. In a report to the Board of Supervisors, Jensen complained that "we find a peculiar situation, and a most unsatisfactory one, where the Mexican alien's monthly budget has been increased 30 percent and yet we refuse to allow him to do any work in return for the same, even if he were willing to do so."[70] Jensen's concern was well founded, for the cost of providing for the county's ten thousand indigent Mexican families amounted to $200,000 per month or $2,400,000 a year.[71]

Faced with this tremendous expenditure, the county sought to alleviate its financial burden by every means possible. Los Angeles County Board of Supervisors targeted the property of repatriates as a source of revenue. The county placed liens on properties of repatriates "to cover the aid received." Francisco and Carmen Esquivel relinquished "their right, title, and interest in and to" a property in the "Artesian Tract" of Los Angeles County "as a guarantee for reimbursement for transportation costs of family to Mexico."[72] The Mexican American Community Association's Executive Director, Siegfried Goetze, castigated the county for adopting this punitive policy. The Mexican community, Goetze complained, would view the confiscation of "their little homes," as destroying their "confidence in American institutions," and experience "widespread indignation."[73] The Jiménez family of East Los Angeles suffered the added indignation of losing their home when repatriated to Mexicali, Baja California.[74]

Besides acquiring properties owned by repatriates, local and state governments obtained some relief from the federal government. In spite of some shortcomings, the various welfare programs introduced by the New Deal helped to relieve the strain on state and local governments. Under the newly established Social Security system, Mexicans were eligible for old-age pensions, aid to dependent children, and aid to the blind. Most of the recipients were concentrated in the states of Arizona, California, Colorado, New Mexico, and Texas. In California, there were reportedly 55,863 Mexicans participating in the Social Security system. The state easily outdistanced its closest rivals, Colorado and Texas, nearly four to one in the number of Mexicans being served. However, the figures indicating how many people were receiving assistance tend to be misleading. In some instances, the data was incomplete or the states did not provide all three Social Security programs. Texas, for example, did not implement either the aid to dependent children or the aid to the blind programs. The number of Mexicans participating in federal-assistance programs remained relatively small. As late as 1937, it was estimated that nationwide only 100,000 Mexicans were working on WPA projects.[75]

The employment situation was adversely effected when the Seventy-sixth Congress succumbed to public pressure and declared that aliens were ineligible for employment on WPA projects. According to Section 3, Title I, of the revised Emergency Relief Act of 1937, the Works Progress Administration "shall not knowingly employ on such projects aliens illegally within the limits of the United States or aliens who have not filed declaration of intention to become citizens."[76] The new restrictions applied to all aliens, not merely to Mexicans. In New York City, 1,873 aliens lost their jobs. In New Jersey the total was 717; and in Pennsylvania, 1,107 foreigners were laid off. While Mexicans across the country were involved in the layoffs, the toll was heaviest in California and in the Southwest. The vast majority of the 100,000 Mexicans employed on WPA projects resided in California and Texas.[77]

In San Antonio, Mexicans protested the layoffs by storming and stoning the local WPA office. In an attempt to defuse the tense situation, representatives of the Mexican embassy in Washington, D.C., met with U.S. State Department officials to seek their cooperation in ameliorating the plight of those who had been discharged from WPA projects.[78] Congressional legislation had simply made a bad situation worse. Due to the new regulations, many of the individuals discharged wound up on county or state relief rolls. In California, state senator Ralph Swing of San Bernardino introduced a bill to exclude aliens from the state relief rolls. Although the proposed legislation was aimed at all aliens, the Mexican press pointed out that in California the largest alien population was of Mexican origin. Governor Culbert Olson subsequently vetoed the measure. The Mexican press hailed the action as a courageous and just stance on the part of the governor.[79]

Governor Olson's action, although hailed abroad as a humane gesture, was damned by many vociferous residents. There was a strong difference of opinion about whether the state legislature could legally appropriate or expend public funds for alien relief. In an attempt to settle the dispute, a legal opinion was sought from the state attorney general's office. In his response, state attorney general Earl Warren pointed out that neither the state constitution nor the codes or statutes of California contained any inhibition or restriction against granting relief to aliens. The attorney general cited Section 17 of Article I of the California Constitution, which stated: "Foreigners of the white race, or of African decent [*sic*], eligible to become citizens of the United States under the naturalization laws thereof, while bona fide residents of this State, shall have the same rights in respect to the acquisition, possession, enjoyment, transmission, and inheritance of all property, other than real estate, as native-born citizens."[80]

It would be assumed that a legal opinion from the state's attorney general would have settled the question and laid the issue to rest. But in Los Angeles, the Board of Supervisors asked the county counsel for an opinion regarding medical aid for Mexican aliens who were patients in the Olive View Sanitarium or those receiving Outside Medical Relief. The chief question posed to the county counsel was whether the county or the Mexican government was responsible for furnishing medical care.[81] However, the opinion of the county counsel was academic, for the position of Mexican government officials remained adamant. They were convinced that many Mexicans who were hospitalized or institutionalized in medical facilities had sacrificed their health to enrich the United States, not Mexico. Therefore, it was now up to the American authorities to provide indigent patients with proper medical care. This point of view was in essence shared by California Governor Culbert Olson. In remarks attributed to him, he reputedly stated: "Many of these people, particularly the Mexicans, were invited to come here and in many ways brought here so they could work to create the wealth of this state. They worked for low wages to help create this wealth and are entitled to share in it."[82]

Not everyone in California or elsewhere shared Governor Olson's generous point of view. Most people did not care about what the Mexicans had contributed; they simply wanted to get rid of them. A leading spokesman vociferously advocating removal of Mexicans from state and local welfare rolls in order to cut the costs of the program was Siegfried Goetze, a housing and planning consultant. In January of 1940, he submitted a detailed plan for getting rid of indigents to the governor, the state legislature, and the Los Angeles County Board of Supervisors. Goetze's plan was prompted by his contention that in Los Angeles County alone there were about 4,000 welfare cases involving Mexican families. These families, he asserted, received approximately two million dollars per year from the state Relief Administration. Goetze cited a study of 188 families, which found that 64.8 percent of those surveyed were headed by an alien. The study also revealed that the families had resided in the county an average of 17.11 years.[83]

Mr. Goetze accused welfare officials and social workers of dragging their feet and not addressing the alien welfare problem. Therefore, he proposed setting up a statewide commission under the direction of a full-time czar. The commission would be empowered to launch a concerted, statewide effort to rid relief rolls of Mexican recipients. To assure the success of the commission, Mr. Goetze recommended that twenty-five thousand dollars be allocated to the agency for its first year of operation. Thereafter, he proposed, "the budget shall not exceed 10 per cent of the actual saving to the state in alien relief, based on 1939 State Relief Administration expenditures."[84] This ploy, he believed, would whet the commission's appetite for going after Mexican aliens in an aggressive manner. Across the country, people who shared Goetze's zeal also clamored for getting Mexicans off of the relief rolls.

In Indiana Harbor, Indiana, social workers threatened Mexicans with loss of welfare aid. "We'll starve," people protested. "No, no you have an alternative; [you can] . . . go to Mexico," was the retort.[85] It was blindly or conveniently assumed that "all Mexicans" would be better off in Mexico, with their own kind. The natural inclination to reduce expenses prompted welfare agencies to cooperate with the Immigration Bureau. Welfare agencies reported the names and addresses of aliens to the Immigration Service, although they were forbidden to do so by welfare regulations. In a scenario endlessly repeated throughout the country, Mrs. Manuel Del Campo agreed to leave in order to obtain release of her husband, who was in jail awaiting deportation. Mrs. Del Campo and her five children were shipped to Mexicali, Baja California. Such procedures were regarded as "practical" for all concerned. However, even though families left through their own volition, the immigration authorities monitored their expulsion. This was done so that their reentry could be prevented on the grounds that they had been public charges.[86]

Despite their ingenious efforts, wholesale repatriation of welfare recipients proved to be a bankrupt policy. In spite of the hardships they faced in colonias around the country, many Mexicans simply decided to stay put and await a better tomorrow. Children played a decisive role in arriving at the decision. Their protestations against going to what they considered a foreign country, often tipped the scales in convincing families to remain in the United States. Resolute parents resolved to do so even if it meant resorting to scavenging in order to survive. They often did not know where their next meal was coming from, but prayer and hope sustained them during their darkest hours.

In August of 1941, the executive director of the Department of Public Assistance of Los Angeles County implored the Board of Supervisors to remove all indigent Canadian and Mexican citizens from the welfare rolls. Including the Canadians, who were few in number, gave the proposal a certain degree of impartiality. However, the few cases of deportation of Canadians were given considerable official attention. The deportation of John McNeil's family with four American-born children, for example, received extensive attention and resulted in lengthy correspondence between the county and Canadian authorities before any action was taken.[87] Conversely, little or no attention was given to the expulsion of hundreds of thousands of Mexican American children. The director singled out those aliens who were not legally eligible to receive emergency aid. He further advised that aliens should be notified that all county aid would be discontinued as of September 30, 1941.[88] However, Wayne Allen, county chief administrative officer, advised the Board of Supervisors that any plan that merely offered indigents a free trip to the border was doomed to failure. Success was dependent upon some form of transitional assistance being rendered to the welfare recipients.[89] John Anson Ford, a member of the Board of Supervisors, privately questioned the county's repatriation policy. "The county's policy of putting unfortunate Mexicans on the train and dumping them somewhere in Mexico," Ford complained, "is neither humane nor in the interest of international good will."[90] However, he publicly supported Wayne Allen's proposal. He advised his colleagues that a sufficient sum of money would have to be provided to each family that volunteered to be taken off the relief rolls and agreed to return to Mexico. According to Ford, "Due to the favorable ratio of five Mexican dollars [pesos] to one American dollar, a contribution of a few months' relief money per family would go a long way toward giving each family... financial aid that would... assure them against suffering in their new environment."[91]

Wayne Allen pointed out that the actual cost of maintaining a family on welfare totaled fifty-six dollars a month. He, therefore, recommended that one hundred dollars be given to each family. The sum would be paid in ten equal monthly installments, either through the auspices of the Mexican government or the nearest American consulate office.[92] Some supervisors believed that one hundred dollars was excessive and balked at approving the amount. They changed their minds when it was pointed out that the

sum was less than the cost of two months of public assistance. It was duly
noted that at the rate of exchange, then in effect, indigent repatriates would
actually get the equivalent of the basic amount they had received while on
relief. The supervisors also agreed to inform the Mexican government that
if a family who accepted the cash settlement returned to the United States
within a period of two years, the county would not be responsible for their
well-being.[93] Supervisor John Anson Ford was selected to travel to Mexico
City to present the plan to the Mexican government. To assist Ford in his
discussion with the Mexican authorities, he requested and received a letter
of introduction from Governor Culbert L. Olson. "I am very much in sympathy with efforts to bring about repatriation," the governor wrote and delegated Ford "to represent me and the State and County Coordinating
Committee on Reemployment."[94]

With support from the governor, the supervisors were elated with their
scheme. On Tuesday, December 2, 1941, they approved the ingenious plan.
Here was a golden opportunity to pare the relief rolls, get rid of the
Mexicans, and save the beleaguered taxpayers money. Pundits wondered
why no one had come up with this brilliant idea before. Why had it taken
so long, a decade, before devising what appeared to be a foolproof plan?
However, when the public learned of the proposed "giveaway" of their tax
dollars, there was wide-spread opposition to the envisioned largesse. One
letter received by the supervisors regarding the payment of one hundred
dollars declared that "it shows you are unfamiliar with conditions in
Mexico, where $100.00 of our money is a small fortune, and it will serve no
good purpose, only making more Mexicans anxious to come here to share
in the easy money."[95] The letter writer urged the supervisors to take a
courageous stand in resolving the problem, and suggested that all employ-
able indigents be put to work in cutting weeds, digging ditches, and collecting beer bottles. Another letter received on Monday, December 8, 1941,
also protested the one-hundred-dollar payment and asked why those on
welfare should be "payed" [sic] to return to their own country.[96]

El Condado
DOCUMENTS

■ ■

SUPERINTENDENT OF CHARITIES REX THOMSON TO BOARD OF
SUPERVISORS OF LOS ANGELES COUNTY, 10 FEBRUARY 1939.
Source: Los Angeles County Decimal File.

OFFICE OF THE SUPERINTENDENT OF CHARITIES
February 10, 1939
Honorable Board of Supervisors
Los Angeles County

Gentlemen:
SUBJECT:
Providing an escort and a doctor attendant for following clients being
repatriated to Mexico:

BLANCO, Barbara   Linc. #328010   Age 4   Jimenez, Chih.
FLORES, Gregorio   Vt. #413588   Arteriosclerosis
                                                            Queretaro, Queretaro
GAREA, Arturo   O.V. M-82681   Tbc   Monterey, Nuevo Leon
HERNANDEZ, Francisca   Elys. #30344   Coronary dis. & V.D.
                                                            Juarez, Chih.
MESA, Emilia and infant   PF #263-815   Infant is incubator baby
                                                            Fresnillo, Zac.
SABORI, Berta   Prob. Case   Luetic   Mexico City, D.F.
ORIGEL, Maria and infant   Elys. #419654   Mental
                                San Francisco del Rincon, Gto.
                                (manic depressive)
MORENO, A.   Ins.II #419855   Blind   Mexico City, D.F.
RIVERA, Benjamin   Prob. #85096   Guadalajara, Gto.
GUTIERREZ, Antonia   Prob. #82337   Mexico City, D.F.

The above will need special accommodations due to physical
condition indicated and in addition we wish to join to the same train
the following persons:

RODRIGUEZ, Ana Maria   Alhambra #406517   Zacatecas, Zac.
and five children
ORIGEL, Felipe   Elysian #419654   San Francisco del Rincon, Gto.
and five children
SABORI, Maria   Cent. Intake #48848   Mexico City, D.F.
and five children
PROSPERO, Ezequia   Cent. Intake #37045   San Pedro, Coah.

RECOMMENDATION:

That your Honorable Board authorize and make it the duty of
Joe Vargas to act as attendant and that Dr. Gordon Rosenblum,
resident physician LACGH, be authorized to act as doctor
attendant to accompany the patients, and any other additional
patients who are being repatriated to Mexico; including round
trip tickets and all necessary personal expenses, and that your
Board authorize waiver of receipts for such attendants, due to
difficulty of obtaining same in foreign country.

[added Minutes, Vol 248 page 322]
[stamp Feb 28 1939]
[signature M M auth.]

The combined monthly budget of this group is $304.27 excluding
institutional care by the State in the case of Maria Origel and we are
anxious to accede to their request for return to their relatives in Mexico.

Respectfully submitted,

[signature: *Rex Thompson*]
Rex Thompson
Superintendent of Charities

RT:RCN:h
cc—Hon. Roger Jessup
Mr. R. C. Newton

■ ■

SITUATION OF MEXICANS IN ROCKDALE, ILLINOIS TO THE
CHICAGO MEXICAN CONSULATE, 30 DECEMBER 1930.
*Source: Mexico City, Archivo de la Secretaría de Relaciones
Exteriores, IV-354–4.*

Con/de México
Chicago, Ill. Dec. 30, 1930.

Respectable Consular representative of our nation. This letter is addressed
to you with the exclusive purpose of communicating the present situation
that prevails among us Mexicans in this town of Rockdale, Ill.

Among us are a number of families and single men without work or
hope of obtaining work in this town. As far as industries, there is a wire
factory and a brick factory. The wire factory has not employed a single
Mexican in years but for those who for the past 10 years already worked
there. The brick factory was our only option, and on the 29th of this
month it laid off all Mexicans in order to hire North Americans and
Europeans instead. This leaves you as our only hope against the
travails of hunger and cold, to intercede on our behalf before the
Prime Magistrate of our country.

Most honorable Consul, we wish that for humanity's sake you will
do whatever possible in order to repatriate us with our families before
we die of hunger and cold or be forced to crime and dishonor over a
morsel of bread for our wives and children. The government denies us
aid and when we ask for it they answer that Mexicans are exempt from
aid. The only way we have managed without work is because those
with jobs have, for a long time, helped those without.

We hope His Excellency will act on our behalf, offer us repatriation
and collaborate towards the enrichment of our beloved nation.

■ ■

REPATRIATION PROPOSAL. SUPERVISOR JOHN ANSON FORD TO
LOS ANGELES BOARD OF SUPERVISORS, 18 NOVEMBER 1941.
Source: Los Angeles County Minutes, Vol. 273: Page 385.

MEMO TO BOARD OF SUPERVISORS RE THE MOST ACCEPTABLE
BASIS OF REPATRIATION OF MEXICANS
BY JOHN ANSON FORD

The working out of a repatriation program for Mexican aliens in Los
Angeles County which will assure fair and equitable treatment for
the Mexicans who voluntarily participate, will benefit both Los
Angeles County and Mexico financially and in many other respects.
Furthermore, such a program can be made the means of engendering
and strengthening bonds of good will between the two republics and
will serve as evidence of sincere good neighborliness, springing from the
people of a great state close to and intimately associated with Mexico.

The program about which we will confer with Mexican federal
officials is designed as a long-range, continuing relationship rather
than a brief or sporadic deportation effort. It can be made an invaluable
contribution to better Pan American understanding.

A factor causing Los Angeles County and the State of California to
give consideration at this time to a new program of repatriation of
Mexican aliens, is the special interest that Mexican Nationals have
shown in returning to their native land. I believe the program can be
worked out so that an increasing number will want to take advantage
of the opportunity.

We find that the Mexican government has been encouraging the
return of its Nationals, if such returns can be accomplished under
conditions which include (a) Settlement of the repatriates where
agricultural lands or industrial occupations are made available in
advance and suitable to the background and experience of said
repatriates; (b) The necessity of providing for each family a sufficient
sum of money either from the Mexican federal government, the local
Mexican government, or from California or Los Angeles County sources,
or both, sufficient to guarantee said families against want during an
adjustment period and/or sufficient to assist said repatriated person

DOCUMENTS

to establish himself with farm or craft tools, or otherwise, thereby giving him further assurance of self-support.

Due to the favorable ratio of five Mexican dollars for one American dollar, a contribution of a few months' relief money per family would go a long way toward giving each family of repatriates that financial aid that would reasonably assure them against suffering in their new environment.

An important step toward the successful operation of such a program of transfer to Mexico would be obtaining cooperation from the Mexican Secretary of Interior and the Secretary of Social Service in Mexico City in conserving and supervising such Mexican and American funds as would be provided to the repatriates.

A careful social survey should be made of each family considered for this program to the end that the Mexican authorities and ourselves may cooperate in giving them reasonable security in their homeland.

Preferable families should be selected where all the members including the young people involved are in accord with the program as a real family opportunity.

After checking the costs carefully—I find that the trip by train will cost somewhat more than by auto. Accordingly I ask for authorization to take a County car because of the greater mobility it will afford, especially if there are land re-settlements to be visited.

John Anson Ford

The repatriation of Mexican men, women, and children from the railway station in Los Angeles on March 9, 1932. Courtesy of the Los Angeles Public Library, Security Pacific Historical Collection.

Repatriation
Afuera

Vamos, vamos caminando	*Let's go, let's be on our way*
A la patria cariñosa	*To our loving homeland*
Que como Madre Piadosa	*Which like a merciful mother*
Sus hijos está esperando	*Is waiting for her children*
—"Adios Paisanos," Corrido	—"Farewell Countrymen," Ballad

Repatriation of unwanted immigrants is not a new or novel phenomena. All nations exercise their legal prerogative to rid themselves of undesirable aliens whenever such action suits an avowed purpose. During normal times, voluntary departures by Mexican immigrants as a result of seasonal employment generated a natural cyclical rotation. The traffic going south was augmented by individuals who were returning home to stay after spending several years in the United States. Some of them were accompanied by wives and young children. A few of the returnees had been able to save enough money to set themselves up in a small business or, hopefully, to acquire a parcel of good farmland. Among the southbound travelers were compatriots who were returning home temporarily to visit family and friends during the off-season. A common yearly occurrence was the pilgrimage home during the Christmas holidays. The festive occasion was marked not only by gifts but often by the introduction of a new bride or newborn children. An effort was made to arrive nine days before Christmas Eve to participate in the *Posadas* (reenactment of Mary and Joseph searching for lodging) and remain until

January 6th, which was when the Magi arrived and gifts were exchanged. After the brief stay, they would undertake the trek north once again. It was not unusual for them to return time and again to the same locale in the United States, often to the same employer.

However, after World War I, the insatiable need for labor began to ebb as the United States returned to a peacetime economy. Such a situation did not bode well for Mexican workers. The first portent of things to come occurred during the short but severe recession of the early 1920s. Faced with an excess of workers, repatriation became an acceptable means for getting rid of unwanted aliens. Repatriation was a cheap, effective way of reducing the suddenly bloated, idle workforce. Mexican immigrants who had lost their jobs were returned home in significant numbers. This successful remedy for getting rid of unwanted workers would not be forgotten.

Fortunately, the depression was short lived and was replaced by a booming economy fed by a spiraling growth, the likes of which had never been seen before. The period became known as the "Roaring Twenties." Optimism pervaded the national mood. Increasing numbers of workers were needed to help feed the voracious needs of the newly unleashed industrial giant. The United States again turned south to tap the great resource of Mexican workers. Many of those who had left during the depression returned to share anew in the abundant life. Then came the stock-market crash in October of 1929. For the second time in a decade, the bottom had fallen out of the American economy.

Once again, it became necessary to rid the country of workers who were no longer needed. Besieged welfare bureaucrats welcomed repatriation as a panacea. Repatriation endeavors, unlike those concerning deportation, as a general rule did not involve the federal government. It was primarily a local undertaking carried out by city, county, and state governments, or by a combination of all three. Civic or private charitable agencies often abetted their efforts. In Indiana, the repatriation program was financed largely by contributions from local businesses, which, in turn, were offered scrip, which could be used for paying local taxes.[1] The intent of repatriation was threefold: to return indigent nationals to their own country, in this case Mexico; to save welfare agencies money; and to create jobs for real Americans. These concepts were reinforced and justified by the prevailing belief that "those people would be better off in Mexico with their own kind." Therefore, repatriation was viewed as a humanitarian gesture.

In actuality, taxpayers resented having their hard-earned tax dollars used to support indolent aliens. This did not set well with property owners and business interests or the general public. Their rancor was further incensed by the knowledge that very few of the Mexican immigrants ever renounced their allegiance to Mexico and became American citizens. Such ingrates were deemed unworthy of receiving any public benefits.

To avoid the humiliation of official repatriation, many Mexican Nationals "voluntarily" left the United States. Vidal Pedrozca requested the assistance of New Orleans Consul Armando C. Amador in seeking the security of the mother country. He elected to face deprivation in his homeland rather than endure the disparagement heaped upon him in El Norte.[2] Buffeted by rampant unemployment, discrimination, and anti-Mexican hysteria, Mexicans sought the security of the mother country. In Mexico, they might suffer hunger pains, but at least they would be treated like human beings and as equals. The repatriates were in for an unpleasant surprise in adjusting to life in Mexico.

Threats of physical violence induced many Mexicans to abandon jobs and long-established domiciles. More than two hundred tenant farmers from different parts of the state of Mississippi including Shaw, Fork, and Essex worried about their precarious situation with the cold season approaching and pleaded for assistance from the New Orleans consulate.[3] In Terre Haute, Indiana, Mexican railroad workers were forced to "give up their jobs" when a mob of one hundred men and women marched on their work camp and demanded that they quit immediately or suffer the consequences.[4] In Malakoff, Texas, a gang of ruffians bombed the headquarters occupied by the Society of Mexican Laborers. Signs were displayed warning Mexican residents to leave town. "There is intense excitement and fear among Mexican Nationals of serious bodily injury," Luis Lupián, Mexican Consul General in San Antonio, informed Texas Governor Ross S. Sterling.[5] The consul demanded that the governor provide adequate protection for Mexican workers. The governor instructed the Texas Rangers to conduct an investigation of the situation. This was tantamount to having the fox guard the chicken coop. In the colonias, the reputation of the *rinches* (Rangers) left a great deal to be desired. Their mistreatment and harassment of Mexicanos was legend. If a ranger approached, it was best to get off the sidewalk.

As the depression worsened, repatriation, deportation, and voluntary or induced departures spread their ominous shadow across the entire

United States. Trains, cars, trucks, and buses streamed southward from every corner of the land. Los Angeles, Phoenix, El Paso, Denver, Kansas City, Chicago, Detroit, Pittsburgh, New York, New Orleans, San Diego, San Francisco, Portland, Seattle, and Fairbanks, Alaska, spewed forth their human jetsam. Those too poor to afford any kind of transportation joined the mass exodus on foot, carrying their belongings on their backs. An article in *Living Age* called the heart-wrenching scene "A Caravan of Sorrow."[6]

No means of transportation was overlooked in expediting the mass migration. Air travel was then in its infancy, but there is one known incident of a repatriate being shipped home by air.[7] In addition to cars, trucks, buses, or trains, ships were also utilized. Nationals whose hometowns were on the western or eastern coasts of Mexico or on the Yucatan Peninsula were often shipped home on empty oil tankers, fruit boats, and coastal cargo steamers.

In New York, the Henry L. Doherty Company made passage available to repatriates on empty Ward Line oil tankers on the ships' return trip to the Mexican gulf ports of Tampico and Veracruz. New Orleans was commonly used as a port of departure by Mexicans who resided in the southern states or in the Midwest. Repatriates from Detroit and throughout Michigan became so numerous during 1932 that the Standard Fruit Company and United Fruit Company no longer had sufficient capacity to accommodate all those seeking passage. Half fares of ten dollars attracted fearful repatriates anxious to return home.[8] In most instances, shipboard employment was provided as a goodwill gesture. It allowed destitute repatriates to earn their room and board for the trip home. Unfortunately, the trips had to be suspended when Mexican stevedores and longshoremen objected to repatriates being used as crew members on the ships. Eventually, Secretaría de Relaciones Exteriores intervened and settled the dispute, allowing the voyages to resume.[9]

Whenever possible, H. L. Doherty and other companies paid the cost of the trip, or funds were solicited from public agencies and private donors. The chief expense was food, which ranged from fifty cents a day for children to one dollar for adults. The voyage home was a difficult trip at best, for the tankers and cargo vessels were not equipped to handle large numbers of passengers. Women with babies and small children were given priority in the limited number of cabins available. Other repatriates found whatever accommodations they could in the empty holds or on the open decks. Galleys and heads (kitchen and restroom facilities) were strained to the maximum. Many repatriates wondered if they had made a mistake in accepting passage on the rusty ships. Mercifully, the trips as a rule were of short duration.

In Southern California, ships were also used to transport indigents to Ensenada, Guaymas, Mazatlán, Acapulco, and other coastal ports. When the shipping service was first inaugurated, it was hailed as a marvelous, if not ingenious, idea. Hopes and expectations soared in anticipation of being able to repatriate large numbers of indigent Nationals at a minimal cost. When the *Progreso*, a naval gunboat, first docked in San Pedro Harbor to pick up passengers, its arrival triggered a series of parties to celebrate the occasion. Relatives and neighbors hosted fiestas to fete and say adiós to those who had been chosen to make the maiden voyage. However, farewell parties often resembled a wake. Half-hearted attempts at gaiety fell flat and were punctuated with sorrowful tears—*abrazos* (embraces), and hugs. The sorrowful scene was repeated at the dock as relatives and friends exchanged tearful farewells.

The Mexican consulates in San Diego and Los Angeles often cooperated with each other in order to maximize the number of repatriates being shipped home. The minimum number on a cost-effective basis was two hundred individuals, and shiploads of five hundred or six hundred were not uncommon. On one occasion, eight hundred were on board the gunboat *Progreso* when it weighed anchor and sailed from San Diego. It was calculated that the average cost per passenger was eight dollars.[10] This meager stipend purchased "uncomfortable accommodations [because] it was not a passenger vessel," recalled repatriation coordinator Adolfo Tapia.[11] Moreover, "the ship was full," making for pitiful conditions, according to Alicia Apodaca, who visited the vessel before it departed.[12] Apodaca stated she will never forget the pitiful screams of a woman passenger as the ship left its berth: "Let us off! . . . I am just going to die, [I have] no money, no one knows me in that town in Mexico."[13] Repatriate Sebastiana Briones Casas and Southern California colonia leader Lucas Lucio sadly recalled the heart-rending experience.[14] Like so many other aspects of the repatriation nightmare, the *Progreso* venture never lived up to its billing. After the vessel had made a few trips, SRE discontinued the service because it was not considered to be cost effective. There was also an occasion when a fierce storm shipwrecked the repatriation ship *Ensenada* in Baja California. However, the Mexican government continued the practice of employing gunboats such as the *Nicolás Avila* for transporting unemployed Mexicans home from Cuba and Central America.[15]

While ships were used intermittently, trains were the most common means of transportation for repatriates being shipped home by welfare authorities. Trains of every type and description were used to expedite the process. Accommodations were usually limited to second-class passenger cars, but sometimes even boxcars and cattle cars were pressed into service. On rare occasions, Pullmans and compartment cars were also utilized. Train trips from such places as Pittsburgh, Chicago, Detroit, Gary, Indiana, and other eastern cities often became tests of sheer endurance. The trip to the border might take over a week, as the trains chugged along at a snail's pace. First-class passenger and freight trains took precedent, and often caused the repatriation trains to be shunted off onto a siding.

Railroads were utilized because they were the cheapest form of transportation. Trains with hundreds, sometimes over a thousand, repatriates aboard regularly left collection centers such as Detroit, Chicago, St. Louis, Denver, Phoenix, Oklahoma City, and Los Angeles. Fares on both sides of the border averaged about a penny a mile.[16] However, in many instances, to encourage repatriates to leave, special fares or deals were worked out. In Chicago, the Inland Steel Company provided free fares to Laredo, Texas, for 170 former employees. In Denver, the Santa Fe Railroad offered half-fares to El Paso. Repatriates from Torrington, Wyoming, demanded a 50 percent reduction in fares. Belzoni, Mississippi, offered Mexicans half-fares to the border in order to induce them to leave. Kansas City, Missouri, also made half-fares available. In Detroit, railroad fares were reduced 60 percent to help indigent Mexicans avoid the onslaught of winter. Not getting in on the discount rate could prove costly. Oklahoma City was forced to pay $1,060.85 to provide passage for eighty-nine repatriates.[17]

Repatriates from the Midwest and Northeast were usually shipped home after the sugar-beet season was over. The sudden exodus from places like Michigan, Minnesota, Nebraska, and Colorado strained the facilities on both sides of the border. County welfare agencies and employers, such as the Great Western Sugar Company, often cooperated with each other in making repatriation arrangements.

They would usually share transportation expenses but there were occasions when Great Western Sugar covered all repatriation costs. Among the beneficiaries was a group of former employees from Bayard, Nebraska. In most instances, fares were paid only to the border. Consuls often entreated welfare authorities to pay the repatriates' fares to their final destination in Mexico.[18] However, they usually encountered rather sporadic success.

In addition to agricultural workers, as factories, shops, mills, and mines closed their doors, the number of unemployed Mexican Nationals grew alarmingly. Such was the case for Mexicans who had worked in the coal mines of Bridgeport, Texas since the 1880s. By 1930, when the coal mines were closing, the Mexican colonia of Bridgeport numbered more than two hundred and fifty miners and their families for a total of 750 individuals. Some observers estimated that two-thirds of the entire community were Mexican Americans, and most of the Mexican Nationals had lived there for "fifteen or twenty years." Even though they had contributed to the prosperity of North Texas, the local community including town officials and the Chamber of Commerce as well as residents of nearby Fort Worth under the leadership of Rev. G. A. Walls, Pastor of the Mexican Presbyterian Church, sought to ship the Mexicans to Mexico. They even sought assistance from the National Headquarters of the Red Cross in St Louis. However, the Red Cross refused to help because they thought a local relief drive was more appropriate and the Mexican miners were no worse off than other miners. The local relief drive was successful in forcing the Mexican miners and their families to leave. However, Pastor Walls correctly observed that many of the Mexicans from Bridgeport were "out of touch in that country [Mexico]. They will be going there as foreigners."[19]

In the northern and eastern states, even though Mexican Nationals also had resided there for decades, large numbers opted for going to Mexico. Among them were 53 individuals from New York City and Brooklyn. The Spang Chalfant Steel Corporation of Etna, Pennsylvania, sought to assist the repatriates by permitting them to work three consecutive days in return for funding their repatriation expenses to their destination. During the same year, 1932, the Inland Steel Company also paid transportation costs for approximately 110 Mexicans who were being repatriated.[20] If possible, it was best to leave before the first snowstorms arrived and made departure virtually impossible. On one occasion, over three hundred Mexicanos from Lucas County, Ohio, boarded a special repatriation train commissioned by state authorities.[21] It seemed that those who needed "relief are more or less compelled to take it in the form of repatriation."[22] In many cases, one of the prime incentives for leaving was the weather. Former railroad workers, migrant field hands, and unemployed factory workers often lived in empty boxcars, abandoned shacks, and makeshift shelters without heat, water, or indoor plumbing. Without food or coal, or the money with which to buy either, winter could become a highly perilous period. Faced with the prospect of not getting their jobs back, destitute Mexicans chose to forego spending yet another miserable winter in struggling not only to keep body and soul together, but also to keep from freezing to death.

Mexicans who left often did so with the unspoken expectation that they would someday return. Ironically, they were leaving with the same expectation with which they had arrived many years before. Lured by the promises of the enganchistas, they had come *por sólo un poquito tiempo* (for only a little while). Now, ironically, they were going back to Mexico hopefully for "only a little while." Although it was the mother country, for many of them Mexico was no longer home. Their lives, their hopes, and their dreams were now rooted deep in the soil of their adopted country. It did not matter that they had never applied for U.S. citizenship or that they continued to honor their native land and clung to its cultural traditions. In most instances, in spite of all the adversity they had suffered, they had developed a grudging affection and admiration for the country they had helped to build.

Even men and women who had been born in Mexico, but had spent most of their lives in the United States, resisted leaving. Sisters Dora Raya and Irma Amparano remember that their mother refused to accompany their father back to Mexico. Their mother had heard that children were dying because of conditions in Mexico. Like any protective mother, she feared for her own youngsters' health and well-being. She preferred to remain in the United States and raise her American-born children alone rather than return to Mexico.[23] Juanita Rodríguez was another mother who refused to accompany her husband when he opted to return to Mexico. She adamantly refused to take her five American-born children to Mexico. When her husband warned her that the family would starve to death if she stayed, Juanita replied confidently, "Dios sabrá."[24] God's will be done. The fears of women who resisted going to Mexico were not groundless. Carmen Martínez's younger brother died of pneumonia when the family was forced to return to Mexico during the winter. She recounted that the family arrived in Cananea on the heels of a terrible winter storm. It was freezing cold and five feet of snow covered the ground. Being from Southern California, the family was totally unprepared for the blizzard-like conditions. They did not even own any warm winter clothing. In his weakened condition, her brother was unable to survive the trip and the bitter cold.[25]

Older children had to deal with the difficult choice of whether or not to accompany repatriated parents. Eliseo Martínez agreed to go with his father, even though he and his brother were earning a combined salary of nine dollars a day. For Mexican workers, this was an exceptionally good income during the depression. Eliseo agreed to accompany his father, even though his uncle advised him against returning to Mexico and his brother elected to stay behind.[26] In this instance, as in many other cases, the family was split when an older son or daughter decided to remain in the United States. Enrique Angel was among those who chose not to accompany his parents. They were returning to Mexico and planned to settle in Aguascalientes. Angel's decision was understandable because he had recently gotten married. However, the choice was not an easy one, for Enrique dearly missed his brother and younger sisters.[27] This traumatic sense of loss was an experience shared by tens of thousands of families.

Yet the repatriation trains continued to roll south. As a result, small barrios virtually disappeared. Once bustling colonias took on the eerie look of abandoned ghost towns. Rows of houses stood empty, lonely sentinels and mute witnesses to the life and laughter that had once filled their small, dingy rooms. Southern California community leader Lucas Lucio recalled that the entire Mexican colonia of "the Bastanchury Ranch [in Orange County] was repatriated. They were very poor... went on the half fare of the Southern Pacific."[28] Urban areas were not spared. In Los Angeles, "many homes in the Belvedere district have been abandoned by their owners," one journal reported.[29] Discarded furniture littered the yards as grass and weeds reasserted their domain. No one was sure where all the residents had gone. In some cases, families simply moved on to some other place in search of work. Although attempts were made to record the mass migration, Mexican consuls, county welfare agencies, and local officials lost track of how many families merely left town or were actually repatriated. The lack of precise figures is not surprising since the majority of the repatriates, contrary to popular myth or belief, paid their own way, provided their own transportation, and left without official intervention. Therefore, there was no adequate way of keeping track of the actual number of people who returned to Mexico.

Most Nationals disdained any official assistance and simply loaded their belongings on overloaded cars and trucks and started the arduous journey southward. Automobiles, especially among Mexicanos in Southern California, were prized possessions. Nearly 25 percent of Mexican families owned an automobile.

American Consul Richard F. Boyce at Nuevo Laredo reported that the cars of repatriates crossing the border were "from nearly every state in the United States." Boyce also observed the repatriates' "old automobiles carried all the household goods, they could have piled in them"[30] Among repatriates traveling by automobile was Francisco C. Barron. Barron was accompanied by his wife Angela and four children Francisco, Fernando, Enriqueta, and Roberto, as well as his mother-in-law, brother-in-law, and a friend, Mr. Vallejo. They were traveling from Fort Luption, Colorado to Chihuahua, Chihuahua in a jam-packed 1926 Chevrolet. In addition to the nine passengers, the car carried 100 pounds of beans, a gas stove, a sewing machine, and 200 pounds of flour.[31] Obviously, where there is a will, there is a way.

Traveling by car was a hazardous undertaking, especially on the roads south of the border. Cars often traveled in caravans and only in the daytime. Due to bandits who preyed on the repatriates, it was not safe to do otherwise. The bandits knew that the repatriates carried all their worldly goods and money with them. The money was hidden under the floorboards of the cars or other safe places. At night the cars would be covered with limbs and brush to conceal them from the bandits roaming the countryside.[32] Sheer safety necessitated that repatriates be armed. There was also the danger of encountering wild animals. On occasion, repatriates were forced to hunt for food in order to survive. Comisión President Catarino Cruz remembered that "many [repatriates] departed in their old cars, risking death by hunger or thirst. Roads were no good in Mexico."[33] The roads were so poor that El Paso Consul General Luis Medina Barrón issued a warning about the road from Ciudad Juárez to Villa Ahumada. Repatriates were instructed to carry twenty extra gallons of gasoline, a gallon of oil, and one of water and bedding or coats in case they had to spend the night on the road.[34]

However, to ease the trip for repatriates who were driving their own cars, arrangements were sometimes made by welfare authorities to ship their household goods and belongings by train at greatly reduced rates. This arrangement induced some who were undecided to abandon their domicile and return to the land of their birth. To help them on their way and to provide an added inducement for them to leave, some communities donated small sums of money to be used to purchase gas, oil, and food along the way.

Such donations seldom covered the journey's actual expenses, and families sometimes found themselves stranded along the road. People were forced to beg for food and handouts in order to survive. The Martínez family from Detroit made it as far as Texas and remained there.[35] Their son, Adolfo, eventually made his way back to Detroit.

In Los Angeles, anticipating the advent of official repatriation, trains bound for Mexico had been leaving every week either on Monday or Thursday from Central Station located between Fifth and Sixth Streets on Central Avenue. Officially, the first repatriation train organized by the county Welfare Department was scheduled to leave on February 10, 1931.[36] However, the inability to obtain ten-dollar fares delayed the departure until March 23. When total expenses were included for item, like food and medical attention, the actual cost per repatriate was $14.70. Children under twelve traveled at half-fare. Reportedly, fifty thousand Nationals and their children were repatriated from Los Angeles during a five-month period. This was estimated to be one-third of the Mexican population then living in the city.[37]

Los Angeles County became the hotbed of the repatriation movement. Whether Mexicans were employed or unemployed, they were targeted by the Los Angeles County repatriation campaign. Even Mexicans not on relief were pressured into accepting repatriation offers. A special group of employees was recruited "to encourage the acceptance of repatriation." They were required to have a variety of qualifications including ability to speak Spanish fluently, mature judgment, and be conversant with labor and economic situations in California and Mexico. The special employees included Fernando España and Joseph Vargas. Both had reputations as tireless recruiters. According to repatriate Rubén Jiménez, "España insisted, connived, and pressured us out of Los Angeles to Mexico." Jiménez's father "finally gave in" when España convinced him that he would lose his "two or three days of weekly employment, because it would go to Anglo employees."[38] Joseph Vargas was another dedicated county welfare employee, who gained a degree of notoriety because he reportedly was able to stay four days in Mexico City and confer with Mexican authorities for a grand total of $18.00.[39] Vargas never revealed the secret of his economical mission.

Local groups tried to make the departure as pleasant and as festive as possible. In Los Angeles, church groups, such as the Mount Hollywood Church's Goodwill to Mexico Committee under the leadership of Ernest

Besig, distributed toys and goodies to the children. Originally, the committee had tried raising money to aid the repatriates, but due to the ever increasing number, that became an impossible task. Reverend Allan A. Hunter stated that he would "never forget getting on the train with Besig . . . and our feeling of injustice. We thought it was utterly unjust what was being done. There wasn't much we could do except make these gestures of friendship."[40] Occidental College students, led by María Bustos Jefferson, recited poems and readings. They also performed dances and skits to uplift the spirits of the repatriates. Mariachis serenaded the repatriates with old favorites. But attempts to inject a sense of festive gaiety into the heart-rending scene at the train station proved futile.[41]

Crusading journalist Carey McWilliams commented on the traumatic scene presented by repatriated families. He observed that "repatriados arrived [at the train station] by the truckload—men, women, and children— with dogs, cats, and goats . . . half-open suitcases, rolls of bedding, and lunch baskets."[42] McWilliams was present when the first trainload of repatriates sponsored by the Charities Department departed from Los Angeles. Lucas Lucio, Comisión Honorífica Mexicana president, also commented on the sobering scene. He noted that "the majority of the men were very quiet and pensive" while "most of the women and children were crying."[43] Abe Morales also recalled the tearful scene when going "down to the Pennsylvania railroad depot in Indiana Harbor and saying good-bye to our classmates."[44] This sorrowful scene was repeated time after time at railroad stations across the nation, as families and friends said tearful goodbyes to loved ones. Sociologist Emory Bogardus also cited the estrangement of family life as a result of repatriation: "The mother is in a dilemma. She wants to go back with her husband to Mexico but does not want to desert her older children, who beg to remain in the United States. She faces a divided family. She is pulled strongly in two different ways at the same time."[45]

As the days dwindled and the date approached for families to leave, bitter arguments erupted as older children tried to talk their parents into letting them remain behind. When parents refused, desperate last-minute solutions or alternatives ensued. Young boys ran away from home or hid, teenage girls got married, older children opted to stay with friends or relatives. Teenagers were determined to face the consequences rather than accompany their families. For distraught fathers and mothers already taxed to the limit of their endurance, this was the final affront. Parents felt personally rejected and betrayed. Entreaties, pleas, and tears proved futile. Adamant children refused their parents' requests to join them. Even threats of divine retribution by a vengeful God failed to deter them. They were Americans, of Mexican heritage perhaps, but Americans nevertheless.[46] The prospect of living in Mexico created tension, anxiety, and consternation among young Mexican Americans. At the train station, a scared and apprehensive "little boy and girl grasping each other's hands, held firmly to their English school books."[47]

However, in spite of bitter or stormy recriminations, as a final gesture of filial piety and respect, grown sons and daughters knelt in the swirling dust and beseeched a final parental blessing.[48] A loving mother's intervention and prayers to the *Virgen de Guadalupe* was something to be sought and cherished in keeping one safe from all evil. The pervasive sadness and shedding of tears were quite understandable. Men concealed their feelings by outward stoicism or a show of bravado. The difference, of course, was that for women repatriation meant making endless preparations for transporting family and hearth to another country. Emilia Castañeda de Valenciana correctly assessed the dilemma faced by women when making arrangements to leave the United States: "A man, well, he . . . just packs up his sleeping bag and throws it over his back and that's good enough for him. Now a woman, she'll think about whether she wants her sewing machine, her bed, and her dishes."[49]

Transportation arrangements sometimes forced families to split up, adding another layer of woe to the turmoil. In Gary, Indiana, officials sent women and children to the border by train, and the men went by truck in order to stretch a limited budget. This made a difficult journey even more onerous. For many individuals, this callous separation from loved ones was the last straw. A young Mexican girl remarked, "This is my country but after the way we have been treated I hope never to see it again. . . . As long as my father was working and spending his money in Gary stores, paying taxes and supporting us, it was all right, but now we have found we can't get justice here."[50] The young lady was expressing a very common lament at having her own country slam the door in her face.

As trains prepared to leave from their respective stations, strains of "*La Golondrina,*" Mexico's counterpart of "Auld Lange Syne," filled the air. It was played in the midst of last-minute abrazos, kisses, and tears.[51] It is doubtful that anyone really heard the farewell song or cared. Everyone was caught up in his or her own thoughts and feelings. Many shook their heads in disbelief at what was happening to them. Mexicans are not strangers to the adage "Life is hard, and then you die!" But the repatriates were determined not to be defeated by adversity. Consequently, in typical Mexican fashion, myriads of *corridos* (folk songs) were composed about the plight, sorrows, and hardships that repatriates were forced to endure. Often composed on the spot and dealing with personal tragedy, only a handful of the corridos have survived. One of the most notable is El Corrido *La Pensilvaña*, recounting the train trip of repatriates returning to Mexico from Pennsylvania: "Now I bid farewell with my hat in my hand, and my loyal companions are three hundred Mexicanos."[52] Perhaps it is better to sing than to cry.

Equally as traumatic as the scenario between departing parents and their children was the pitiful sight of hospital and mental-asylum patients who were being repatriated.[53] The Welfare Department of Detroit retained a medical doctor to accompany repatriation trains, "owing to the fact that several of these Mexicans were taken directly from the hospitals or had been removed from the hospitals shortly before the trip."[54] On the other hand, in Milwaukee, the García family's three children were suffering from tonsillitis. Arrangements were made to have the tonsils removed before the family was shipped to the border.[55] Seeking to reduce expenses at the County General Hospital and other medical facilities, the Los Angeles Welfare Department initiated a campaign to ship as many "Mexicans as possible to Mexico."[56] Bedridden and terminally ill patients did not escape the repatriation dragnet. Included among the patients repatriated were cripples, lepers, elderly individuals afflicted by the ravages of old age, and those suffering from tuberculosis. Genevieve Valencia, a leper case, for instance, was sent by county car with a "deportation" worker and nurse to Mexicali, Mexico. There were also occasions when escort-attendants, matrons, and doctors accompanied groups of patients to the border. One such group included tubercular Frank Sepulveda, paralyzed Fermin Quintero, and eighty-six-year-old Narcisa Renteria. Also included were the five Robledo and two Miranda children.[57] Expelling tuberculosis cases to Mexico required extensive diplomatic negotiations. Special arrangements had to be made to place the patients in Mexico's only tubercular hospital, Talapam, Huipulco, because it had a limited capacity of only 180 beds.[58]

Typical of the indignities suffered by families with ill members was that undergone by Miguel Muriel's family when they and a paralyzed son were escorted home. Traveling by car or truck from Los Angeles to Ensenada,

Baja California was not an easy journey in the 1930s. Due to road and other conditions, even short trips were fraught with problems. Making matters worse for the Muriel family was the fact that the open, stake-bed truck was severely overcrowded. In addition to the family, a driver, and hospital orderly, the vehicle carried all of the family's personal belongings. The orderly was sent along to help care for the ill youngster until the family reached its destination. Once back home, the family was abandoned and left to look out for itself.[59] Across the Southwest, the proximity of the border made Mexico a convenient dumping ground for counties anxious to cut their welfare costs.

Mentally ill patients were also summarily repatriated. Petra Sánchez Rocha, for instance, was induced to accept being repatriated after suffering a nervous breakdown. The staff at the Los Angeles County Mental Health Center convinced her family that "her recovery could only be achieved in Mexico."[60] Even though Los Angeles County provided hospital orderlies to escort ill patients, it was not regarded as a humane gesture. Her son, Librado, thought the hospital personnel were sent along as guards rather than as orderlies to assure they arrived at their destination.[61]

One incident among many featured an elderly, bedridden couple who were being ejected after having lived in the United States for nearly forty years. Beset by the infirmities of old age, they were being sent to Mexico to die.[62] In some instances, burial costs were included as an incentive to return home. Gravely ill individuals often clung to life until they reached their final destination. Among many of the elderly, there was a prevailing belief and fear that if they died in the United States they would be cremated or buried as paupers in a county cemetery. In either case, they believed they would lose their souls and be denied entry into Heaven. For true believers, only interment in a Catholic cemetery would assure being welcomed at the Pearly Gates. That is why many elderly, infirm Mexicans agreed to be repatriated.

Encompassing another significant group of repatriates were women who were traveling without their husbands. Often, they were widows or abandoned wives accompanied by several young children. These women faced a series of seemingly insurmountable obstacles. The perverse system seemed designed to thwart their efforts to return to Mexico and join their relatives or husbands. At the onset, they encountered difficulty in registering children with the Mexican consulate. Since a father was not present to verify that the children were actually his legitimate offspring, detailed verification and proof was required. Birth certificates or baptismal records were not always readily available. At times such records were nonexistent. This was especially true among families of migrant or itinerant farmworkers.

Another problem encountered by women being repatriated was that they were not legally considered to be heads of households. Mexican consuls sometimes refused to extend Certificates of Residency "to señoras whose spouses wanted to stay here."[63] Thus, they encountered many difficulties in obtaining Certificates of Residency. In most instances, the certificates did not entitle them to full *franquicia* privileges, dispensation of custom duties. Male heads of households, for example, were permitted to import a gun or rifle for each adult member in the family. A woman traveling alone was allowed to import only one weapon or firearm. Even this right was grudgingly granted. Primarily, it was done as an acknowledgment of the dangers that she and her family faced on the long, perilous journey home. There were always unscrupulous individuals willing to take advantage of unescorted women or their young daughters.

Women whose husbands had been deported or had returned to Mexico agreed to repatriation in order to rejoin them. This was a common occurrence because the raids of the Immigration and Naturalization Service frequently resulted in families being torn apart. Relief agencies became concerned that due to the loss of their breadwinners the families would become dependent on welfare. The Federal Emergency Relief Administration came to the assistance of the relief agencies by providing transportation for destitute family members of deportees. Although they had initially refused to accompany their husbands, many women found they could not provide for their families by themselves. They were left with no other recourse than to rejoin their husbands already in Mexico. That was the case with Louise Delgado and her five children. She accepted the offer of the Los Angeles County charities office to drive them to Manadero, Baja California, in order to rejoin her husband. Ramona Ulloa was also escorted to the border because Los Angeles County officials feared "her stopping off en route" and "thus preventing her return to this country."[64]

Adela S. Delgado was among the brave women who made the hazardous trip to Mexico alone. Delgado drove from Pueblo, Colorado, to Santa Eulalia, Chihuahua, in an old Dodge automobile. She was accompanied by her three young daughters, Margarita, Catarina, and Virginia, who were thirteen, twelve, and nine years old, respectively. The car was jam-packed with personal belongings. Among the treasured items were a stove, mattresses and bedding, a carpenter's toolbox, and boxes of dishes and books.[65] It was a trip that would have taxed the endurance of most men, yet Señora Delgado took the long, perilous journey in stride. Another woman who traveled to Mexico by herself was Mariana Villaseñor. A strong-willed woman, she agreed to be repatriated only if permitted to take all of her household belongings. A truck was provided because her destination was not easily accessible by train or bus transportation. Besides, her departure made "possible a substantial saving" in welfare payments.[66]

Cases like those of Señoras Delgado and Villaseñor were not aberrations or rare exceptions. The Mexican consul in San Diego reported that of nearly one hundred cases of repatriates registered at the consulate in 1933, twenty-seven of them were women traveling alone. Eleven of the twenty-seven women were accompanied by young children. Final destinations in Mexico ranged from nearby border towns like Tijuana to distant Mexico City and beyond. It took a great deal of courage for women, especially those with little children, to undertake the long trek home. No woman knew what fate awaited her on the journey south. Modes of transportation often left a great deal to be desired. Interruptions and delays were commonplace and the journey to isolated rural or mountain villages often had to be completed on foot. Discarded belongings often littered roads and trails as women struggled to complete the journey. Many a tear was shed in frustration, doubt, and desperation.

Repatriation of Mexican women without spouses was not confined to those in the United States. One of the most memorable instances involved some four hundred Mexican women married to Chinese. The women had accompanied their husbands when they returned to their homeland. However, in China, they suffered many hardships because they did not understand the language, cultural traditions, or social customs. According to the Secretary of Foreign Relations, the women and their children were stranded and had no money or any means of support. Help was urgently needed to avert a disaster. At the specific request of President Lázaro Cárdenas, the government appropriated seventy-one thousand pesos to cover transportation costs from Hong Kong to the port of Manzanillo in the state of Colima. Railroad transportation to the interior was arranged so that the women could be reunited with their families.[67] Ironically, the tragic experience endured by the women returning from China resulted because their husbands had been expelled from Mexico.

Children in county orphanages did not escape the repatriation noose. In their eagerness to reduce expenses at all levels, counties often tried to find homes for orphaned children. If that proved unsuccessful, they attempted to return the children to relatives in Mexico or to transfer them to orphanages south of the border. In one instance, Los Angeles County spent nearly two years trying to find a suitable home for orphans, Ramón and Luz Martínez. Their tenacious efforts finally paid off when the Martínez children were placed in "Casa del Niño" in Mexico City.[68] In Globe, Arizona, the Public Welfare Department also sought an orphanage for Salvador Ramirez, Alicia Alfonso, and Melita Landeros when a distant relative became ill and was unable to care for them after the death of their parents.[69] For such children, it certainly seemed as if they were homeless waifs without a country. No attention was paid to the fact that the majority of the children were American citizens. In part, this was due to the doctrine of dual citizenship. Ostensively, children born in the U.S. of Mexican parents were considered to be American as well as Mexican citizens. That is, they were Americans by birthright and Mexicans due to their parentage. As such, they were legally deemed to have full rights and privileges in both countries. In actuality, the paper guarantees turned out to be meaningless.

Among the repatriates were individuals who were independent businessmen, merchants, shopkeepers, farmers, and property owners. They operated "mom-and-pop" grocery stores, retail furniture outlets, movie theaters, barbershops, secondhand stores, and other small businesses. In most instances, these enterprising individuals catered to the special needs and interests of the colonias. Faced with the wholesale deportation and repatriation of their customers, business fell off dramatically. Many struggling Mexican entrepreneurs faced economic disaster and had to liquidate their properties. Among those forced to sell or lose their holdings were José M. Otero, who was forced to sell his movie theater valued at fourteen thousand dollars, and his neighbor Augustín Maganas, who had to sell his commercial building assessed at ten thousand dollars.[70] Another individual was Juan Caldera in Colton, California who had to liquidate extensive holdings valued at over $100,000.[71]

Also adversely affected were prosperous colonias in the Midwest. Prior to the outbreak of the depression, the Chicago district of Hull House boasted a thriving colonia of some twenty-five hundred persons. The neighborhood Atlas Bank counted some six hundred Mexicans among its depositors, and another four hundred Mexicans who regularly purchased money orders to send money to families in Mexico. Among the colonia residents was a fairly large middle class that owned and operated a variety of small-business establishments, including fourteen restaurants, five pool halls, five grocery stores, a barbershop, a shoemaker, four bakeries, a meat market, a print shop, two sign-printer shops, a photograph gallery, a tailor shop, and a music shop. Especially successful in the Mexican community were two cartoonists on the staff of the *Daily News,* ten doctors and dentists as well as an instructor of Spanish at Crane College.[72] Many of these individuals did not survive the combined onslaught of the depression and repatriation.

Colonia businesses and services suffered because of the rampant unemployment in the barrios. Anticipated purchases were delayed indefinitely. Unsecured credit buying, even of foodstuffs, became a way of life. It was a risky venture since store owners had no assurance they would ever be paid. Carmen Martínez recalled the loss of the family grocery store, due largely to overextending credit to fellow compatriots. As a result, she and her family eventually joined their former customers in boarding the county repatriation train.[73] Compounding and adding to shop owners' woes were the rumors and scare-head tactics launched against Mexican places of business. In some instances, Mexican shopkeepers were harassed by Anglo competitors in an attempt to discourage patronage.[74] Barrio grocery stores were targets of a rumor—which later proved to be unfounded—that only U.S. citizens would be allowed to cut or butcher meat.[75] This was an effort to deter Mexicans from patronizing stores and meat markets that catered to their demands for particular cuts or types of meat.

Unable to make a decent living or to get a fair return on their investment, many Mexican businessmen and craftsmen decided to join the exodus. Consequently, established businesses, choice property, draft animals, farming equipment, and the tools of their respective trades went on the auction block. Possessions and property that had taken a lifetime of hard work to acquire now had to be disposed of for a few cents on the dollar—if one were lucky enough to find a buyer. Even at cut-rate prices, no one had any money to invest and sales often went begging. As a last resort, attempts were made to exchange commercial real estate for property of equal value in Mexico. A major problem in effecting an equitable trade was the scarcity of good farmland south of the border.[76]

Regardless of the repatriates' personal status or reason for leaving, nothing could make up for the devastating anguish they underwent in getting ready to leave. From one end of the country to the other, the tidal wave of abject humanity seeking assistance swamped Mexican consulates. Although the consuls lacked funds to provide monetary aid, they did offer several vital services to members of the colonia. Parents were urged to register their children before leaving the United States. This served a dual purpose. It established and verified the fact that the children had indeed been born in America. This proof would prove invaluable when youngsters grown to maturity or to legal age decided to return to the land of their birth. Registration was also instrumental in assuring children of the rights and privileges accorded all Mexican citizens regardless of their place of birth.[77] Ironically, but for different reasons, the view prevailed in both the United States and Mexico that "once a Mexican, always a Mexican!" The United States Bureau of the Census shared the common view of who was a Mexican. In 1930, it classified "as Mexicans all persons born in Mexico or having parents born in Mexico."[78]

Consuls also tried to make sure that individuals were not abusing the franquicias granted by the Mexican government. This privilege was granted to repatriates to facilitate their return to the mother country. They were allowed to bring in their personal belongings without having to pay customs fees or import duties. Many Mexican businessmen objected strenuously to this practice because they viewed it as giving repatriates an unfair advantage. They suspected that many of the goods, especially those in new or nearly new condition, were scheduled for resale. In some instances, their fears were well founded. But, in most cases, repatriates were merely taking advantage of the opportunity to bring in items they feared would not be readily available in Mexico.

In order to discourage the abuse of franquicias, consuls were authorized to grant Certificates of Residency only to Nationals residing in their respective districts. The certificates listed the names of the parents, the names, sexes, and ages of the children, respective places of birth, and the family's final destination. A detailed enumeration of the household and personal belongings of the repatriates was also included. Tools, equipment, animals, and plants, as well as vehicles and spare parts, including tires, were duly noted. Only two new spare tires were permitted per car or truck. Some items such as bedding, stuffed mattresses, and pillows were often excluded from the list of allowable imports.[79] As might be expected, repatriates complained bitterly when these indispensable items were confiscated at the border. In most instances, a *mordida*, or bribe, convinced customs officials to relax enforcement of the punitive measure.

Along with bedding, one of the most cherished items among women was their precious Singer sewing machine. Of all their belongings, it was the one thing they were determined not to leave behind. Many mothers also potted their favorite plants, including those used for medicinal purposes. *Yerba Buena, ruda, té de limón*, and other plants with curative powers were packed in crates for the trip south. There was often a problem at the border because the *aduanas* (customs officials) refused to let plants come in unless they were certified to be free from disease or parasites. The same problem occurred with animals ranging from household pets to farm or draft animals. A certificate attesting to the animal's clean bill of health had to be obtained from a veterinarian. The cost for livestock varied. Prices for horses, cattle, and mules ranged as high as ten dollars. Fees were less for smaller animals. Due to the added burden the fees placed on the repatriates they were gradually reduced and eventually most of them were eliminated. One woman objected bitterly to paying $4.70 to bring in her seven laying hens. Equally as galling was the fact that a fee of $10.00 was charged for the Certificate of Residency.[80] Eventually, due to the cries of protest by returning Nationals, the Certificate of Residency fee and other charges were abolished or drastically reduced for all indigents.

Although most of the repatriates were destitute and in dire straits, railroad and aduana officials were amazed at the tremendous amount of household goods and personal belongings that each family owned. It was, to say the least, impressive despite the fact that many household furnishings had to be left behind. However, due to their cost, special status was accorded to pianos and Victrolas. They were exempted from all restrictions, so repatriates could bring in their cherished musical possessions.[81] The Mexican government also permitted the entry duty free of "a used car and four used tires."[82] Old iron or brass beds were too heavy and cumbersome to transport. So too were stoves, iceboxes, dressers, and chests. In most colonias, discarded furnishings were so plentiful that it was impossible to give away household goods. Even secondhand stores refused to pick up items unless they were brand new. Rather than discard their hard-earned furnishings, some families stacked their furniture and set it afire. They simply had no choice since aduana officials allowed only fifty kilos of duty-free goods per family.[83] Excess weight and baggage had to be paid for by the repatriates.

Like the women with their prized sewing machines and treasured momentos, the men too had their priceless belongings. In most instances, they were the tools of their trade. Barbers, shoe repairmen, plumbers, tailors, leather workers, musicians, carpenters, mechanics, and other journeymen insisted on taking their equipment with them. It represented their one hope of being able to reestablish themselves in Mexico and avoid becoming a burden to the government. Some tradesmen attempted to import enough supplies to enable them to establish a business and hire local workers. As prospective employers, they sought special concessions from the Mexican government. In most instances, since Mexico sorely needed economic development, dispensation was granted. However, in instances when demands were excessive—as in the case of one Juan Rodríguez, who wanted to bring in enough lumber and plumbing supplies so he could build a large home—the request was denied.[84]

The deluge of repatriates and their mountainous accumulation of goods, tools, and animals swamped aduana facilities all along the border. Entry ports like Tijuana, Nogales, Ciudad Juárez, Nuevo Laredo, and Matamoros felt the full impact of the onslaught. The border cities reeled from the weight of the sheer numbers storming their gates. Customs facilities, food supplies, housing, medical attention, and railroad transportation creaked, groaned, and in some cases finally collapsed. No one had foreseen the advent or enormity of the human tide flowing south from every corner in the United States. A major cause of problems at the border was due to the fact that there was very little cooperation between Mexican and American authorities. As a result, it was virtually impossible to control the mass migration back to *el terrenazo*. American officials usually ignored the situation unless there was rioting. According to *Excélsior*, Mexicali and Tijuana officials were afraid outbreaks of violence might happen in their cities, as had occurred in Ciudad Juárez. There, it had been necessary to call on American police and the National Guard for assistance to quell unrest at the border.[85]

Making matters worse, the repatriates often arrived at the border in the most pitiful circumstances. Babies, the elderly, pregnant women, and the sick suffered the most from the ordeal. Deaths occurred daily along the way and in repatriation centers at the border. Too often, the forced repatriation of individuals not fit to travel became a virtual death sentence. *Excélsior,* one of Mexico City's leading newspapers, reported that on board one repatriation train, twenty-five children and adults had died of illness and malnutrition during the trip to the border.[86] The same newspaper in another edition reported that some repatriates had arrived in such an ill and pitiful condition that they had to be hospitalized before being permitted to continue on their journey.[87] Despite the suffering, misery, and deaths, repatriation officials continued to maintain that efforts were made to assure the comfort and well-being of the repatriates.

A factor contributing to the sad plight of the repatriates was that vast numbers left the United States without ever contacting the Mexican consul in their respective districts. The vast distances and lack of transportation often prevented them from contacting the consulate. They, therefore, arrived at the border without Certificates of Residency or any documentation needed to facilitate their processing by the aduana service.[88] In their haste to get rid of indigent Mexicans, county welfare agencies often sent them on their way without notifying the local consul. Repeated violators, like welfare administrator Mary Grace Wells of Gary, Indiana, caused consternation and unnecessary problems for their charges even though she contended that repatriation "would be a blessing to the community, a kindness to them to help them go back home."[89] Attempts by Mexican Consul Rafael Aveleyra to gain Wells' cooperation or that of the county trustees proved futile. Delays, heartbreak, and prolonged detention at the border were the end result. Official insensitivity and intransigence made a bad situation even worse. However, according to Mary Grace Wells, the Gary, Indiana, repatriation program was a splendid success, for "all [repatriates] were happy en route and were delighted to set foot again on their native soil."[90] How Wells was able to surmise or arrive at that conclusion is a mystery, for she never made a trip to the border.

For each group of repatriates, the train trip to the border was different, yet the journey assumed a certain commonality. Whether from Detroit, Chicago, Kansas City, Denver, or Los Angeles, after the initial excitement of getting under way, a dull monotony settled over the human cargo. Only the younger children who did not fully comprehend what was happening to them viewed the trip with glee and good spirits. As on the repatriation ships, amenities aboard the trains were limited. Individuals and families laid claim to their particular spot in the crowded coaches and tried to make the best of it. Some napped, some played cards, others roamed through the cars looking for old friends or relatives. Every car or coach had one or more self-styled musicians. Repatriation coordinator Lucas Lucio remembered that "from Los Angeles to El Paso some sang with guitars trying to forget their sadness and others cried."[91]

The boredom and monotony of the trip was interrupted by breakfast, lunch, and dinner. In order to save money, food portions were usually strictly adhered to and second helpings were seldom available, even though Los Angeles repatriation director Rex Thomson claimed the trains were "full of food."[92] This was a sore point with many of the men who, due to a life of hard work, were hearty eaters. There were also occasions when repatriates were told to bring their own food. This was good advice because at times arrangements for sufficient food were not made. A repatriation train from Detroit, Michigan made no provision for feeding 78 children and only provided them "a pint of milk three times a day." The children had no other option but to drink water to quench their hunger and "soon emptied the water coolers."[93] Immigrant Inspector Harry G. Yeager was concerned about this situation, because there "was considerable delay" in rewatering the coolers. Fortunately, night punctuated each day and brought a much needed respite. Thankfully, for the bone-weary repatriates another miserable day was behind them. Troubles, cares, and increasing apprehensiveness could be momentarily set aside. María de la Luz Sánchez was six years old at the time, but she can still remember that "one would sit, eat, and sleep in the same location."[94] Morning began the dismal routine and ordeal all over again. The only consolation was that the miserable trip would soon be over.[95]

Repatriates and their families arriving at the border from Detroit, Pittsburgh, Cleveland, Chicago, and elsewhere complained bitterly about the hardships encountered on the extended trip which often took a week or more. Their sentiments were echoed by those arriving from the Midwestern states of Iowa, Kansas, Nebraska, and Minnesota, or from the northern states of Washington, Idaho, Montana, and the Dakotas. Arrival at the designated port of entry was greeted with mixed emotions. It signified the end of the first leg of the journey and the beginning of the final lap. Repatriation coordinator Lucas Lucio recalled the "terrible cry among the repatriates upon reaching the border." Lucio deduced that some repatriates "did not want to cross the border because they had daughters or sons who had stayed behind."[96] Conditions at the border towns were certainly not reassuring. Lucas Lucio was horrified when he saw repatriates who were sick, starving, and dying at the border. Especially shocking was "the abuse by the immigration authorities not respecting their [repatriates'] rights to bring goods in duty free."[97] Emilia Castañeda remembered as a young child being ordered to "disinfect her shoes as a safeguard for protecting cattle from infection."[98] The young girl thought the Mexican government's actions were "shameful" and showed that the cattle industry was more important than people. A trainload of repatriates from Detroit also received a cold welcome when they arrived in Laredo: "The engine was turned off and the people [were] required to remain on the train all night without light or heat."[99]

One proud, eighty-two-year-old National disdained all offers of help and returned to Mexico on horseback, accompanied by his grown sons. In one final gesture of bravado and defiance, he shouted "Viva México" as he rode across the Rio Grande. After having lived in the United States for more than twenty-five years, he chose to return home even if only to die on native soil.[100] Such incidents produced dramatic press coverage. Newspapers underscored the fact that extended years spent contributing to the prosperity and economic development of the United States was not enough to gain Mexicans either permanent residence or acceptance in their adopted country. Instead, the Mexican worker and his family were ousted without any concern for citizenship status, length of residency, health conditions, or age factors. Neither was any thought or attention given to problems a family faced at the border or at their final destination. The adage, "Out of sight, out of mind," was never more applicable.

In the border cities, all amenities were sorely lacking. Food, water, and shelter were in extremely short supply, and prices were sky-high. Sanitary facilities and medical care were primitive by any standards. There were simply too many people vying for the same spaces, goods, and services. People were reduced to begging and even stealing in order to survive. Conditions worsened as more repatriates arrived to join those already awaiting transportation into the interior. One journalist described the terrible conditions that prevailed during the winter of 1931 in Ciudad Juárez, across the International Bridge from El Paso: "Up at the customs house, there is a large corral, where early in January more than two thousand *repatriados* camped and starved, huddled together, waiting for a kind government to provide them with transportation so that they could move on. . . . Women swarmed about the warehouses picking up one by one the beans spilled through the holes in the [gunny] sacks."[101] A group of repatriates from Des Moines, Iowa was forced to beg for food while they waited for transportation to their destination.[102]

In light of such deplorable conditions, there were rebellious individuals who decided to forego the remainder of the trip. A dozen Mexicans being shipped by train from Saginaw, Michigan, to Nuevo Laredo, Mexico "requested permission to leave the train at San Antonio. They had changed their minds about returning to Mexico," according to the U.S. Immigration Inspector who accompanied the train. Their request was unilaterally denied. Two youths, however, escaped by jumping out of the windows when arriving at Laredo, Texas. Inspector R. W. Gangewere reported proudly that "our officers" captured the youths and "both [were] returned to Mexico."[103] Los Angeles County officials responded to the problem of escaping repatriates with a policy of escorting reluctant repatriates who might attempt to return. County cars and even private vehicles were authorized for employees to accompany families to the border towns of Tijuana and Mexicali, Baja California. These employees made sure the repatriates were checked at the border to prevent their return.[104] There also were occasions when trains from Indiana Harbor, Indiana, included American Legionnaires volunteers who were "on the train to see that nobody jumped off all the way to Texas."[105] To reduce this possibility, it became common practice for trains not to stop at the railroad station on the American side, but proceed directly to the Mexican side of the border.

For the majority of repatriates, in spite of doubts and misgivings, there was no other option but to continue the arduous journey. Having come this far, there was no turning back. There was nothing to go back to! They waited stoically for trains to carry them south. No one knew when the next southbound train would arrive. A lucky few left within days of their arrival, others waited endless weeks and months. One group of forty exasperated repatriates refused to tolerate any further waiting. They stormed a train and demanded that they be allowed to ride on the roofs of the cars. "We are repatriates and the government has offered us help," the nearly starving and desperate group pleaded with the engineer.[106] When trains finally came, many locomotives and coaches looked like relics left over from the Revolution, which indeed many were. Repatriates doubted whether the antiquated trains could survive the tortuous mountainous terrain on the journey south. The prospect of another lengthy, jolting train ride was less than appealing to the bone-weary repatriates. Librado Sánchez lamented the prospect of "the long train ride from Juárez to San Francisco del Rincón, Jalisco in wooden boxcars."[107] Long train rides in uncomfortable cars was not the only humiliation facing repatriates. The trip south was plagued by many perils whether you went by car, truck, or on the train. In one particular case, a trainload of repatriates believed they were on their way to their destination in Guanajuato. Suddenly, in the middle of the night, the train stopped and they were dumped in the isolated, mountainous desert in the state of Sinaloa. No explanation was given them for the hasty action. In the pitch black darkness, the repatriates had no idea where they were. There was no town or any signs of habitation.[108]

As the repatriados proceeded south and drew nearer to their final destinations, new fears and doubts began to trouble them. What lay ahead was anyone's guess. Had the decision to pull up stakes and leave the United States been the right choice? That perplexing question would have to wait for a final answer. However, doubts about the wisdom or folly of returning to Mexico were not confined solely to the Mexicans who were forced to depart. Even at the depth of the depression, there were groups and individuals who vehemently opposed mass repatriation. Businessmen were impacted by the loss of loyal customers, and ranchers and industrialists decried the loss of dependable workers. Warnings were heard about the negative consequences of such a rash and hasty action. The cure could be worse than the supposed illness, claimed the doomsayers.

Echoing local business sentiment, Pablo Baca, president of the Los Angeles Mexican Chamber of Commerce, enumerated twelve reasons why repatriation ought to be stopped. Baca's critique was submitted to Clarence H. Matson, of the Los Angeles Chamber of Commerce.[109] Baca's report and recommendations were prompted by the fact that fifty thousand Mexicans allegedly had been shipped home during the previous five months. Both Chambers were concerned about repatriation, but for different reasons. Baca was sensitive about the injustice being done to the Mexican population and wanted it stopped. Anglo employers feared that if the mass exodus continued, soon there would be very few Mexicans left to do the dirty, backbreaking, monotonous work at which they excelled.

In addition to loss of workers, repatriation was bad for the merchants' pocketbooks. Local retailers pointed out that the Mexicans were dependable and loyal customers. In good times or bad, "come hell or high water," they paid their bills. Their rate of default on credit purchases was surprisingly low. Merchants in every community noted a significant drop in sales with the sudden departure of their loyal clientele. Belatedly, the establishment began to realize that Mexicans were not only producers whose work benefited the entire society; they were also consumers of goods and services who contributed to the economic well-being of the community. Consequently, in Los Angeles, businessmen led by the Bank of America and the Chamber of Commerce joined in asking authorities to desist in their repatriation efforts. Repatriation, they insisted, should be limited to those who volunteered or requested to be sent back.

Bankers were concerned because large amounts of money were being withdrawn by Mexican clients in anticipation of being repatriated. According to one financial statement, in Los Angeles alone banks had lost more than seven million dollars in deposits.[110] The same was true about banks across the nation that serviced barrio residents. Contrary to being stereotyped as spendthrifts who lived for the moment or who were not able to defer instant gratification due to their childlike ways, Mexicans formed a significant part of the savings community. Attesting to the truth of that statement were small banks and savings and loan companies that felt the financial pinch. To prevent loss of accounts, they often stonewalled or delayed processing requests for withdrawal of funds. In one such instance, it took Antonio de Alva six months to withdraw his savings of $209.73 from the Maritime Building Loan Association in San Pedro, California.[111]

Ranchers and growers, as might be expected, were another group opposing repatriation. They had always opposed any immigration restrictions on their source of cheap, dependable Mexican labor.[112] Now they viewed the increased repatriation efforts with alarm and feared for the loss of their crops. As a result, surprising as it may seem, repatriates often arrived at their destination in Mexico, only to find enganchistas busy recruiting workers to pick cotton and other crops in Texas and Arizona. It must have been the final irony for repatriates or perhaps it was poetic justice. "Bring back the Mexicans" resounded throughout the Southwest, where they formed a vital link in the agrarian economic chain.

An early advocate of fair treatment for Mexican Nationals was Ernest Besig, head of the Goodwill to Mexico Committee of the Mount Hollywood Church. The committee directed its efforts and attention to ameliorating the plight of those forced to return to Mexico. Originally, the Mount

Hollywood Church attempted to pay for fares and to provide clothing and other basic necessities to needy repatriates. In this endeavor, Mr. Besig found that he was battling against the tide. There were simply too many families who needed help. In desperation, he appealed to other civic agencies and religious groups for assistance. Besig also attempted to persuade local officials to respect the repatriates' civil rights and not make them convenient scapegoats.[113] His pleas, unfortunately, fell on deaf ears.

The Mexicans themselves did not remain passive or acquiescent in the face of the ominous threat facing them. Various organizations in the colonias such as the Comité Pro-Repatración and the Cruz Azul, joined in protesting what they viewed as disparate treatment of Nationals. After repeated trips to the train station to see their relatives and neighbors off, resentment began to mount in the colonias. Why, many demanded angrily, were there no train loads or caravans of other aliens leaving? Why weren't other foreigners being rounded up and repatriated? Mexicans were not the only people out of work or on relief! Why were recent newcomers from Europe being treated better than Mexicans whose ancestral roots went back to the exploration and settlement of much of the southern portion of the country? To residents of the colonias, it did not make sense or seem fair. Citizens groups, such as the Confederación de Sociedades Mexicanas, denounced repatriation and demanded that it cease immediately.[114] They viewed it as nothing more than a contrived, racist plot to get rid of all Mexicans.

Joining in exposing this racist point of view and adding their moral support in behalf of *México de afuera* (refers to Mexicans residing outside of Mexico in the United States) was the Mexican press and radio on both sides of the border. The entire repatriation episode was closely monitored by the Spanish-speaking news media. In the Southwest, newspapers such as the prestigious *La Opinión* in Los Angeles, *La Prensa* in San Antonio, and *El Heraldo* in San Diego printed articles and published editorials critical of the repatriation movement and its racial overtones. In Mexico, the media added its own shrill cry as calls for justice and restraint were ignored. In addition to speaking out in behalf of their compatriots, the repatriation debacle was tailor made for engaging in biting, often vitriolic Yankee baiting.[115] The media pursued several avenues in mounting its attack. It argued that Nationals had worked to enrich the Colossus of the North. Therefore, it was the responsibility of the beneficiaries of their labor to care for them in their hour of need. Why should Mexico serve as a convenient dumping ground for America's rejects? These attacks increased when the infirm, lame, mentally deranged, or terminally ill patients began to arrive from as far away as Philadelphia. Many of the returnees, the press claimed, had suffered job-related injuries or had ruined their health and wasted their youth in enhancing the economic interests of the United States.

The inhumane treatment was particularly galling to the repatriates because they viewed themselves as honest, industrious workers. Their renown and reputation as a reliable workforce spoke for itself. They had performed their tasks admirably. Why, then, were they being heartlessly expelled? Mexico City's prestigious *Excélsior*, in an editorial published June 2, 1932, commented on this aspect. It attributed repatriation to blatant racism. As proof of America's racism, it cited a statement attributed to the International Relations Committee of the Federal Council of the Churches of Christ in America: "Racial discrimination in these times not only makes more painful the downfall of racial groups previously placed in a disadvantageous position, but they increase the responsibility of the communities because of the suffering of those groups."[116] Quite obviously, the U.S. was not fulfilling its moral responsibility.

Consuls usually advised their beleaguered compatriots to remain where they were, if at all possible, and ride out the economic tempest. Better times were bound to come. Patience! Don't give up hope, were constant words of advice and encouragement. Since the consuls had no funds with which to aid potential repatriates they were wary of creating false hopes or expectations among their charges. Resentful of the treatment accorded them, repatriates lodged vehement protests with SRE about the inability of local consuls to act effectively in their behalf. "The Los Angeles consul does not know nothing," a repatriate complained in *La Opinión* of Los Angeles, when he arrived at the border and learned "they [repatriates] were hated in Mexico."[117] The protestors did not understand, nor did they care, about the constraints under which the consuls were forced to operate. Caught up in their own desperate plight, repatriates had little tolerance for bureaucratic explanations. Yet, in spite of how their performance may have appeared to their compatriots, the consuls were indispensable. In most instances, they interceded in a very aggressive manner in behalf of their countrymen. They were instrumental in pressuring local authorities to provide better care and treatment for Mexican Nationals and their families. Many humane changes were made as a result of their efforts.[118] Concessions were often obtained from railroad companies for reduced rates, or employers were induced to pay part or all of the train fare for their former workers. Some consuls actually accompanied the repatriation trains to look after their charges and to assure prompt service at the border. The mere presence of a consul official had a salutary effect in dealing with bureaucrats in both countries.

In spite of protests and recriminations, the flow southward continued. How many people were actually repatriated? Hundreds, thousands, tens of thousands, hundreds of thousands, a million, two million? In all honesty, it is virtually impossible to cite a specific figure as to the number of Mexicans and their children repatriated during the Great Depression. There are official and unofficial estimates and "guesstimates." Both the American and Mexican government played the numbers game. American officials cited one set of figures, but the Mexican government arrived at conflicting counts. Several problems contributed to this dilemma. In many communities in the U.S., no figures were kept regarding the exodus. That is understandable since, in many cases, departures were due to local harassment. It is unknown how many Mexicans simply got fed up and left, often in the black of night. Some returned to Mexico as they had come: They simply waded back across the river. This maneuver had several advantages: It was free, it was convenient, and it bypassed all the bureaucratic and legal hassles. As far as its advocates were concerned, it was nobody's damn business anyway as to who came or went. Other individuals made several trips across the border, adding to the confusing statistics.

Nonetheless, bureaucrats in all countries love statistics. They thrive on them. Collecting them is vital to their well-being. In fact it often constitutes the only justification for their existence. Consuls dutifully accounted for the number of Certificates of Residency issued. Welfare agencies kept records of indigents shipped home, detailed the cost of repatriation, and justified it in relation to the amount of money saved in the course of a month or a year. The figures were impressive, to say the least. In Mexico, SRE (Secretaría de Relaciones Exteriores) solicited repeated counts and studies from its consuls concerning the repatriation movement. Its purpose was to enable the government to cope with current and projected arrivals.

American consuls in key Mexican cities also monitored the repatriation flow and reported the figures to the State Department in Washington, D.C. The American consul in Nuevo Laredo reported to his superiors that during the combined months of October and November of 1930, 8,250 repatriates had passed through his jurisdiction. It should be borne in mind that Nuevo Laredo constituted one of the lesser entry ports. The consul duly noted that 20 percent of the repatriates were from Texas, Michigan, and Illinois, each contributed 15 percent, while Indiana and Missouri accounted for 10 percent apiece. Ohio was credited with 8 percent of the total, while Minnesota and Colorado were credited with 5 percent each. Massachusetts, New York, Wisconsin, and Pennsylvania, respectively, accounted for 2 percent of the 8,250. Three percent were attributed to Oklahoma. The state of Alabama was credited with only 1 percent. The astute consul also noted that the repatriates owned 813 cars.[119]

In a subsequent dispatch, the consul in Nuevo Laredo reported that 21,700 repatriates passed through his station between July 1 and December 31, 1930. He estimated that 51.1 percent were from the old South, with the overwhelming majority from Texas. The north central states had been home to 40.7 percent of the returnees. The mountain and Pacific Coast regions and the northeastern Atlantic area, respectively, accounted for 6.2 percent and 2 percent of the repatriates during that period.[120] Contributing to U.S. State Department figures were dispatches from the American Consulate General in Mexico City. A report transmitted on September 18, 1936, alleged that a total of 356,723 Mexicans had been repatriated, during the period of 1930 to 1935, from countries around the world. The United States accounted for 345,839 individuals, or 96.95 percent of the total. According to the report, 1931 was the peak year for repatriation, when 123,247 Mexicans were shipped home. As economic conditions in the United States slowly improved, the tide of repatriation receded. By 1935, according to the official count only 16,196 Nationals were repatriated.[121]

According to figures attributed to the U.S. Labor Department and cited by *El Universal*, on August 22, 1932, 2,000,000 Mexicans had returned home during the past fifteen months. It was asserted that 1,600,000 had arrived during 1931, and another 400,000 repatriates had entered Mexico in the first three months of 1932.[122] A rival newspaper, *Excélsior*, claimed that 75,000 Mexicans had been repatriated from Los Angeles alone during the past three years. In its official publication, *Memoria*, SRE reported that 126,154 people had been repatriated during 1931–32. It categorized them into five distinct groups according to their repatriation status: 547 had been assisted by the Mexican government; 13,462 had been aided by American authorities; 3,519 were helped by civic organizations; 6,166 had paid their own way; and for 102,460, it was not specified how they had returned. The SRE indicated that most of the repatriates were from 15 major American cities and some were from Cuba and Guatemala. Among the major American cities listed were Los Angeles, Denver, Chicago, Milwaukee, Detroit, New York, Kansas City, Dallas, Salt Lake City, and Phoenix. The official repatriation tally for the years 1930 to 1940 was 422,831. With deference to the official tally, it should be borne in mind that many repatriates returned, as has been previously stated, without contacting the Mexican consulates or seeking anyone's assistance. They left as they had come, unobtrusively![123]

Taking the conservative middle ground, it is reasonable to estimate that the total number of repatriates was approximately one million. Statisticians have also attempted to determine the cost of getting rid of the brown horde. Based primarily on transportation costs, the minimum amount is estimated at 15 million dollars. However, if the cost of food, medicine, escorts, and financial inducements to leave are added, the price escalated between 25 million dollars to 30 million dollars. As with the number of estimated repatriates, one can only speculate as to the exact figures. Perhaps even more important than sheer numbers, in either case, is the question of how a country like Mexico, with its limited financial resources, was able to cope with this enormous problem. While the United States, which, in spite of the depression, remained the richest nation in the world, refused to share its bounty with those who had worked so hard in helping to create its vast wealth. A review of the effort and policies of the Mexican government may illustrate the differences in attitude.

Afuera
DOCUMENTS

■ ■

REPATRIATION CERTIFICATE. DENVER, COLORADO.
Source: Mexico City, Archivo de la Secretaría de Relaciones Exteriores, IV–354–40.

CERTIFICATE OF RESIDENCE

Number 17.   File 524.5   Fee GRATIS

ISMAEL M. VAZQUEZ Mexican Consul in Denver, Colo., U.S.A. CERTIFIES—That according to proofs presented at this Consulate, Mrs. *Adela S. de Delgado* of Mexican nationality, who is being repatriated from *Pueblo, Colo.,* has resided in the United States for more than six months, required for enjoying the exemptions established by Circulars A-54–167 and 14–103–132 of the General Customs Office. The foregoing is registered by petition of the applicant for the consequent objectives, with the understanding that said applicant is being repatriated with the destination of *Santa Eulalia, Chih.* MEXICO, bringing the following items of personal property.

Truck of make ——— , ——— Engine No. ———

Automobile of make *DODGE BROS.,* Engine No. *H-9126*

A trailer.

Used household items and, in addition,

1 carpet and some rugs.

1 oil stove.

1 trunk of used clothing.

3 mattresses, blankets, and pillows.

2 used spare tires.

1 box of utensils.

__ valises of used clothing.

1 box of crockery. —1 bed.

1 bundle of used clothing.

1 box with carpenter's tools.

_ musical instruments.

1 box of books.

NOTE: She is accompanied by her daughters Margarita, Catarina, and Virginia ages 13, 12, and 9, respectively.

EFFECTIVE SUFFRAGE. NO REELECTION

Denver, Colo., Feb 13 1932.

Consul,

[Adela S. de Delgado.]

Signature of Applicant

NOTE: Applicants must provide themselves with all such proofs as vouch for the ownership of the objects which they are attempting to bring with them into the country, so that they may be presented at the Mexican Customs of the port of entry.

■ ■

MOVEMENT OF MEXICAN RESIDENTS OF UNITED STATES TO MEXICO. NUEVO LAREDO CONSUL RICHARD F. BOYCE TO SECRETARY OF STATE, 26 NOVEMBER 1930.

Source: Washington, D.C., National Archives, Department of State, RG 59, 311.1215/17

AMERICAN CONSULATE

Nuevo Laredo, Mexico,

November 26, 1930.

Subject: Immigration.

1—1055 G P O

THE HONORABLE

THE SECRETARY OF STATE,

WASHINGTON.

Sir:

I have the honor to report that thousands of Mexican residents of the United States have been returning to Mexico during the past two months through Laredo, Texas. In crossing the international bridge each day one can always see a line of cars with licenses from nearly half the states of the United States filled with household effects of Mexicans returning and waiting to make the necessary registrations with the Mexican authorities. Most of the cars are dilapidated in appearance and show the effects of the long journey from northern sections of the country. Those travelling in cars however are less than half of the total who are returning. Many of them are returning to lake up land at the Don Martin irrigation project, attracted by the advertisements of the Mexican National Irrigation Commission. But about 805 are returning because of lack of work in the United States. A Mexican coming from a large Mexican settlement of about a thousand in Colorado stated that almost all were planning to return to Mexico because of lack of work.

No figures are given for those who were legally in the United States and those who were illegal residents. The Mexican immigration authorities do not record either the length of residence in the United States or whether legal admission was made. The American authorities do not "check out" those aliens unless they have proof of legal entry, an identification card from the Mexican consul in the United States and voluntarily call at the American immigration office. The Mexican consulate at Laredo has no other figures than for the number of Identification Cards issued—to legal and illegal residents indiscriminately and have no data regarding length of residence in the United States or legal entrants. Those legal entrants who do not register their departure with the American immigration authorities are unable to reenter without visas within six months as they have no acceptable proof to claim reentry under Rule 1, Subdivision K, Paragraph 1-H, of the Immigration Rules of January 1, 1930.

While no figures, or even estimates, are obtainable of these Mexicans who have lived over five years in the United States it is believed quite a number have lived in the United States more than five years. Some claim eight, ten, fifteen, even thirty years American residence.

Number of Mexicans returning to Mexico from the United States through Laredo, Texas:

   October, 1930 4,255
   November 1–24, 1930 3,995

Number of automobiles entered Mexico as effects of repatriated Mexicans, Nuevo Laredo, Mexico:

October, 1930 372
November 1–24, 1930 441

Estimated American residence of Mexican repatriates:

Texas 20%	Oklahoma 3%
Illinois 15%	Massachusetts 2%
Michigan 15%	New York 2%
Indiana 10%	Wisconsin 2%
Missouri 10%	Pennsylvania 2%
Ohio 8%	Alabama 1%
Minnesota 5%	
Colorado 5%	

If the Department of State is interested in reports concerning this interesting and important movement of Mexican residents of the United States back to Mexico, I shall be glad to forward further information.

Respectfully yours,
[signature: *Richard F. Boyce*]
Richard F. Boyce,
American Consul.

855/811.1
cc–to Embassy
cc–to Consulate General

RFB/ep

■ ■

EL PROGRESO REPATRIATION ANNOUNCEMENT AND
PASSENGER LIST. SAN DIEGO CONSUL ARMANDO C. AMADOR.
11 AUGUST 1932.
*Source: Mexico City, Archivo de la Secretaría de
Relaciones Exteriores, IV–360–38.*

[seal of the Mexican Consulate in San Diego, Cal.]
**RE: REPATRIATION OF MEXICANS
ABOARD TRANSPORT *PROGRESO.***

San Diego, California
August 11, 1932

Sir

The Government of Mexico, with the cooperation and aid of the Welfare
Committee of this County, will effect the repatriation of all Mexicans
who currently reside in this County and who might wish to return to
their country. This repatriation will be effected aboard the Mexican
Transport *Progreso*, which will leave from San Diego the 23rd of this
month at two o'clock in the afternoon, with destination the ports of
Mazatlán and Manzanillo.

Those persons who are repatriated will be able to choose among
the States of Sonora, Sinaloa, Nayarit, Jalisco, Michoacán, and Guanajuato
as the place of their final destination, with the understanding that the
Government of Mexico will provide them with lands for agricultural
cultivation in any of the aforementioned States and will aid them in the
best manner possible so that they might settle in the country.

Those persons who take part in this movement of repatriation may
count on free transportation from San Diego to the place where they
are going to settle, and they will be permitted to bring with them their
furniture, household utensils, agricultural implements, and whatever
other objects for personal use they might possess.

Since the organization and execution of a movement of repatriation
of this nature implies great expenditures, this Consulate encourages
you, if your circumstances so require, to take advantage of this special
opportunity being offered to you for returning to Mexico at no cost
whatever and so that, once established anew in our country, you might

dedicate all your energies to your personal improvement, that of your family, and that of our country.

If you wish to take advantage of this opportunity, please return this letter, duly signed, with the information requested on the reverse; with the understanding that, barring notice to the contrary from this Consulate, you should present yourself with your family and your luggage on the municipal dock of this port on the 23rd of this month before noon.

In case of any doubt or wish for clarification on your part as to the particulars, I would be grateful if you would direct yourself immediately to this Office, which would be more than happy to provide you with whatever information might be necessary.

With all due consideration.

EFFECTIVE SUFFRAGE. NO REELECTION.

Consul.

ARAMANDO C. AMADOR.

Junta Patriótica Mexicana del Pueblo Obrero, Santa Ana, California, 1919.
Courtesy of Yolanda Alvarez, Mary García, and the Orange County
Mexican American Historical Society.

Revolutionary Mexico
Para los Mexicanos

Mexicanos, la Patria nos llama	*Mexicans, the country calls you*
A luchar con denuedo y valor	*To fight with boldness and valor*
Por la causa del Pueblo	*For the cause of the people*
Que aclama Libertad,	*That proclaims Liberty,*
Democracia y Honor	*Democracy and Honor*
—"Canto al Obrero," Corrido	—"Song to the Worker," Ballad

Nationalism is commonly regarded as a dynamic phenomenon of modern life. In Mexico, the 1910 Revolution revitalized the ideals of nationalism, which embodied social justice, land reform, Mexicanismo, and anti-Americanism as cardinal principles. These concerns were manifested during the Revolution with the cry *México para los Mexicanos* (Mexico for the Mexicans). This great upheaval, in which an estimated 10 percent of the 15 million population perished, was the first social revolution of the twentieth century, boldly advocating socialistic concepts and programs.[1] The Revolution of 1910 vibrantly depicted downtrodden masses battling not only foreign economic domination and exploitation, but also political tyranny and social injustice at home. Mexico's Revolution served as an inspiration for oppressed people everywhere, particularly in Latin America.

For the Mexican people, only their proximity to the United States, commonly viewed as both a blessing and a curse, rivaled the impact of the Revolution. A lament commonly heard in Mexico intones: "Poor Mexico, so

far from God and so close to the United States!" Both realities had a decisive influence on the lives and attitudes of Mexicans in the United States.
Individuals like community activist Lucas Lucio and farm worker Celso
Medina joined those who fled the chaos and aftermath of the Revolution
for the peace and security provided by the United States.[2] The 1910
Mexican Revolution was much more than merely a force propelling Mexicans across the border. Immigrants fondly reminisced about the Revolution and minimized the political differences and divisions engendered by
the violent struggle. "Pancho Villa, Emiliano Zapata, and [Venustiano]
Carranza," José Santos Herrada told his family, "were all good men with
the right ideas."[3] Many Mexican children in the United States also shared
the experience described by the distinguished Mexican scholar and historian Ramón Eduardo Ruiz: "I would listen to my father . . . discuss what
had taken place in the country he had recently fled. A magnificent story
teller, my father eagerly shared his wealth of anecdotes and opinions with
all of his children."[4]

Tales of the revolutionary heroes and aims of the Revolution served as
more than a form of family entertainment. Residents of *México de afuera*
avidly debated the government's ability and commitment to carry out the
goals espoused by the Revolution of land reform, social justice, and the regulation of foreign investments. Mexican communities in the United States
were imbued with the revolutionary zeal and the demand for change. A core
of dedicated activists and labor groups provided invaluable leadership during the turbulent decade. Among those actively participating in the activities of the *Confederación de Uniones y Obreras Mexicanas* (Confederation
of Unions and Mexican Workers) were president Celso Medina, executive
officer Nicolás Avila, and secretary Evelyn Velarde Benson. Farm workers
Emilio Martínez, Alejandro Casto, and their coworkers cited Article 123 of
the Revolution's 1917 Constitution as the Mexican workers' Magna Carta.
They acknowledged that the Revolution's pledge of fair treatment for workers inspired them, as well as compatriots everywhere, to participate in
union activities of all types, including labor strikes. Throughout the nation,
individuals with a similar orientation assumed a vital leadership role in
their colonias.[5] The tenets of the Revolution had a strong and compelling
effect on the Mexican community north of the Río Bravo del Norte. They
were proud of the leadership role Mexico was assuming in promoting and
protecting the rights of the working class.

At home, war-weary Mexicans celebrated the end of the civil war by embracing a new and dynamic national rebirth. The nation's new vibrancy could be heard in the music of pre-Columbian scores composed by Carlos Chávez; read in novels like *Los de abajo* by Mariano Azuela; and viewed in the public murals painted by Diego Rivera, David Alfaro Siqueiros, and José Clemente Orozco. New ideas also permeated Mexican intellectual thought. Anthropologist Manuel Gamio applied an innovative approach to studying Mexican Indians in *La población del valle de Teotihuacán* (1922). Historian Martín Luis Guzmán chronicled fresh chapters of the Revolution in *El águila y la serpiente* (1928). Philosopher José Vasconcelos formulated an original vision of mankind in *La raza cósmica* (1925). Mexico's revolutionary nationalism was fervently extolled in its art, music, literature, and the social sciences.

Mexican revolutionary nationalism also made inroads north of the border. Noteworthy examples were artists David Alfaro Siqueiros and Diego Rivera being commissioned to paint murals in the United States. In 1932 at the historic Olvera Street of Los Angeles, Siqueiros dedicated the mural "América Tropical" to the local Mexican community. "America Tropical" portrayed a Native American impaled on a crucifix with a screaming American eagle hovering on top. During the same year Edsel Ford, President of the Ford Motor Company and the Detroit Institute of the Arts, retained Diego Rivera to decorate the courtyard walls of the institute. The Ford Motor Company's Rouge plant inspired Rivera to create what he thought was his best work—"Detroit Industry Frescoes." It is a microcosm of the industrial age depicting its positive and negative contributions. To make certain that Rivera did not inject his socialist ideas in the mural, every day after Rivera quit painting at 4:00 P.M., Edsel Ford's father, Henry Ford, would send his personal photographer to photograph the day's work. Each night, Ford would review the film in his private projection room. Despite the precaution, civic and business leaders in both Detroit and Los Angeles demanded the "white-washing" or destruction of the murals. They were successful in having "América Tropical," in Southern California painted over and concealed but the "Detroit Industry Frescoes" remained intact and served as an inspiration for the Midwest Mexican community.[6] Auto worker José Santos Herrada, for example, would routinely take his granddaughter to visit the "Detroit Industry Frescoes" on Sunday mornings. "This is our art, it belongs to us, the people," he would proclaim to his offspring.[7] His granddaughter recounted that her grandfather viewed the mural with reverence akin to a religious experience despite the fact that he was adamantly anti-Catholic and anti-religion.

The spirit of revolutionary nationalism that swept across Mexico and spilled over into the colonias in the United States became the decisive force in determining the policies and practices of the Mexican government. This influence became apparent when the new, post revolutionary government was confronted with its first major international crisis: the deportation and repatriation problem, as a result of the brief but severe economic recession in the United States during 1920–1921. This unexpected return of large numbers of immigrants severely strained the capabilities of the debt-ridden government. Coinciding as it did with the end of Mexico's civil war, the governmental apparatus, financial resources, and economic infrastructure required to handle the influx were not available. Yet the government felt compelled to assist its Nationals and their children. Neglecting the unfortunate repatriates might be construed as profaning the principles of the Revolution.

Mexico had always welcomed its Nationals as they routinely returned to *la madre patria*. However, the 1920–1921 repatriation involved a sudden and significant surge in the number of individuals entering the country. Reportedly 111, 979 repatriates returned in 1921. The sheer numbers created a sense of urgency and a demand for government intervention. Unemployed immigrants found themselves stranded in a foreign land, with some of them on the verge of starvation. The emergency was so grave that all foreign immigration to Mexico was suspended until the repatriation crisis could be resolved.[8] However, there was no established policy or administrative structure available for dealing with repatriation on such a massive scale. Providentially, the repatriation movement of the early 1920s occurred during the presidency of Alvaro Obregón. His public images as a "reasonable man" and a "peacemaker" served him well in dealing with the repatriation emergency. Obregón received numerous requests for assistance and often directed the Secretary of the Treasury, Adolfo de la Huerta, to utilize government funds to aid Mexicans stranded in the United States.

Increased demands for help made it impossible to assist all potential repatriates who requested aid. A severe problem was that repatriation expenses escalated because Mexico had to bear the cost of repatriating its destitute Nationals. In an attempt to share the burden, American businesses and local authorities were asked to assist in funding passage to the border. Most employers proved unwilling to assist or cooperate in the venture. A few compassionate employers, among them the Ford Motor Company, agreed to provide free transportation to the border for their former employees. Ford shipped more than three thousand of its workers back to Mexico.[9]

Most Nationals were not as fortunate and had to fend for themselves. In order to assist destitute repatriates, Mexico was forced to spend nearly three million pesos within a period of five months.[10] Rapidly dwindling treasury reserves convinced the government that financial assistance should be limited to repatriates facing life-threatening situations. This view became established government policy and was adopted by the Department of Repatriation created by Obregón within the Ministry of Foreign Relations. The Mexican government had learned an invaluable lesson in dealing with repatriation: Its stance against assuming fiscal responsibility for repatriation remained a guiding principle during the repatriation influx of the 1930s.

By 1923 the American economy had begun to recover, and economic conditions quickly improved. Mexicans once again began to migrate north in large numbers. The renewal of Mexican immigration after the repatriation crisis of 1920–1921 led Mexican writers to examine the dilemma of Mexican emigration. Several of the authors were government officials, and this gave their writings an aura of official sanction. Publication of these works during the 1920s indicated an awareness, if not an acceptance, by the government that the diaspora was now a permanent rather than a temporary or intermittent phenomenon. Mexicans were not only leaving the country in large numbers; more of them were doing so with the intention of establishing permanent residence in the United States. The literature attempted to explain *México de afuera* within the framework of the nation's revolutionary nationalism. Social justice, Mexicanismo, and anti-Americanism remained prevalent themes in the semi-official works published during this period.

Various aspects of immigration and the life of Mexican Nationals and Mexican Americans north of the Río Bravo del Norte were carefully examined in Andrés Landa y Piña's *La migración y protección de mexicanos en el extranjero*. The author urged his compatriots to stay home and contribute to the economic development of *la madre patria* rather than emigrating to the United States. This would not only benefit Mexico; it would spare them from being exploited and discriminated against by the Anglo society.[11] This point of view was generally regarded as representing the government's official position because Landa y Piña was head of the Migration Service Department in the Ministry of the Interior. As an official in Mexico's strict governmental hierarchy, it is inconceivable that he would have expressed any contrary or personal opinions. In fact, the treatise had been written at the behest of the Secretary of Foreign Relations.

Another significant commentary on immigration life in the United States was Alfonso Fabila's *El problema de la emigración de obreros y campesinos Mexicanos*. It delivered a vehement attack against American society. Fabila portended to see little benefit to be derived by Mexicans emigrating to the United States. Fabila's book was based on firsthand observations made while living in Los Angeles. He reported scandalous and widespread discrimination against Mexicans, regardless of whether they were native or foreign born. Copies of the book were distributed to Mexican consuls in the United States. Its acceptance and use as a reference source gave the book legitimacy and fostered the view that it was an officially approved version of conditions in the United States.[12]

In sharp contrast to Alfonso Fabila's work was the reasoned academic discourse in *Emigración de mexicanos a los Estados Unidos* by Gilberto Loyo. His interpretation presented a demographic outlook based on analytical computations. Loyo stressed the fact that immigrants should remain in Mexico because the nation needed a population density large enough to support the development of modern industrialization. He too concurred that Nationals in the United States were not contributing to Mexico's economic growth, but to the prosperity of the United States. Loyo also contended that in America Mexicans earned their living by enduring terrible working conditions and suffering acrimonious discrimination by the Anglo society.[13] In this respect, he agreed with Fabila's observations. Gilberto Loyo's views were particularly influential because he had powerful friends in the government.[14]

Taking a different approach than the one pursued by his colleagues was Dr. Manuel Gamio. Trained in anthropology and archaeology at Columbia University, Gamio developed a comprehensive analysis of the Mexican immigration experience. His *Mexican Immigration to the United States: A Study of Human Migration and Adjustment* and *The Life Story of the Mexican Immigrant: Autobiographic Documents* were based upon extensive original research.

The findings of these studies were presented at U.S. Congressional Hearings on Immigration during the 1920s. If the U.S. acted to restrict

Mexican immigration, Gamio feared a "repatriation" of Mexicans and a "revolution of starvation." He proposed that the U.S. Congress establish a temporary Mexican immigration program as a solution. Gamio, unfortunately believed that his "voice was isolated and of little authority" in the United States.[15] Regretfully, Gamio's works were not translated or available in Mexico until many years after his death. Gamio's works may have been ignored because rather than engaging in gringo bashing, he emphasized the positive aspects of both immigration and repatriation. He contended that when the national economy recovered its strength and achieved its full potential, Mexicans would no longer have to seek work as braceros in the United States. Gamio also asserted that Mexico would be well served by repatriates who "have acquired during their stay in the United States valuable experience in agriculture or industry; they learned to handle machinery and modern tools; they have discipline and steady habits of work."[16] In spite of his expertise, Gamio was never instrumental in formulating Mexico's immigration policy. This oversight is difficult to understand unless his divergent views are taken into account.

In nationalistic Mexico, it was not wise to disagree with or challenge government sanctioned views or dogma. A more cautious position on repatriation, and one which contradicted Dr. Manuel Gamio's positive assessment, was taken by Enrique Santibañez, Consul General in San Antonio, Texas. Santibañez was not convinced that repatriates had learned any useful or substantive skills which would prove beneficial to them in Mexico. The consul's opinion undoubtedly reflected the situation with which he was familiar in Texas rather than with the occupational opportunities Mexicans found elsewhere in the United States. In Texas, with its caste-like employment patterns, job opportunities were extremely restrictive. Mexican workers had little opportunity to acquire new skills. Santibañez also reasoned that higher wages in the United States would deter skilled workers from returning to *la madre patria*. The Consul General's views first appeared in a series of articles written for the *Excélsior* in Mexico City. Later, the columns were published in *Ensayo acerca de la inmigración mexicana en los Estados Unidos* at the request of then President Emilio Portes Gil.[17] Regretfully, Santibañez died at his post just as the repatriation movement of the 1930s was getting under way. His expertise and insight would have been invaluable in dealing with the ensuing repatriation crisis.

The political situation in the 1930s was markedly different from the one existing in 1920–1921. Then, the presidency had been under the vigorous leadership of Alvaro Obregón. He had been succeeded by another assertive individual, Plutarco Elías Calles. In 1928, the president's term of office was extended to six years, with no reelection possible. Obregón was reelected to succeed Calles as president. Unfortunately, he was assassinated before taking office, whereupon the nation was plunged into a quick series of three presidents. Upon Obregón's untimely death, Congress appointed Emilio Portes Gil to serve as interim president form 1928 to 1930. President Portes Gil did restore a semblance of political order, and a general election was held to select a successor. Pascual Ortiz Rubio and Abelardo Rodríguez each served two of the remaining four years of Obregón's unexpired term.

As a result, during the critical period of the early 1930s, Mexico's political leadership failed to implement a concerted program to deal effectively with the issues of deportation and repatriation. However, in the waning days of his administration, President Portes Gil conferred with American Ambassadors Dwight Morrow and Josephus Daniels about the matter. All three gentlemen believed the problem could be resolved in a harmonious manner with a minimum of inconvenience or disruption.[18] While Portes Gil was meeting with the American ambassadors, his successor, Ortiz Rubio, promised "that his administration would make every effort possible . . . to permit the return to the country of all Mexicans desiring [to do] so."[19] Upon assuming office, Ortiz Rubio carried out part of his pledge by issuing a presidential decree granting franquicias (exemptions from custom duties) to the repatriates. His successor, President Abelardo Rodríguez, expanded the list of articles that repatriates could bring in duty free.[20] Even though the ruling government was in a state of disarray, Mexico could not risk ignoring the need for action presented by the vexing repatriation dilemma.

The reemergence of repatriation as a socioeconomic issue reawakened deeply imbedded revolutionary sentiments for social justice, feelings of Mexicanismo, and a strong anti-American sentiment among the general populace. This sensitive controversy provided opportunistic politicians with a clearly defined issue upon which to vent the emotional ideals of revolutionary nationalism. To defray the expenses of repatriation, a law was enacted requiring all foreigners residing in the Republic to register and pay a ten peso fee.[21] Repatriation was a political football made to order for extolling the virtues of Mexican nationalism. Rather than dealing with the nation's problems, politicians diverted public attention by pointing the finger at the transgressions of the Colossus of the North. The national press kept the public informed about repatriation and other developments involving México de afuera. The negative conditions encountered by compatriots who had migrated north was a favorite, ongoing feature in Mexican newspapers. For the nationalist-oriented press, repatriation became a major chapter in the continuing saga of tension and discord between the United States and Mexico. Incidents, no matter how trivial, were described and analyzed in detail. Mexico's leading newspapers ran sensationalized repatriation stories on a regular basis.

Among the numerous episodes recounted by the press were stories of destitute Mexicans hopelessly stranded in Alaska or Kansas; of compatriots suffering the ravages of a perilous winter in Chicago or Detroit; of patient Nationals anxiously awaiting transportation in Juárez or Nogales. Provincial newspapers throughout the country joined in highlighting repatriation incidents. There was never a lack of tragic stories to report as the "caravans of sorrow" headed south. Some of the most extensive coverage appeared in Guadalajara's *El Informador* and Monterrey's *El Porvenir*. Mexican newspapers also published accounts appearing in the Spanish-language press of México de afuera. *La Prensa* in San Antonio, *Hispano-Americano* of San Diego, the *Continental* in El Paso, and *La Opinión* and *El Heraldo de México* in Los Angeles were newspapers often cited.[22]

Some historians have severely criticized the Mexican press for its lack of objectivity in chronicling and reporting the repatriation crisis. Much of the criticism centers specifically on allegations that they did not always distinguish between fact, fiction, and rumor.[23] While there are legitimate grounds for this charge, Mexican press coverage must be assessed and understood in its role as the voice of revolutionary nationalism and the constraints under which it operated. A wary eye always had to be kept on the fact that the government controlled the supply of newsprint. Woe to any newspaper that became overly critical of national policies. "Yankee bashing" provided an acceptable way for the press to vent its spleen or displeasure. Criticism notwithstanding, the press performed an invaluable service in keeping the repatriation issue in the public's eye and conscience. Due to its vigilance and aggressive, semidocumentary reporting, the press often spurred a reluctant government into taking action.

It must be borne in mind that the Mexican people remained highly conscious of past transgressions against their country by the United States.

To them, repatriation was simply one more example of the callous attitude that the United States continually exhibited toward its southern neighbor. Repatriates themselves contributed to the discourse by stating their plight in patriotic jargon. Some Nationals seeking to return frequently requested assistance from Mexican consuls, the Secretary of Foreign Relations, the Secretary of the Interior, and other departments. In some instances, their impassioned pleas were addressed directly to the president of the republic. Requests for assistance often extolled the virtues of la madre patria and asserted the repatriates' undying love and devotion to the nation's revolutionary ideals, and promised to be loyal and productive citizens.

Luis N. Vera wrote to President Pascual Ortiz Rubio that the Comité Pro-Repatriación, consisting of one hundred Mexican families in Wyoming and Nebraska, wished to return home and establish an agricultural colony. These supplicants, who formerly worked for the Great Western Sugar Company, laced their plea for help with specific references to the nation's revolutionary Constitution of 1917, and adopted the nationalistic motto of "Union, Progress, and Country" for their organization.[24] Another fervent letter sent to President Ortiz Rubio was a petition from Santiago L. Gómez, representative of the Agriculture Colony of Goodyear, Arizona. Señor Gómez wrote of his group's desire to return to their "beloved country," in particular to the state of Sonora. Their intent was to develop an agricultural colony under the patriotic banner of "union, progress, and country."[25]

The president of the Comisión Honorífica Mexicana of Wiley, Colorado, Rosalio Araiza, in a letter to Manuel C. Téllez, Secretary of Foreign Relations, bemoaned the fact that a lack of funds prevented them from telegraphing the president directly. According to Señor Araiza, the Comisión's members were truly in a desperate state: "We are hungry, shoeless, and unclothed . . . without a miserable piece of bread for our children." Despite enduring their miserable situation and without any help from local charities, these stalwart compatriots maintained that they were "preserving the romantic and glorious traditions of our race." And as loyal Mexicanos, they pledged their continued dedication to "Unity and Country" upon returning to Mexico.[26] Neither the government nor the press could ignore such noble and patriotic requests.

While the government received numerous requests for assistance, it was the Consular Service which was forced to deal with the initial stages of the repatriation tragedy. Although the Consular Service had been numerically increased, the immensity of the repatriation movement of the 1930s completely overwhelmed the consulates. Mexican consuls throughout the United States realized that new strategies and tactics were required to enable them to deal with the disaster. Unable to wait for directions from Mexico City, some consuls exercised their own judgment on how to handle immediate problems. Recommendations and changes were proposed to Secretaría de Relaciones Exteriores. Some of the innovative procedures instituted by consuls were adopted system-wide to facilitate servicing the repatriates.

Due to the efforts of Consul Rafael de la Colina, the Los Angeles consular office surpassed most others in the nature and quality of services rendered. A perennial problem facing a surprising number of repatriates was the need to get rid of property, usually on very short notice. Consuls everywhere attempted to assist prospective repatriates concerning the sale of their property or its exchange for holdings in Mexico of comparable value. Yet the Los Angeles consulate was the only one that formally organized a special colonization desk to advise Nationals involved in complicated property transactions. Mexican officials, including Mexico's ambassador in Washington, D.C., were not pleased with the mission undertaken by the Los Angeles consulate's colonization desk. They feared that recommendations from the consulate might be misconstrued as denoting official sanction of the transaction. They were afraid the government might be held legally responsible if compatriots were dissatisfied with the eventual results.

There were also concerns that land exchanges or purchases encouraged the exodus of Mexican property owners from the United States. Such individuals were deemed to be an important moral force in the colonias. It was therefore feared that the loss of their leadership and stability would have a very negative impact on the Mexican communities. Opponents also claimed that the colonization desk's actions ran counter to the government's policy of encouraging Nationals with any viable means of support to remain where they were. Secretaría de Relaciones Exteriores (SRE) eventually overruled all opposition and reaffirmed that the colonization desk in Los Angeles was acting in accordance with the federal government's "propositions and recommendations."[27]

Consul Luis Medina Barrón in San Antonio convinced his superiors that repatriates should be allowed to bring with them, duty free, all articles needed to earn a livelihood. As a result of his efforts, items such as carpenter tools, shoe-repair equipment, barber chairs, plumbing, and other trade tools were exempted from custom fees.[28] New Orleans Consul Armando C. Amador proposed purchasing an automobile to transport penniless repatriates who lived near the border. Salt Lake City Consul Raúl Domínguez demonstrated personal initiative by publishing a newsletter informing his constituents about repatriation issues and other pertinent matters. It proved to be an effective way of reaching the far-flung colonias in the mountain states of Utah, Colorado, Idaho, and Montana.[29] In spite of their Herculean efforts, the consuls encountered serious problems in attempting to assist the repatriates. Adding to their dilemma were the confusing and often contradictory regulations received from various government departments in Mexico City. This confusion and delay added to the repatriates' turmoil and suffering. At times, the government bureaucracy seemed mired in its own red tape and appeared confused over which course of action to pursue. Government snarls and intrigue challenged the ingenuity and resourcefulness of individual consuls.

The situation faced by Consul General Eduardo Hernández Cházaro in San Antonio is illustrative of the problems faced by some consuls in discharging their duties. His jurisdiction included Karnes County, located in southern Texas between San Antonio and Corpus Christi. The area was primarily inhabited by destitute tenant farmers and agricultural workers. During the summer of 1931, prolonged unemployment caused many Nationals in Karnes City and the surrounding area to opt for returning home. In assessing the situation, the Consul General visited more than four thousand idle farm workers. He reassured them that the government was prepared to do everything possible to ameliorate their plight. On their behalf, on two separate occasions, Consul General Cházaro solicited travel funds form the Secretaría de Gobernación (Secretary of the Interior). Both requests were denied.[30]

Aggravating the situation was the fact that any assistance by Texas relief authorities required the repatriates to verify residency. This presented a formidable hurdle because many Karnes County residents were migrant workers, who simply used the area as a home base during the off-season. Unable to verify continuous residency, they were denied any type of public assistance. In sheer defiance brought on by frustration, the desperate Karnes County repatriates declared their intention "to walk to the border," if necessary. Hernández Cházaro was determined to avoid the "shameful spectacle" of twenty-seven hundred men, women, and children, many of them suffering from malnutrition, hiking over 250 miles to Nuevo Laredo, Mexico. As a last resort, the Consul General appealed to the colonia to help their compatriots return to the motherland. Cházaro couched his appeal in revolutionary rhetoric because he viewed repatriation as a nationalistic issue.[31] Before being appointed Consul General, he had publicly confirmed this belief in an exclusive interview published in *La Prensa,* San Antonio's leading Spanish-language newspaper. Repatriation, Hernández Cházaro declared, presented an opportunity for bringing back Mexico's prodigal sons and daughters. Successful repatriation, he believed, would preclude any future exit of compatriots to the United States.[32]

Mexican Nationals and Mexican Americans throughout Texas responded generously to Hernández Cházaro's plea for help. Typical of the overwhelming response was the contribution made by colonia residents in San Antonio. In a surge of nationalistic fervor, they provided vehicles as well as gasoline, oil, and food for the trip to the border. The San Antonio colonia was in a unique position to help their fellow paisanos, for it was home to a sizable number of affluent Mexicanos. These individuals, "largely from Mexico's upper classes," were a unique minority in the United States.[33] Although they distrusted the revolutionary Mexican government, they maintained a compassionate attitude toward their less-fortunate countrymen. Empathy, combined with their nationalistic spirit, compelled them to support humanitarian projects like the one initiated by the Consul General for destitute repatriates. Their sense of righteous indignation was particularly aroused in behalf of compatriots suffering exploitation at the hands of *norteamericnos.*[34]

Hernández Cházaro personally directed the registration of compatriots and assigned consular staff to accompany units of the mercy caravans to the border. The convoys of human cargo were given extensive coverage in the Texas and Mexican press. A death and three births were chronicled on the trek to the border.[35] Repatriates who were too proud to accept charity packed their bags and toted their belongings on their backs. They were determined to walk the entire distance to the border, if necessary. Some dropped by the wayside. Men, shaken by the suffering of wives and children, swallowed their pride and belatedly accepted rides from fellow travelers. Observers who witnessed the tragic exodus criticized Consul General Hernández Cházaro for not vehemently protesting repatriation and the treatment accorded to Mexican Nationals by American authorities.

This was a common complaint often lodged against the Consular

Service, and against local consuls in particular. Desperate and frustrated Nationals suspected the consuls were not doing their job in an aggressive manner. The explanation for their seeming inaction was quite simple: Consuls were forbidden to denounce repatriation publicly. There were two main reasons for this restriction: First, the Mexican government viewed repatriation as the right of any sovereign nation to determine who could reside in their country. Mexico could hardly object to repatriation because it was also involved in expelling hundreds of Chinese and other unwanted aliens. Second, was the belief that returning Nationals would contribute immensely to the nation's well-being, due to the skills and experiences gained abroad. In addition, the international canons of diplomacy required that consuls conduct themselves in a neutral, non-threatening manner at all times.

In short, the consuls must maintain the respect of the host authorities or incur the risk of recall. If formal demurs were lodged concerning the plight or maltreatment of repatriates, it was the responsibility of the ministers in Mexico City or the Mexican Embassy in Washington, D.C. to convey complaints via diplomatic channels. Occasionally, Mexico's ambassador did deliver formal protests expressing his government's displeasure about specific incidents to the U.S. Secretary of State. It was not considered proper protocol for local consuls to express any personal or political opinions critical of the host nation.

Nonetheless, due to the constant pressure and stress of dealing with massive repatriation, there were occasions when consuls ignored official protocol and vented their wrath or frustration with surprising candor. Among those who dared to voice their opinions was Consul Rafael de la Colina in Los Angeles.[36] He was able to exercise greater personal discretion because his consular jurisdiction had the largest concentration of Mexican Nationals and Americans of Mexican descent.

Personally, Consul de la Colina approved of the country's repatriation efforts, but he also called for the repatriation of other foreigners. Although selective repatriation was strongly resented by all consuls, few would have dared to be so candid in their remarks.[37] While cooperating with local welfare and repatriation authorities, de la Colina sent a confidential memorandum to SRE. In it, he expressed his genuine concern for social justice and fair treatment. Consul de la Colina resented how agriculturalists and industrialists viewed the Mexican worker. They saw him, he averred, "as a docile beast of burden, hardworking, economical, and cheap." As a result,

the "welfare [of the Mexican] is never the concern of the [Anglo] community," except when "it affects the efficiency of his labor."[38] In courageously
proclaiming his views and opinions, de la Colina was in a select minority.
Most consuls feared that any condemnation of the repatriation process
might result in charges of meddling in the domestic affairs of the host
nation. Such an offense could lead to being labeled a *persona non grata* and
the possibility of being recalled. Therefore, few consuls openly criticized the
treatment accorded their compatriots.

In Detroit, Consul Ignacio Batiza enjoyed the singular advantage of
being able to call upon famed muralist Diego Rivera for support and assistance. Rivera was in Detroit, working on the "Detroit Industry Frescoes"
mural. Not only did he assist in raising money for repatriation, the artist was
also instrumental in obtaining humane treatment for compatriots from
welfare authorities. Moreover, Rivera exhorted his countrymen to return to
Mexico and avail themselves of the opportunities offered by a benevolent
government, rather than wasting their energy and talents enriching the
United States. Not all Mexicans shared Rivera's views. Roberto Galvan
labeled his utterings as those of "a crazy old man."[39] In addition, Rivera
played a critical role in establishing the *Liga de Obreros y Campesinos*
(League of Workers and Farm Laborers). The League's purpose was to assist
the consul in protecting the welfare and employment rights of local
Mexicans. On one occasion, Batiza and the League came to the aid of Pedro
González when he was threatened with repatriation. The former Ford
Motor Company employee had been dragged out of his home and escorted
to the train station by police officers. Authorities justified their action by
claiming that repatriation "was in the best interest of all concerned."[40] Due
to the protests of the consul and Rivera, Pedro González was allowed to
remain in the United States.

Consul Rafael Aveleyra in Gary, Indiana, ably demonstrated the Consular
Service's concern for social justice. Despite his efforts to assist repatriates, he
failed to secure the cooperation of the local welfare department. During the
summer of 1932, Mary Grace Wells, welfare administrator, shipped several
contingents of repatriates to the border without informing the consulate.
After repeatedly protesting this illegal practice to no avail, Consul Aveleyra
lost his patience. Diplomatic rules and regulations serve a useful purpose, but
they have their limits. A consul could elect to observe protocol or risk all and
do his duty. Aveleyra reasoned that protecting the rights of a country's

citizens was the sole justification for having consulates. Therefore, even though it was counter to Consular Service policy, Aveleyra concluded that there were times when it was necessary, even imperative, to violate protocol and speak up forcefully.

The situation in Gary, Indiana, clearly called for extreme measures. An exasperated Aveleyra visited Wells and lectured her regarding her repeated transgressions. He reminded her that the repatriates had contributed to the nation's progress and "regardless of their nationality are members of your community," rather than Mexico's. Even though the "problem may be easily solved by shipping these people to the border," the welfare department could not summarily abrogate its responsibility, he asserted. Furthermore, Aveleyra admonished Wells, "These people are going to be subject to all kinds of hardships, if you do not show your cooperation."[41] Unfortunately, as in other similar instances, the consul's entreaties were ignored.

The efforts of consulates in Los Angeles, San Antonio, Detroit, and Gary were not unique. They reflected the actions of consuls across the country who intervened aggressively in behalf of their constituents. All of them tried in various ways to ameliorate the dire plight of the repatriates. They would have been derelict in the performance of their duty if they had let protocol deter them from demanding justice and humane treatment. Consul S. J. Treviño, in Denver, summarized the feelings and dedication of his colleagues when he stated: "you realize the sufferings and oppression which confronts our connacionales in this country, [by repeatedly] having the opportunity to see and hear their laments and to feel the pain of their disgrace." With the pleas and complaints of their co-nationals ringing in their ears, Treviño and other consular agents had no other recourse but to respond in a vigorous and energetic manner. "We help as much as possible our people . . . trying to return to our country," Consul Treviño asserted.[42]

In spite of the criticism directed at them, the consuls earned the gratitude of the repatriates. Some became immortalized in corridos, or historical ballads. Consul General Cházaro's efforts in San Antonio were recounted in the corrido "Despedida de Karnes City": "The Consul General has worked without rest in order to repatriate us," ran the tune. Cházaro's lack of success with SRE did not diminish the appreciation for his efforts in behalf of his charges. Consul de al Colina was also immortalized in verse and song: "Mr. Rafael de la Colina was chartering a train" went the refrain in the ballad "Adiós Paisanos."[43] Countless corridos, many of them composed impromptu, echoed the sentiments, suffering, frustration, and dreams of the faceless masses being swept south into Mexico. Many corridos were laced with protests against the injustice to which repatriates were subjected.

Just as nationalistic concerns characterized consular action in behalf of the repatriates, this same spirit was apparent in organizing the National Repatriation Committee, the NRC—commonly known as the *Comité*—in Mexico City. This organization attempted to bring together private and public agencies as well as business and charitable institutions. The committee was organized under the leadership of experts familiar with México de afuera. Among them were Andrés Landa y Piña and Alfonso Fabila, who, as has been noted, were also respected authors. Landa y Piña and Fabila were serving as assistant secretaries in *Gobernación*. Together, they drew up a list of "who's who" of political leaders to comprise the organization's executive committee. Given their political and literary status, they were in a unique position to recruit select individuals to the august body. Many potential members considered being asked to join the Comité as a political plum.

Among the distinguished members of the Comité's executive committee were Albert J. Pani, Secretary of Public Credit; Narciso Bassols, Secretary of Education; Eduardo Vasconcelos, Acting Secretary of the Interior; Francisco S. Elías, Secretary of Agriculture; and Manuel C. Téllez, Secretary of Foreign Relations. One puzzling omission was Dr. Manuel Gamio, Mexico's foremost authority on immigration. He was not included in either the executive committee or on the board of directors. Regretfully, as would become apparent, the executive committee delegated operation of the NRC to a board of directors who found it difficult to cope with the problems facing the Comité. Yet, in all candor, it is doubtful that any group, no matter how distinguished or capable it might have been, would have been able to resolve the repatriation crisis. The Herculean task literally defied all solutions that were attempted, regardless of who initiated or directed them.

Some Mexican politicians reacted negatively to the founding of the Comité de Repatriación and the accompanying publicity regarding repatriation. They denied or refused to assume any responsibility for resolving the crisis. Repatriation "is not a problem of [created by] the Revolution," Mexican Congressman Gilberto Fabila stated emphatically. Rather, he declared, "responsibility rests with the preceding governments before the revolutionary movement."[44] Regardless of who was to blame or whose responsibility it was, most politicians demanded action. Given the magnitude of the problem, precious time could not be wasted in assessing blame. People had to be trans-ported, fed, housed, and cared for. Action and immediate assistance, not political rhetoric or bickering, was what the repatriates needed. The Comité responded with a fund-raising campaign to collect a half-million pesos. This endeavor assumed the aspects of a crusade and was launched with an air of patriotic ardor and zeal via radio and the press.

In their appeal for financial assistance, Comité spokesmen utilized the revolutionary rhetoric of social responsibility, but also heralded repatria-tion as an opportunity which the Mexican nation "can and should profit from."[45] This approach enjoyed some success as a fund-raising strategy, and contributions were received from a variety of donors. Among the con-tributors were President Abelardo Rodríguez, government employees, mil-itary personnel, Spanish industrialist José González Soto, and other local as well as foreign businessmen.[46] Based on their generous contributions, the Comité appeared to be well on its way to raising or even exceeding its goal of a half-million pesos. However, as is often the case in fund-raising efforts, the initial euphoric support soon began to abate.

While soliciting monetary contributions, internal dissention, political controversy, and public criticism engulfed the Comité. This was partially due to the fact that the Comité's operational procedures and goals were not clearly defined when it was organized. Differences over procedures and objectives soon emerged. Some members proposed the establishment of dormitories or employment agencies for the repatriates. A variety of other suggestions were proposed, discussed, and summarily rejected for one rea-son or another. Sponsoring the establishment of agricultural colonies even-tually emerged as the Comité's primary objective. Colonization, particularly of Mexico's underdeveloped hinterland, had originally been proposed by Dr. Manuel Gamio as an effective program for incorporating repatriates into Mexican society. Although he had been overlooked as a committee mem-ber, Gamio's ideas definitely influenced the Comité.

Despite the revolutionary zeal and fanfare, the Comité's colonization projects were not successful. Rafael González, representing repatriates who had joined the League of Workers and Farm Laborers, complained that the government's assistance was irregular and insufficient. Farm machinery, tools, and equipment, as well as mules critically needed for cultivation, never arrived. Disgruntled repatriates often threatened the use of violence to achieve their objectives and promote their interests. Colonization agent

Manuel Chávez remarked that "the life of a repatriate only costs 25 pesos,"[47] meaning that for all intents and purposes they were expendable. Widespread discontent among the colonizers occurred because repatriates were not consulted or involved in the planning or decision-making process. Consequently, insurmountable problems that eventually arose led to the dissolution of the National Repatriation Committee by President Abelardo Rodríguez on June 14, 1934.

In a final attempt to resolve the repatriation and colonization issue before leaving office, Rodríguez established a National Repatriation Board by presidential decree on July 26, 1934, to replace the discredited Comité de Repatriación. Unlike its predecessor, the Board was an official agency of the federal government. Six ministries were directly responsible for its creation and operation: Foreign Relations, National Economy, Interior, Public Health, Labor, and Agriculture and Development. The agency was to operate under the direction of the Secretary of Agriculture, Francisco S. Elías. This arrangement placed the repatriation issue at the presidential cabinet level and assured it top priority. The National Repatriation Board continued the defunct Comité's colonization projects. The Board's rationale was that colonization remained the best way to resettle repatriates and utilize the farming skills they had acquired in the United States. Both Mexico and the repatriates would ultimately benefit by participating in the venture.[48]

Formation of the National Repatriation Board in 1934 coincided with General Lázaro Cárdenas's campaign for the presidency. Cárdenas had gained national prominence due to the reputation he established while serving as governor of Michoacán. He distinguished himself by aggressively attacking the bleak poverty rampant in his home state. Guided by the ideals of revolutionary Mexico, he built schools for children, championed the cause of the landless peasants, and responded to the needs and interests of the working class. He used his power and influence to redress the injustices afflicting the people. While his reforms were notable, General Cárdenas's innate political acumen was responsible for his emergence as a national leader. The young and energetic Cárdenas presented himself as the champion of the people dedicated to promoting proletarian causes. If elected, Cárdenas promised to distribute the nation's wealth more equitably, raise living standards, and provide the common people access to political power. Cárdenas's promises of revolutionary changes in existing socioeconomic conditions were warmly received by the poverty afflicted masses.

Upon assuming office on November 30, 1934, Cárdenas inherited a nation reeling from the effects of the world-wide depression. Although Mexico had begun to recover from the dismal abyss of the combined presidencies of Portes Gil, Ortiz Rubio, and Abelardo Rodríguez, enormous problems remained to be solved. The depression had brought widespread misery and suffering to Mexico's working class. However, unlike the United States, government welfare or assistance programs were virtually nonexistent. Plagued by their suffering, rural campesinos and urban laborers demanded action and immediate fulfillment of the promises of the Revolution. Many members of the ruling class feared that violence, perhaps even a second revolution, might erupt if something were not done to improve the wretched situation. The influx of repatriates armed with democratic ideas could trigger a social uprising. Fortunately for all concerned, Cárdenas's commitment to improving the status of Mexican workers was evident from the onset of his presidency. He supported demonstrations and strikes for better wages and improved working conditions. Cárdenas's nationalist endeavors, including the expropriation of the British and American oil properties in 1938, were enthusiastically approved by Mexicanos residing on both sides of the border.

Among the many changes favored by Cárdenas was a proposal to allow Mexicanos in México de afuera to retain their Mexican citizenship if forced to forsake their national allegiance in order to secure employment in the United States. The proposal never became law and, as a consequence, many Nationals lost their jobs rather than give up their Mexican citizenship. The citizenship question would remain a sore point and a bone of contention throughout this period.[49] Also of particular importance to Mexicans and Mexican Americans in the United States was the repatriation policy of Cárdenas's administration. A promise to assist Nationals in returning to la madre patria had been made during the presidential campaign. To emphasize his commitment, the pledge was boldly reiterated in the party's platform. Resettlement of repatriates was an integral component of Cárdenas's plan for instituting land reform and promoting agricultural development. A top priority of the program was the redistribution of the vast landholdings amassed by *hacendados* during the era of Porfirio Díaz. Due to Cárdenas's personal zeal, his administration redistributed more than twenty million hectares, or about fifty million acres of land. This dwarfed the combined total distributed by his predecessors. The acreage amounted to more than 10 percent of the farmland available in Mexico.[50]

The issue of land reform was of foremost concern to Cárdenas. He believed ownership of land was the key to the nation's stability and well-being. If a peon had his own plot of land, there would be no need for him to emigrate, and if land were available, it would serve as an incentive for repatriates to return home. Farming would offer them a means of providing for their families and prevent them from becoming wards of the government. Repatriates were expected to play a decisive role in the agrarian transformation of Mexico. President Cárdenas shared Dr. Gamio's view that the repatriates had acquired skills and experience that would prove beneficial to Mexico's agricultural development. They were, after all, familiar with the latest farming techniques, machinery, and pesticides needed to increase food production. Cárdenas expressed this belief in his presidential address and praised the repatriates who while "struggling to survive have remained loyal to the land of their birth, [and] represent a valuable resource for the progress of the country."[51]

According to the plan envisioned by the government, development would be tailored to each area's unique potential. The coastal and subtropical states of Michoacán, Guerrero, Oaxaca, Chiapas, Veracruz, and Tabasco were deemed capable of supplying the nation and the international market with a wide variety of tropical and subtropical fruits and vegetables.[52] This was viewed as a natural course to pursue since many repatriates had worked in groves and orchards in the United States. Being familiar with the latest techniques in the care of fruit trees, they would assure production of high-quality fruit. The building of modern roads and railroads would facilitate the distribution of the exotic produce to local and foreign markets. On the return trip, manufactured products could be shipped into the region. A modern transportation network would enable the government to ship newcomers into the various regions of the country without delay. This would relieve the border areas of the annoying socioeconomic problems created by the repatriates. Dispersion to the interior would also make it more difficult for dissidents or malcontents to return to the United States.

Resettlement ventures failed to ameliorate existing conditions. Problems continued to plague the repatriates throughout the decade. In April of 1939, Chihuahua Governor Gustavo L. Talamantes called a conference of ranking government officials and large landowners in an attempt to find a solution. The meeting was held in response to President Cárdenas's directive that state and local authorities assume greater responsibility for dealing with the readjustment issue on a local level. At the conclusion of the conference, it was recommended "that the head of each repatriated family having at least five dependents be given 3,500 pesos for the purpose of building a home, sufficient farming, and agricultural implements, two cows, twenty chickens, four pigs, four mules, and economic assistance until the crops enabled them to be self-sustaining."[53] The *Banco Nacional de Crédito Ejidal* (National Bank of Communal Land and Credit) was to finance this generous, if unrealistic, plan. No one explained how the bank was supposed to raise the tremendous sum of money required to implement the grandiose scheme. Nor was there any provision for the bank to be repaid, other than the stipulation that the repatriates should pay back the advancement as soon as they were able to do so. When the proposal was sent to Mexico City for review and approval by the chief of Agricultural Colonization, it was quietly allowed to die.

As evident from the above proposal, state governors were anxious to cooperate with the federal government in assisting the repatriates, but none was in a position to respond effectively. In the hope of breaking the impasse, Governor Talamantes suggested that the federal government resume construction of the irrigation works that had been canceled in the Bachimba region. He argued that not only could skilled repatriates be gainfully employed, but once the project was finished the local *ejido* (communal lands) could be enlarged by ten thousand hectares. According to the governor's estimate, this would permit the settlement of an additional one thousand families. Attention was also called to the fact that ejidos in the municipality of Galeana, Chihuahua, were willing to accept repatriates to fill the vacancies created by unsuccessful settlers. Governor Talamantes also recommended that the federal government energetically pursue the construction of Las Lajas Dam in Villa Humada. The site was deemed capable of accommodating numerous farm families. The same claim was made regarding Lagunas de Casas Grandes and La Boquilla de Plazuela, near the town of Buenaventura, if the irrigation systems were extended.[54] To appreciate Governor Talamantes's concern with dams and irrigation, it must be borne in mind that the northern part of Mexico does not receive enough rainfall to sustain an intensive farming economy.

In addition to the dams and irrigation systems, two major projects designed to improve the infrastructure and put repatriates to work were also contemplated for the state of Chihuahua. It was proposed that an all-weather road be built to connect the border town of Ciudad Juárez with the city of Chiuahua. Work on the highway was scheduled to begin as soon as the federal government appropriated the 3,500,000 pesos needed to get the project under way. Subject to a similar fate was a scheme to build the Kansas City, Mexico, and Orient Railroad to the Pacific Ocean.[55] In both instances, repatriates possessing the necessary skills in laying track and maintaining the right of way could have been put to work if the monies had been available. Sadly, this situation was neither unique nor limited to the state of Chihuahua. It seemed that no matter where they turned for help, the repatriates suffered one bitter disappointment after another.

Commenting on the efforts to resettle repatriates in the state of Chihuahua, American Vice Consul Robert K. Peyton filed a confidential, not-for-publication report with the State Department. Peyton's candid, if unflattering, commentary stated: "Like so many other schemes of this nature in Mexico, the repatriation program seems doomed to failure. There is a lack of persistency in the Mexican human nature, a lack of organizing ability in carrying out big plans of this character, and a weakness in the colonizing spirit of the rural farmers, all of which factors will tend to thwart the consummation of such a laudable endeavor."[56] Vice Consul Peyton's assessment was in stark contrast to American Ambassador Josephus Daniels glowing report a couple of years earlier. "Mexico's economic recovery," the ambassador had proclaimed, was "advancing swiftly."[57]

Nonetheless, Secretary of Foreign Relations Eduardo Hay continued to publicize Cárdenas's repatriation policy via radio broadcasts and press releases. Hay directed his appeals to return home at the "million and a half Mexicans living beyond our boundaries." Minister Hay's entreaties were embellished with patriotic music and sentimental corridos or songs. It was hoped that arousing feelings of nostalgia would induce Mexicans residing abroad to "return to their own country, as an integral and vital portion of our people."[58] In spite of such entreaties, it was not until the latter years of Cárdenas's presidency that the government implemented and earnestly pursued an aggressive colonization policy. Part of the reason for the delay was that requests for repatriation assistance had begun to abate notably. The decline was due to the fact that the American economy had begun to improve and stabilize in the mid-1930s. Infusion of New Deal programs helped to ease the worst aspects of the economic crisis, although the hard and trying times brought on by the Great Depression persisted. Implementation of Cárdenas's

repatriation policy was also hindered because it was dependent on other government programs and projects. Chief among them was the construction of
dams and the building of essential irrigation systems. Highways and railroads
also had to be built to transport farm produce, goods, and people in order for
the colonization projects to be successful.

Resettlement of repatriates in agricultural colonies was not a new or
innovative policy. It had been proposed and tried by the National Repatriation Committee, the National Repatriation Board, Obregón's administration,
and even during the Díaz dictatorship. However, in the past, colonization had
been a haphazard operation. Under President Lázaro Cárdenas, colonization
became a national priority. The program, however, was not intended to
encompass all repatriates. It was to be directed specifically at Nationals who
had acquired the agricultural skills essential for success. Past colonization
failures were blamed on the fact that too many of the repatriates lacked the
background and skills necessary to succeed as colonizers. Those familiar with
Cárdenas's character can readily understand that he would not embark upon
or tolerate projects destined to fail.[59]

Cárdenas's emphasis on repatriation and colonization coincided with
efforts to provide asylum for refugees fleeing the Spanish Civil War. While
the Western democracies remained steadfast in their neutrality, Mexico
supported the Spanish Republic during the bloody conflict. Mexico not only
provided crucial diplomatic assistance for the loyalist government; it also
allowed volunteers to fight for the Spanish republic. During the spring of
1939, the Mexican government arranged for the arrival of the first shipload
of Spanish exiles. Approximately 1,599 Spaniards were due to arrive in
Veracruz on June 13. Some historians have charged that a renewed interest
in repatriation was merely a convenient means to deflect criticism about
allowing Spaniards to settle in Mexico. This allegation has never been
proven or conclusively verified. Altruistic motives, rather than pragmatic
interests, may well have prompted Mexico's action in both cases.[60]

In the drive to recruit Nationals from México de afuera, Sub-Secretary
of Foreign Relations Ramón Beteta was ordered to tour the colonias during
the summer of 1939. His mission was billed not only as a "trip of investigation but also of action." The selection of Ramón Beteta was significant
because he was much more than a Sub-Secretary of Foreign Relations. He
was a very prominent and influential member of the administration, who
enjoyed a unique relationship with President Cárdenas. Beteta's father was

a successful lawyer and his mother came from a wealthy, landowning family. Beteta was not only a graduate of the University of Texas, with a degree in economics; he also had a law degree from the National University. In addition, he held the distinction of having received the first Ph.D. in social science granted by the Universidad Nacional Autónoma de México.

Beteta's rise to power and influence under Cárdenas was due in part to family ties, personal friendships, and education.[61] Another key factor contributing to Beteta's eminent position within the administration was Cárdenas's reluctance to deal with the much older Secretary of Foreign Relations, General Eduardo Hay. Cárdenas preferred to bypass Hay and deal directly with Sub-Secretary Beteta.[62] An American journalist commented on the situation: "Cárdenas's Minister [of Foreign Relations] was General Eduardo Hay. . . but it was openly acknowledged that the brilliant Beteta was the real policy maker for his ministry."[63] Beteta was also head of the Cárdenas "brain trust" and served as the secretary of the important Committee of Studies for the president's office. It is therefore understandable that American authorities viewed Beteta not as a Sub-Secretary of Foreign Relations, but rather as a special plenipotentiary diplomat.[64]

In the United States, Señor Ramón Beteta was accorded the red-carpet treatment. Cognizant of the unpleasantness that several previous Mexican officials had encountered, the U.S. State Department requested state and local officials to extend every diplomatic courtesy possible to the distinguished visitor. Beteta made numerous stops in Texas, New Mexico, and Arizona, due to the large number of Nationals residing in those states. He advised them that he was authorized to offer immediate assistance to those who wished to be repatriated. Transportation for themselves and their belongings, including automobiles and farm animals, would be paid for to their final destination. Each family would receive twenty acres of irrigated land and fifty acres of temporal land. Monies would be provided to tide them over during the first year. After that, bank loans and private credit would be available. Colonizers could elect to settle in El Fuerte, Sinaloa, in El Río, Tamaulipas, or in Mexicali, Baja California.[65]

In Karnes City and Kenedy, Texas, Señor Beteta informed his audience that the government was prepared to spend forty million pesos to assure their successful repatriation and resettlement.[66] In spite of such assurances, few Nationals believed that the government would be able to honor all of its promises. That may explain why, even though Beteta was enthusiastically received in the various colonias, the number of individuals signing up as potential colonizers was far less than government officials had anticipated. In an attempt to induce more people to return, interested individuals were given extensions ranging from six months to a year. This would allow them the time to harvest crops, complete labor contracts, sell their property, or simply get their personal affairs in order. The sub-secretary offered to transport repatriates to their place of origin or anywhere in the republic where they could earn a living, even though this was contrary to official government policy.

On the eastern swing of his trip, Beteta visited Mexican enclaves in New Orleans, Chicago, Pittsburgh, Philadelphia, New York, Boston, Providence, and Norfolk. His most successful stopover was in Chicago, where 140 destitute families indicated a desire to be repatriated. Nationals who had become naturalized American citizens posed a particular problem. They feared the loss of their U.S. citizenship if they returned home. To allay their fears, it was recommended that Article 37 of the Mexican Constitution be revised to allow them to retain dual citizenship.[67] However, no action was taken on this issue.

In spite of all his efforts and promises, Señor Beteta convinced very few Mexicans to accept his generous offers. In most cases, the only ones who signed up were totally indigent and had no prospects of improving their situation in the near future. During the initial portion of his trip, fewer than 20 families were actually repatriated and only 415 expressed any interest in returning to Mexico. In total, only about 5,000 potential repatriates agreed to return home.[68] This poor showing placed Beteta in a very embarrassing position. It also gave credence to the charge that his recruiting trip had been undertaken primarily to pacify the rising tide of criticism leveled against the government for admitting the Spanish refugees. Nonetheless, although disheartened by the results, Beteta redoubled his efforts. Failure or even a hint of it was completely unacceptable to the sub-secretary. He was also well aware of how important his mission was to President Cárdenas.

In Mexico City, the government attempted to prevent any embarrassment or misunderstanding as a result of Beteta's actions and statements. President Cárdenas sent SRE a directive reaffirming the Sub-Secretary's power to take whatever action was necessary to accomplish his task. Beteta, Cárdenas asserted, was authorized to assist all Mexicans who wished to return to the mother country. According to the presidential directive, designed to support his emissary, the repatriates could return to their original homesite or settle in any of the proposed colonies. The decree stated that at least four hundred families could be accommodated immediately at previously prepared sites. President Cárdenas reiterated the guarantees made by his emissary.[69] The urgency of the communiqué may be noted by the fact that it was sent to SRE from the presidential train during its stopover in Matamoros, Tamaulipas. In the month of May, Beteta and President Cárdenas held a private conference in Ciudad Juárez.[70] Although the personal or confidential details of the meeting were not disclosed to the press, several pertinent facts were readily available. Repatriates were to be given all possible assistance in returning to Mexico and to facilitate their resettlement. President Cárdenas and Beteta toured the proposed colonization site to assure its appropriateness. To maximize the colony's ability to succeed, the chief engineer of the project, Eduardo Chávez, was to coordinate the efforts of all the government agencies involved in the *18 de Marzo* (18 of March) colonization project. In addition, 800,000 pesos were to be allotted to assure that all transportation costs, settlement needs, and initial agricultural expenses of the repatriates would be met. Cárdenas was determined to avoid the problems and eventual colonization failures at Pinotepa in Oaxaca, El Coloso in Guerrero, and La Esperanza in Tamaulipas.[71]

The repatriation drive conducted by Sub-Secretary Ramón Beteta enjoyed very little success and marked the final major effort of the Mexican government to assist repatriates wishing to return home.[72] With his mission completed, if not accomplished, Sub-Secretary Beteta returned home. In evaluating the efforts by Cárdenas's government and other administrations to assist repatriates and their children, it should be borne in mind that they were undertaken during a period of political instability and in the midst of a severe economic crisis. Therefore, despite the government's good intentions, Mexico lacked not the will but the resources to provide a haven for the repatriates. Yet, the nation and its political leaders, imbued with the spirit of revolutionary nationalism, made a valiant effort in assisting repatriates returning to la madre patria. This was especially true regarding endeavors at colonization.

Para los Mexicanos
DOCUMENTS

■ ■

COMPLAINT AGAINST LAKE COUNTY REPATRIATION PROGRAM.
CHICAGO CONSUL RAFAEL AVELEYRA TO MISS MARY GRACE WELLS,
22 JULY 1932.
*Source: Mexico City, Archivo de la Secretaría de Relaciones
Exteriores, IV-354–12.*

> Departamento de Protección
> No.–
> Exp.—73.10/524.5
> Asunto.—Repatriaciones.–

Chicago, Ill., July 22nd. 1932

Miss Mary Grace Wells,
Township Trustee.
Lake County, Gary Sup. Court Bldg.
Gary, Indiana

Dear Madam:
Through a mistake of your office, your letter addressed to the Mexican
Consul at Laredo, Texas, was placed in [an] envelope addressed to this
Consulate. In that letter you advise that "you are returning fifteen
Mexican families who have become public charge and desire to return
to Mexico"; that they will leave Gary at 2.30 on July 27, 1932 and will arrive
at Laredo on July 29 at 2.30.

Please refer to my note No. 2493 of June 9th, 1932 and to the note of
the Consul at Laredo No. 1520 of June 13th. where we both advise you that
Gary, Indiana is under the jurisdiction of this Consulate and that this
Office is the proper channel through which repatriations in this territory
should be transacted.

I very much regret to be in the case to state that contrary to the attitude of Authorities and Institutions of the rest of my jurisdiction, yours has shown little desire to cooperate in a matter where complete accord and understanding should exist.

I have been very clear in previous occasions pointing out that the simple fact that Mexicans in your country have become public charges does not warrant your action in sending them back to Mexico with only a few days notice and in a rather authoritative way compelling our Authorities to take care of them without consultation or advice.

Besides this, I have received complaints that "your policy is to send all of those who are receiving relief without regard to the time of residence in the United States or means of subsistence upon arriving in Mexico. Those who are unwilling are refused relief. That it is causing great privation in some families who have been in this County many years and who are entitled to support from the community to whose progress they contributed when they were working. That the people who are refusing to go to Mexico are refusing because they have no means of support in Mexico; because of their long residence here feel that they are entitled to some consideration; and that this forcible return of people is unjust from every angle."

Very different has been the attitude of the Authorities and Institutions of east Chicago who are working in complete accord with this Consulate and who are receiving our fullest cooperation in the benefit of all concerned and avoiding difficulties and harshnesses.

I very earnestly call again your attention to the fact that the Mexican Government is in no way obliged to take care of those people who, regardless of their nationality are members of your community. In taking these repatriates who for long time have contributed to the progress of your Country and not to the progress of Mexico, my Government is showing a friendly gesture of cooperation towards the United States in its hour of adversity. Of course, we welcome our fellow countrymen going back to Mexico, but the Mexican Government feels that we are entitled to some attention and consideration from you in return for our willingness to take from your shoulders a problem that is not ours.

When we ask to be notified through the proper channels and with reasonable anticipation we intend to introduce order and facilitate things in a matter which is not simple at all and which, if not properly handled, shall involve many grievances and unpleasantnesses. You must take in consideration that while your particular problem may be easily solved shipping these people out to the border, these very people are going to be subject to all kinds of hardships if you show not your cooperation by enabling this Consulate and the Mexican Government to be properly prepared to take care of them upon their arrival, or if you use not a little discrimination and humanitarianism by not placing those unwilling to leave in the quandary of being denied of relief.

Had you only asked my cooperation in these latter cases I would have endeavored to convince those people to return to Mexico where they belong rather than to remain in a community where they are no longer welcome.

I sincerely regret to have to write you this letter but I must exhaust every effort in my endeavor to establish a sound and sincere cooperation between you and this Consulate before referring the matter to our Embassy in Washington to be taken up with the Federal Government.

In this present case I will do my best to secure opportune transportation to the party scheduled to leave on the 27th inst. by writing to my Government asking them to rush cars for the 79 people you are sending, but I earnestly trust in future occasions you will be kind enough to advise this Consulate with a more reasonable anticipation and to show a little more consideration to the Country which is so cheerfully helping its neighbor in its times of hardships.

Yours truly.

Rafael Aveleyra

Consul of Mexico

c.c.p. la Secretaría de Relaciones Exteriores

c.c.p la Embajada de México en Washington, D.C.

c.c.p. el Cónsul de México en Laredo, Tex.

RA/IRA

▰ ▰

REPATRIATION PETITION. MINATARE, NEBRASKA. LUIS N. VERA TO
PRESIDENT PASCUAL ORTIZ RUBIO, 15 MAY 1931.
*Source: Mexico City, Archivo de la Secretaría de Relaciones
Exteriores, IV-353–38.*

To the President of the Mexican Republic
Engineer Pascual Ortiz Rubio
Palace of the Federal Executive

Luis W. Vera   May 15, 1931
P.O. Box 267
Minatare, Nebraska

Your Excellency:

Because of the highly patriotic and moral labor with which you have
initiated your administration, the Pro-Repatriation Committee, which
today has become a Farmers' Cooperative, responding to the sense of
its membership, all of Mexican nationality, residing in this part of the
Platte Valley and the states of Nebraska and Wyoming of the United
States of America, declares absolute allegiance to the First Magistrate
of the Nation, Engineer Pascual Ortiz Rubio, wishing him the best of
luck, in personal matters as well as in the nationalist and constructive
policies on which the intentions of his administration are based.

Turning to your noble sentiments, to the proposals you have raised,
and to your honorable and high ideals, this Cooperative, recently formed,
requests from your Supreme Government assistance in the complete
repatriation of all its members, more than one hundred families and an
additional large number of single individuals, as we desire to establish a
settlement of rural farmers, since here we are without sufficient work,
without resources of any kind, and only with the prospect of assistance
from him who alone can provide for those in need.

Our worthy Consul, Mr. Carlos M. Gaxiola, in Kansas City, Mo.,
has made a visit to these parts, and we owe him a vote of thanks for the
interest which he demonstrated by presenting our case to the authorities

and highly placed employees of the sugar company, Great Western Sugar Co., so that they might provide us with work at least for this year, while our Government assists us in our repatriation, and promising us to do everything in his power to assist us.

Luis N. Vera
Farmers Pro-Repatriation
Committee

[Translation of Petition sent with preceding letter, May 15, 1931]

Foundations and articles on which are based the petition of this Committee, converted to Farmers' Pro-Repatriation Cooperative.

First—By the right conceded to us by Article 32 of our Magna Carta, that Mexicans will be given preference over foreigners, in equal circumstances, [and] passes all types of governmental concessions, charges, and commissions, in which the status of the citizen is immaterial;

Second—By the right also conceded to us by Article 24 in its subparagraph V to exercise in all types of affairs the right of petition;

Third—By availing ourselves of the guarantees which Our Mexican Constitution grants, beginning a group bearing the name "Pro-Repatriation Committee" and with the motto of: Union, Progress, and Country and whose objective is to work with assiduous constancy in regard to our Mexican Government to secure Repatriation, by means of [whatever] efficient assistance it might offer us in [whatever] sense it might deem appropriate, we beg:

    (a) That this group, which in its totality consists of small farmers, respectfully requests of our Secretary of Development that he apportion to us a small plot of public land to form a settlement of plots (rural settlement).

    (b) That attention be paid to our necessities as the Mexican rural class, that in our own country we were in an unstable situation, and now outside it, we are suffering damage that we are going to waste our youth and our energies in a foreign land, being well able to obtain on our own soil the well-being to which we are entitled.

(c) That we wish to form a farming settlement in one of the irrigation systems, in order to be one of the organizations which, once in operation, might regulate production and at the same time be one of the unbreachable barriers to hold back the onslaught of heavy importation of staple comestible agricultural products.

(d) That we be considered as brothers in the struggle with the problem of settling the lands we might wrest from the desert, assisting us with the fundamental requirements, which are to provide from this country, in some appropriate manner, stability and security in the plots we acquire at a convenient site and under fitting conditions; assistance necessary for the promotion of our farming work and for the encouragement of our personal efforts and initiatives.

(e) We accept the adoption of modern systems of cultivation; the beneficial example of experimental fields; rational systems for organizing the operation of small agricultural industries; the adoption with great pleasure of instruction regarding profitable crops appropriate to the soil and climate of the region.

(f) That we be provided with knowledge concerning modern systems of selling agricultural products and the technical means for struggling to conquer markets and to search for centers of consumption that present advantageous conditions and that require for all these necessities the assistance of technical experts to successfully solve the problems that arise, so that we settlers who have a small plot might receive the same profits as those who have a larger plot.

Bearing in mind the foregoing, this cooperative recommends that it be remembered that this settlement is planned to be carried out solely by citizens, and that repatriation be arranged for them. Upon the acceptance of our petition, we will provide the requisite information which

our Secretariat needs to know: number of persons who are ready to
immigrate as settlers; their background and attitude toward work, that is,
information regarding their previous and present occupations; readily
available economic capability, through an accounting of the goods and
general resources which each one of us has at our disposal. etc., etc.

In the meantime, we offer our respects and allegiance.

UNION, PROGRESS, AND COUNTRY

Minatare, Nebr., May 15, 1931

Luis N. Vera [signed]
Representative

■ ■

REPATRIATION PETITION. MEXICANS FROM NEW YORK, NEW YORK TO
PRESIDENT ABELARDO RODRÍGUEZ, 5 OCTOBER 1932.
*Source: Mexico City, Archivo de la Secretaría de Relaciones
Exteriores, IV-341–39.*

New York
Oct. 5th, 1932.

To
The President
Mr. Abelardo Rodriguez:
Federal District of Mexico.

Dear Mr. President:
It is practically impossible to describe in writing the sorrow and misery
we are currently experiencing. The telling would be a tale of terrible
destitution and distress. Due to the difficult crisis bearing on this country
for the past three years, all companies have decreed the employment of
none but American citizens or legal aliens, making it impossible for us
to continue earning a living.

For the reasons previously stated, we address you, Mr. President,
that you might act on our behalf with the government over which you
so judiciously preside. We ask that an allotment of land be facilitated
to us somewhere so that we, as a community, may dedicate ourselves to

agriculture, raising cattle or poultry and that we may count as well with government provisions of the necessary materials and monies with which to begin.

We commit ourselves to reimbursing all originated expenditures, from travel expenses to agricultural equipment, heads of cattle, etc. After the land starts producing, that is, by the second year, we will make annual payments proportional to our crops.

As to location of the land, we ask it lay not far from communication routes and that it be fertile with water for irrigation, even if seasonal.

We address you well aware of the vicissitudes of life and we are willing to begin a new chapter. All we need is the foundation, that we may guarantee you with our stability, constancy and favorable outcomes, achieved only through hard work and perseverance.

There is one other point we feel obliged to address which is our stance in national politics. To begin, we are ready to cooperate with the current government as far as our citizenship allows. That is, we will dedicate ourselves solely to our labor without mingling in any political matter outside of voting, since we are bound by law to vote.

Due to the urgency of our present moment, we request that your answer, Mr. President, be known to us as soon as possible, since with each passing day it proves more difficult to remain together, as we await evicted from our present home for past due rent of several months. In addition to this, we must face the impending harsh winter with no means whatsoever of procuring the most basic provisions. Thus you will understand, Mr. President, our plea for your reply since we are not able to remain united much longer. Life is already very difficult for one or two and impossible for three or four not to mention ten or fifteen.

We impart our most anticipated gratitude to you, Mr. President, for your actions on our behalf.

We take our leave.

    Most Faithfully Yours,

Bulmaro Delgado	*José A. . . .*
Luis Martinez	*José García Fernández*
José Alvarado	*Esteban Ramírez*
José P. R. . . .	*Louis Diaz*
Ramiro Muñoz	*J.V.G. . . .*
Alejandro García	*Jesús Aguirre*

"El Argil" took passengers from San Pedro, California, to Baja California, Mexico, in September 1935. Courtesy of Los Angeles Public Library, Pacific Historical Photograph Collection.

Colonization
Pan y Tierra

Nuestro lema es el trabajo	*Our motto is work*
Queremos tierras y arados	*We want land and plows*
Pues la patria necesita	*For the nation needs*
De sus campos cultivados	*Its fields cultivated*
—"Corrido del Agrarista"	—"The Ballad of the Agrarist"

During the 1930s, due to the economic onslaught of the Great Depression, approximately one million Mexican Nationals and their children were deported or repatriated to Mexico from the United States. This compelled Mexico to explore ways and means of assimilating the mass of indigents suddenly foisted upon her. One of the options was to utilize the agrarian skills acquired in El Norte to open up and colonize new regions of the country. Baja California, the northern border states, the Yucatán Peninsula, and the southern, subtropical region of Mexico, including the states of Oaxaca and Guerrero, became prime targets for colonization efforts.

With a population of less than fifteen million, Mexico was anxious to acquire additional settlers. It envisioned the repatriates as the impetus that the nation needed to promote agricultural growth and to achieve industrial development. Both aspects were viewed as conducive to the emergence of a dynamic and affluent middle class and a higher standard of living for the entire nation. The inevitable demand for goods and services would generate increased productivity and correspondingly higher profits. Given

Mexico's substantial natural resources, the introduction of modern technology and a resurgent work ethic would infuse Mexico with a new orientation and sense of self-worth. Optimists viewed the return of Mexico's
prodigal sons and daughters as a positive good. Some individuals warned
that while repatriation represented an opportunity, it also posed a danger
if the returnees were not fully assimilated.[1]

The National Revolutionary Party adopted an official stance of welcoming and assisting the repatriates. Under the party's guidance, Mexico
would be transformed from a rural, agrarian nation into a modern industrial giant. The slogan *México para los Mexicanos* (Mexico for the Mexicans)
took on new meaning. Grandiose plans and fanciful schemes were introduced to facilitate the perceived changes and to hasten their fulfillment. A
series of dams and irrigation canals were to be built to provide a reliable
source of water for the colonizers. Farmers would no longer be at the mercy
of the capricious elements. The dams would also provide the electrical
power needed by an expanding industrial economy. Adversity, seemingly,
could be turned into a national triumph.

In order to induce repatriates and local unemployed residents to settle
in isolated, desolate areas, farmland would be made available to prospective settlers on very generous terms. Bank loans and other financial support
would be guaranteed. Seed, farm implements, draft animals, and livestock
would be furnished. No payments or interest charges would be levied during the first year. As an added inducement to colonizers, the nation's infrastructure would be modernized to support and enhance both colonization
and industrial growth. The ability to reach local and distant markets was
deemed vital to the success of the government's colonization efforts.
Realists pointedly proclaimed that one key ingredient was missing from the
equation: money! Much to the government's chagrin, it had to acknowledge
that adequate funding was the weakest aspect of the envisioned project.

To those with vision, however, the prophecy of expansion was self-
fulfilling. Two key factors would assure the success of colonization. First,
since the central government lacked the necessary funds, state governments
would be instructed to become directly involved in the nationalistic
endeavor. Governors were to extol the myriad benefits that would accrue as
a result of economic growth. Their nation was in a position to free itself from
the bonds of foreign exploitation and domination, which had robbed the
country and the people of their rightful inheritance for much too long. Under

such circumstances, how could patriotic *hijos del país* (loyal sons and daughters) resist or refuse to contribute to the well-being of *la madre patria?*[2]

The second factor contributing to the success of colonization was obvious. The expanding economy would generate ever-increasing sources of revenue. By shrewdly reinvesting the newly acquired wealth, additional investment capital would be created. This would fuel the ever-expanding economy. The growing economy would support a population double or triple the fifteen million people then inhabiting the country. It would be a more affluent society able to afford quality goods and services. In addition, the web of poverty and unemployment that had forced people to emigrate would at last be broken. There was a certain national pride in the anticipation that Mexico finally would be able to provide the material amenities and quality of life which, in the past, had been denied to so many of its citizens.

As if anticipating the forthcoming avalanche of repatriates who needed to be resettled, in August of 1929 the Secretaría de Agricultura y Fomento (Department of Agriculture and Planning) initiated a farsighted project. The Secretaría requested that a thorough survey be made regarding the status and availability of lands that could be used for colonization purposes. Commissioning the study can only be deemed as providential. Results of the survey were to be shared with Secretaría de Relaciones Exteriores for its information and consideration. The SRE was interested in the status of the Don Martín and Calles Dams. It wanted to know how soon the lands would be ready for occupation, and which portions would be irrigated, and which would be dry farmed.

The Department of Water, Land, and Colonization, under the direction of Gumaro García de la Cadena, informed SRE that the Calles Dam was completed. For all practical purposes, de la Cadena assured his superiors, the region could be considered ready for colonization. He also reported that the Don Martín Dam was expected to be finished by the end of the year, and the land would be ready for cultivation as soon as the irrigation system was in place. According to the Department of Irrigation, the canal system would be in operation by the following March (1930). Colonists could then begin buying land and settling the area. It was estimated that the irrigation system would deliver enough water to irrigate thirty thousand hectares, about seventy-five thousand acres.[3] The SRE later asked for more detailed information regarding not only the Calles and Don Martín Dams, but also the sites of La Sauteña and El Xapote. The information would be distributed to consuls in the United States to aid them in advising and assisting repatriates who desired to become colonizers.[4]

Acting in the same vein of trying to encourage and support colonization efforts, the Secretaría de Agricultura y Fomento's representative, Marte R. Gómez, made a trip to Los Angeles. While in the United States, he purchased a million dollars worth of farm implements, tools, and equipment. They were to be used exclusively in colonizing the Zona del Mante in the state of Tamaulipas. According to official reports, the Zona contained approximately forty thousand hectares that could be distributed among thousands of farmers. While in Los Angeles, Gómez revealed that the government was prepared to make available a maximum of fifty acres, or twenty hectares, to all who solicited land. Nationals living in the United States were eligible and encouraged to apply.[5]

Coincidentally, Marte R. Gómez's trip was made in October of 1929. The stock-market crash was already turning the corner and coming into view. On his trip home, Gómez scheduled a stop in Tijuana to consult with the territorial governor, Abelardo Rodríguez, on how to improve agricultural production in Baja California. Before Gómez arrived back in Mexico City, the depression had received its initial impetus. Black Friday was history; the American stock market had collapsed, and with it the American dream of peace, prosperity, and plenty. Although the land and colonization survey commissioned by the Secretaría de Agricultura y Fomento was not complete, it provided a certain degree of orientation on how to deal with the advent of repatriation. Also, the colonizing efforts of the Mexican government during the 1920–1921 depression would prove to be beneficial during the hectic period unleashed by the Great Depression.

For Mexico, the respite before the repatriation onslaught commenced would be brief indeed. Caught in the abysmal throes of the nation's worst depression, many Nationals residing in México de Afuera decided that it was an opportune time to return to Mexico. Colonization promises presented an opportunity to escape the worst travails of the depression and to put their agricultural skills to personal use. The dream of owning their own small farms seemed within their grasp, at last. Rather than enriching the gringos, they would be working for themselves. The possibility of being their own *patrón* (boss) was heady wine indeed. It also represented their stake in the future. Here was a legacy they could leave to their children. With substantive roots in their own nation, there would be no need for future generations to emigrate to El Norte to seek an illusory fortune. Imbued with the hope and expectation of potential success, unemployed Nationals flocked to apply for acceptance as colonizers. In colonias throughout the United States, a panorama of groups sprang up to aid and encourage those seeking to return.

Most of these *sociedades mutualistas* or *beneficencias* (self-help or benevolent charitable groups) endeavored to obtain assistance from local American agencies or the Mexican government. During the incipient years of the 1930s, interim presidents Ortiz Rubio and Abelardo Rodríguez received numerous petitions seeking various forms of assistance. The petitioners usually requested lands for colonization and cultivation as well as franquicia privileges, the free import of household goods, free railroad passage, and monetary assistance. Typical of the requests for assistance was a letter sent to President Rodríguez by a group of Nationals residing in New York City. In requesting aid, they promised to be good, law-abiding citizens. As proof of their good intentions, they asserted their intention to vote in all elections.[6] Other groups pledged not to become involved in partisan politics or to promote discontent among the general populace. All they wanted was to be allowed to return and become good farmers and loyal citizens. Their profession of not becoming a disruptive influence was meant to allay fears and suspicions harbored by many Mexicans that the repatriates might not fit in or accept a more authoritative government. In short, they had become addicted to the "Yankee way."

Despite their nationalistic oriented pleas, repatriates found that obtaining help from the government was not easy, nor could it be taken for granted. Tact and innovation often had to be used to get the government's attention and arouse its interest. A group of campesinos in Brawley, California amply illustrated this approach. They identified themselves as the "*Vanguardia de Colonizacíon Proletaria* (Vanguard of Proletariat Colonization)." According to a news article in Mexico City's *Excélsior* of April 6, 1930, the organization claimed it had acquired 40,000 members within two months. Reportedly, the Vanguardia hoped to eventually encompass the majority of the 3,500,000 Mexican Nationals estimated to be living in the United States. Given the number of clandestine border crossings, no one was certain how many Mexicans actually lived in México de afuera. The total count could be misleading because Nationals and Mexican Americans were customarily lumped together. Even the Vanguardia made no distinction between the two groups. As previously stated, for all intents and purposes a "Mexican was a Mexican." This view prevailed among residents in the colonias.

In addition to increasing its membership, another avowed purpose of the Vanguardia de Colonización Proletaria was to raise twelve million to fifteen million dollars within four or five months. How it hoped to accomplish this in an economically destitute community was not made clear. However, according to the newspaper article, the group had already collected the enormous sum of forty thousand dollars. This princely sum and all other monies collected were to be deposited in the *Banco de Tesoro Común* (Common Treasury Bank) in Mexico. Upon the group's resettlement, the money would be used to assist in the development of industry and the creation of jobs, which would contribute to the enrichment of la madre patria.[7] Obviously, the group was convinced that the prospect of contributing a large sum of money would induce the government to grant them special consideration. Their representative, Alejandro Saucedo Salazar, was sent to Mexico City to meet with government officials and elicit their support. In San Antonio, Texas, Antonio Villarreal Muñoz hatched a colonization plan with a unique and innovative twist. He wrote to President Herbert Hoover asking him to impound all Mexican funds in the United States and let him use the money to colonize one million Mexicans in their native land.[8]

One of the most active and persistent groups was the *Comité Pro Repatriación* (Pro-Repatriation Committee) in Vroman, Colorado. The group first appealed to the consul in Denver for help, but he was not in a position to render any financial assistance. At his suggestion, however, they decided to appeal directly to the president of the republic. In their letter, the board of directors enumerated the various problems facing the group and the mistreatment to which they were subjected. In the petition, they noted that the group consisted of only forty-five families, but estimated that membership would increase to eighty or a hundred families within a month or two. Appended to the Comité Pro Repatriación's two-page letter to President Pascual Ortiz Rubio was a six-point statement outlining the organization's position. In summary, the prospective colonizers asked to be admitted as settlers and to be given good farmland, and they requested the government to select the colonization site. In exchange for franquicia privileges, they promised to provide their own passage to the border. Their final request was for financial assistance and credit during the first year of the colonizing venture. The letter emphasized that they were all experienced farmers.[9]

Due to the growing clamor for aid, the Secretaría de Agricultura y Fomento published a massive document containing the regulations governing all colonization ventures. In its decree, the Secretaría established the requirements that had to be met by prospective colonizers and the order of preference in which applicants would be considered. Also stipulated were the duties and responsibilities incumbent upon the Comisión Nacional de Irrigación, acting as the government's contracting agent, and the settlers. Since the Comisión was to be responsible for the colonization projects, it developed an extensive application form that all interested settlers were required to fill out in detail. No aspect of the applicant's life was overlooked.[10] Prospective colonizers were not only required to have prior agricultural experience and the means to succeed in the venture, but must also be of sound moral character. The thorough procedure was intended to discourage incompetents and to assure the success of the colonization efforts.

Equally as important, the Comisión established a uniform price for a hectare, or 2½ acres. First-class land would sell for 300 pesos, second class for 285 pesos, and third class for 275 or 270 pesos per hectare. Applicants were required to pay an initial sum of 5 percent down on their parcel of land. The remainder was to be paid within a period of twenty-five years, at an interest rate of 4 percent annually on the balance. For the first three years, colonizers were obligated to enter into a partnership with the Comisión. All rights and privileges of the participants were outlined in exacting detail in an eight-page, sixteen-clause, iron-clad contract. Even the maximum as well as the minimum amount of water to which colonizers were entitled was spelled out. So were the amounts of various kinds of seed that the Comisión was obligated to provide, if requested to do so. To qualify for a partnership, settlers were required to cultivate at least 50 percent of the land upon acquisition.[11]

During the obligatory three-year partnership stipulated by the contract, the Comisión was entitled to a percentage of the yearly harvest. This, too, was duly stipulated in the agreement: If the settler received only the land and water rights, he would contribute 20 percent of his crop to the Comisión; if he also received seed, he owed the Comisión 25 percent of the crop as its rightful share. If, in addition, farm tools and implements were provided, the Comisión was entitled to 30 percent of the harvest.[12] At the end of three years, if the cash value of the crops received by the Comisión amounted to at least 10 percent of the value of the land, the colonizer had the option to terminate the partnership and buy his farm outright or on monthly terms. Credit would be extended for a period of twenty years at 4 percent interest, in order to facilitate and encourage personal ownership of the property.[13] Hopefully, outright ownership would serve as an incentive to industrious farmers to increase production and reap the benefits thereof. It would also enable the Comisión to utilize its limited resources to help new settlers.

No doubt, the regulations governing colonization, as implemented by the Comisión Nacional de Irrigación, were intended to foster the best interests of the settlers and assure their success. However, the contractual rules and regulations imposed upon the colonists tended to be too restrictive and oppressive. In some instances, they led to widespread abuse by the zealous overseers. As a result, virtually all of the colonizing endeavors ended in dismal failure. Yet colonization efforts must be viewed in perspective. Mexico faced a deluge of approximately one million people in less than a decade, with the majority of them arriving within the span of 1931–1933. Attempting to resettle or colonize such an immense number of people would have strained and taxed the resolve and commitment of even the most affluent society. To her credit, Mexico welcomed her returning sons and daughters, and in spite of her limited resources, she chose to share what little the nation had with returning compatriots and their children.

The government efforts are manifested by the fact that colonization projects for repatriates read like a Mexican road map: Valle de San Quintín in Baja California; San Pedro in Coahuila; Hacienda Silva in Romita, Chihuahua; Tamarindo Hacienda in Sinaloa; Rancho la Gloria in Durango; Comarca in San Luis Potosí; and Mazapil in Zacatecas. There were also colonization attempts in La Misa in Sonora; Lampazas in Tamaulipas; Villa Humada in Chihuahua; Hacienda Los Pozos in Choix, Sinaloa; Calles Dam in Río Santiago, Aguascalientes; and Río Salado in Coahuila. Other resettlement projects could be found in virtually every state in the union. The state governors heeded the federal government's "suggestion" to become aggressively involved in promoting colonization in their respective states. In all candor, they really had no choice but to comply if they wished to remain in office. Open dissention would have been unthinkable, and the refusal to cooperate would have been politically disastrous.

The government needed the cooperation of the state governors, for colonizers arrived in a steady and almost uninterrupted stream. Individual families, small groups, and large cadres often arrived virtually unannounced at the border. Typical of the groups returning in the hope of colonizing was one interviewed on March 7, 1930, by Maurice W. Altaffer, American consul in Nogales, Sonora. He reported that 40 families, comprising a total of 149 individuals, had passed through on their way to settle in the Colonia "Emilio Carranza" in La Misa, Sonora. They were the vanguard of some 400 families expected to settle in the La Misa area. To help repatriates acquire needed farming equipment, the governor of the state had deposited a sum of ten thousand pesos in a Guaymas bank. The La Misa property formerly belonged to General Francisco Manzo, but it had been confiscated because Manzo had been one of the leaders of a brief insurrection in the previous year. Under similar conditions, additional lands were available in Cananea, Sonora.[14]

According to Consul Altaffer's dispatch, most of the families were from the area of Phoenix, Arizona. However, the group also included fourteen individuals from Tustin, California, a small citrus and farming community in Orange County. As a point of interest to his superiors in Washington, D.C., Consul Altaffer noted that there were eighty-one males and sixty-eight females in the group. He judiciously observed that fifty-nine of them were under twenty-one years of age, eighty were between twenty-two and fifty years old, and only ten were over fifty.[15] The consul also reported that most of the people had been in the United States for a period of five to ten years or longer. Judging from the ages cited in the report, a sizable number of the repatriates must have been children born in the United States, but the report failed to enumerate them.

The influx of colonizers continued to grow at a rate that no one had foreseen. On April 3, 1930, the *Excélsior*, in Mexico City, reported that four hundred families had recently arrived and were settling in the state of Nuevo León. They were the first wave of several thousand settlers who were expected to colonize the sparsely populated northern region of the country. The newly completed Don Martín Dam, or "La Gran Presa" as it was known locally, would provide the water necessary to make the desolate countryside bloom. The newspaper proclaimed that the area had the potential to become one of the nation's major granaries. The article asserted that not only was there ample room for repatriates from the United States, but for individuals from areas in Mexico who were experiencing difficulty in earning a living in their present locale. In addition to Nuevo León's proximity to the United States, there was an added inducement for settling in the area: oil had been discovered in the region. One hundred oil wells were expected to be spudded and drilled. Settlers not addicted to farming could possibly find good jobs as oilfield roughnecks.

In November of the same year, Consul J. M. Vázquez in Denver, Colorado, reported that a group of 1,160 repatriates from the area had left the city and were headed south. Since they were all paying their own way, there were no expenses to be borne by the national treasury, the consul reported proudly. Of the 1,160 repatriates leaving Denver, 860 had asked for and received Certificates of Residency from the consulate. Some had not bothered to apply for certificates because they did not have enough personal belongings to warrant paying the $4.72 fee for the certificate.[16] There were repatriates who simply could not afford to pay the nominal fee. This was understandable since most of those electing to return were either out of work or their wages were so low that they could not eke out a decent living. In his report, the consul informed his superiors at SRE that the vast majority of all Nationals in the Rocky Mountain area were in very dire straits.

With apparent satisfaction, the Denver consul noted that he had been instrumental in convincing many compatriots to return home and take advantage of the generous colonizing opportunities available. Their hopeless situation, plus the specter of a Rocky Mountain winter, undoubtedly facilitated the task of inducing indigent Mexicans to leave. Most of the repatriates, Consul Vázquez reported, were planning to join families already settled in the Don Martín Dam site in Nuevo León. Others were bound for the President Calles Dam in the state of Aguascalientes. A lesser number were en route to the state of Chihuahua. The repatriates were primarily interested in settling in areas where irrigation systems were available. They were well aware of the fact that dry farming was a risky venture and not worth the gamble in arid regions of Mexico. In concluding his dispatch, the consul assured SRE that all the prospective colonists were honest, hard-working individuals with ample farming experience. He opined that they would prove a real boon to the colonizing effort and make an important contribution to the nation's economic well-being.

Not all repatriates were as fortunate as the group from Denver in getting settled in the area of their choice. Repatriates sent to colonize in Mexicali, Baja California, "found nothing, bare land, no living quarters, no running water, no electricity," according to survivor Rubén Jiménez.[17] One group from Maricopa County in Arizona requested assistance in obtaining land in the state of Sonora. Their aspirations were shattered when the Secretaría de Agricultura y Fomento informed them that the government did not have any funds left to help finance their resettlement. In addition to this depressing news, the group was also advised that no more lands were available for cultivation in the state of Sonora at that time. A heavy influx of colonizers had overtaxed the area's capabilities. Demands for irrigated land had simply outrun the construction of irrigation works undertaken by the Comisión Nacional de Irrigación. Once again, limited resources had undermined efforts to resettle repatriates on suitable farmland. As the Maricopa group pondered what to do about their situation, they received a communiqué from the Secretaría.

The Secretaría de Agricultura y Fomento informed the Maricopa County group that the Banco Nacional de Credito Agrícola in the state of Chihuahua had 1,500,000 hectares for sale at the bargain price of three pesos each. The drawback was that it was all pastureland, fit only for grazing livestock. According to the bank, all acreage fit for cultivation had been sold and there was no more prime agricultural land available in the entire state. Any individual interested in ranching rather than farming could buy up to 40,000 hectares. A down payment of 10 percent was required, and the balance was to be paid in ten- or fifteen-year terms at an interest rate of 5 percent, or 6 percent, respectively.[18] One aspect that apparently escaped everyone's notice was that approximately 225,000 of the hectares were located near San Miguel Babícora. The Lake Babícora area would later gain notoriety when the government attempted to confiscate forty thousand acres of the Babícora Ranch. William Randolph Hearst, head of the powerful newspaper empire, owned the property. Hearst was not prepared to lose or cede one inch of land without a fight. The action might have been in retaliation for Hearst's anti-Mexican stance and his avid support of deporting and repatriating Mexicans.

Overwhelmed by the demand for land by Nationals being ousted from the United States, Mexico was forced to turn a deaf ear on numerous requests from foreigners who wished to emigrate and colonize. Russians, Slavs, and Chinese were among the groups seeking asylum in Mexico.[19] Opposition to allowing foreigners into the country was based primarily on the fact that, in nearly every instance, these groups did not make any effort to assimilate into the Mexican culture. To avoid such situations, it was deemed best to give preference to returning repatriates.[20] In support of this advocacy, one newspaper commentary pointed out that in more than thirty years there had been only two instances of intermarriages in the Russian colony of Santo Tomás in Baja California.[21] There was also widespread resentment that rather than applying for Mexican citizenship, the Russians opted to become American citizens.

As incongruous as it may seem, also seeking asylum and permission to colonize in Mexico were twenty-nine thousand World War I American veterans. President Ortiz Rubio sent a personal telegram to Doak E. Carter, former head of the American Legion and leader of the group. The telegram stated that it would be inappropriate to allow foreigners to colonize when the government was having difficulty in securing enough land for Nationals being repatriated from the United States.[22] In commenting on the president's action, *El Universal* praised the decision as representing the national will. The editorial also castigated the United States for having turned its back on veterans, who had given so much in the nation's hour of need.[23] In another editorial commenting on American and foreign requests for permission to colonize, *El Universal* pointedly recalled that Mexico had lost Texas and nearly half of its territory by allowing destitute Anglos to settle in the area following the American depression in 1820. Mexico should not make the same mistake twice, the newspaper editorialized.[24] The Mexicans viewed the Americans as ingrates whose attitude was best summarized by a remark attributed to Sam Houston who allegedly asserted that "I didn't come to Texas to live under the Greaser's yoke." Mexicans never forgot or forgave such disparaging remarks.

Contrary to requests seeking permission to colonize in Mexico during the 1930s, eight thousand Mennonites decided to leave the country. Originally from Canada, they had emigrated to Mexico in 1926–28, and had been granted asylum in the state of Chihuahua. Thrifty, honest, and hard working, they had been welcomed by the government. Due to their efficiency and tireless efforts, thousands of desolate acres were converted into productive farms. For a time, they enjoyed prosperity and religious freedom. Unfortunately, a groundswell of antireligious propaganda made it difficult for them to practice their religious beliefs in peace. Sadly, it was a repetition of the problem they had faced in the Canadian provinces of Manitoba, Saskatchewan, and Alberta. They hoped to return to Canada and settle in a rural section of the province of Quebec, where hopefully they would not be harassed.[25] While the Mexican government regretted their departure and the loss of their stabilizing influence, the vacated lands could be put to good use.

According to figures attributed to Galindo y Villa, a noted Mexican geographer, concerning the availability and utilization of land, 80 percent of Mexico was considered to be unfit for intensive cultivation. He warned ominously that the land would not support an extensive increase in population. However, Villa emphasized that only one-twentieth of the available farmland was being cultivated. There were, he declared, 150 million hectares that were not being used effectively. He classified land utilization into three major categories: 10 percent could be cultivated without irrigation; 20 percent would require irrigation; and the remaining 70 percent was declared unfit for cultivation. The latter acreage could be utilized only for reforestation purposes or for the pasturing of livestock.[26] This was certainly not the kind of news that either the government or the public liked to hear. Land, especially the lack of it, was a sore point for Mexico's demographers. In a society that was still primarily rural and agrarian, land was the key to the nation's future prosperity and well-being.

Commenting on Galindo y Villa's observations, *El Universal* editorialized that various agencies should join in a cooperative effort designed to educate the populace and enhance agricultural production. The select group should include not only the Comisión Nacional de Irrigación, but also the Comisión Nacional Agraria; the Oficina Federal para la Defensa Agrícola; the Dirección de Estudios Geográficos y Climatológicos; and the Dirección de Aguas, Tierras y Colonización. It was apparent that only a unified and concerted effort would resolve the nation's agrarian problems. In its editorial, the newspaper pointed out that, under an uncoordinated approach, land considered unproductive nearly twenty years before was still being cultivated. The newspaper asserted that if science and technology were harnessed, wastelands could be converted into fruitful zones. To turn the situation around, it proposed that new impetus be given to the agricultural development of the entire country.[27] In essence, that was precisely what the government attempted to do as the hordes of repatriates continued to pour into the country.

In emphasizing the extent of the calamity, a report by United Press, attributed to Consul Rafael Aveleyra in Chicago, estimated that 60 percent of all Nationals in Iowa, Wisconsin, Minnesota, Indiana, and Illinois had returned home during the past twelve months. According to the consul, many barrios in South Chicago, Illinois, and in Gary, Indiana, were virtually deserted. Faced with the loss of jobs in the steel mills and manufacturing plants where they were formerly employed, many families opted to leave. To facilitate their departure, Consul Aveleyra negotiated reduced railroad fares of fifteen dollars for passage to the border. *Comités de beneficencia* (Benevolent Committees) in the colonia assisted those unable to afford the fare. From the border to their final destination, the Mexican government provided transportation at the flat rate of a penny per mile.[28]

In the same article, *El Universal* headlined the fact that forty thousand Americans had left the United States and were seeking to settle in Mexico. The figures were attributed to the American Chamber of Commerce in New York. According to the Chamber, 14,000 Americans had entered Mexico during 1931, and the number had swelled to 37,074 by 1932. Alarmed by the rapidly growing influx, the newspaper urged the government to take stringent steps to halt the invasion from the United States. As noted, the Mexican government had been denying foreigners permission to settle in Mexico. Exceptions were made if the individuals could contribute significantly to the nation's commercial growth and industrial development. With impoverished Nationals flooding across the border, Mexico had no need to create more problems for itself by admitting penniless norteamericanos.

With the great number of repatriates seeking homes, jobs, and land, problems abounded. Prospective colonizers hounded their local consulates in seeking information about available lands and prospective sites. Secretaría de Relaciones Exteriores (SRE) was beseeched for help in verifying the condition and status of lands proffered for sale or trade by individuals or private companies. Many of the properties were offered by absentee landowners, primarily Americans, who were not always aware of the true nature of their holdings. Ascertaining such aspects as land titles, soil fertility, water rights, tax status, and actual boundaries often developed into a maze of complex legal problems. The SRE repeatedly advised consuls not to become directly involved in matters dealing with the transaction of property. In accordance with SRE instructions, they were forbidden to become entangled, or to participate, in lawsuits filed by either of the contracting parties. Consuls were to limit their involvement to providing information that was already public knowledge or which had been approved for release by the Secretaría de Industria, Comercio y Trabajo.[29]

Affluent Nationals who wished to dispose of their property in the United States and return to Mexico faced the problem of finding a reputable buyer. Compatriots who were in arrears in their taxes or had fallen behind in their monthly payments tried desperately to sell their holdings. Many of them were facing foreclosure and the loss of their properties. Forced to sell and often facing immediate explusion, repatriates had no choice but to accept a mere fraction of what their properties were actually worth. Consuls across the nation were bombarded with pleas for help from desperate compatriots who had no one else to turn to. In spite of SRE's directives, consuls could not ignore their moral responsibility and the pleas of their constituents who were already at the end of their rope. Risking SRE's ire and perhaps the loss of their jobs, consuls quietly and unobtrusively followed Los Angeles Consul Rafael de la Colina's example and did their best to assist repatriates in settling property matters. In most instances, although it was aware of the transgressions, SRE wisely looked the other way. It was the old bureaucratic dodge, employed since the days of the Spanish viceroys: *¡Obedezco, pero no cumplo!* (I obey, but I do not comply!)

Given the dire nature of the situation facing Nationals on the eve of their departure, humane compassion took precedence over legal prerequisites. A report forwarded to SRE by the consul in Denver, Colorado, vividly illustrated the dilemma. The consul's communiqué included copies of a poster announcing a forthcoming farm auction. For sale were the draft animals, farm machinery, and equipment belonging to Rito Rangel and Frank Acosta. Both men had leased and successfully farmed substantial acreage for many years. Caught in the onslaught of the depression, and buffeted by falling farm prices, they faced ruin. Attempts to borrow money or gain an extension on loans proved to be futile. Instead, they were being dunned by creditors to make good on their arrears or face foreclosure. Both men harbored a strong suspicion that the refusal of any financial accommodation was designed to force them to vacate their respective farms. Once this was accomplished, the land could then be leased to deserving Americans. In an effort to pay off his creditors, Mr. Rangel was forced to sell his livestock and equipment, worth 9,000 dollars, for the mere pittance of $1,426.[30] After fifteen years of hard labor, Rangel wound up landless and virtually destitute. Señor Acosta also suffered the same fate.

The fate suffered by Rito Rangel and Frank Acosta was not atypical. Lack of investment capital, plus the large number of properties up for sale,

made for a buyer's market. Unscrupulous real estate agents plagued beleaguered property owners. These con artists sought to reap a handsome profit
by taking advantage of the seller's desperate plight. Scare tactics, fraud,
deceit, misrepresentation, and outright scams were their stock in trade.
Representatives of the La Vally and Grant Company approached Mexicans
who owned property in Clearwater, California (now incorporated into the
city of Paramount). As bait, the agents claimed that the consul in Los
Angeles had given them permission to engage in the sale and exchange of
properties in behalf of Mexican Nationals. When contacted by suspicious
residents, the consul vehemently denied having ever spoken with the
agents or having had any contacts or dealings with the company.[31] Consuls
everywhere received similar complaints. It was but one of many attempts
to capitalize on the misery and misfortune of others.

To avoid being duped, wary individuals, like Manuel Mendoza, relied
upon their consul for help in selecting reputable real estate agents.[32]
Others, who were being forced to depart suddenly, feared that they would
have to abandon their hard-earned property. In most instances, it was a
modest wooden bungalow, which they had acquired after years of great personal sacrifice. Unable to bear the thought of this final indignity, consuls
were implored to act as the executors of the property. Among those taking
that course of action was Señor J. C. Pasillas, who approached Consul
Fernando Alatorre in San Bernardino. Alatorre was reluctant to assume
direct responsibility for the property. He advised his superiors that Mr.
Pasillas's request was not an isolated case, and he requested SRE instructions on how to proceed in such instances. Alatorre's dilemma was typical
of that faced by other consuls. As a rule, for their own protection, consuls
refused to assume the liability and responsibility that such an arrangement
would entail.[33]

Unable to dispose of their property at a fair market value, some Mexicans attempted to exchange their holdings for land in Mexico. In order to
arrange for or to negotiate a better deal, some of them banded together and
combined their separate plots. However, it was always difficult to locate
property of equal or comparable value in either country. There simply was
no benchmark that could be used to determine the actual worth of disparate properties. The Mexican government received repeated requests to
verify the condition of various parcels of land. It became impossible for the
federal government to comply with the huge volume of requests. However,

not wishing to ignore the inquiries, the governors of the respective states in which the properties were located were asked to ascertain and report on the status of the parcels in question. Unavoidably, the long-range, sight-unseen transactions were bound to produce some disappointments. In some instances, angry repatriates who felt they had been swindled accused property appraisers of being in cahoots with prospective buyers or vendors. Appraisers were accused of making false or erroneous evaluations regarding property values, soil conditions, or agricultural potential.

Illustrative of the problems and heartbreak encountered by potential colonizers who wished to effect a land exchange was the experience of a group from Colton, California. During a period of three years, the "Grupo Nacional Mexicano," led by Isaac López, negotiated for the transfer of the Hacienda La Gloria, situated within the adjacent states of Chihuahua and Durango. This dual location exacerbated the negotiations, and efforts to resolve the impasse concerning the proposed trade proved to be futile. In desperation, the group asked the consul in San Bernardino to use his good offices and intercede in their behalf. Personally, Consul Fernando Alatorre had doubts and misgivings about the deal. However, in responding to pleas for help in effecting the exchange, he promised to pursue the matter with SRE. By becoming involved, he hoped not only to protect their rights and interests, but to give the Colton group an opportunity to reconsider acquiring the property.

Consul Alatorre warned the Grupo Nacional Mexicano to use extreme caution in pursuing the venture. While waiting for a reply from SRE, he advised them to obtain more information directly from the Secretaría de Agricultura y Fomento before proceeding with the proposed trade. Alatorre also suggested that rather than merely acting in concert as members of a loosely knit group, they should form a corporation. This, he advised them, would enable them to deal more effectively with John D. Carlton, representing Loftus, Dysart Development Company of Los Angeles, the alleged owners of the property. Consul Alatorre also instructed them to have the parcels independently surveyed and insist that Mr. Carlton deliver legal titles to the individual owners. This, he cautioned, would prevent future squabbles among themselves regarding boundaries and ownership of the said property.[34] In light of the misrepresentation or fraudulent schemes to which international land transactions are privy, the consul's sound advice was worth heeding.

As a result of his inquiry, Consul Alatorre was advised by SRE that Rancho La Gloria consisted of approximately 15,893 hectares, the equivalent of 35,000 to 40,000 acres. The property's total value was estimated at 31,736 pesos. Yet Mr. Carlton was offering to sell or exchange the land at a rate of 10 dollars an acre, and this would enhance the value of the land between 350,000 or 400,000 dollars. Given the fact that much of the land was alkaline and fit only for grazing and that sweet water could be obtained only by drilling to a depth of 100 to 125 meters, SRE deemed the price per acre to be excessive.[35] The Secretaría de Relaciones Exteriores instructed Consul Alatorre to share its findings with members of the Grupo Nacional Mexicano. Based on this information, Alatorre warned the group not to rush into any contractual agreement with Mr. Carlton, and not to release title to their property prematurely.

In order to verify the physical condition of the land comprising Rancho La Gloria, a delegation from the Grupo Nacional Mexicano went to Mexico to inspect the property firsthand. Upon their return, the emissaries reported that the land was suited for cultivation of corn, wheat, oats, beans, alfalfa, and other crops. Portions of the land could also be used for raising livestock since there was ample pasture. The investigators reported that the 15,893 hectares in the state of Durango were in addition to 10,140 hectares located in the adjacent state of Chihuahua. To Consul Alatorre's astonishment, the proposed price of ten dollars per acre was not considered excessive by members of the Grupo Nacional Mexicano. Their reaction was due to the fact that they feared losing their property either as a result of bank foreclosures for failing to make payments on their loans or as a result of their failure to pay property taxes. By entering into a deal for Rancho La Gloria, they hoped to salvage something from their hard-earned holdings.[36] Anything providing a glimmer of hope was better than watching their dream of owning a little plot of land turn to dust before their very eyes. In truth, the deal represented a last, desperate effort to preserve some vestige of their dignity and self-worth. The dreams, hopes, and aspirations of a lifetime die hard!

Advised by Consul Alatorre of the Grupo Nacional Mexicano's determination to proceed with the Rancho La Gloria exchange, Consul Joaquín Terrazas in Los Angeles decided to intervene in an attempt to resolve the issue. He arranged a meeting between members of the group and John D. Carlton and William Loftus, associates of the Loftus, Dysart Development

Company. When questioned about the excessive price of ten dollars an acre, Mr. Carlton replied that although the ranch consisted of approximately sixty-five thousand acres, they were selling the Colton group only forty thousand acres. The sixty-five thousand acres figure included the combined 40,000 acres in the state of Durango plus an additional 25,000 acres in the adjacent state of Chihuahua. The additional twenty-five thousand acres would be deeded to the group free of charge. The impact or effect of this new development was not lost on the purchasers. If the bonus acreage were added to the total, a quick mental calculation indicated a reduction in price to $6.15 per acre. In addition, the agents revealed, the company was willing to pay $1,000.00 to have the land surveyed, and it was prepared to reimburse the colonizers $365.00 for each $100,000.00 worth of land they bought. This would help the buyers defray transportation expenses. As a further indication of the company's goodwill, Mr. Carlton offered to donate two trucks, two tractors, some farm implements, and a machine for drilling water wells.[37] To the Grupo Nacional Mexicano, the deal seemed too good to pass up.

At the behest of Consul Joaquín Terrazas, both groups agreed not to enter into any contractual agreement prior to July 5, 1932. Ostensibly, this would allow Consul Terrazas time to obtain more detailed information from the Secretaría de Agricultura y Fomento. An urgent telegram was sent to SRE, requesting them to expedite an immediate response because the colonizers were anxious to conclude the deal. Throughout the entire Rancho La Gloria episode, the governors of the states of Chihuahua and Durango had been kept apprised of the situation. Their cooperation and input had been sought at various stages of the delicate negotiations. Both governors had responded to queries for information from the Grupo National Mexicano and from various departments of the Mexican government. Their participation was part of the federal government's plan to actively involve states and municipalities in resolving the gnawing problem of resettling the repatriates.

In December of 1933, the Grupo Nacional Mexicano from Colton, California, finally concluded the purchase of the portion of Rancho La Gloria located in the state of Durango. The land was surveyed and lots deeded to the members. However, the feeling of euphoria was short lived. Enrique Vega, co-owner of the adjacent ranch, Hacienda Jaral Grande, filed a legal protest. Vega claimed that only 7,357 of the 15,893 hectares actually belonged to Rancho La Gloria.[38] He threatened to sue the Grupo Nacional Mexicano in order to regain rightful ownership of his property. Stunned by the unexpected development, the Grupo threatened to file a lawsuit against Mr. Carlton and Mr. Loftus. The Mexican consul in Los Angeles was asked to contact Carlton and Loftus and elicit their cooperation in settling the dispute.[39] It appeared that a long, bitter legal conflict was in the making. Seemingly, the colonizers from Colton had traded one set of problems for another one that was equally as compelling. This resultant fiasco was the very reason why SRE did not want its consuls to become embroiled in property transactions.

To avoid the recurrence of problems similar to the Rancho La Gloria situation, state governors were instructed to survey carefully all the lands available for colonization in their respective states. They were to redouble their evaluation efforts and take every precaution necessary to avoid subjecting the government and its departments to a repetition of the embarrassment suffered as a result of the Rancho La Gloria debacle. State governors were advised that the occurrence of problems between colonization ventures and the settlement of government-sponsored ejidos would not be tolerated. Every governor would be held strictly accountable for errors of omission or commission regarding colonization efforts in his state. To assure compliance with the decree, the Consejo Consultivo de Migración in the office of Secretaría de Governación would be responsible for overseeing all surveys and reports. All governors realized that failure to comply with the federal government's directive could have dire implications for their political careers.

As might have been expected under the circumstances, hoping to ingratiate themselves with the federal government, the governors began sending in reports without delay. In the state of Veracruz, twenty-four hundred hectares in the vicinity of Orizaba were offered for sale at one hundred pesos each. The governor of San Luis Potosí claimed that his state would provide sufficient land to settle one thousand financially independent repatriates. In addition, acreage for five hundred indigent families would be made available. The governors of Michoacán and Guanajuato also offered to make good lands available.[40] Subsequently, other governors offered lands for colonization purposes. In some respects, among the zealous governors the commitment to survey and make lands available became a game of one-upmanship. None of them wanted to be overshadowed by their political rivals or to appear to be less patriotic. In the realm of Mexican politics, that would have been a cardinal sin, if not a fatal mistake. As a consequence, in many instances, the land proffered was marginal and unfit for intensive agricultural development.

In April of 1933, under the auspices of the National Repatriation Committee, or NRC, the government assumed direct involvement in carrying out the colonization program. The semiautonomous committee was to be instrumental in establishing a colony at Pinotepa Nacional, near Minizo, Oaxaca, in southern Mexico. Other sites contemplated for future settlement included El Coloso Ranch near the port of Acapulco, Santo Domingo, near Magdalena Bay in Lower California, Cobano in the state of Colima, and Canton de Autlan in Jalisco. All these sites, including Pinotepa Nacional, were located on the West Coast. Only one site was proposed for the Gulf Coast and would be located at San Andres Tuxtla in Veracruz.[41] The Minizo site was selected to be settled first because it was far removed from the United States–Mexico border. Experience had shown that when repatriates were allowed to settle along the border region, many of them eventually pulled up stakes and returned to the United States. The proximity of the border provided a convenient escape valve for those who became frustrated or discouraged with the rigors of leading a pioneer life.

In an attempt to avoid defections, all of the men selected for the Minizo, Oaxaca, project were required to be experienced farmhands familiar with modern farming techniques. The NRC wanted to capitalize upon the full range of knowledge and skills which the men had acquired during their stay in the United States. A total of one thousand braceros and their families were chosen to establish the experimental agricultural colony. A sanitary brigade preceded the colonizers to prepare the site for occupancy. The parcels of land were surveyed, and crude, temporary huts were built by using fronds from the plentiful palm trees. This would enable settlers to begin the immediate task of clearing and preparing the area for cultivation. To assure the venture's success, the federal government promised to furnish the settlers with modern agricultural tools and machinery.[42] Understandably, the government was anxious for the first officially conducted colonizing effort to succeed. It was hoped the Minizo project would set a precedent and serve as a model for erecting future government-sanctioned settlements.

Unfortunately, by the end of 1933 colonizing efforts at the Pinotepa Nacional settlement in Minizo had come to naught. Of the five hundred original settlers, only eight remained. After so much fanfare and high hopes, the failure was a bitter blow and disappointment to all involved. In August, Andrés Landa y Piña, the colony's provisional director and chief of the Ministry of the Interior's Migration Department, had issued a glowing report lauding the colony's progress. Obviously, no one had envisioned the possibility that the project would fail. What had gone wrong? Citing various issues of *El Universal* as his source, American Vice Consul John Littell, stationed in Mexico City, stated: "The causes for the failure of this colony were given as (1) the attempts of certain persons to exploit the colonizers for personal profit; and (2) dissension among the members of the National Repatriation Committee."[43]

Charges levied against the National Repatriation Committee accused it of mismanagement and the misuse of funds. The committee strenuously denied all allegations of misconduct or ineptness in discharging its duties. Smarting from the charges, its members met to consider disbanding. However, they decided to take no action until after accounting for the 300,000 pesos they had collected. The question of what had happened to the money was a very sensitive issue and provided ample fodder for the committee's critics. In March of 1934, the National Repatriation Committee accounted for the 318,221.65 pesos collected. NRC reported that 202,777.48 pesos had been spent to aid the colonizers and 14,008.84 pesos had been incurred as general operating expenses. On deposit in the Bank of Mexico were 101,407.09 pesos, and cash on hand amounted to 28.24 pesos.[44] Failure of the Pinotepa Nacional project discredited the committee's endeavors in southern Mexico. However, plans to colonize in Baja California were still in effect.

In May of 1934, American Vice Consul John Littell filed a surprisingly detailed account of the Pinotepa Nacional colonizing failure. He prepared the report for the Department of Labor at the behest of the U.S. State Department. In the report, he pointed out that not one but two colonies actually had been abandoned. They were colonies "No. 1 and No. 2 located in Minizo, Guerrero, and Pinotepa Nacional, Oaxaca," respectively. This appears to be an error or oversight, since the Pinotepa Nacional colony was located near Minizo, Oaxaca. The vice consul undoubtedly had reference to El Coloso Ranch, located near Acapulco in the State of Guerrero. In his dispatch, the vice consul cited two reasons for the colonies' failure: (1) the arbitrary government thereof, and (2) the starvation rations given to the colonists.[45] Some of the former colonists complained of the overly strict discipline imposed by the administrators. They claimed that they were often berated and insulted, but they did not dare to protest because the overseers were protected by armed guards. The straw that seemingly broke the colonists' back was when the corn harvest was fed to swine rather than being divided among the settlers, as had been promised. The Pinotepa colonists also endured terrible health risks. While interviewing repatriates from July 1933 to February 1934, researcher James Gilbert was dissuaded by former colonists from visiting the area. To do so could not only endanger his health, but could prove fatal, they warned him. Some sixty colonists were reported to have died there within twenty days. The colony was situated in the same area where Dictator Porfirio Díaz had often exiled political opponents to a certain death.[46]

Unable to tolerate the deadly conditions, the residents of the Pinotepa Nacional colony left en masse and made the arduous twenty-three-day trek to Acapulco on foot. When the destitute, bone-weary colonists arrived in Acapulco, General Lázaro Cárdenas happened to be in the area campaigning for president. He took pity on them and paid their bus fare to Mexico City. Once in Mexico City, the beleaguered colonists planned to present their case to the proper authorities. They hoped to circumvent the bureaucracy by meeting directly with the Secretaría de Agricultura y Fomento (Department of Agriculture and Planning) after lodging a formal protest with the Ministry of the Interior. Attesting to their strength of character and purpose, in spite of their sad experience, most of them were unwilling to give up on their dream of owning a plot of land.[47] Hopefully, the Secretary of Agriculture would be able to help them get reassigned to another government-sponsored colonization project. Although they did not want to become a burden to the government, the disposed colonists had no other alternative but to seek help.

A region that the government retained an interest in colonizing was the territory of Baja California. It hoped to contribute to the area's development by encouraging mainland Mexicans as well as repatriates to settle in the territory. Because it was adjacent to the state of California, where many indigent Nationals resided, Baja California seemed made to order for colonization purposes. Los Angeles County welfare authorities and the State Relief Administration (SRA) were anxious to sell indigent Mexicans on the idea of settling in Baja. Both agencies viewed it as a means of saving money by cutting welfare expenses. In neighboring Arizona, the same view prevailed. The "Unionist Confederation" in Nogales demanded immediate expulsion of "all

Mexicans."[48] The prime objective in both instances was to get as many Mexicans as possible resettled in Baja California.

Two areas in Baja California received particular attention as possible sites for settling the repatriates. One was the Valle de las Palmas, located about fifteen miles inland from Ensenada. The other was Valle de San Quintín, near the Bahía de San Quintín located further south. From all indications, the two sites seemed to offer the best possibility of being successfully developed by colonizers. In 1930, efforts were made to colonize the Valle de San Quintín. The bleak, forbidding region posed a grim challenge because rainfall averaged only about five inches per year, making it dependent on dry farming. It was the classic struggle of man against nature. In 1930, nature emerged triumphant and the desert returned to its pristine state. Concerted settlement efforts had to await a more urgent or compelling reason. The worsening depression provided that impetus.

In September 1932, the Santa Monica settlement in Valle de las Palmas informed William R. Harriman, superintendent of charities for Los Angeles County, that they could accommodate one hundred indigent families. He relayed the information to the county Board of Supervisors. However, Harriman advised the Board not to take any action until conditions at the settlement had been verified. Harriman proposed sending his assistant, Rex Thomson, to investigate. Upon his return, Thomson filed an extensive report on the status of Valle de las Palmas. While there, he interviewed the territorial governor, the president and vice president of Baja California Light, Water, and Telephone Company. He also met with the vice president of the Tijuana Light and Power Company, who was also president of the local Rotary Club. The territorial governor, Señor Olachea, expressed opposition to foreign interests using the valley as a dumping ground for indigents.[49]

Governor Olachea was willing, however, to accept colonists who were experienced in modern farming. He favored giving preference to self-reliant families who were able to colonize without becoming a burden. His government did not have the funds to assist either repatriates or local residents. Olachea confided to Thomson that to prevent local indigents from becoming a problem, hundreds of unemployed workers had been rounded up and shipped to the mainland. This was done, the governor explained, as a humanitarian gesture, not as a cold-blooded deed. Baja California officials believed that opportunities for assimilation into the general labor force were much better in the mainland. Putting the colonization venture in perspective, the governor pointed out that even the industrious, hard-working Japanese had given up trying to earn a living from the harsh environment.[50] Governor Olachea was convinced that extensive colonization ventures were doomed to failure.

Governor Olachea's observations and conclusions were borne out by the officials of the Light, Water, and Telephone Company. They, too, had investigated the possibility of promoting colonization in the Valle de las Palmas in order to increase their sales and services. They had abandoned the effort when their agricultural experts reported that prolonged irrigation depleted the water table and brought harmful alkalines to the surface, rendering intensive farming impossible. This boded ill for any concerted attempt at extensive colonization. The vice president of Tijuana Light and Power concurred with the conclusions of his colleagues. He reiterated the fact that any major colonizing attempt would be "impracticable and disastrous." Experienced farmers could eke out a living and meet their personal needs, but the best they could hope for was a bare level of subsistence farming. All of the businessmen and officials interviewed by Mr. Thomson were of the opinion that repatriates would be much better off in mainland Mexico than in Baja California.[51]

To dispel any false notions among the Mexican populace about the facility of colonizing in Baja California, Governor Olachea sent a representative to Los Angeles. The governor's agent collaborated Rex Thomson's dire findings. Despite all advice and evidence to the contrary, the important thing to welfare officials was to get rid of the indigent Mexicans. Whether the repatriates succeeded or failed was of no consequence to welfare bureaucrats. Therefore, in spite of the ominous warnings, Mexico City's *El Universal* reported on March 2, 1933, that two thousand hectares of first-class farmland in Valle de las Palmas were being offered to repatriates. According to the article the federal government was prepared to furnish the necessary farm equipment and provisions needed by the colonists. In a belated show of concern, Rex Thomson visited the colony at least twice and, on one occasion, was accompanied by Vice Consul Ricardo Hill. Based on his observations and findings, Thomson continued to regard the region as virtually worthless for intensive farming. He remained adamantly opposed to sending repatriates into the area.[52]

A view contrary to Governor Olachea's and Rex Thomson's dismal appraisal of the area's potential was expressed by Dr. Ramón Puente. Puente claimed that the area around Ensenada was excellent wine country and simply needed the proper development. Although the area lacked adequate rainfall, artesian wells could be drilled to meet farmers' needs. Puente also recommended recruiting Italians since, according to him, they had no peers in cultivating the vine and enhancing its related industries. As proof, Puente cited their success in Argentina, Chile, and Brazil. An added inducement was that Italians assimilated easily into the Mexican culture and lifestyle. Unlike other foreigners, their Latin temperament enabled them to feel at home in Mexico. This was in sharp contrast to the Russians in Santo Tomás, below Ensenada, who, as previously noted, had intermarried only twice in thirty years. It galled Puente that the Russians had opted to apply for U.S. citizenship rather than becoming naturalized Mexicans. Because of the threat posed by the Russians, Puente concluded that it was imperative that colonization be undertaken to counteract their influence in the area.[53]

Dwarfing the two thousand hectares originally made available in Valle de las Palmas, in 1934 the government deeded four million hectares to the new Junta Nacional de Repatriación. The acreage was located in an area known as "El Centinela," and was deemed capable of supporting thousands of repatriates and their families. Much of the land formerly had been leased and cultivated by foreign investors. In order to facilitate settlement and permit immediate cultivation, it was recommended that funds left by the defunct National Repatriation Committee be used to develop the new venture.[54] The extent of the government's commitment in colonizing Baja California was apparent in two presidential decrees issued early in 1935. The first decree established a commission, comprised of several key government ministries, to study the feasibility of channeling repatriates to designated sites in the region. The second decree authorized using the remaining funds, approximately thirty thousand dollars, from the disbanded NRC for carrying out the colonization effort.[55]

The decrees attested to President Cárdenas's personal resolve to succeed in colonizing the repatriates. Upon assuming office in 1934, Cárdenas had called for the Secretaría de Gobernación, Mexico's Department of the Interior, to do everything possible to facilitate the transportation and settlement of repatriates in the areas designated by the Secretaría de Agricultura y Fomento. During the second year of his administration, Cárdenas provided critical support for repatriation colonization. He initiated three large irrigation projects at a cost of eighty million pesos designed to irrigate some 600,000 hectares, or 1,500,000 acres in the states of Durango, Coahuila, Tamaulipas, and Sonora. Cárdenas was especially interested in settling Baja California and Quintana Roo in the Yucatán Peninsula. Eager to carry out Cárdenas's wishes, in addition to sites in Baja California and Quintana Roo, the Junta Nacional de Repatriación also identified areas in the states of Hidalgo, Jalisco, Nayarit, and Morelos that were considered suitable for colonization.[56]

Colonization efforts were experiencing a new impetus and undergoing revitalization. In March of 1937, it was reported that the government had received nearly fifty thousand colonization petitions. Most of the prospective settlers wanted to relocate in Baja California. In order to adequately accommodate that huge number, per presidential decree, a commission made up of doctors and engineers was authorized to study and evaluate the conditions that prevailed in the area. This would be done in an attempt to correct beforehand whatever problems or deficiencies existed. Hopefully, preplanning would assure the success of the colonizing ventures.[57] All government agencies were determined to avoid the mistakes made in the Oaxaca and Guerrero settlements. Federal ministers were also aware of the fact that President Cárdenas would not brook failure. Their very jobs could well depend upon the success of whatever colonization projects were undertaken.

For obvious reasons, welfare authorities in the United States also wanted Cárdenas's resettlement efforts to succeed. The ever-resourceful Helen Murray, of the California State Relief Administration office in Los Angeles, solicited colonization information and literature directly from the Mexican government. She used the material as propaganda to induce more Mexicans to return home. Murray also identified a number of local groups and organizations that could be helpful in promoting the return of immigrants to Mexico.[58] Murray resolved not to overlook any avenue or opportunity to give repatriation a boost. Thus, although the Mexican government tried to anticipate and respond to problems before they occurred, it had no control over the biggest problem of all: the huge number of people being repatriated. In many instances, there was little or no cooperation forthcoming from American authorities. Like Helen Murray, they were interested only in getting rid of the indigents.

In order to assist in the colonization effort, consular offices repeatedly asked SRE for detailed reports concerning available lands. The information, they advised SRE, should include site location, soil conditions, water and irrigation status, sale price, and conditions of purchase and payment. Prospective settlers were also concerned about the availability of consumers' markets for their produce.[59] In many instances, adverse information dissuaded repatriates from making irrational decisions. But hope and despair compelled some individuals to make the best deal possible. Those eager to colonize agreed to settle wherever the Mexican government assigned them. Their basic demands were threefold: fertile farming land, adequate government support, and sale terms that could be reasonably met. Despite its altruistic efforts, there were limits to what the government could do. Recognizing this fact, newspaper editorials called upon private institutions, business firms, Chambers of Commerce, and labor groups to cooperate in the ventures.[60] Unfortunately, support from the private sector was not always forthcoming.

Glossing over or ignoring this fact, newspapers tried to promote an optimistic outlook. They frequently editorialized that as inopportune as it appeared to be, repatriation could be turned into a national benefit. "Mexico needs all her sons," Mexico City's *Excélsior* proclaimed and the repatriates with "habits of industry and frugality would make them very helpful to the development of their country."[61] Other newspapers observed that lands that lay idle due to lack of population could now be transformed into productive acreage. Energetic repatriates schooled in the latest agricultural techniques "will create in places now unpopulated, verdant agricultural centers, and new centers of population and wealth," one newspaper waxed eloquently.[62] Another newspaper, however, pointed out that in order to assure the success of the ventures, the government must establish clear title to the properties deeded to the settlers. Colonization, it warned, must not be allowed to become a political issue exploited by unscrupulous individuals. The editorial advocated providing campesinos with adequate protection against gangs of ruffians who might seek to terrorize or victimize them.[63] In some instances, repatriates had encountered harassment and physical abuse not only from local marauders, but from local residents who resented the intruders.

In the waning years of the repatriation crisis, the Spanish Civil War added a new and unexpected dimension to the problem of colonization. Spanish refugees fleeing the ravages of civil war sought refuge in Mexico. Mexico opened her doors and her heart to the less fortunate. However, many Mexicans were fearful that due to the urgency of the Spanish situation, the plight of their own people might be temporarily ignored. Addressing this concern was an editorial published in *Ultimas Noticias*. The editorial reported that several hundred Spaniards had departed from the French port of Saint Nazaire on the steamer *Flandre*, destined for Veracruz, and that an additional eight thousand Spaniards were awaiting their turn to emigrate. The Spanish immigrants, the editorial stated, compound an old problem: "We very much fear, however, that the repatriation of compatriots... and their location on lands in Mexico will be much more difficult now than it was before."[64]

It was to allay such growing fears and misgivings that the government redoubled its efforts to recruit indigent Nationals who were still in the United States. As noted earlier, it authorized Ramón Beteta, Sub-Secretary of Foreign Affairs, to visit all cities in the United States that had large Mexican populations. Coincidentally, the *Ultimas Noticias* editorial appeared on the very day, April 5, 1939, that Señor Ramón Beteta departed for the United States on his recruiting mission. The Sub-Secretary was authorized to take whatever action was necessary to recruit and transport volunteer colonists to their destination. Lands were being reserved for them in the states of Tamaulipas and Sinaloa. The National Bank of Agricultural Credit had been alerted to be prepared to assist the colonizers in financing land purchases.[65] Once again, editorials applauded the government's actions and praised its efforts to relocate both Nationals and Spaniards. In doing so, the government was determined to avoid any charges of preferential treatment. Spanish immigrants would be selected on the basis of the contribution they could make to the nation's well-being and would be assigned to settle in areas where their skills were needed.[66]

As a result, in August of 1939, a contingent of 570 families, primarily Spaniards, was sent to Valle de Mexicali in Baja California. The intent was to have the Spaniards develop local vineyards. It was envisioned that Baja had the potential to become a premier wine-producing area. In addition to grape production, the area was seen as a source of cereals, beans, potatoes, and such fruits as pomegranates, mangoes, and watermelons. Sugarcane, cotton, and wheat could also be grown commercially. Some areas could be used for the grazing of various kinds of livestock or developed into forestation enterprises. With an area of 152,000 square kilometers and barely fifty-three thousand inhabitants, Baja was the least populated area in the country. Therefore, it was considered a national and a patriotic duty to colonize and civilize the raw peninsula.[67] Like virgin lands everywhere, the region invited exploitation and awaited the plow's intrusion. Joining the effort to develop Baja California was a Southern California group primarily from the cities of San Pedro and San Fernando. They settled Ejido Erienda in San Isidro, Baja California. The early days were very difficult with "no roads . . . nothing, . . . no water" according to pioneer settler Ramona Ríos de Castro. There were times when the colonists were even at the point of starvation and barely survived. On occasion, we were reduced to "eating beans by the spoon without tortillas."[68] Fortunately, letters about their desperate situation written by Ríos de Castro to the Governor of Baja California prompted him to save the ejido. He supplied the colonists with provisions of corn and other supplies as well as basic farming equipment. Knowing about President Cárdenas's keen interest in settling and developing Baja California, the governor could not afford to let the colony fail.

The government was also busy acquiring additional lands in various states. A total of 488,977 hectares were obtained in the states of Durango, Oaxaca, Veracruz, San Luis Potosí, Sonora, Tamaulipas, and Nuevo León. Officials estimated that 20,100 families, approximately 100,000 repatriates, could be readily accommodated. One of the new colonies was to be established in La Sauteña, near Matamoros, in the state of Tamaulipas. La Sauteña consisted of thirty thousand hectares, and five hundred families were slated to be settled there.[69] Other repatriates would join the "18 de Marzo" settlement in Matamoros. Letters received by friends and relatives in San Antonio, Texas, indicated that the colonists already at the site were extremely happy in their new home. Based on the colonists' optimistic letters and reports, the Consul General in San Antonio was directed to recruit at least one hundred families a month to join the "18 de Marzo" colonia.[70]

Officials were lulled into a false sense of accomplishment as a result of letters like the one sent by Isabel de la Cruz to her brother in San Antonio, boasting of conditions and the well-being of the colonia.[71] However, contrary to glowing letters and official reports, the Spanish-language newspaper *La Prensa*, in San Antonio, reported that conditions at the "18 de Marzo" colony were deplorable.[72]

In 1939, 15,925 Mexican Nationals and their children were repatriated. Of that number, 627 families comprising approximately 4,000 individuals mostly from Texas, settled in the 18 de Marzo colony. Despite the efforts to coordinate all aspects of the venture, the colonists were plagued by many of the same problems that had beleaguered other attempts at colonization. Once again, the funds and support that had been promised failed to materialize. No one had anticipated the number of repatriates seeking help or the wretched condition in which many of them arrived. The limited medical staff was overwhelmed by the extent and types of illnesses that victimized the new arrivals. Nothing had gone according to plan![73]

Similar information concerning the plight of the colonists was transmitted to the U.S. State Department by the American consul stationed in Matamoros. The United States, of course, was responsible for the exodus of Mexican Nationals and their children. However, in the report, the consul attempted to absolve the U.S. of any blame or responsibility for the dire situation in which the repatriates found themselves. The consul's communiqué read, in part: "in a sense I suppose it is no concern of ours whether these Mexican nationals are properly treated upon their return to their own country." As an afterthought, the following statement was added: "However, it is obvious that there are humanitarian considerations involved, and it is probably the case that some of these so-called repatriates are citizens of this country [the United States] by birth. Therefore, we are at least morally interested in an attempted solution of the plight of the people involved when such a solution threatens to be no solution at all." The dispatch's final paragraph declared piously, "I suppose that for the moment there is nothing to do but observe developments, but I thought you would want to know of the seemingly very unfortunate trend which threatens."[74] In light of the fact that approximately 60 percent of the repatriates were children born in the United States, there certainly was ample reason to be concerned about the welfare of American citizens. The tragedy is that an official expression of concern was so late in coming and, even then, nothing was done to ameliorate the tragic injustice. Shouldering the burden of resettling the repatriates was left to Mexico.

In the continuing quest for land that could be colonized, an agent of the Secretaría de Agricultura y Fomento informed the Babícora Development Company that the government planned to establish a colony on the company's property. The American-owned company was a division of the William Randolph Hearst enterprises. The property manager was advised that approximately forty thousand acres would be required for the project. The property in question was deemed to be the only remaining area in the state of Chihuahua that was suitable for successful colonization.[75] When his protests came to naught, the manager contacted the American consul in the city of Chihuahua to elicit his aid. He explained that the property was being confiscated because the Mexican government claimed the company was not running enough cattle on the acreage in question to warrant the "inaffectability-of-petitions" clause that applied to grazing lands.[76] That is, the lands were not protected or immune from the right of eminent domain. Loss of the acreage, the manager contended, would mean the end of the company's ranching activities. The company manager also alleged that Pedro Saucedo Montemayor, the General Federal Agent representing the Secretaría de Agricultura y Fomento, had offered to settle the matter for the sum of thirty thousand pesos. The offer had been refused, and the company was seeking to negotiate a settlement.[77]

On both sides of the border, the repatriation issue was quietly fading into the background and the torrent of repatriates was subsiding. In 1938 only about 12,000 Mexicans were repatriated.[78] Colonization had lost its sense of urgency. The worst of the depression was over, and more important events in Europe were beginning to demand serious attention. For many repatriates already in Mexico, the demanding ordeal of adjusting to a different lifestyle which had been the bane of their existence was also hopefully drawing to a close.

Pan y Tierra
DOCUMENTS

■ ■

REPATRIATION IN CHIHUAHUA: CONFIDENTIAL SUMMARY
VICE CONSUL ROBERT K. PEYTON TO AMERICAN CONSUL,
UNITED STATES EMBASSY, MEXICO CITY, 19 MARCH 1939.
Source: Washington, D.C., National Archives,
Department of State, RG 59, 311.1215/128.

VOLUNTARY
REPATRIATION IN CHIHUAHUA

From   Vice Consul [signature]
                                        Robert K. Peyton

Chihuahua, Mexico.   Date of Completion: March 19, 1939
                                        Date of Mailing: March 19, 1939

APPROVED:
[signature]
Lee R. Blohm
American Consul

Great interest has been taken by the public in the Chihuahua consular district in the plan of the Mexican national administration to bring back into this country, particularly to the State of Chihuahua, as large number as possible of destitute Mexican citizens who are now residing in the United States. Up to this time only a few scattering families have returned to this district to live and many of these have been unable to locate themselves happily; in fact a certain percentage of them has even attempted to return to United States to take up residence there again. This State therefore has had no large experience in repatriation as have other districts in Mexico such as the Matamoros sector, which it is understood attempted to effect the settlement of repatriates several years ago.

While sympathetic with the idea in a general way, the Mexican citizens, particularly big ranchers, do not believe that there is sufficient land available in the State to bring in a large body of migrant farmers. Employers of labor in the various mining centers likewise do not believe that their industries can absorb more labor just at this time, their businesses being somewhat discouraged by the unfriendly attitude of the national administration toward capital and investment.

Leaders of political thought here do feel, however, that the President and his Under-Secretary for Foreign Relations are sincere in their work for development of the repatriation program. They do not believe that it is a political move to meet any criticism directed against the administration because of its friendly attitude toward immigration of Spanish refugees. Up to the present time of course no significant number of Spanish or Jewish refugees have taken up residence in this district.

Report on Available Lands

On April 12, 1939, it will be recalled, President Cárdenas, in cognizance of the increasing demands from Mexican citizens living abroad in destitute circumstances for repatriation—presumably inspired by the sanctuary reported to have been offered to Spanish refugees by Mexico—issued a request to the governors of the several states of the Republic and to the Banco Nacional de Crédito Ejidal to study the problem of repatriation and to report as soon as possible on the number of families which existing ejidal communities and new colony projects could absorb.

In compliance with the President's request and that of Governor Talamantes of Chihuahua, the General Agent of the Secretaría de Agrucutura y Fomento in Chihuahua City called a meeting of the representatives of several large estates, ranches, and land companies on April 24, 1939, to discuss the problem and to ascertain the amount of private land available for colonization by repatriates.

The meeting was attended by representatives, among others, of the Cía. de Palomas, Ojo de Federico, Testamentaría de Pedro Zuloaga, Cía. Agrícola del Norte, Corralitos and Santa Clara. A representative of the extensive Babicora Ranch, although summoned, did not attend. The meeting proceeded with the other members of the committee who discussed the suitability of Babicora (a Hearst property) as a locale for settlement along with the other properties. At the meeting it was decided that some of the properties under consideration could provide arable and pasture land sufficient to the colonization of some three thousand repatriated families, the manner of settlement to be left to the Agrarian Commission.

The Babicora Ranch, the chairman pointed out, could provide 30,000 hectares of arable land around the lake section accommodating one thousand repatriated families with thirty hectares apiece. It was further pointed out that the Babicora land under consideration was exceptionally productive since a preliminary study had revealed that a yield of crops from seed planted would approach a ratio of 15:1 in corn, and 80:1 in wheat, and that water could be found at depths ranging from three to eight meters throughout the section. The committee also stated that Babícora could easily provide 50,000 hectares of grazing land to be dedicated to cattle raising. The representative of Babicora Ranch, who later attended the meeting, proposed a grant of 70,000 hectares of arable land situated in a different section than that under consideration which he declared was equally as good as the land in the vicinity of Babicora Lake. It is not known which of the two plans discussed the committee finally submitted to Mexico City.

The representative of Ojo de Federico Ranch offered 1,500 hectares of arable land to accommodate one hundred and fifty colonists each with ten hectares of land suited for farming. Further offers consisted entirely of grazing land, the Cía. Agrícola del Norte proposing a grant of 1,000,000 hectares and the Rancho Las Palomas offering another small parcel. It was estimated that these two properties could accommodate several thousand families desiring to engage in the cattle raising industry.

The committee finally suggested that the head of each repatriated family having at least five dependents be given 3,500.00 pesos for the purpose of building a home, sufficient agricultural implements for farming, two cows, twenty chickens, four pigs, four mules, and economic assistance until the crops should prove self sustaining. The project is presumably to be financed by the Banco Nacional de Crédito Ejidal and the money to be refunded by the repatriates as soon as they are able to do so. The plan as drawn up by the committee has been submitted to the Chief of Agricultural Colonization in Mexico City and instructions from that point are being awaited before further action is taken in the premises.

Governor's Report on Available Land

Governor Talamantes of this State, in submitting a reply to the presidential message, laid more stress on the necessity for enlarging existing
ejidal districts and the employment of repatriates, skilled in various
types of labor, on construction projects rather than their settlement
in new communities which might be formed on private lands.

The Governor suggested that Irrigation District No. 5, situated near
Bachimba, Chihuahua, where construction has been suspended, could be
enlarged by 10,000 hectares so that the ejidal community now existing there
could be increased by a thousand families. He also proposed the immediate
construction of the "Las Lajas" dam, recently under consideration, in the
Municipality of Villa Ahumada whereby a large zone of first quality land
could be irrigated to provide for a large number of colonists. The extension
of the Laguna de Casas Grandes and also of the system at la Boquilla de
Plazuela in the Municipality of Buenaventura would, along with the foregoing improvements and additions, provide sufficient territory for the settlement of agriculturally inclined repatriates in the opinion of the Governor.

In reference to construction work in Chihuahua the Governor reported
that skilled highway laborers could be easily placed on the central highway
from Ciudad Juárez to Chihuahua City where construction and oiling of
the road is now only awaiting a federal appropriation of 3,500,000 pesos.
He further stated that work on the completion of the Kansas City, Mexico,
and Orient railroad (to the Pacific Ocean), which has long been held in
abeyance, could absorb a large number of railroad and construction
workmen, who could thus be assimilated into the community gradually.

Some of the ejidal groups in the Municipality of Galeana, the
Governor also reported, have volunteered to accommodate a small
number of repatriates in their communities to fill vacancies left by
unsuccessful settlers. This proposal, it appears, has the approval of
the local authorities since it would mean settling the repatriates into
organized zones where it is hoped they will be more easily assimilated
at less expense to the government.

Activities of Banco Nacional de Crédito Ejidal

The Banco Nacional de Crédito Ejidal in a preliminary report to the
President on the ability of existing ejidal zones to fill vacancies with
repatriated Mexican families, reported that the State of Chihuahua could

immediately accommodate thirty families throughout the area. That this plan is moving forward is evidenced by the activities of the local Agrarian Department in ordering a revision of the census in the communities involved to facilitate the inclusion of new arrivals.

A telegram to the local agency of the Banco Nacional de Crédito Ejidal on May 1, 1939, from the headquarters in Mexico City indicated that the matter of the colonization of repatriates is urgent since it called upon the chiefs of the several ejidal communities concerned to report within three days the number of families that each could accommodate and name the various railroad stations most conveniently situated near their communities. However, the plan for repatriation in Chihuahua apparently is not limited entirely to settlement in existing ejidal zones since the local Secretary of the Departamento de Agricultura y Fomento accompanied by an agrarian engineer and a veterinarian departed from this place on May 1, 1939, to study the lands of the Santa Clara, Ojo de Federico and Babicora areas with a view toward ascertaining the number of repatriate families which could be settled in those sections immediately.

Active Immigration

Although no immigration of repatriates into Chihuahua has yet been reported, as mentioned above, the movement may begin in the very near future. The Mexican Consul at El Paso, who has been studying the economic conditions of Mexican families in that area, has reported to the American newspapers that between seven and eight hundred Mexican families in El Paso are now only awaiting instructions from the Mexican Government before proceeding to the designated locations within Mexico, and that another two thousand families in the area immediately surrounding El Paso desire to return to Mexico as soon as possible.

CONFIDENTIAL
Sources of Information.
Personal observation and deduction unless otherwise stated.

File No. 855
RKP/
In quintuplicate to the Department.
Copy to the Embassy.
Copy to the Consulate General.

Colonization Application. Comisión Nacional de Irrigación, 4 September 1930.
Source: Mexico City, Archivo de la Secretaría de Relaciones Exteriores, IV–354–40.

NATIONAL IRRIGATION COMMISSION

QUESTIONNAIRE TO BE COMPLETED BY THOSE WHO DESIRE TO BE ADMITTED AS SETTLERS IN THE NATIONAL IRRIGATION SYSTEMS

The National Irrigation Commission requires information concerning persons attempting to acquire irrigated plots of land within the National Irrigation Systems set aside for settlement. To this end, whosoever desires to be admitted is to complete the following questionnaire and mail it to this address:

NATIONAL IRRIGATION COMMISSION
Department of Irrigation Systems
Calle de Balderas No. 94
México, D. F.

The sending of this questionnaire confers no right whatsoever to the sender, and the Commission accepts it solely as an indication that the sender desires to be admitted into the National Irrigation Systems.

1. Name_____
(complete name)

2. Place and date of birth _____

3. Address_____

4. Married or single _____

5. Number of dependents _____

6. Number of Children_____

7. Number of male Children_____

8. Number of working age_____

9. Physical condition of family members_____
(indicate invalids or chronically ill)

10. Are you able to read and write? _____

11. What other instruction have you received? _____

12. How much cash do you have?_____
(Mexican currency)

13. List your farm equipment, machinery, and vehicles:_____

14. Current value_____
(Mexican currency)

15. Other goods and value_____

16. Occupation _____
(indicate previous and current jobs)

17. Annual income _____
(Mexican currency)

18. Types of farming with which you have experience_____

19. Where have you done farmwork? _____

20. What types of farming would you engage in and what plan of work would you follow if accepted as a settler? _____
(give full details regarding: work you would carry out, distribution of money and equipment, number of farmworkers you intend to employ, etc., etc.)

21. Irrigation System in which you desire a plot _____

22. Amount of land desired_____

23. Would you prefer to acquire the land by means of a simple Promise of Sale (Promesa de Venta), or would you prefer to enter into an Agricultural Tenantship and a Promise of Sale? _____

24. If you elect a tenantship, would you prefer case **a**, **b**, or **c** of Foundation 2 of Presidential Accord No. 646?_____

25. When would you be able to come to the System if you were accepted as a settler? _____

26. Would you be in favor of the organization of cooperatives, and would you want to take part in them? _____

27. List references regarding your farming skills_____

     name _____ address _____

     name _____ address _____

     name _____ address _____

28. Indicate in detail places and periods of residence during the last 25 years, and the reasons which forced or induced you to change residence in each case_____

     Place and date of completion_____

     Signature _____

NOTE: The information submitted herein by the applicant will serve as a means for the National Irrigation Commission to judge the level of education, agricultural status, social status, and financial capability, so as to determine whether the applicant is capable of cultivating the area applied for, or, if not, to diminish the area of the plot that might be awarded.

Repatriate Juan Rodríguez and his family in Long Beach, California, c. 1936. Courtesy Raymond Rodríguez.

Adjustment
Agringados

Ya llegaron los Norteños   *The Northerners have arrived*
Del punto de la Fronteria   *From the border*
Todos vienen presumiendo   *All come bragging about*
Que son la chucha cuerera   *How rich they are*
Porque ahora traen pantalón   *Just because they wear pants*
Ya se creen que son catrines   *They think they are dandies*

—Los Norteños   —The Northerners

An experience common to all immigrants is the challenge of adjusting to the demands imposed upon them by their new environment. It can often be a devastating experience. This is particularly true when people are forced to emigrate by circumstances beyond their control. For the million or more Mexicans who were repatriated or deported during the Great Depression, readjustment became a unique double-edged experience. Parents and children had faced the difficult task of adapting to a life plagued by discrimination in the United States. Then, as a result of being summarily expelled, they faced this problem anew when they returned "home" to Mexico. Their situation was aggravated by the fact that there were several diverse groups involved in adjusting to life in a stratified and authoritarian Mexican society. There were the adults who had been born in Mexico, but had left the country as young men or women and lived a major portion of their adult lives in the United States. Lengths of stay ranging from five to thirty years were not uncommon. Many had left Mexico to escape the horrors of the Revolution or in quest of jobs during the World War I era. Occasional brief visits home, often as the result of a parental death, were the only real contacts with the mother country. Steady jobs, marriage, a family, and material conveniences all had a seductive effect.

Imperceptibly, Mexican immigrants had changed during their sojourn in the United States, and a form of estrangement had quietly occurred. Although they enthusiastically celebrated *Las Fiestas Patrias* (Patriotic Celebrations), and mariachi music and Mexican food were thoroughly enjoyed, a new dimension had been added: they had become *agringados* (Americanized) in many ways. Their mode of life, including style of dress, speech, and manners, assumed an American flavor. Tex-Mex and Caló, a mixture of Spanish and English, were fused into new speech patterns. No aspect of life escaped the dominant American influence. Sunday comics, Hollywood movies, popular radio programs, and daily soap operas left their indelible mark. Is it any wonder that even adult repatriates often felt as if they were returning to a foreign country?

Mexican women underwent their own particular transformation and did not escape the effects of their American experience. Movies, fashion magazines, and their American sisters served as role models to be envied and imitated. Greater personal freedom became a key aspect of their enfranchisement. Without the consent of fathers and husbands, some women worked outside the home. "My wife does not want to stay home and take care of the baby," a confused husband complained. "She learned how to make money in a beauty parlor and now she wants to start a beauty parlor and make money."[1] Husbands, along with parents, brothers, and mothers-in-law, looked askance at the changes taking place. They were sure that women in America had entirely too much freedom. Many conservative Mexican women were certain that a woman's place was in the home. But even in the home, the acculturation process was accelerated by hot and cold running water, indoor plumbing, gas stoves, electricity, and the popular sewing machine. The advent of sheer stockings, bobbed hair, lipstick, nail polish, and cosmetics reinforced the transformation process. Returning to Mexico and a more conservative lifestyle posed many problems for women who had become accustomed to American ways.[2]

Also faced with the difficult task of adjusting to life in Mexico were the children of the repatriates. Children who had been born in the United

States, or had arrived at a very young age, were often the impetus or catalyst in hastening the adoption of "American ways." One Mexican mother deplored American influence and its impact on her daughter: "She is getting American ways; she will not wear the earrings that hang on her ears. They are not the same kind that the American girls wear in their ears. Oh! Our children get so different here."[3] Primary among these changes was the preference for speaking English. Like many other young repatriates, Carmen Martínez "spoke very little Spanish in the United States and learned to read and write Spanish in Mexico."[4] Spanish-speaking parents often viewed the use of English as an affront to them and as a means of showing disdain for the mother tongue. Parents with a very limited command of English feared that their offspring might actually be talking about them.

As one youngster sagely remarked when questioned about her ancestral background: "I'm an American with a dash of Mexican heritage!" That insightful comment succinctly summarizes how most children of Mexican immigrants felt about themselves, their lifestyle, and the United States. They viewed themselves as first-generation Americans. To them, their ancestry, like the color of their eyes or hair, was simply due to the accident of birth. Their heroes and idols were American sports heroes and Hollywood stars, who caught their imagination and fired their dreams.[5]

The average Mexican family returning to Mexico consisted of five persons. In most instances, three of them were children. However, there were larger families. Gregorio Rosales, for example, was accompanied by his wife Juana Carmona and their nine children: Elias 17, Cesarea, 15, Francisca 13, Genaro 10, Catalina 8, Antonio 6, Margarita 4, Esperanza 2, and Ricardo 4 months. All the children were born in the United States except for Elias who had been born in Mexico but had spent most of her life in the U.S. It was a long arduous trip for the Rosales family who were residents of Etna, Pennsylvania. They left on the Baltimore & Ohio Railroad, passed through Laredo, Texas to their final destination in Tarimoro, Guanajuato.[6] Repatriation created a new and distinct group of "reluctant emigrants." For the children born in the United States, the Mexico they were "returning to" was a foreign country.[7] While it was the land of their parents and ancestors, it was not their home. From their perspective, they might as well have been banished to Mars. Upon reaching the border, traumatic scenes often occurred as children, especially teenagers, made a final desperate effort to avoid the inevitable. There was the sudden, chilling realization that once the *línea* (international boundary) was crossed, it was all over, and there was no turning back. Many older children balked and refused to go any farther. Among those who agreed to accompany their parents, foreboding and disaffection increased as the trip south continued. Travel conditions, transportation, accommodations, and food left a lot to be desired.

The situation rarely improved when repatriates reached their final destination. "There are thousands," the newspaper *Porvenir* observed who were "in misery, dirty, hungry, and sick."[8] In Mexico City, *El Universal* reported that another group arrived at the capital starving, unclothed, and sick.[9] Squalid and crowded living conditions, prolonged unemployment, and cultural adjustment were some of the many problems encountered by those who were forced to return.

For many, the disenchantment became more aggravated and protests grew more vitriolic after settling in their new environment. Adjusting to a different lifestyle entailed changes that were never imagined during family discussions or arguments about life in Mexico. Things certainly were not what the repatriates had expected. Some parents began to quietly share their children's doubts and misgivings. Disillusionment prompted alienated individuals to seek ways of returning to the United States. For the young, as well as for many of their elders, Mexico simply was not, nor would it ever be, home. One young repatriate spoke for many of his contemporaries when he observed that "no matter how long I stay here, I can never be a Mexican. I just can't get used to calling this place home. Honest, I just can't tell you how much I want to go back to the United States."[10]

Even individuals born in Mexico found their villages and *pueblitos* very different from how they remembered them when they had migrated north many years before. Most startling was how different living conditions were from what they had become accustomed to in the United States. Contrary to popular belief, most Mexican emigrants became city dwellers, and the harsh countryside life no longer appealed to them. Rural areas lacked many of the material and social amenities they had long taken for granted. For those who had been away a long time, relatives and old friends were like strangers. Differences between local residents and the *recién llegados* (newcomers) led to discord. Repatriates everywhere experienced similar disappointments and frustrations.[11] To their dismay, official promises turned out to be empty bureaucratic gestures.

In spite of the government's official position of welcoming the repatriates back to la madre patria, resentment against them manifested itself in subtle and covert ways. Repatriates resented being treated as social lepers and considered the nation and its people to be sheer ingrates. In years past, while gainfully employed in the United States, they had generously remitted millions of dollars to families and relatives in Mexico. Their hard-earned dollars had helped to fuel the economy, making it possible for many potential immigrants to remain behind. Now the repatriates' pleas for help were being ignored. Aggrieved by their plight, the *Excélsior* newspaper in Mexico City recommended that the repatriates organize themselves and present their case and complaints to the Secretaría de Gobernacíon.[12]

Not all returnees required governmental assistance; a surprising number brought substantial savings with them. The work-and-save ethic was well embedded in the national character. One prominent Los Angeles banker, Mr. K. Hingson, revealed that Mexicans that departed from the western United States during 1931 had withdrawn more than seven million dollars from local banks. He also declared that "the Mexican worker is intelligent, readily accepts the American standard of living and believes in saving his money either to acquire property in this country or to enable him to return to Mexico in this time of crisis." A copy of the article containing Hingson's remarks was sent to *El Universal* in Mexico City by United Press. According to the article, the repatriates had taken with them a total of twenty million dollars in actual cash or personal property.[13] The sum total of the wealth accumulated by the repatriates probably amounted to twice as much as the twenty-million-dollar estimate. Many Mexicans had a very low opinion of banks, were suspicious of their motives, and did not trust them. Given the bank failures of the period, their fears appear to have been well founded. The fact that many Mexicans were migrant farm laborers or mobile railroad workers, and without a stable home base, meant that customary banking practices were out of the question.

Not only did some repatriates have money in their pockets, which buoyed their self-esteem; all of them had something even more important: their self-respect. Although forced to return by circumstances beyond their control, these proud people were not returning home *con el sombrero en la mano* (with hat in hand). They were ready to lend their muscle, skill, and knowledge to enrich la madre patria. As potential benefactors, they expected to be treated with respect. Once back among friends and relatives, they hoped to start life anew. The discrimination, pain, and anguish they had endured abroad would be left behind and forgotten. However, the unending influx of newcomers placed a burden on local resources, and the warm welcome that greeted the initial arrivals soon turned to grumbling and scorn. Feelings of disaffection began to surface. Repatriates, as well as local residents, began to feel aggrieved and put-upon as the novelty of returning home wore off. The noticeable differences began to grind upon and annoy everyone. It was a clash of two dissimilar cultures.[14]

There was certainly ample reason for the pervasive feelings of betrayal and dissatisfaction rampant among recent arrivals. One of the most discomfiting aspects was living space, which was at a premium. For those forced to live with relatives temporarily, the small homes were not capable of accommodating two families. Ten or more people were often forced to share one or two rooms. Bedrolls and mats replaced beds. To make matters worse, many repatriates arrived without pillows and mattresses since these items were often confiscated at the border. A woman who had been repatriated as a teenage girl recalled years later, "We just had a bedroom for all of us [the entire family]. But it was practically summer so that didn't bother us too much. 'Cause we could sleep outdoors, you know. 'Cause we couldn't fit all of us in that bedroom."[15] Another repatriate, who was then a young girl, recalled that they lived with relatives and getting along was very difficult. She wistfully remarked that in California, even if you were poor, you had a place to sleep and more to eat. Her family later moved to an isolated ranch with only six inhabitants and no stores or any amenities. The isolation was depressing but her greatest fear was "rats that would crawl on me and bite me."[16] In her mind, even as a grown woman, she equated her repatriation experience with terrible suffering.

In this respect, the experience of both girls mirrored those of their contemporaries. Repatriation and suffering seemed to go hand in hand. Try as they might, many of the newcomers simply did not fit in. It was the classic case of the square peg in a round hole. Inadvertently, remarks and observations would be made comparing living conditions in the United States and Mexico. In the United States, the presence of material amenities had made poverty somewhat easier to bear. In the rural areas and small towns or villages where many of the repatriates settled, utilities such as running water, electricity, natural gas, and indoor plumbing were usually nonexistent. Harmless comments about the lack of facilities were often misunderstood or misconstrued, even when there was no desire or intent to offend.

Native Mexicans who had never been to El Norte were quick to take offense or umbrage at any real or imagined slight. Relationships often became strained. Derogatory barbs and negative aspersions were traded and sometimes resulted in violent confrontations.[17]

Wives forced to live under the watchful eye of critical and distrustful mothers-in-law found their lives transformed into a siege of quiet desperation. Their fate was to suffer in silence, which constituted the worst kind of penance. Daughters-in-law with "American ways" were considered as being too independent and strong willed. In rural areas, they were viewed as free thinkers by women accustomed to more traditional and cloistered ways. Their behavior was considered brazen and unbecoming to decent women. It was difficult to accept women openly chatting and joking with men as if they were equals. A shaking of heads and clucking of tongues greeted such unorthodox conduct. Some of the criticism and faultfinding was undoubtedly due to envy tinged with jealousy. American hairstyles, mode of dress, use of makeup, and personal deportment were aspects that contributed to resentment and ill feelings. Preparation of meals was also a cause of friction or open conflict between mothers and daughters-in-law.

Although adjusting to their new environment was difficult for adults, it was the older children who bore the brunt of the Mexicanization process. Children can be very cruel, and *pochos* (American-born children) were often teased and ridiculed unmercifully about their status. They were not allowed to forget that they had been rejected—kicked out—by the land of their birth, and were actually kids without a homeland. Children hampered by a lack of fluency in Spanish were jeered at because of their Tex-Mex or Caló jargon, a mixture of Spanish and English. Many repatriated teenagers often lapsed into English. "We never stopped speaking English" Josefina Pérez confessed proudly. "Everyone knew my sister and I were Americans because we started every sentence with "you know, you know."[18] Many American children avoided speaking Spanish because they did not know the proper words or phrases to use and did not want to be embarrassed by making childish or foolish mistakes. Native-born children accused the pochos of putting on airs and acting as if they were better than local Mexicans. Ironically, in the United States, Mexican American children were always referred to as Mexicans, but in Mexico they were commonly called *gringos, yanquis,* or worse. Fernando Pérez recalled being referred to as "el guero" by the other children because he had a very fair complexion.

The "American kids," of course, retaliated and took a devilish delight in vexing their tormentors. One of their favorite techniques was to converse among themselves in fluent English. Another effective ploy was boasting about their lifestyle in the United States, often unhindered by the truth. Pochos also needled their antagonists by deriding Mexico's backwardness and its extremely low level of material development. Trading insults often led to trading blows. Each side got in its licks and gave as good as it got.[19]

For many children, schooling posed a particularly embarrassing problem, and often proved to be their most disheartening experience. Most youngsters, with the exception of some itinerant migrant children, had attended school while in the United States. To their dismay, attending school in Mexico was not a right or privilege to be taken for granted. Many isolated ranches and small villages did not have schools. This was a shock to many of the children. María Ofelia Acosta, José López, and other repatriates lamented the fact that education, which they had always taken for granted in the United States, was over for them and their brothers and sisters after they arrived in Mexico. In many instances, not only education but their childhood also ended abruptly. Due to the harsh economic times, there was no choice but to go to work at a very young age or starve to death. Hortensia Nieto recalled that her grandmother would get her up at four in the morning so she could do her household chores before going to work in the fields. Her father or grandmother showed up every payday and collected her wages. On one occasion, a payday, her coworkers, also young girls, decided to splurge and go to the village store and buy sodas. They invited Hortensia to go with them. Since she did not have any money, she charged the soda. When her grandmother learned of her willful and extravagant transgression, Hortensia was severely punished.[20]

For Ignacio Piña who was penniless and homeless when he arrived at his family's ancestral village, there was no alternative but to go to work. From sunrise to sunset, he worked at various jobs including herding livestock, carrying baskets and packages, shining shoes, or doing whatever was available. The only thing he did not do was beg! However, he recalled that at one time he was reduced to eating "animal feed" in order to survive. On another occasion, Piña was forced to steal produce so that he and his brother could quell their hunger pains.[21]

Repatriates did whatever was necessary in order to survive, including engaging in unlawful practices. Along the border, smuggling contraband was a common occurrence. For example, Albino Piñeda revealed that between Nogales, Arizona and Nogales, Sonora, items were concealed by putting "them in our socks and in our waists while wearing a coat."[22] Silk items were in great demand, and women often donned underwear, dresses, and other apparel and simply walked across the border. Such illegal activity allowed Piñeda's family and other destitute repatriates to survive, but he decided to give it up after he and one of his chums were caught. Fortunately, since they were only children, they were released and not charged with a crime.

Children who were fortunate enough to attend school often had to walk several miles along dusty, unpaved roads. Rubén Jiménez of Mexicali resented having to walk what seemed endless miles to school.[23] Destitute parents found they could not afford the enrollment fees, nor could they pay for books and other materials.[24] Children fortunate enough to attend school encountered a series of embarrassing ordeals. One was the matter of grade placement, a primary concern of youngsters everywhere. It was rather embarrassing for older students to be placed in a lower grade simply because they were deficient in Spanish. While most of them spoke Spanish in varying degrees of proficiency, few of them could read or write as fluently as their native counterparts. A few parents were able to hire tutors to help their children become fluent in all phases of Spanish.[25] School discipline proved to be another sore point in more ways than one. Discipline was more akin to that of the famed Hoosier schoolmaster than the relaxed atmosphere to which most children were accustomed in American schools. Without meaning to, due to cultural differences they often ran afoul of strict regulations. Violations were swiftly and heavy-handedly punished. Sparing the rod and spoiling the child was not a charge that could be levied against Mexican schools.

The easy manner and casual lifestyle to which the American-bred children were accustomed also got them in trouble outside of school. Native peers and elders often considered them to be rude and ill mannered. They had no training or upbringing; *no estaban bien educados* was the general conclusion. Teenage boys and girls raised in the United States were accustomed to greater personal freedom. In many rural towns and isolated villages where the old customs and social mores still prevailed, their conduct was considered shocking. Nonetheless, teenagers clung to their American ways as long as they could. But gradually they began to adopt local styles and customs, and their use of English grew less and less frequent.[26] Fortunately, children seem to be

endowed with a resiliency not possessed by adults. They have an inner buoy-
ancy that allows them to adapt to whatever situation they find themselves in.
Being natural survivors, in due course of time, a truce or *modus vivendi* was
worked out with their peers. Young people had a natural interest and curiosity about each other. Informal family gatherings and social occasions provided an opportunity to become better acquainted. Local fiestas and dances
provided opportunities for positive interaction. There was a grudging tinge of
pride in having cousins or relatives *del otro lado* (from the United States). At
parties and dances, a certain fleeting notoriety could be attained by chatting
or dancing with "los americanos" or "las norteñas."[27]

While most children would have preferred to remain in the United
States, some, like Enrique Vega, viewed the entire episode as "a new adventure." Unlike his sisters, who had lived in Mexico and did not want to go
back, Enrique was anxious to "return." When the eventful day arrived, ten
family members piled into the family car and began the ten-day journey to
Zacatecas. The family also owned a truck, which carried all their personal
belongings. Portions of the highway, Enrique recalled, were mere trails. The
area was barren wasteland, and there were no provisions or water available.
Somehow they managed to keep going, although the trip was "really rough
and hard." In Zacatecas, Enrique's father bought a ranch with money that
he had saved, and the family settled down to a life of farming and cattle
ranching. Enrique Vega enjoyed riding horseback and roping, and did not
recall suffering any great hardships. "In my case the change was not drastic. I never regretted going back," he asserted. Having their own ranch made
life easier for the Vega family. Initially, at least, Enrique Vega felt that "we
were home among our own people."[28]

In many cases, such euphoric sentiments were dispelled by reality and
the passage of time. Slowly but steadily, a growing number of repatriates
began to realize that Mexico, beloved in song and memory, was not what
they had envisioned, hoped for, or expected. Several factors contributed
to the demise of the hopes and expectations that had buoyed their spirits
and made the repatriation ordeal more bearable. Many arrived in ill health
and were easy prey for diseases. Malnutrition, a poor monotonous diet,
and unsanitary, crowded living conditions contributed to prolonged illnesses. Unaccustomed to the food and water, many became victims of
diarrhea, dysentery, fever, and black vomit. Those who went to the subtropical areas encountered malaria and yellow fever. The quinine needed

to combat the malady was often not available, in which case cheap rum was used as a substitute. Homemade remedies often proved futile and, in some cases, actually aggravated the patient's condition. Deaths among babies and the aged who could not develop a strong immunity to local plagues were a common occurrence.[29]

Arturo Herrada contacted smallpox in Mexico as a four-year-old child and "remembered there are no doctors, no hospitals." His only treatment was being placed in "the corner of his grandmother's one room hut to await death and others stayed away from you. If you survived, you were lucky because ninety percent of the children died." Arturo, his brother, and two sisters lived with their grandmother. Their father had returned to Detroit to find work so he could support the family in Mexico. As a young child, Arturo wondered "why he was there . . . and why he was sick and where his dad and mom were?"[30]

The death toll among repatriates led to severe criticism of the United States in the Mexican press. "All was not gold that glittered," harped an article in the *Excélsior*. The newspaper bemoaned the fact that Mexicans were returning from the "promised land" with their pockets empty and their stomachs sticking to their ribs. The scathing article accused the U.S. of lacking any moral character, which, it stated, cannot be purchased with dollars but constitutes the real wealth of a country.[31] Even more vocal in its denouncement was the *Ideal Liberal* of Cananea, Sonora, a newspaper with a definite socialist orientation. It stridently condemned the heartless action of the United States against Mexican Nationals. An editorial charged that the cruel mistreatment was tantamount to a vendetta which callously ignored basic human rights.[32]

Such outcries and condemnations were to be expected and even justified if the dire situation in which many of the repatriates found themselves were taken into consideration. Mexican authorities estimated that at least 25 percent of the returnees arrived home penniless.[33] In cities such as Monterrey and other dispersion centers, repatriates often arrived on the verge of starvation. The sorrowful sight prompted the ladies' auxiliaries to pool their resources in order to provide free food to the penniless mendicants. For a time, the ladies in Monterrey even provided railroad fares to the final destination. However, their financial resources were limited and were soon depleted as thousands of needy repatriates inundated the city. In desperation, the ladies' auxiliary was forced to call upon the governor of the state, Francisco A. Cárdenas, for help in furnishing transportation to the destitute horde. Sensing the urgency of the situation, Governor Cárdenas contacted the Secretaría de Gobernacíon, and within fifteen minutes authorization was given to provide rail passage for all who needed it.[34] Other beleaguered cities followed Monterrey's lead and took similar action.

In some instances, communities attempted to prevent the human jetsam from invading their city. Such action was taken in an attempt to prevent the repatriates from becoming a local burden. Mexico City and other towns established soup kitchens, and meals were provided to the hungry repatriates for ten centavos (three cents). In an attempt to mitigate the situation, the federal government tried to discourage the new arrivals from settling in the cities. It encouraged them to return to their villages and ranchitos by paying their fare to their destination. However, many repatriates felt that their skills could best be utilized in commercial or industrial centers, rather than in small villages or rural areas.

This was especially true of tradesmen and craftsmen who needed to ply their trade in well-populated areas. Shoemakers, tailors, plumbers, barbers, and store owners naturally gravitated toward the larger cities where their services, hopefully, would be in greater demand. Many entrepreneurs also preferred to settle in larger towns or cities because they offered some immunity against the resentment felt by local merchants and tradesmen. Local businessmen feared that better equipment and advanced techniques possessed by the repatriates would adversely affect their economic survival. Repatriates with money, tools, equipment, and a car or truck usually eschewed grubbing out a living in some small village where payment for their services might be made through the barter system. They had become accustomed to a monetary economy. To them, a dollar was a dollar, even if it took three and a half pesos to equal one dollar.

In the countryside, there was widespread opposition to the government's encouragement of repatriates to settle in rural areas. Ejido leaders complained about the lack of land and felt threatened by the presence of the newcomers. Most rural communities simply did not feel that they could support an expanded population. A repatriate from Idaho who had returned to Penjamo, Guanajuato remarked, "I can't understand how many of these people live here. There's no industry, nothing but agriculture. And that's no good—no irrigation, just raising corn once a year."[35] Rural politicians were also concerned about large concentrations of repatriates. They feared it could bode ill for the political future of the area, and the ruling clique in particular. The Governor of Sinaloa regarded the repatriates as such a threat that he placed guards at the Rio Colorado with instructions to stop their entry into the state. Reacting to pressure from the federal government, he rescinded the action.[36] Accustomed to American ways, some government officials feared that the returnees might find it difficult to work quietly in the traces and accept the established order. Their numbers and special interests could cause severe problems. Therefore, many political leaders felt it was best to disperse the repatriates to virgin frontier settlements. This could be done under the patriotic guise that their skills and expertise were needed to develop remote parts of the country. The lure of "pan y tierra" (bread and land) induced desperate repatriates to answer the nation's call.

Mexican government officials readily embraced the plan of relocating repatriates in remote areas. The government worried about the growing tide of discontent and disenchantment. It felt threatened by the social ideas and democratic beliefs that the repatriates were bringing with them. Aware of the criticism levied against it for its failure to deal effectively with the plight of the repatriates, the government looked for ways to defuse or counteract their influence. In a primary reader, *Vida Rural*, children in rural schools were instructed on how to react to and treat the repatriates in their midst.[37] At one point, the Office of Education seriously considered instituting a curriculum that new residents would be required to complete. It would emphasize Mexican culture, history, language, and geography. The intent was to make "good Mexicanos" of the newcomers by indoctrinating them with the socialist goals and objectives of the 1910 Revolution.

The newly returned children would receive an indoctrination into the social and political life of the new, emerging Mexico. This was deemed absolutely essential for successful assimilation. There were even occasions when authorities requested that children deny their American citizenship upon entering Mexico. María Ofelia Acosta's mother refused to comply. She had insisted that her children "will be adults someday and can decide then what they will be."[38] Officials were fearful that the rumblings of discontent might spread among the native population.

Among male repatriates, the lack of jobs was the major cause of disgruntlement and resentment. Unable to find gainful employment, repatriates were forced to live on their savings until the funds ran out. Organized labor, through the Junta Federal de Conciliacíon y Arbitraje, voiced its opposition to employing the repatriados. Many local workers had managed to retain their jobs only by agreeing to a reduction of eight to sixteen hours per week. Their wages, correspondingly, had been reduced by five to twenty pesos a week.[39] Under such circumstances, they were in no mood to be generous or hospitable to potential rivals. Hostility was also bred by the widely held view that those who had gone north to earn big money were now returning to take the bread out of the mouths of those who had stayed behind. If it had not been for *la crisis*, the ingrates would never have come home.

As the situation grew worse, many newspapers joined the chorus of criticism. Newspaper editorials lamented the intrusion of the repatriates into the labor market. Mexican authorities estimated that at least 89,960 workers were unemployed. The hardest-hit states included México, D.F. with 13,995, Zacatecas with 10,743, and Jalisco with 6,930.[40] With a teeming pool of unemployed residents, there was no need to add another layer of idle workers. Given the economic situation, the unemployment figures appear to be unrealistic. However, it should be borne in mind that 90 percent of the population tilled the land or lived in rural, isolated hamlets not included in the official count. One editorial sagely observed that the influx of such great numbers of people would have been difficult even during normal times. It was even more so now, due to the economic crisis gripping Mexico. Although the editorial praised the government's valiant efforts in offering repatriates assistance in a sincere and energetic manner, the newspaper lamented the great cost that had to be borne by the national treasury. In spite of its misgivings, the newspaper supported providing the repatriates with jobs in order to reduce the possibility that they might become a disruptive influence. It pointed out that those who had emigrated to the United States and were now returning constituted the most energetic and enterprising members of the community. Therefore, the editorial concluded, the initial cost should be viewed as an investment in assuring the future agricultural and industrial growth of the nation.[41] All Mexicans did not share the newspaper's viewpoint. Seemingly, both the nation and the repatriates were having difficulty in coping with the problems of readjustment.

Another newspaper cited the statement made by the Secretaría de Gobernacíon, Manuel C. Téllez. He assured the media that there would be work available for the repatriates. The Secretary had met with the state governors and elicited their help and support for the government's program to assist destitute returnees. The Secretary suggested forming an advisory board comprised of repatriates who had returned and adjusted successfully. Their role would be to advise on the best and most effective manner of dealing with the assimilation of their fellow compatriots. Consideration would be given to the trades or skills that they had acquired while living abroad.[42] The theme of taking advantage of the expertise acquired by Nationals in the United States recurred repeatedly in government releases and newspaper articles. However, a few objective writers pointed out that most of the work performed by the returning compatriots had been of a very menial nature. Most were day laborers rather than skilled artisans. Their "expertise" was decidedly limited, as the critics noted.

Some writers suspected that the government was simply using the patriotic rhetoric to make the return, transition, and assimilation as easy as possible for the disheartened repatriates. Tossed from pillar to post in the United States, many repatriates had expected that once in Mexico, jobs, land, and a better life awaited them. Promises—real, imagined, or implied—were wisps of hope grasped at by the repatriates. Cast adrift by a cruel and fickle fate, they desperately needed something to believe in. As they had done so often while in the United States, various groups and individuals sent letters and petitions to the Secretarías, the federal departments, begging for help. Ultimately, some appealed to the president of the republic imploring his benign intercession. By and large, official replies tended to be sympathetic, but actual results left a great deal to be desired. That was certainly the case regarding gainful employment.

The government had envisioned establishing a vast public works program to develop and improve the infrastructure. The building of all weather roads, railroads, dams, and irrigation canals was seen as the cornerstone of the "make-work" projects. To a degree, they would be patterned after the WPA projects launched in the United States. Aware of such projects, repatriates pleaded for employment in the proposed public work programs. Like her prodigal sons and daughters, Mexico desperately needed to find its place in the economic sun. By working together, both the nation and the returnees had the potential to achieve their respective yet mutual goals. The costs incurred by the projected developments would be amply repaid in future years by the substantial economic growth that would subsequently result.[43] However, in spite of the inherent potential, the dream failed to materialize. This was not due to lack of moral commitment or resolve. The painful truth was that the federal government, no matter how well intentioned or noble in its endeavors, simply did not have the money required to provide funding for the proposed projects.

A few work projects were begun, but hiring preference was usually given to local residents who were out of work. Among the repatriates, only experienced craftsmen or those possessing a skill not readily available were hired. Ironically, because they were repeatedly subjected to discrimination in hiring in the United States, the repatriates had not expected to receive the same kind of treatment at home. In an attempt to counteract the worst aspects of the situation confronting them, the repatriates formed the "Union of Mexican Repatriates." Led by Secretary General Manuel Olmos, the union was headquartered in Mexico City. Its first order of business was to call upon all labor organizations to demand the immediate cessation of repatriation. The basis and justification for the demand was that the economic problems posed by those already repatriated had not yet been resolved.[44] It did not make any sense to continue to augment or aggravate the situation. Union leaders asked, why allow the United States to indiscriminately and summarily continue to repatriate people simply to relieve its own unemployment problem?

The Union of Mexican Repatriates severely criticized the efforts of the then-active National Repatriation Committee. It charged that the committee was taking too long to raise its avowed goal of 500,000 pesos and was not responding to the needs of the repatriates.[45] The failure of the Repatriation Committee to act in a timely and effective manner was a major reason why the repatriates' union had been formed. In actuality, ill feelings generated by the growing number of repatriates was a prime factor preventing the committee from raising the 500,000 pesos necessary to help needy compatriots. In an attempt to raise the badly needed funds, it was suggested that a surcharge or excise tax of five centavos be levied on the price of each ticket sold by theaters, bullfights, and other entertainment events. The money would be earmarked specifically for the benefit of the repatriates.[46] Fierce vocal opposition forced the idea to die aborning. The general public resented taxing themselves to help ingrates who had chosen to enrich *los yanquis* rather than their own country. Many local residents experienced a covert feeling of satisfaction in seeing *vende patrias* (sellouts) get their comeuppance or just desserts.

Due to the widespread opposition, the efforts of the repatriates' organization came to naught. The union found it impossible to coordinate the diverse needs and interests of the different groups. Immediate survival became the paramount issue, and few repatriates had time to join or participate in an organization that did not deliver concrete solutions. The continued arrival of new repatriates compounded existing problems. The enormous horde of refugees inundated communities in the northern states and in the central plateau. As more people returned to their place of origin, resettlement grew more difficult. Unable to cope, areas that had formerly welcomed the *repatriados* now shunned them.[47] By the end of 1932, the prime irrigated land available to the government for colonization purposes had been virtually exhausted. All that remained to be parceled out was marginal or temporal land fit only for grazing animals or precarious dry farming.[48] The contentious situation fed the festering undercurrent of resentment and ill will.

It was not difficult to find reasons for real or imagined grievances against the repatriates. In the slower-paced Mexican society, repatriates were often viewed as being too ambitious, too assertive, and too demanding.[49] There were also charges of being *muy agringados* (Americanized) in their speech patterns and in their habits. Mexicans resented Spanish words being Anglicized by the repatriates. Native speakers accused repatriates of *hablando a lo mocho*, of shortcutting or bastardizing the language. Among young repatriates, reared in the American culture, it was a very natural way of expressing themselves. For adults, the use of such words denoted their attempt to learn basic English words. Without formal schooling, many adults had simply learned English phonetically. They pronounced English words the way they heard them. Thus, it was surprising that their limited command of English should have caused adult repatriates any problems when they returned to Mexico. Repatriate Emilia Castañeda de Valenciana remembered that "the poor people used to pick on us but the middle class people spoke English and wanted to learn more."[50] In a few instances, repatriates were hired as tutors.

Repatriated women discovered that in a male-dominated society the freedoms of movement and expression, which prevailed as a matter of course in the United States, were severely curtailed. In small towns or rural villages, their excursions outside the home were limited to going to the market and to church. Husbands whose status as the head of the household had been eroded by prolonged unemployment or the acceptance of welfare now began to reassert themselves. The oft-cited statement *en mi casa yo mando* (in my house I am the boss) assumed new vigor. In their cloistered existence, women had no need for their American-styled clothes. One Mexicana found that "many of my friends went back to Mexico only to be laughed at for wearing short dresses until they had to use them for underclothes. Now they are in rags and have no shoes."[51] In many instances, the treasured dresses and shoes were set aside and saved to be worn only on special occasions. Giving up their finery was one thing, but younger women adamantly refused to stop using cosmetics while they lasted or they could afford them. This elicited a great deal of criticism from the older, traditional, rural Mexican women. They viewed the use of lipstick, rouge, or fingernail polish with disdain. Only loose women called attention to themselves by parading around in such a fashion. Modesty and self-effacement were the hallmarks of a decent wife and mother. There was also the underlying fear that young local girls might emulate their more worldly and sophisticated sisters.

Repatriates soon learned to avoid problems by not calling attention to themselves. They may have arrived at their destination wearing American-style clothes and with a few dollars in their pocket, but within a few months, outwardly at least, they began to assume the styles and modes common to friends and relatives. Among adults, it was deemed ill mannered to stand out from the crowd. Adaptation also protected them from being looked at askance because they had lived in El Norte and had been forced to leave the United States. Men packed away their suits and wore the blue bibbed overalls or the white loose-fitting outfits worn by the poorer class. By blending in, repatriates found it easier to get along and eke out a living.

Although wages and earnings were low by American standards, a family could get by on very little. Rents, for example, were relatively cheap. In rural communities or small towns, a modest home could be rented for a couple of pesos a month. Since the houses did not have running water, indoor plumbing, electricity, or gas, there were no utility bills to pay at the end of the month. Clothing—the traditional white cotton camisa and pantalones worn by the campesinos, or the black rebozo, skirt, and blouse worn by local women—could be purchased very cheaply. Food staples were also relatively cheap. A kilo of beans could be purchased for six centavos, and *masa de maíz* (corn meal) for making tortillas cost five centavos a kilo. A liter of milk was eighteen centavos, and a dozen fresh eggs were thirty centavos. Fruit in season, depending on size and quality, was five centavos for several pieces. Three bananas could be had for five centavos. It is evident that by adroit bargaining and shrewd shopping, fifty centavos could be stretched a long way. Meat was the most expensive item. Chicken tended to be the cheapest, followed by pork and then beef, which ranged from fifty centavos to a peso per kilo.[52] Meat was a rarity and when a snake was killed, it would be cooked and eaten. According to Hortensia Nieto, the meat tasted like chicken but was slightly sweeter. Hortensia compared it to the meat of the iguana, which was often sold as chicken. Since meat was scarce, both added a welcome change to a bland diet. Out of necessity, many repatriates followed the local custom and grew much of their own food and raised animals to add to their meager food supply. Fernando Pérez recalled that on the farm purchased by his father, they had orchards and grew a variety of fruits. They also grew vegetables and sold the excess to neighbors who did not have farms. Chickens and other farm animals were common. Consequently, his family never went hungry.

The experience of Arturo Herrada was quite different and more nearly resembled that of many of his fellow repatriates. He and his brother and two sisters lived with their elderly grandmother in a one room hut. There was no room for raising more than a few scrawny chickens and a pig, which had the run of the house. At night, the pig slept in the house with the rest of the family to prevent someone from stealing him. One of Arturo's most traumatic experiences as a four-year-old occurred when the pig was slaughtered. There was blood everywhere, he recalled 74 years later and vividly remembered the pig's plaintive, human-like cries. After that horrible experience, Arturo had a terrible time eating pork.

José López recalled that his family often had nothing to eat, not even beans or tortillas. On one occasion, driven by hunger and desperation, José went to a neighbor's house and told the woman that his mother had sent him to borrow some maize so she could make tortillas. The woman took pity on him and gave him some corn. That evening, the tortillas were all they had to eat. José remembers often going to bed hungry and being unable to sleep.[53]

Very little was spent on entertainment, because commercial amusements, including movie houses, were a rarity. Actually that did not really matter because most of the children who were repatriated, recalled that they were so busy working to eke out a living that they did not have time to play games or enjoy themselves. At the end of a long, hard day's work, they were ready to collapse and go to bed. The same dull, physically taxing routine awaited them when they got up in the morning. Repatriation had deprived and robbed them of their childhood. The future appeared dark and dismal.

Compared to the United States, living in Mexico could be rather inexpensive. Therefore, repatriates who had saved some money and were able to purchase a small cantina, dry-goods store, pool hall, or similar businesses, providing them with a modest but steady income, enjoyed a comfortable living. So too did those who could turn skills acquired in the United States into an asset and open small repair shops. Men with mechanical skills were welcome in small communities that formerly had been without such services. These individuals previously may have been mere laborers or assembly-line workers, but their new-found status and affluence earned them the respected title of "Don Ramón" or "Don Juan." They became pillars of their communities, and their advice and wise counsel were sought on a variety of subjects. These individuals and their counterparts in larger towns and cities usually found it easier to make the transition and adjust to life in Mexico than did most of the indigent repatriates. Least well adjusted were their wives, who complained because there was nothing for them to do. Walking around the plaza in the evening was not their idea of entertainment or recreation. But they were loathe to voice their displeasure publicly, lest it hurt their husband's modest business. They had to comport themselves "como damas," like ladies, befitting their new situation in life. For most of the repatriates, however, affluence of any kind eluded them.

The trials and tribulations suffered by the refugees and their children were enormous and unending. Even those who sought to return and had gone back with a modest amount of money, found it impossible to adjust. Albino Piñeda recalled that when they arrived in Nogales, Sonora, they lived in a house with a cement floor. As their money dwindled, they moved to a house with a dirt floor. Eventually, they ended up living in a ravine in the poorest section of town. The shack they lived in did not even have a door. They had to nail up cardboard to cover the gaping cracks between the boards forming the walls of the house. Like many of the other repatriates they began to wonder if they had made a terrible mistake in going to Mexico after their father died.[54] Nostalgia began to play tricks upon their memory and selective recall. Individuals like Francisco Castañeda, who was about ten years old when he returned to Mexico with his family, observed: "I would have preferred to have stayed here [in the U.S.], life is better here."[55] Echoing Castañeda's feelings was Teresa Martínez Southard. When interviewed, she vividly recalled, "I used to miss the States a lot. I used to cry every night 'cause I was real lonely. But still, what could I do?"[56] The sadness and yearning she had experienced as a young girl were still evident in her soft voice forty years later. She also recalled that she did not like corn tortillas, and her father, at great sacrifice, would buy a sack of flour so she could make her own tortillas. Teresa Martínez Southard's and Francisco Castañeda's experiences were repeated a thousandfold. Tears and disenchantment proved to be the lot of many repatriates of all ages and gender. No one claimed that life in America was a bed of roses, but there was no denying that even with its alleged short-comings, the United States was truly the home or adopted homeland of many of the repatriates. This mood and the deplorable conditions in which they found themselves led to a longing to return "home" to the United States.

The reasons for desiring to return home to El Norte were as varied as the individuals who espoused them. Enrique Vega who had enjoyed coming to Mexico as a young man, decided to return to the United States in order to "raise my boys as I grew up." He specifically cited the differences in the type and quality of education available. "If I had to do it over again," he reminisced, "I would have stayed [in the U.S.]."[57] He explained that his whole family had returned to the United States, but in order to emigrate they had to obtain a sponsor and the promise of a job. It was possible, he stated, to be able to return in as few as six weeks. However, this was the exception rather than the rule. The quest to return often took years. For some, there was no return possible. Indigents who had been on welfare, or had become public charges for any reason, were not permitted to return despite promises or assurances to the contrary. The back of their departure card identified them as aid recipients, which precluded them from ever legally reentering the United States. Much to their dismay, welfare recipients who had agreed to leave "voluntarily" discovered that they had been blacklisted. Welfare officials had conveniently neglected to inform them of this critical point. Most repatriates were under the impression that they would be eligible to return to the United States as soon as economic conditions improved.

Among those sharing the expectation of being able to return was Pablo Guerrero, who, with his wife and five American-born children, had been repatriated in December of 1932. The family had settled in Mexicali, Baja California. Although many Mexican customs had been modified due to the area's proximity to the border, the children found it impossible to adapt to a new and different lifestyle. Ranging from six to fourteen years of age, the youngsters implored their parents to return to the land of their birth. Consequently, Señor Guerrero sent a letter to Los Angeles County welfare authorities.

He explained his situation and asked them to contact the Department of Labor, which had jurisdiction over the Immigration Service. Señor Guerrero wanted American officials to authorize the consul in Mexicali to issue his family immigration papers and pay the eighteen-dollar fee required for each passport.[58] His contention was that he wanted everything arranged and done legally so he would not violate any immigration laws.

In his laborious, handwritten letter, Pablo Guerrero stated that he had worked in the United States since the age of nineteen. He had even registered for the draft in Johnson, Arizona, during World War I. Like other unhappy repatriates, he cited the disparity between the educational system in the two countries and stated that he wanted his children to be educated in American schools. He complained bitterly about the fact that the Mexican government had not given him or his family any assistance. Guerrero also decried the government's lack of protection of children who, like his own, had been born in the United States. For that reason, he stipulated in Spanish, "I ask that my children and myself be allowed to return to the country in which they are entitled to live."[59] The letter, along with countless others, was received and filed by the Board of Supervisors. Apparently, the Board ignored Señor Guerrero's eloquent plea, for no action or response was recorded.

By the mid 1930s there was a growing number of disillusioned repatriates seeking to return home to the United States. Among them were Ramón Sánchez and his family. His children had found it impossible to adjust to life in San Julian, Jalisco, the family's ancestral home. Acquiescing to his children's pleas, Sánchez decided to return. However, when the family arrived at Ciudad Juárez, they were denied visas even though ten of the thirteen children were American citizens. While waiting for American consulate authorities to resolve their case, which could take months or even years, Sánchez peddled candies and cigarettes, and his sons, Librado and José, sold newspapers, shined shoes, sold rings made of bull horns to the tourists and carried parcels for American women shopping in Juárez. Yet, despite their efforts to survive there was never enough money for food and other basic necessities. Seeing his family suffer, Señor Sánchez grew desperate. Their marginal existence was taking its toll. Something had to be done! Although he wanted to enter the United States legally, to avoid problems for his children, he realized that was virtually impossible. The resourceful Sánchez "borrowed money to buy a secondhand suit, shaved off his mustache, and relying on his fair skin and green eyes, he simply walked across the border."[60] As soon as he could afford it, he paid a coyote to smuggle the rest of his family into the country. Tragically, in the interim, his youngest daughter, Catalina, had died of malnutrition.

The dire fate of Ramón Sánchez' family was not an isolated case. For many families, the attempt to return to the United States was as tragic and frustrating as their expulsion had been. Some families lost loved ones on both segments of the arduous journey, according to the National Catholic Welfare Conference, which chronicled the experiences of various families. In one particular instance, a family had returned to their hometown, but after an absence of more than thirty years, they did not find any relatives or friends. Sadly disillusioned, the family began the fifteen hundred mile trek back to the border on foot. The journey proved to be a harrowing experience. The father died in the city of Torreon, but the family pressed on. In Chihuahua, the youngest daughter, only four years old died, worn out by the trip. The following day, the mother gave birth to a baby boy, adding to the hazards of the journey. Still, the family persisted in their efforts to return to the United States. Three weeks later, the family finally arrived in El Paso. Having kept her promise to return her children to the land of their birth, the weary and physically exhausted mother died. The four American-born children were placed in an orphanage in El Paso and the newborn baby was given to a Mexican family in Ciudad Juárez.[61]

By the late 1930s, as more young, American-born repatriates reached legal age, the trickle of those wanting to return home became a torrent. Mexico, simply was not their home and the yearning to return to the United States was not to be denied. Ignacio Piña recalled that he made up his mind to go back when he saw Judy Garland singing "Over the Rainbow" in the film *The Wizard of Oz* in a theater in Mexico City. Memories of home overwhelmed him and he began to cry uncontrollably. Piña wanted to go back home where he belonged.[62] So did many other of his contemporaries. Once of age, they were unwilling to tolerate or submit any longer to a different culture and lifestyle. Fortunately, they came of age during the advent of World War II, which in essence, ended the deportation and repatriation terror. The "better day" the Mexicans had hoped and prayed for, had arrived. Once again, Mexican labor was in demand. In many ways, it was a repetition of the scenario that had drawn their grandparents and parents north during and after World War I. The elders who stayed behind wondered what fate awaited those repatriates who returned home.

Agringados
DOCUMENTS

■ ■

REMAINING AMERICAN AND RETURNING TO THE UNITED STATES.
EMILIA CASTAÑEDA DE VALENCIANA.
Source: Christine Valenciana Interview with Emilia Castañeda de Valenciana. Courtesy of Emilia Castañeda de Valenciana.

Yes, we were a novelty, because, I guess, we spoke mostly English. We used to go to the store and we used to refer to the money as pennies, not centavos. So you know, the people used to laugh at us. They didn't really laugh at us, but they used to get a kick out of it. So I think we spoke more English than Spanish.

I used to speak English to my brother, especially a lot of times when I didn't want anyone to understand what I was talking about. But he used to get embarrassed. He's been the type who's not a show-off. Well, I'm not a show-off either, but I felt I didn't need to hide the fact that I could speak English. I mean, why should I deny the fact that I was an American citizen? My dad was pretty proud that we were American citizens. . . . He always used to tell people that we were American citizens and that we didn't belong there in that country.

So my dad said, "Well, why don't you plan to arrive in the United States, in your native Los Angeles, for your birthday?" I said, "Gee, that'd be nice." So I did. When I came, it wasn't easy for me to come by myself. I was a young girl, and you know how it is when you're brought up to watch out for this guy and watch out for that guy. I was a little bit frightened to come, on my own, to the United States. . . . So when I was close to the border, the Mexican Immigration boards the train and they ask you if you have a tourist card. What tourist card was I going to have? (laughter) So I had to pay the money for a tourist card because, according to them, I was a tourist.

Well, they knew what I had been doing after they asked me. So I didn't see any reason to pay for the tourist card, but I ended up paying

for a tourist card, to Mexican Immigration. Can you imagine me
a tourist, all those years over there? I wouldn't call that the life
of a tourist. (laughter)

Anyway, I was on a very crowded train coming back to the United
States. This was during the war, and the trains were crowded. There
was no place to sit since servicemen came first. The seats were for them.
But there were some kind servicemen who let me use their seats. They
would stand up in the aisles and visit with each other and talk to me.
I talked to them, and I guess that I was a novelty to them, because
they were trying to get all this information out of me. Here was this
girl coming back to the United States who had lived there. They were
surprised that I could speak a little bit of English.

■ ■

TRYING TO SURVIVE IN MEXICO. TERESA MARTÍNEZ SOUTHARD
Source: Christine Valenciana Interview with Teresa Martínez Southard.
Courtesy of Teresa Martínez Southard.

So we stayed with my aunt. Can you imagine we just had one bedroom
for all of us. Since it was still summer time when we arrived that of
having only one bedroom didn't bother us too much. So with the warm
weather and we couldn't fit in that one bedroom, we slept outdoors.

While we were living with my aunt she would make those corn
tortillas. They looked good, but I didn't like them. I had to eat my flour
tortillas. Poor Dad he would sacrifice himself and buy a special sack of
flour so I could make my own tortillas. Otherwise, I wouldn't eat.

Everything was so different. I wasn't used to this life. It was so
tough on me.

I used to play baseball with my high heels on. I wore them when
I carried water when I did everything. I loved heels. The people didn't
like the way I dressed. They didn't like for us to wear lipstick, rouge,
or anything.

I would always say, oh what if I could go back to my country,
again. . . . I always had intentions of going back home.

DOCUMENTS

■ ■

TRYING TO RETURN. PABLO GUERRERO TO LOS ANGELES COUNTY.
TRANSLATION FROM SPANISH TO ENGLISH A. G. RIVERA. 1 JUNE 1934
Source: Los Angeles County Decimal File.

OFFICE OF THE COUNTY CLERK

Translation from Spanish to English

INTERPRETERS' DIVISION   *A. G. Rivera   Date 6/1/34*

31336

V. LYLE   DEPUTY CLERK IN CHARGE

5/28/34. Mexicali, Low. Calif. Mexico

L.A. County.

Los Angeles, Cfa.

By these presents I hereby make it known that my family and myself
were deported into Mexico on 12/8/32, on the S.P. trains that left Los
Angeles, Calif., and in view of the fact that all of my children were born
in the U.S. of A, they do not like the Mexican customs and wish to
return to the U.S. in company with their parents and ask the Los Angeles
County authorities, as a favor to address the Department of Labor
in Washington, requesting that the American Consulate in Mexicali,
Low. Cfa. be ordered to grant me immigration papers, paying the
$18.00 for each Passport.

   I want to arrange everything legally; I do not wish to violate the
frontier Immigration Law, and I want my Passport issued with the
seal of an American citizen. I worked in the U.S. of A. since 1904 with
different companies. I registered in the world war in Johnson, Arizona,
Cochise Co. I have never given my services to the Mexican government
nor to the Mexican capital. I have worked all of my life, since I was
19 years of age in the U.S. of A., and that is why I wish to return to
the country where I am entitled to live with my children so that they
be educated in the schools of your country and not in Mexico.

   Besides, the Mexican Government here does not give any assistance
nor protection to children born in the U.S. of A., and for that reason

I ask that my children and myself be allowed to return to the country in which they are entitled to live.

FATHER.   My name.   Pablo Guerrero.

MOTHER.   Refugio R. Guerrero.

CHILDREN.

Miss Bessie Guerrero; born 5/6/18 in Johnson, Ariz., Cochise Co.

Miss Felix Guerrero, born 6/9/20, Johnson, Ariz. Cochise Co.

Emilia Guerrero, born 4/5/22 in Downey, Calif., Los Angeles County.

John Guerrero, born 5/6/24, Clearwater, Cal., Los Angeles County.

Victor Guerrero, born 3/23/26 in Clearwater, Calif., Los Angeles, Co.

My address:

Pablo Guerrero,—Gen. Delivery.

Mexicali, Low. Calif. Mexico.

"Americanos Todos Luchamos por la Victoria / Americans All Let's Fight for Victory." Courtesy of Yolanda Alvarez and the Mexican American Orange County Historical Society.

Accommodation
Al Otro Lado

"Donde es me tierra,	*"Where is my country,*
Donde me vaya bien."	*Where things go well for me."*
—Dicho Mexicano	—Mexican Proverb

The story of humankind is filled with tragic tales of peoples being displaced or uprooted by wars, famine, racial or ethnic purges and natural catastrophes. In most instances, there is a persistent yearning and quest by the survivors to return to the land from whence they came. However, with the passage of time and the changing of fortunes, the dream of returning to the beloved homeland tends to diminish. The elders remember the past fondly but succeeding generations find it more difficult to identify with or share in the odyssey. Yet, there are always those hardy souls for whom the dream will not die. During the decade of the 1930s, the coerced repatriation to Mexico of Mexican Nationals and their American-born children produced a similar situation. Many repatriates who were American citizens by birth, yearned to return to the land of their birth.

How many repatriates actually returned to the United States is impossible to verify. This is not surprising because scholars on both sides of the border cannot agree on the number of individuals who were repatriated or scare headed into going to Mexico "voluntarily." The U.S. Labor Department cited a figure of two million. The official figure compiled and cited by the Mexican government is slightly less than 500,000.[1] As previously noted, the total of approximately 1,000,000 individuals is considered a legitimate figure. Incomplete, lost or destroyed files, or the failure to compile any records, especially of surreptitious or illegal actions by zealous officials, present an insurmountable quandary for researchers. Due to the shame and trauma of the ordeal, many of those who returned home to the United States, after living in Mexico for various periods of time, seldom told their children about their horrendous experience. As María Robles related, "When my Dad read *Decade of Betrayal*, he cried and for the first time told us about the ordeal he had endured as a youth."[2] Many others took their sad story to their graves. Consequently, only recently, have their children and grandchildren begun to explore the history and background of repatriation, and the role their particular families played in the ordeal.

Although the total or exact number of repatriates who left or returned is important, it is not the critical issue. The key aspect is the trauma and the havoc that the repatriation movement created in the Mexican American community. The heart-rending impact was felt by families and individuals throughout the United States in colonias large and small. Families caught in the repatriation dragnet struggled to understand what was happening to them. Why were they being singled out? Why were none of the other racial and ethnic groups being expelled to their ancestral lands? Children, especially teenagers, found it impossible to believe, let alone accept the fact that the land of their birth was callously dispatching them to a foreign country. Mexico, was the land of their parents and forefathers, but it was not their home. Understandably, when asked if he wanted to go back to Mexico, one ten-year-old youngster responded candidly, No! It is like being sent to Mars. This was a common reaction shared by children who had been born and had spent their entire lives in the United States. Going to Mexico held no illusions for most of them.

Since approximately 60 percent of the 1,000,000 persons who were expelled were children born in the United States, the traumatic impact they underwent cannot be trivialized or ignored. In truth, these children were actually forced to endure three horrific experiences: First, there was the frightening realization that they and their parents were being kicked out of the United States. Secondly, they had to endure the frustrations and anxieties of trying to adjust to life in Mexico. And third, for some of them, there was the accommodation and reconciliation to a new way of life when they returned to the United States, the land of their birth. The first two aspects have already been covered. However, the latter aspect has not been dealt with in a comprehensive manner. The fears and the anguish these children endured are extremely difficult to ascertain and comprehend nearly seventy years later. Repatriation and its aftermath was a different experience for every individual. In many instances, the sudden loss of family stability produced by the dysfunctional nature of the repatriation ordeal was overpowering. This was true even for those who were not sent back. Beatrice Ortega, related that "once my husband, Nick, started reading *Decade of Betrayal*, I could not get it away from him."[3] As a youngster, her husband had lived through that period and readily identified with the sad plight of the people involved.

The series of experiences were so traumatic and devastating, that in order to maintain their dignity and sense of self-worth, repatriates commonly suppressed their bitter memories. Persuading some survivors to talk about their experiences is akin to getting combat veterans to recount their ordeals on the battlefield. Repatriation survivors have to be persuaded to relate their painful tale. This is often accomplished by emphasizing that it is the only way their posterity will ever know what they went through and how much they suffered. They also have to be convinced that an important aspect of history will be lost if they do not speak out. Their story is a vital part of both American and Mexican American history, and it must not remain untold any longer. Among the victims of repatriation are those who chose not to return to the United States. Perhaps nothing demonstrates more vividly the extent and the depth of their trauma than the fact that some children born in the United States, and who were American citizens, rejected returning to their native country and chose to remain in Mexico. Their psychological scars of betrayal and rejection never healed.

For many of the victims of repatriation, the events were so devastating that seventy years later, it is painful for them to recall or vocalize them. As José López, from Detroit, Michigan, pitifully lamented, "It is such a painful period. It is something personally, I would rather not even think about, much less talk about it."[4] López's sentiments capture the disposition and the attitude of the overwhelming majority of the victims of repatriation. López did not learn the details of the forced repatriation of his family until late in life. "It is something that I did not learn until I retired," he related.[5] He had heard bits and pieces and whispered comments but he never knew the true extent of the tragic event because his parents never talked about it.

As in the case of María Robles, many parents never talked about the traumatic experiences they had undergone as children. However, once retired, José decided to research the subject and learn more about how repatriation had effected his family. López was surprised at how little material the public library in Detroit had on the topic, and how few U.S. history books even mentioned repatriation. "I want future generations to be able to find out a lot more than what is now in the history books," López declared.[6] Aware of the need for more information, he became active in organizing an informal group of people with a similar interest, primarily the children and grandchildren of repatriates. Typically, consistent with the attitude prevalent among some repatriates in the Mexican community, José's older brother told him to forget about it. "Why dig up the past. Let it be. Life goes on," his brother admonished him.[7] However, José López was determined to proceed because he wanted his grandchildren to know about the ordeal of repatriation, and to bring it to the attention of the general public.

José López returned to the United States after an absence of 14 years. He was only five years old when his father was deported in 1931. Unable to support the children by herself, his mother had no choice but to accompany her husband with their five children. José's older brother was ten and his youngest sister was only a year old. Once José became of legal age like many other repatriation survivors, he fulfilled his ever persistent desire to return home. When he arrived in Detroit, in 1944, he went to work for the Ford Motor Company and retired after 40 years. Having a steady job enabled him to get married, buy a modest home and send his three daughters to college. He is exceptionally proud that his oldest daughter is an attorney in Toledo, Ohio. José has been active in the affairs of the Mexican American community and volunteers to help newcomers adjust to life in their new surroundings. Despite the number of years that have passed, José López still resents the fact that the U.S. government allowed such a grave injustice to be done to him and his family. He particularly regrets being "deprived of an education, deprived of medical care, deprived of food. All the necessities that growing children need."[8] His comments were punctuated by tears and emotional outbursts. In his mind, repatriation was a wrong that can never be righted. In failing health, he now lives in a senior citizens home.

Although many repatriation survivors were young children, some babes in arms, when they left, they have never fully recovered from the painful experience. On more than one occasion, upon being interviewed, repatriation survivors burst into tears and needed time to regain their composure. In some instances, individuals were so wrought up emotionally, that in order to lessen the painful heartache, the interview had to be rescheduled for another time. It was often necessary to spend a substantial amount of time chatting informally in order to establish positive rapport and credibility with the survivors. Now in their old age, their late seventies and eighties, they are a generation for whom being *bien educado*, well educated, means observing proper decorum and showing due respect and deference to one's elders, regardless of their station in life. Therefore, only after observing *la cortesia mexicana*, proper Mexican courtesy, did the individuals feel comfortable in baring their souls during an interview. In some instances, they refused to be photographed or allow the interview to be taped. The experience was just too painful and personal for them to display their emotions and inner feelings publicly. Insightful, personal questions often had to be postponed until a second interview session was arranged. Even then, there were times when they had to be reassured that certain aspects of the interview would remain strictly confidential. Especially when women were interviewed, proper protocol had to be religiously observed.

Emilia Castañeda, painfully recalled her expulsion and return to the United States. During the entire ordeal, she never understood why she and her older brother had been treated in such a manner. After all, they were American citizens. To this day, she believes that they were done a grave injustice. Seemingly, no one cared what happened to her or her family. North or south of the border, she was not assisted in any way by either government. Fortunately, upon turning eighteen, her godmother located and sent her a copy of her birth certificate and other documents that proved she was an American citizen. She also sent Emilia money to enable her to come home in 1944. The train from the border to Los Angeles was crowded with servicemen. That gave her an opportunity to practice her limited English. Although she was thrilled to be home again, her joy was tempered because her brother and father adamantly refused to return to the United States. Emilia had been forced to spend half of her young life in Mexico. Upon her return, she got a job in a candy factory and attended an adult school to learn English. Ironically, the classes were held in the same elementary school she had attended as a child. Emilia visited her father and her brother as often as possible, and in 1953, she finally convinced her brother to return home. That made her very happy, but she was saddened by the fact that her father never came back to the United States. Starting life anew, her life has been fulfilled by a happy marriage blessed with three wonderful daughters. All are college graduates and one has earned a Ph.D., and is a college professor. Still, despite her blessings, the memories of her repatriation experience continue to haunt her.[9]

As they say in Spanish: *"Cada cabeza es un mundo."* Each head is a different world. That is especially true in relation to the reaction and manner in which the survivors of repatriation view their unique experience. Their reactions run the gamut of human emotions. Arturo Herrada, who now lives in Sandusky, Ohio, was very stoic, almost matter of fact, when asked how he viewed the fact that his father had taken the four youngest members of the family to Mexico but left his four older brothers and sisters in the United States so they could continue their education. Arturo was only four years old at the time. "My Dad did what he had to do in order for our family to survive," he responded without rancor and refused to cast any blame or aspersions on his father. However, he confessed that he often wondered why he was subjected to being separated from his family. It was a painful separation. "Too depressing every day nothing to be happy about . . . a miserable time," Arturo remembered.[10] He also recalled missing and crying out for his father and mother, but was comforted by the knowledge that he had not been abandoned. He knew that his dad would come and take him back to Detroit as soon as the economy improved and he had a steady job so he could once again support the family. Perhaps the fact that he was only four years old made it easier for Arturo to accept a situation over which he really had no control and perhaps did not fully understand. Not having a job and being unable to support the family was a traumatic and shameful situation for fathers who were used to paying their own way. It is one of the reasons why most fathers never talked to their children about repatriation. They had never gotten over their sense of guilt and shame.

María Ofelia Acosta had an entirely different reaction than Arturo Herrada. She could not understand why her parents, who were legal residents, and her brothers and sister who were all born in the United States, had been rounded up and shipped to Mexico. María Ofelia was adamant in her belief that her family had suffered a great injustice. She particularly resented the fact that her education and that of her brothers had been interrupted and their future jeopardized as a result of being repatriated. "I could have gone to school . . . I could have had a better life," she lamented emotionally.[11] Her reference to the loss of her education was a recurring theme among interviewees who had been unceremoniously pulled out of school when their parents were repatriated. They believed, without exception, that they had been deprived of a decent education. María Ofelia's statement captured that feeling very emphatically. For school age children who were being repatriated, the aspect of being deprived of their education was compounded because in many instances they were unable to attend school in Mexico. Either no schools were available in the village or ranchito where they settled, or their parents were unable to pay the tuition or buy necessary school supplies. Children also often had to go to work in order to help support the family. The low, prevailing wages made it necessary for everyone to work in order for the family to survive. Albino Piñeda regretted that he was able to attend school only one or two days a week while in Mexico. His family was so poor that he had to start working at a very young age. Conversely, in the United States he had gone to school full time. José López also bemoaned having to give up school in order to go to work while only eight years old.[12]

For young repatriation survivors, getting an education when they returned to the United States was often a major problem. Many of them found that their English had deteriorated to the point where they could not attend classes at their appropriate grade level. "I could not speak English," Arturo Herrada recalled. "It took me three semesters to know what was going in school."[13] His father did not allow him to speak Spanish at home in order to force him to learn English. To her dismay, Hortensia Nieto learned that she could not enroll in her local high school in Gardena, California because of her lack of proficiency in English. She was forced to enroll and commute daily to Central High School in Los Angeles. The school had an English program designed especially for students, like herself, who had been expelled to Mexico as youngsters and could not cope with the standard school curriculum when they returned.[14]

Unfortunately for Hortensia, the class was taught by a teacher from Oklahoma with a very noticeable drawl and heavy accent, and who had no knowledge of Spanish. Neither did she have any idea about how to deal with students who had only recently returned from Mexico. Utterly frustrated and feeling that she was not learning anything, Hortensia quit school after one semester. Rubén Jiménez underwent a very similar experience when he returned to the United States. In his English class, the teacher passed out copies of *Readers Digest* and picked them up at the end of the period. She never asked them anything about what they had read or assigned any written work. Realizing that he was not learning anything, Rubén also dropped out of school and decided to join the army. Ironically, in Mexico, the repatriates' lack of fluency in Spanish had been a detriment, now the lack of fluency in English had the same dire effect in reverse.[15]

While education was a major concern of the school age survivors, there were other equally painful aspects that had to be faced. One of the most difficult was reestablishing relationships with relatives and family members who had remained behind. In some instances, the familial relations had become so frayed that it was impossible to establish a kindred bond. Residency in Mexico varied from a few months to more than ten years, and the longer the absence, the more difficult it was to reestablish personal relationships. As Elena Herrada stated sadly in describing the situation in her family, "a dissimulation had set in."[16] In some instances, families no longer functioned as cohesive units. Some of the returnees, for any number of reasons, ranging from psychological or sociological maladjustment, sibling rivalry, jealousy or envy, alienation and a different cultural orientation, simply abandoned attempts to fit into the existing family mode. In many cases, as in Mexico, they once again felt like outsiders and intruders.

Unable to cope, some of them rejected their Mexicanismo, including the use of Spanish, in an attempt to assert their independence and establish their own identity. Feeling rejected, they even renounced family ties, married outside of the Mexican culture and moved out of the colonias. All four of Elena's aunts, repatriation survivors, for example, married non-Mexican men. One of her cousins even changed her name. It seemed that women had a more difficult time in making the transition and adjusting to life in America. However, it was not easy for men either. Elena's father, Alfredo, also married an Irish girl. Their self-imposed ostracism was their way of coping and putting behind them all the bitter and negative memories that haunted and continued to bedevil them. Consequently, if possible, it was best to suppress the past. As is said in Spanish: *Ojos que no ven, no llorran*, eyes that do not see, do not cry. Out of sight, out of mind. It is difficult to determine to what extent such behavior was based on rebellion, frustration, or a sense of rejection or perhaps all three. One thing was certain, as all repatriates attested, as much as they desired to return to the land of their birth, adjusting anew to life in the United States was not an easy task. In some instances, it was exacerbated by the difference in the level of success between children who had been repatriated and those who had remained in the United States.[17]

Adjusting to the return of family members after long absences was not an easy task for family members who had remained in the United States. Their lives too had changed. In some instances, like in Hortensia Nieto's family, her mother had remarried and there was now a stepfather and half-sisters and brothers. Fortunately for her, they accepted her with open arms.[18] However, as might be expected, that was not the case in all instances. There was often open resentment of the newcomers, especially when bedrooms and other amenities had to be shared. There was also a degree of embarrassment for Americanized teenagers in having siblings or relatives who were noticeably "different!" Some teens also resented the fact that it became their responsibility not only to run interference for the new arrivals, but to Americanize them so they would fit in and not stand out like sore thumbs. This was particularly true when it came to the use of English. The moment the former repatriates opened their mouths and attempted to converse or express themselves in English, they butchered the language, much to the embarrassment and chagrin of their teenage relatives. And, conversely, when Mexican Americans reared in the United States attempted to converse in Spanish, their pochismo or Tex-Mex sounded crude and infantile. As had occurred in Mexico, once again a modus vivendi had to be worked out. Until they were able to acculturate, the repatriation survivors had to rely on the goodwill of family members to help them adjust and fit back into a society and a way of life that was vastly different from what they had experienced in Mexico. Understandably, they felt like misfits in both countries!

Consequently, for the survivors who returned, to a degree, it was déjà vu all over again. Therefore, it is understandable that some of the repatriates, especially the younger ones who had no concerted memories or only a vague recollection of life in the United States, chose to remain behind and live in a culture to which they had adapted. Also, Mexican Nationals who had been public charges, had no choice in the matter, they were forbidden to ever return to the United States, although they had been led to believe that if they left "voluntarily" they could return at any time. Some of the repatriates had married Mexican Nationals, started their own families, and perhaps even owned a small business. For them, there was no compelling need or reason to return to the United States. A new life beckoned them.

That was the case regarding Ramona Ríos de Castro. Her family had settled in and helped colonize Ejido Erienda near San Ysidro in Baja California.
She had married "a Mexican National who spoke no English." Ramona utilized her ability to speak English to help her husband establish a tourist
fishing business catering to Americans. The business is still flourishing today.
In spite of their success, Ramona, wistfully confessed that, "I love the United
States and I wish I could go live there again, but I had to stay here and raise
my children."[19] Another individual who chose to remain in Mexico was Marta
Ornelas de Manrique. Marta had arrived in Mexico with her three-year-old
son, Jesús. When he became of age, Jesús wanted to return home but due to
the uncertainties of the war years, his father had advised him to remain in
Mexico rather than returning to the United States. "And so I became very disillusioned," Jesús confessed. Perhaps recalling his own sad experience, he
observed that "the victims of repatriation are the children."[20] Both Jesús
Manrique and his mother rued the fact that he had lost the opportunity for a
better life and a brighter future by not returning home. Francisco Castañeda
refused to come back, stating bitterly, after spending nine years in Mexico,
"Why return to a country that took away my homeland, that rejected me?"[21]
Years later, Francisco's sister, Emilia, finally convinced him to return.

For other repatriation survivors, returning to the United States was no
longer an option. They had become Mexicans. They might be poor, but
once they became acculturated, they were usually treated as equals, rather
than as second class citizens, as was usually the case in the United States,
regardless of how long one had lived there. Besides, for others, especially
those who had lost everything when they were repatriated, there was really
nothing to go back to. For the older repatriates, it was often too late to start
over again. They viewed venturing north into an uncertain fate as something best left to adventuresome young people. Furthermore, due to the
shame and trauma that they associated with their repatriation experience,
many did not want to expose themselves to the possibility of undergoing
the same ordeal at a future date.

Many American-born repatriates were not able to return home because
the burden of proving American birth and citizenship rested solely on them.
In some instances, their parents had died, and having arrived in Mexico as
babies or as very young children, they did not even know where they were
born or if they had a birth certificate or other valid papers. Unable to offer
tangible proof, there was no possibility of them ever returning home.

Other survivors of repatriation found their efforts to return to the United States frustrating due to the legal documentation required by American authorities. This was the case of Mexican National Natividad Castañeda who wanted to reunite with his son Francisco and daughter Emilia in Los Angeles where he had lived for over twenty years before being repatriated by Los Angeles County. Sadly, Natividad died before he could be reunited with his son and daughter. Even though Natividad's daughter Emilia had made a special trip to Mexico to plead her father's case at the American Consulate, birth records were not found in time. Emilia was convinced that her family's experience with repatriation had made her family "a broken one." Moreover, she also blamed the ordeal of repatriation for keeping her from the bedside of her dying father.[22]

Even with proper documentation, reentry into the United States often took time. Such was the experience of María Ofelia Acosta whose mother had carefully safeguarded her children's American birth certificates when they were deported. However, these documents in themselves never guaranteed returning to the United States. It took weeks for the Acosta siblings to be granted visas because they were also required to provide witnesses attesting to their identity and moral character. Furthermore, María Ofelia felt going to the American Consulate was like "begging them for something" which was rightly hers.[23] In many instances, the time required for processing the paperwork strained the limited financial resources of the repatriates. The cost of relocating relatives to the United States posed a very severe burden on Carmen Martínez who was the only member of her family who was not repatriated. She had visited her siblings in Mexico and was alarmed about the extent of their poverty and misery. Carmen pledged to help her brothers and sisters by locating birth records and offering financial help despite the fact she was a single parent working as a domestic.[24] Another individual who decided to return was Juan Caldera of Colton, California. Before being repatriated, Caldera disposed of property valued at "$100,000, and purchased 5,000 acres in Mexico."[25] However, he was left virtually penniless when Yaqui Indians claimed ownership of the land he had purchased, and the failure of a bank in San Diego wiped out his life's savings. An enterprising individual, Caldera returned to the United States hoping to recoup his fortune, but was unsuccessful in doing so. His was another tragic tale attributed to the injustice suffered by many individuals as a result of repatriation.

The return to the United States tended to assume a common pattern. Occasionally, the entire family returned together, except for siblings who had gotten married and chose to remain behind. If parents did not wish to return, the older, more adventuresome siblings came back first. Such was the experience of Hortensia Nieto. At the age of fourteen, she came back with her older brother and a cousin, and over a period of time, she persuaded her younger brothers and sisters to join her in the United States. In similar instances, family members or relatives who had remained in the United States, took it upon themselves to reunite the entire family. As in the case of Emilia Castañeda, José López, and Ignacio Piña, their relatives were instrumental in locating birth certificates and other documents verifying legal residence, as well as sending repatriates money for the trip north.[26] Some of those who returned home, made periodic trips back to Mexico to visit elderly parents and family members or relatives who had remained behind in the hope of persuading them to return home. On the other hand, some repatriates unable to gain readmission to the United States, settled in communities along the border so they could be closer to loved ones even though separated by the border. The Jiménez and Acosta family endured this separation but gathered at the border to maintain their family ties and their overpowering desire to be together. However, there were repatriates who never went back to Mexico even for a visit. Hortensia Nieto was one of those who never wanted to set foot in Mexico again. Given the horrendous nature of their experience and the adjustment ordeal that they were subjected to, their attitude is readily understandable.[27]

As 80-year-old Ignacio Piña painfully revealed, "Today, many years later, I still have nightmares." He has simply been unable, nearly seventy-five years later, to put the tragic ordeal behind him. "It's a feeling I will have until I die," he said. "The government did a very wrong thing."[28] Piña, who was only six years old and living in Montana when his family was repatriated, had previously only shared or divulged his inner feelings to his wife and children, but the horrible memories have plagued him all his life. Piña is not alone in that regard. It is an awesome burden that many repatriates have borne their entire lives and, like him, will haunt them until the day they die. Hortensia Nieto, reluctantly revealed that she had been forced to undergo therapy in overcoming health and adjustment problems arising from her repatriation and return to the United States. She also related that for a time, she had been confined to a sanitarium suffering from tuberculosis, which she contended she contracted in Mexico due to the poor diet and terrible living conditions. She weighed only 90 pounds when she returned to the United States. Coincidentally, Hortensia was admitted to a Catholic sanitarium on the same day a young man named Cruz Nieto, she had met at a party, enlisted in the U.S. Navy. He wrote to her daily, but she declined to answer his letters in order not to be a burden or a bother to him. Fortunately, one of the nuns at the sanitarium convinced her that she should respond to his letters. The letters' therapeutic value and the power of love undoubtedly played a major role in her recovery. Their correspondence resulted in their becoming engaged and getting married after Cruz returned from the service.[29]

As a teenager without any job skills, Hortensia worked on several vegetable farms, but the work was too strenuous for her and she was forced to quit. After she got married, she worked cleaning homes and an office building in order to help her husband pay for a home they were buying. He was working as an x-ray technician at the local VA hospital. One day one of her neighbors informed her that the filtration plant where she worked was hiring. Hortensia's husband did not want her to work full time, but she convinced him that it was only for the summer, so he relented. Eighteen years later she retired as the floor supervisor. After she got married and became involved in working and raising three children, Hortensia did not have time to dwell on her repatriation experience. Like most others, she put it out of her mind and went on with her life.

A life of hard work, at least initially, seemed to be the fate of many returnees. Upon returning to Detroit at age 8 from Mexico, Arturo Herrada related that in order to contribute money to his family, he had started selling newspapers on a street corner. "I used to sell papers in below zero weather and was lucky if I sold six papers in an evening. The newspapers sold for three cents and I kept a penny," he said ruefully.[30] He was not making much money so while still in elementary school he bought a paper route from another carrier. He had to pay the boy 25 cents a customer to get the route. Eventually, he built the route up to 200 customers. His efforts won him several prizes, including a bicycle and a trip to Chicago and one to New York City. One harrowing experience occurred when a gang of young toughs, accosted him and his older brother as they cut through the park on their way to pick up their newspapers. The gang knew they had paper routes so suspected they had money on them because they had to pay for the newspapers. Although outnumbered, Arturo rammed into the biggest boy and knocked him down. Thereupon, the other boys turned tail and ran. Arturo claimed the incident taught him a lesson he abided by all his life, to stand up for himself. "If you do that," he asserted, "people will respect you."[31]

Arturo believes that he was fortunate to attend and graduate from an excellent, technical high school. Back then, he recalled, many kids only went to the sixth or eighth grade before quitting school and going to work. His technical education enabled him to get a job with the Ford Motor Company. He started as a laborer, but Ford offered night classes for those who wanted to learn and advance themselves. Due to his math ability, Arturo became a tool designer and during World War II, he got a deferment because he was deemed essential to the war effort. After the war, he and a select group of men were sent to Sandusky, Ohio to set up a plant producing all types of auto parts. He worked for Ford for 37 years and is now retired. Working for Ford was considered quite an accomplishment, and "even on Sunday, men wore their Ford ID badges with pride."[32] Arturo is extremely proud of his family. He got married when he was thirty years old and he and his wife had eight children. All finished high school and several went to college. He sincerely believes that the United States is truly the land of opportunity if you are willing to apply yourself and work hard.

As stated, not all the repatriates were anxious to return to the United States. Some were haunted by the terrible memories of their life as youngsters in the U.S. and the way they had been treated. For that reason, Josefina Pérez did not want to come back, ever. In fact, when her husband, Fernando, also a repatriate, suggested that they return to the United States, she rejected his suggestion outright. She was so adamant in her stance that she told him that he could bring one of her cousins instead. Life in the United States had no magical allure for her. Josefina recalled that while growing up in a migrant family, they barely had enough to eat. "We were so poor," she recalled, "that I never had a store toy or a little doll to call my own."[33] The bittersweet memories were as vivid to her a lifetime later as they had been when she was a child. She recalled picking cotton with her mother in the Central Valley, as an eight-year-old, and lying down on the big cotton stuffed sack and taking a nap when she got tired. Despite the added weight, her poor mother continued to drag the huge sack down the seemingly endless rows of cotton. Josefina had her fill of picking crops in the fields under a merciless sun and wanted no part of that horrid lifestyle. Fortunately, her husband finally convinced her to set aside her fears and negative memories and join him in the trek north.

Fernando Pérez was insistent about coming back home because his rec-ollection of life in the United States was quite different from that of his wife. His family lived in Pittsburgh, California and his father was earning a dollar an hour working piece work in a shop, extremely good wages during the depression. Having a well-paying job enabled Fernando's father to buy a farm in Encarnación, Jalisco in Mexico. He had always wanted to be a farmer so when he was offered the opportunity to go back to Mexico at government expense, he took his wife and eight kids, all born in the United States, and left. Fernando, who was fourteen years old at the time, was the oldest of the children. His baby sister was only two months old. While his recollections of life in the United States were happy ones, Fernando "hated living in Mexico." When asked if there was anything at all that he liked about Mexico, "my wife," he exclaimed, his face beaming with affection.[34] He was not cut out to be a farmer and hated farm work. Luckily, his father let him go live in town with his grandmother. He got a job making serapes and blankets, but he was only earning five pesos a week. When he got married, he realized that there was no hope or future for him in Mexico. Although he convinced his wife to return to the United States, they had no money for the trip north so it took them a couple of years to work their way to El Paso, where he got a job work-ing in a copper smelter for the Phelps Dodge mining company. Fernando was not sure if he was 22 or 24 years old when he returned. However, one thing he was certain about, was that he was extremely happy to be back in the land of his birth. "Besides," he stated proudly, "in El Paso, I was making $5.00 a day."[35]

However, like many other individuals, Fernando Pérez was attracted by the job opportunities available in the mushrooming defense industry on the West Coast. Lured by the high wages, he went to Long Beach, California and got a job in the shipyards. The opportunity to get hired in the defense industry was made possible by two tremendously important decrees: President Franklin D. Roosevelt issued an executive order declaring that dis-crimination in hiring in the defense industry was illegal and would not be tolerated. This enabled blacks, Mexicans, other minorities and women to get hired on jobs that had not been available to them before. And to help increase production, the War Labor Board declared that foreigners who possessed vitally needed skills could be employed in the defense industry even if they were not citizens. Once gainfully employed, Fernando's life was very similar to that of other repatriation survivors who had returned to the

United States during World War II. Many of them readily found jobs in the booming defense industry. Isabel and Elvia Solís, recounted that "women who were small and thin were hired because they could crawl into small, cramped places on the ships."[36] Laborers and skilled workers of all types were needed to build the biggest naval and merchant marine fleets ever assembled. According to Isabel Solís and her sister Elvia, everyone worked nine hours a day, six days a week, plus as much overtime as you wanted. The story was much the same in the booming aircraft industry in Southern California. Teresa Martínez and her two children returned to Los Angeles during the war. Teresa and her five sisters readily found employment in an aircraft plant and joined the ranks of gainfully employed women.[37] It was rather ironic or perhaps poetic justice, that many repatriates who had left the United States virtually penniless and often returned the same way, suddenly found themselves employed at jobs and wages surpassing anything they had ever envisioned or deemed possible.

When the war ended, most defense workers managed to transfer to peacetime jobs. The economic slowdown or depression that many analysts had predicted would accompany the end of the war, failed to materialize. Instead, industry struggled to convert to peacetime pursuits and meet the needs of a society with ready cash and eager to purchase scarce consumer goods of all types. Economist Jack Kyser, head of the Los Angeles County Corporation, observed that after the war, many of those who had been repatriated or deported started coming back due to unstable conditions in Mexico and the lure of good jobs. Kyser also noted that the repatriates are people who are willing to take risks to seek the opportunity to work, "and this country needs them because they contribute to the economy."[38] One of those who took advantage of the opportunity was Fernando Pérez. After being laid off at the shipyard, Fernando went to work for the Ford Motor Company. He worked there for two years then went to work for U.S. Steel. He retired after 30 years. He proudly boasted of the fact that his three children had gone to college, and that he and his wife still live in the same house they had purchased nearly fifty years ago.[39]

Not all of the young male repatriates who returned home found jobs in the defense industry. To the surprise of many of them, they learned that as American citizens, they had to register for the military draft and were compelled to serve if their number came up. Some of them, understandably, had an ambivalent attitude about doing so. Why should they fight for a country that had turned its back on them when they needed someone to fight for them and defend their rights as American citizens? In some instances, young men such as Jesús Manrique decided against returning to the United States until a more propitious time. When Manrique applied for a visa, he was told he must report directly to a military base so he chose to remain in Mexico. Undoubtedly, some repatriates resented the callous manner in which their families had been treated during the depression.[40] To counteract evasion of military duty, there are reports of American military personnel visiting border towns such as Tijuana and informing Mexican American men that they were obligated to render military service.[41] Surprisingly, most of the young men, perhaps eager for adventure and a chance to see the world, either signed up for the draft or volunteered for military service. Machismo, pride, and patriotism played a part in convincing many of them to enlist. Due to family pressures and the cultural orientation pervasive in Mexican families, only a small number of young Mexican American women served in the women's military auxiliary units.

Albino Piñeda returned home from Mexico in 1942, when he was seventeen years old. An adventurous young man, tall for his age, he hopped a bus in Nogales, Sonora, bound for Phoenix, Arizona where he had a sister, Josefa. After spending a couple of weeks with her, he took another bus and went to the quaint little town of Santa Paula, California, to visit another sister, Dolores. Lacking any skills, Albino worked on the surrounding farms and orchards and did odd jobs as a day laborer. He recalled that when he worked on the farms, he often had to spray the crops with insecticides without wearing a mask or any other protective gear. When he turned eighteen, he received a notice to register for the draft. He was sent to Fresno for a physical and was classified 1-A. Rather than waiting to be called, he volunteered to go with a local group that was being inducted into the army. Since he was only seven when his family was sent to Mexico, and he did not return until ten years later, Piñeda was afraid he might not be able to understand or follow orders. His English ability had virtually disappeared during his stay in Mexico. Albino laughed self-consciously when he was told about the recruiting sergeant who said to another recently returned repatriate, who also worried about his lack of English, "Son, as long as you shoot straight, we don't care what language you speak." Piñeda's battalion commander advised him, "if anyone makes fun of your English, kick them where it hurts and I will support you."[42]

After basic training in Texas, Albino Piñeda was assigned to an artillery unit and encountered firsthand prejudice and racism. He recalled that the battery had a black Portuguese soldier. Since black soldiers were assigned to segregated units, everyone wondered how he had been assigned to their outfit. Albino recalled, sadly, that when they went to town, the black soldier was not allowed in the local restaurants. Another thing that bothered Albino was that at Fort Sill, Oklahoma, they had to attend a series of lectures on minority relations, delivered by an army captain. The captain repeated the usual stereotypical comments prevalent at the time: "Mexicans were dirty, lazy, and were devoid of any social or moral values."[43] As an army private, Albino did not dare complain or contradict his superior. While at Fort Sill, Albino enrolled in an English correspondence course to improve his English. He felt he had missed out on the opportunity to go to OCS, Officers Candidate School, because of his lack of English ability. Due to his correspondence course, he discovered the works of classic writers and fell in love with reading. From then on, his "duffle bag was always half-filled with books."[44] The battery saw action in Europe, and Piñeda's unit was at the Elbe River in Germany when the American and Russian forces met. However, his most memorable and terrifying experience occurred when two successive German 88 shells landed on his gun emplacement. Luckily, both turned out to be duds! "Otherwise, I wouldn't be here," he said, laughing self-consciously.[45]

Upon his return to civilian life, Albino Piñeda decided to be a radio repairman and started taking a correspondence course because he was working full time as a longshoreman. When he got laid off, he drew unemployment checks for nine weeks, as part of the 52/20 Club that the federal government had set up to assist veterans in making the transition to civilian life. He also enrolled in the local community college, but dropped out when he married and started raising a family. He eventually got a job with a heavy construction company. On the job, Albino became a "powder man." He became adept at using dynamite to blast roadways or any large obstacles that need to be removed so the construction crews could do their job. A hard worker, he was soon promoted to a foreman's position. The pay was good but at times, he would be laid off until the company obtained another contract. The jobs took him to various places throughout California and even out-of-state. He often took his wife, Naomi, and their two children with him. A dedicated family man, he wanted to be near his beloved family. After he married, Albino converted to Protestantism and became active in the Methodist Church. At one time, he served as the Sunday school superintendent. Steady work enabled Albino to buy a home in Santa Paula and he has lived there for more than fifty years. Active in the community, he was elected to serve on the county school board, and later became its chairman. Since his retirement, Albino has served as the director of his Church's southern area Spanish outreach ministry. In part, due to his efforts, his mother and his two brothers, Tony and Isidro, obtained a visa from the American consul in Nogales, Sonora, and returned home. That made Albino's life complete.

Alfredo Herrada, whose family had been repatriated in 1930, when he was only two years old, was a repatriation survivor who also saw military service. He had spent less than three years in Mexico because his father José Santos Herrada had returned to Detroit and landed a job with the WPA, Works Projects Administration, a federal work program. Although he was not an American citizen, an exception was made for noncitizens who had served in the military. Herrada qualified because he had been drafted in World War I. As soon as he was gainfully employed, he had retrieved his four children. At seventeen, Alfredo lied about his age and obtained employment with the Chrysler Motor Company. The company trained him to be a tool and die designer. His career was interrupted when he was drafted during the Korean War. He served there as a radioman for two years, then he was assigned to duty in Japan. While in Japan, he learned Japanese by teaching little children Spanish. He readily picked up the language because often Spanish speakers find Japanese easier to learn than English. This was perhaps best exemplified by one of the most amazing feats of World War II. Private First Class Guy Gabaldón who could speak Japanese induced more than one thousand Japanese, on the island of Saipan, to surrender.[46]

When Herrada returned home from the war, he did not get his old job back immediately, so he drove a Good Humor ice cream truck until he was rehired. At Chrysler, he became one of two Mexicans working as engineers in the tool and die department. Unlike Ford who hired and trained any qualified Mexicans who wanted to be engineers, Chrysler kept its Mexican hires to a minimum. Alfredo worked at Chrysler for forty-three years. During forty of those years, he served as a strike captain, although he was a white collar worker. He became active in the UAW, United Auto Workers, union after being passed up for promotion. The "fair haired boys" got the job again, he would complain. He wanted to put an end to that preferential and discriminatory hiring practice. On one occasion he even called a wild-cat strike in order to get his demands met. Alfredo was particularly proud of the fact that he was instrumental in designing and developing the collapsible steering column. In that respect, he followed in the foot steps of his father, José Santos, who had designed a labor saving conveyor system at the Ford Motor Company. His father had received a substantial bonus for his idea and it allowed him to move his family to a better neighborhood.

Other repatriation survivors, like Fernando Pérez and José López, also wanted to serve their country, but found that they were unable to pass the physical. Neither Pérez nor his three brothers qualified for military duty because they suffered from asthma. López was declared to be too small and underweight and unfit for military duty. López blamed his stunted growth and poor physical condition upon the malnutrition and deplorable living conditions he was forced to endure while in Mexico. Although López regretted being unable to serve his country due to his poor physical condition, he thought it rather macabre that after having rejected him and denied him residency for 14 years, the American government had the audacity to ask him to serve in the military. López and Pérez were not alone in not qualifying for military service.[47] Due to the poor diet and malnutrition that was rampant among poor families during the depression, many of the recruits, regardless of nationality failed the physical. Given their meager diet, common in Mexican families, it is amazing that so many Mexican American youths passed the physical. Letters about life in the service from hometown boys induced many young males to enlist. Once in the service, they commonly volunteered for the most dangerous duty. Enlistment in the marines or qualifying for the paratroopers was considered a badge of honor, and they wore the uniform proudly. When one young man was asked why he had joined, despite the discriminatory treatment accorded Mexicans, he replied simply, "it's my country, too!"

The tales of sacrifice and heroism are endless. Raul Morin's classic account, *Among the Valiant*, details the heroism of young men of Mexican and Latino ancestry who won the Congressional Medal of Honor during World War II and the Korean War.[48] At a discussion on repatriation, a middle aged man held up Morín's book and pointed to the picture of Staff Sergeant Joseph Rodríguez. "That's my brother," he announced proudly.[49] According to him, part of the family had been repatriated, but like so many individuals he did not know the details. That was understandable, since as mentioned earlier, parents and grandparents seldom discussed their ordeal with their children. The unpleasant experience was best left dormant in the inner recesses of the mind. Why punish yourself by reliving the past, besides nothing could be undone or gained by it.

Rubén Jiménez was among the repatriated Mexican Americans who voluntarily answered the nation's call. "Although I regretted what the American government did to me and my family," Jiménez asserted proudly that "I am an American and I wanted to serve my country."[50] While serving in the Army Air Force, he was sent to radar school. Since he was a high school dropout, he had no idea how he had qualified or been chosen for one of the top secret operations in the service. Radar was considered such a top secret weapon, that students were not even allowed to say the word "radar" outside of class. The classroom building was ringed with barbed wire and armed guards were posted around the perimeter. Rubén served in the army from 1943 until 1946, mainly in the Burma Theater. After the war, he wanted to go to college but his ability to use English effectively had been severely curtailed due to being repatriated. As stated previously, when he returned to the United States from Mexico, he had received very little help or encouragement in learning English. Frustrated, he had dropped out of school and joined the service.

However, going to school in the service built up Rubén Jiménez's self-confidence and after being discharged, he was determined to avail himself of the GI Bill and get a college education. Like other Mexican American veterans who lacked adequate preparation to pursue a college degree at a four year institution, Jiménez enrolled in a community college. There, he earned an AA, Associate of Arts, degree. Armed with his degree, he went to work for the CYA, California Youth Authority. His college education was interrupted when his wife developed cancer of the throat. Fortunately, after two operations, they were successful in curing her. The fates seemed to be smiling on Rubén! The CYA had a program that encouraged employees with AA degrees to attend UCLA and earn a BA degree. After applying several times, Rubén was selected for the program and earned a BA in Sociology. This enabled him to have a very successful career in his chosen field.

Now retired, Rubén Jiménez holds no rancor in his heart for the treatment accorded him and his family, regardless of the fact that he believes it was totally unjustified. He is justifiably proud that he answered his country's call and served honorably. The GI Bill enabled him and many other

Mexican veterans to enroll in college and become professionals. In nearly every instance, like Rubén, they were the first in their family to go to college and earn a degree. They became known as the "GI Generation," and as Dr. Ralph Guzmán, late provost of UC Santa Cruz stated proudly, "They kicked down the doors and proved it could be done."[51] This select group of Mexican American college graduates went into education or civil service types of jobs because those were among the few professional fields open to them at that time. Discrimination in hiring in the private sector was still rampant. The advent of the struggle for civil rights and affirmative action programs awaited a future date with destiny.

Not surprisingly, and as ironic as it may seem, upon returning home from the war, many Mexican American veterans found that they were returning to a society that still regarded and treated them as second class citizens. There are many incidents of Mexican American soldiers being refused service in restaurants, even while in uniform. It irked them that some of those same restaurants had no qualms about serving German prisoners of war. There are also media accounts of Mexican American veterans being refused burial in certain cemeteries. One cemetery in Texas had a fence separating Mexicans from the white burial area. Such discrimination was not uncommon. In some instances, returning Mexican veterans had to establish their own Veterans of Foreign Wars and American Legion posts because they were not allowed to join the lily white ones. Such was the case in Silvis, Illinois. When Mexican American veterans of 2nd Street returned home they had to build their own VFW post. Ironically, when the white VFW post burned down, the white VFW held their meetings in the post built by the Mexican American veterans. Years later, 2nd Street was renamed Hero Street because the twenty-two Mexican families living there sent eighty-eight of their young men to war. Eight never returned. No other street of comparable size, only a block and a half long, sent so many to war.[52] Discriminatory practices also extended to the ability to purchase a home on a low interest GI Loan. Due to restrictive real estate covenants, Mexican American veterans could not buy homes in certain areas. One woman, whose four sons had served their country honorably, resented the fact that she and her husband could not buy a home in the neighborhood of their choice. Mexicans may have been considered good enough to fight and die for the United States of America, but they were not deemed worthy to buy a home wherever they wished to live.

However, after having fought for liberty and freedom overseas, Mexican veterans were determined to fight for equality and their rightful place as American citizens. They believed they had earned their rightful place in the sun, and were not going to tolerate being forced to live in the shadows. But given the rampant prejudice that prevailed at the time, premier civil rights organizations such as LULAC, League of United Latin American Citizens and the American GI Forum avoided using the word "Mexican" in their titles. As one individual astutely remarked, the proclamation after the attack on Pearl Harbor, that we were all Americans, did not apply to the Japanese Americans or to the Mexican Americans. But if times had not changed, the attitude and expectations of Mexican veterans had. The community was slowly realizing its potential. Although they would have to wait until the explosive 1960s era for the advent of the Chicano Movement, their spirits and expectations were buoyed by the apparent change in the relationship between Mexico and the United States.

Regretfully, the Good Neighbor Policy espoused by the Roosevelt administration was more effective abroad than it was at home. During the summer of 1943 in Los Angeles, sailors and marines went on a rampage against Mexican youths wearing zoot suits. While the police arrested the Mexican victims, local newspapers portrayed the servicemen as heroes. Ironic as it may seem, the relationship between Mexico and the United States had never been more cordial than during World War II. Mexico became the source of much needed raw material to fill the voracious needs of America's war machine as it assumed the role as the arsenal of democracy. Mexico also activated Air Squadron 201, which served with American forces in the Philippines. It became the only Mexican unit to actually see combat during the war, and suffered two casualties. However, of greater importance in helping to win the war was the Bracero Program initiated in 1942, under the cooperative auspices of both governments. Mexicans were once again actively recruited to come and work in the United States. With 16,000,000 men and 350,000 women in the armed forces, a source of dependable labor was sorely needed. In 1942, only 4,203 Braceros were brought in, but by 1944, the number had swelled to 67,860.[53] Although it began as a temporary measure, the Bracero Program lasted until 1964. Ironically, some of the Braceros had been among those who were repatriated a few years earlier. Perhaps it was poetic justice that some of them returned to work in the same mines, factories, fields, and railroads, from which they had once been unceremoniously expelled. It is not surprising that, according to some estimates, 30 percent of the Braceros failed to return home after their contracts expired. In the case of Ignacio Piña, for example, he "never told his in-laws that he had been repatriated."[54] Instead, he led them to believe that he was a former Bracero worker. Perhaps, even more ironic was the fact that a repatriation program was initiated to make sure that Braceros returned to Mexico. Mexicans with long memories feared that a new chapter regarding repatriation might be starting again.

However, for most Mexicans and Mexican Americans, the repatriation epoch faded into the scrapbook of old memories. Most of them, including the former repatriates, were too busy working to achieve a better life in postwar America. Judging from the foregoing accounts, the repatriates who returned home arrived at a most opportune time. Jobs, at decent wages, were available in all types of occupations. For the former repatriates and the rest of the Mexican community, it seemed that anyone who was willing to work hard could improve their station in life from what they had known during the depression even though they still battled prejudice and discrimination. The repatriation survivors were especially aware of the changes, perhaps because they could compare them with the miserable living conditions many of them had encountered in Mexico. They seemed determined to work hard as if attempting to make up or compensate for lost time. Having their children succeed was a leading priority for them. That may explain why they seldom, if ever, talked to their children about their repatriation ordeal. Why burden them with the horrid ordeal of repatriation, when a brighter future beckoned. Reopening that particular chapter of their lives had to wait until their children had established themselves and were ready to seek out the truth for themselves.

Al Otro Lado
DOCUMENTS

■ ■

ACCOMMODATION TO LIFE IN LOS ANGELES. HORTENCIA ZAVALA NIETO.
Source: Interview with Hortencia Zavala Nieto.
Courtesy of Hortencia Zavala Nieto.

Hortencia was born in Los Angeles in 1930 and had a brother and three
sisters. All five of the children were born in the United States. After her
mother and father separated, her father decided to return to Mexico
after having resided in the U.S. for ten years. His decision was due in
part to the anti-Mexican hysteria rampant in the United States during
that period. Her father went first in order to find a place for them to
live. At his direction, her paternal grandparents took the five children
to Mexico in 1932. Since Hortencia was only two years old at the time,
she was not in a position to object or even understand what was
happening to her. However, her oldest sister, who was already in grade
school, objected strenuously to going to Mexico and cried constantly.
She finally relented and agreed to go when she was promised a piano
as soon as they got settled. "Needless to say, she never got her piano,"
Hortencia related sadly.

Although their father had supposedly gone to find a place for them
to live, he was somewhat of a drifter, and irresponsible, so the children
ended up living with their grandparents. According to Hortencia, the
living conditions were horrible and her grandmother was a cruel, heartless woman who never showed them any love or affection. As soon as
she was old enough to do chores around the hut that served as their
home, her grandmother put her to work. Hortencia recalled that she
would wake her up at three o'clock in the morning so she could do her
household chores before going to work in the local fields, despite the
fact she was still only a child. Due to the wretched condition under
which they were forced to live and lacking any opportunity to improve
their miserable lot, "We kids complained constantly and begged to be
allowed to return home to the United States," Hortencia recalled. After

all, regardless of their parentage, Mexico was not their home. They were Americans and wanted to return to the land of their birth. Therefore, when they got older, they contacted their mother, who had remained in the United States, and asked for her assistance in returning home. Eventually, their mother was able to arrange for Hortencia, who was then fourteen, and her brother and a cousin to come back to the United States. The year was 1944, and World War II was raging. Later, two of her older sisters, who had married young repatriates, also returned home. However, some members of the family were not able to gain admittance to the United States and they settled along the border so they could at least be closer to each other.

When Hortencia returned to the United States, she joined her mother who lived in Gardena, a small community on the outskirts of Los Angeles. She was surprised to learn that her mother had remarried and started a new family. That placed Hortencia in a unique position, for it meant that she now had stepbrothers and sisters on both sides of the border. Her father had also acquired a new family in Mexico. Eventually, two of her step brothers also immigrated to the United States and she saw them occasionally. In reality, the development of a dual family situation was not uncommon when families were separated for prolonged periods of time due to being split up by repatriation or deportation. Hortencia readily accepted the fact that her mother had remarried because during the Depression, it was virtually impossible for a woman to survive alone, especially if she had young children.

Although her new family welcomed her with open arms and treated her well, as she had in Mexico, Hortencia felt like an intruder, or as is said in Spanish, "una arrimada," a freeloader. She has never forgotten their kindness and patience as she adjusted to her new life in the United States, and to this date she remains very close to them. After an absence of twelve years, there was much for Hortencia to learn. As with so many repatriates who came back, a major problem she faced was learning English. To help her in that endeavor, her mother tried to get her enrolled in high school. However, due to her lack of proficiency in English, none of the local high schools would allow her to enroll. She learned that there was a high school in Los Angeles which had courses designed to help students who had been repatriated and then returned home. Anxious to learn English, Hortencia enrolled in Central High

School in Los Angeles and made the daily, time consuming trip via the red trolley cars that provided cheap, public transportation to virtually all parts of Los Angeles County and beyond. Riding the jostling, lurching red cars was an uncomfortable and often arduous experience. The cars were usually crammed with servicemen, so seating was scarce. Hortencia remembered that her teacher, "was a lady from Oklahoma who spoke no Spanish and really had no idea what to do with the kids from Mexico." In addition, she spoke English with a heavy drawl and her pronunciation made it difficult for the students to understand her. Convinced that she was not learning anything and was just wasting her time, Hortencia quit school after one semester.

Lacking an education and with a very limited command of English, Hortencia got a job working at one of the local vegetable farms that surrounded the City of Gardena at that time. She was anxious to pay her own way and also be able to help her family financially so she would not be a burden to them. However, being diminutive in size and weighing only ninety pounds, (All her friends called her Tiny, for obvious reasons.), the heavy labor and long work days took their toll upon her fragile health. Also, the trauma of having to adjust to two different cultures caused her many emotional problems, and at one point she was forced to seek medical attention in order to cope with her situation. "Despite taking the medication, I always felt tired and run-down," Hortencia commented. When she refused to continue taking the prescription, the doctor discharged her. Thereupon, her older sister, who was gainfully employed, became concerned about her ill health and decided to take her to a different doctor. The new doctor examined her and determined the pills she had been taking were primarily sleeping pills. More importantly he diagnosed her as suffering from tuberculosis. Hortencia was convinced that she had contracted the disease while living in Mexico, due to the poor diet and unsanitary conditions she had lived under. Fortunately, she was able to gain admittance to Santa Teresita, a sanitarium run by Catholic nuns. She remained there for eighteen months before being pronounced cured and being discharged.

Hortencia attributed her recovery to the loving care she received from the nuns and to the fact that before going to the sanitarium, she had met a young man at a party. Coincidentally, the young man, Cruz Nieto, enlisted in the U.S. Navy on the very same day that Hortencia

entered the rest home. He began writing to her and inquiring about
her condition and her health, despite the fact that they had only met
once. However, given the uncertainty of her health and not wanting
to be a bother or a burden to him, she did not answer his letters. She
relented when one of the nuns counseled her to respond to the letters.
Undoubtedly, the letters played a role in her recovery. When Cruz
returned from the service, their relationship blossomed into a romance
and they were eventually married.

Cruz got a job working as an x-ray technician in the VA Hospital in
Long Beach. Hortencia was happy being a housewife and mother. The
marriage was blessed with three children. When she and her husband
decided to buy a home, Hortencia went to work part-time, so she could
contribute financially. Lacking a formal education, she worked cleaning
homes and at a couple of commercial establishments. While she enjoyed
her thriving and wonderful family, Hortencia often thought about going
to work full-time, but her husband was opposed to the idea. Then, when
her oldest daughter was fourteen, a neighbor told her that the industrial
filtration plant where she worked was hiring new workers. Hortencia
decided to apply and overcame her husband's objections by convincing
him that it was only a summer job. Eighteen years later, she finally quit
her "summer" job. By then, she had become the floor supervisor working
directly with the plant foreman. She enjoyed her job and is proud of the
contributions she was able to make to her family. She always made sure
that despite her job, she did not neglect her husband or her children.

A highly Christian woman, Hortencia looks back on her life with
mixed emotions, but she is not bitter about the hardships she was forced
to endure at a very young age. In fact, she believes that they have actually
made her a better person. She is more compassionate and understanding
of others and is appreciative of the little things so many people take for
granted. Despite her sorrowful experiences in Mexico and later in the
United States, there is no rancor in her heart. Hoping to penetrate her
benign demeanor, I asked how she felt about being repatriated. After
pondering the question for a moment, she replied thoughtfully, "I think
the Mexican government should have taken a more active and forceful
role in opposing the expulsion and the inhumane treatment accorded its
nationals and their children. The children, through no fault of their own,
had their basic rights violated and were sent to live in a foreign country

without any consideration for their safety and well-being." Many, like her, she observed, had suffered the loss of their families and had a portion of their lives destroyed. Hortencia wondered pensively, how any society could treat innocent children so cruelly and subject them to years of misery and suffering.

Noting her emotional state, I asked if a financial settlement or a public apology would help to compensate her for the ordeal she was forced to endure? "How can any amount of money ever compensate me for all I lost and all the suffering I went through?" she replied. "The sum is bound to be small, as in the amount paid to the Japanese," she added thoughtfully, "so what would I gain?" Hortencia then declared, "I'm afraid it is too late to compensate me or to ever make amends for all I suffered." Just the mere thought of those terrible years brought tears to her eyes, her voice quivered and she fought to regain her composure. "Maybe an apology would be more acceptable than any amount of money," she added wistfully.

■ ■

ACCOMMODATION TO LIFE IN DETROIT. ARTURO HERRADA.
Source: Interview with Arturo Herrada. Courtesy of Arturo Herrada.

Arturo was only four years old when he and his brother and two sisters were taken to Mexico. As so often happened in such circumstances the family was forced to split up. His older siblings remained in Detroit so they could continue their education. In Mexico, Arturo lived with his grandmother. He did not like Mexico because they lived in extreme poverty. He felt that he was lucky to survive and always wanted to return home to the United States. "I always intended to return to the U.S.," Arturo declared emphatically. After being forced to live in Mexico for two years, Arturo's father got a job and was able to reunite the family.

Arturo returned in 1932, when he was six years old. Upon returning to Detroit, one of his biggest problems was that he could not speak English. "But I had to go to school, ready or not," he stated sadly. In school, he recalled that the other kids would not talk to him because of his language difficulty. "I sat in the corner because I did not understand

what was going on," he related, shaking his head as if to wipe away the
memory. Arturo remembers that his kindergarten teacher was good
to him, but the kids left him alone since there was nothing much
he could do.

It took Arturo about a year and a half to two years before he learned
enough English to be able to get along fairly well. "Eventually, you
learn to speak," Arturo commented wistfully. He recalled that his father
would not let him speak Spanish at home. "Speak English, speak English.
You have to learn to speak English," he would admonish him. His father
was adamant about that because he wanted his children to get a good
education. He wanted them to at least get a high school diploma. Back
then, Arturo commented, many kids went only to the sixth or eighth
grades before quitting school. As soon as you were old enough to get a
job, you went to work so you could help your family. Some big kids lied
about their age so they could get a job in one of the manufacturing or
assembly plants.

When asked if he had encountered any other major problems in
adjusting to life in America, Arturo said he did not recall being picked
on or teased by the other children for "being different." He believed
that was due to several factors. He did not live in a predominately
Mexican or barrio community. There were Irish, Italians, Polish, and
other Europeans, all struggling to earn a living. So we just got along.
If you did not bother anybody, no one bothered you, he asserted.
Having a large family helped in getting readjusted, plus the fact that
he was young enough to learn English readily.

One aspect that he found difficult and very trying was going to
work at a very young age, while still in elementary school. "I had a job
selling newspapers at night. I still remember standing on the corner in
sub zero weather for hours and maybe selling five or six papers. I paid
two cents apiece for the newspapers and sold them for three cents, so I
made a penny profit," he related. "It was a tough way to make a buck," he
declared laughing self-consciously. "I realized that the only way to make
money was to get a paper route, but you had to buy them from boys who
had the routes. I had to pay a boy 25 cents a customer to get his route."

"I started out with 10, 20, 30 customers and built it up to 50, 100
and eventually I had 200 customers. We always had contests to get new
customers and we won prizes. I got to go to New York City, to Chicago,

and I also won a new bike," Arturo said proudly. "It got to the point where I could give my Dad money. He always took half, that was his rule, he got half of the money. I think it helped me to go through that. It helped the family and it made you aware of what you spent," he added as an afterthought. When asked if he was then in high school, Arturo reacted in surprise. "Oh no, I was about eight years old, I was still in elementary school," he declared emphatically.

The only negative incident during his childhood that Arturo could recall, occurred when he and his brother, Bob, were on their way to pick up their newspapers at the distribution office. They took a shortcut through the park and ran into a gang of six boys loitering there. They looked mean, Arturo recalled. The boys knew we had paper routes and that we must have money to pay for the papers, Arturo asserted. When the biggest boy approached them, Arturo knew that he was going to have to fight him. Although he was afraid of getting beat up, Arturo felt he had no choice. He seized the initiative and rammed the larger boy in the stomach several times while pummeling him with his fists. When he knocked their leader down, all of the other boys turned and ran.

Arturo claimed he learned a very important lesson as a result of that experience: "If you stand up for yourself, people will respect you. You have to look out for yourself and do what you can to defend yourself, if you don't, you're going to get beat up anyway, but if you stand up for yourself, they may leave you alone." You have to make up your mind not to be pushed around, but you don't pick on anyone, either, he stressed. It is a belief he has abided by all his life and which has influenced the way he treats people and expects to be treated in return. In talking with Arturo, you could sense his self-confidence and his feeling of self-worth.

Due to his father's prodding, Arturo continued on to junior high school and then high school. He attended Lawrence Tech, a highly selective and difficult school to get into. When it was suggested that he must have been an outstanding student in order to be admitted, in his candid and frank manner, Arturo explained, "I lived in the district, otherwise I would never have been able to get in. They had to take me in," Being admitted had a profound and lasting effect on his life. "You got exposed to advanced math, metallurgy and a lot of things that you did not get in a regular high school. Things that were useful to you for the rest of your life," he said with quiet pride.

As a result of his technical education, Arturo became a tool and die maker, He worked on designing tools and weapons modifications for the army. He received an award for one of his designs, but in typical fashion, he was reluctant to talk about it and claimed he did not remember the event. However, he did get an exemption from the draft because he was declared essential to the war effort. In 1955, the Ford Motor Company sent him and two of his friends to Sandusky, Ohio to establish a design department. The plant did not produce any cars but designed and manufactured all kinds of automotive parts.

Arturo is very proud of his work experience at Ford. He worked for the company for 37 years before retiring. Eventually, he rose to the rank of supervisor and had 50 to 70 people working under his supervision. He felt really "fortunate to have been able to work at a job I liked and being involved in making key decisions regarding which parts to produce. It was interesting. You had to approve whatever was made there." Years later, his pride in having been a trusted Ford employee, was still apparent in his voice and demeanor.

When asked about his married life and his family, Arturo revealed that he had gotten married in 1955 and he and his wife had eight children. He was proud of the fact that they had all finished high school and some of them had gone to college. Based on his experience, he felt that the Mexican community was doing all right. They were growing in numbers and in the future would have a powerful voice in how things are done. They will go from being a minority to being equals, he observed. "When people respect you," he added insightfully, "you can get ahead." He stated that in his case, surviving the Depression and everything that had happened to him, had helped to make him a better person. You have to keep a positive attitude. Life is what you make it, he professed. If you are a pessimist, you are always going to be pessimistic about everything. But if you are a positive person, you will always think and react that way. Arturo hesitated for a moment as if gathering his thoughts or perhaps thinking he had said too much already. Then, he added somberly, "If you are going to be a defeatist, and say I can't do that and you give up and never try, then you will never make it. You may try and get your butt kicked, but at least you tried." When he finished expounding his deeply held beliefs, Arturo laughed self-consciously, as if surprised by his own candor and audacity.

Since he seemed to be on a roll, I asked Arturo what had impressed him most during his eventful lifetime, and having lived for more than seventy-five years. I expected him to mention his repatriation experience. But Arturo is not a man who fits into convenient molds or modes of thinking. Literally without hesitating and almost as if he had anticipated the question, he replied, "The progress the colored people have made. They came up from being slaves, from being stepped on, and being taken advantage of, but they never gave up and have elevated themselves, in spite of everything." As he spoke, I could sense the admiration and respect he felt for the black people as fellow human beings. I wondered if in some way, whether he was aware of it or not, was his empathy influenced by the suffering he had endured during his repatriation experience.

Determined to find out, the question was asked about how he felt regarding his repatriation experience? Was he bitter; did he hold the government responsible; did he feel the government owed him anything? Without hesitation, Arturo replied firmly, "No, I don't hold anybody accountable, or feel bad about things." Then he added pensively. "You live your time on earth and how you react to the time is up to you. Everybody has the power to think what he wants and to live the way he wants." When pressed about how he felt about being separated from his family at such a young age (he was only four at the time) and being forced to live in Mexico in dire poverty, Arturo maintained his upbeat nature. He believed that his father had to make a tough decision and that he did the best he could. Arturo did not blame him for what had happened. Instead he praised him. "My dad could have gone on relief or cried all day or maybe revolted and been a troublemaker, but he didn't!" Although not a trained historian, Arturo felt that while repatriation was a tragic event, it should be considered in the context of the Depression. People had come north to make a living and when the Depression hit, they had to make a choice. In typical fashion, he concluded, "If you are bitter, you only hurt yourself!"

Town hall meeting of repatriation survivors at Our Lady Queen of Angels Catholic Church at Olvera Street Historical Monument, Los Angeles, California, September 13, 2003. Courtesy of Steve Reyes.

Repatriation in Retrospect
¿Qué Pasó?

No les pedimos perdón
Justicia es lo que queremos
Porque tenemos razón
Por eso la exigemos

—La Caravana

We did not ask for pardon
Justice is what we want
Because we have reason
That is why we demand

—The Caravan

Give us this day our daily bread, is a supplication heard around the world, for there is no greater need or desire than to sustain life. However, as has been sagely observed, man does not live by bread alone. In order to realize their true potential, human beings strive to attain an ever higher social order. Since we are gregarious by nature, we form societies to enhance that purpose. Among the basic principles that govern us, and for which we strive, are the concepts of liberty and justice. In the history of humankind, those two concepts have always been in the process of becoming. That is why the phrase, "liberty and justice for all," is not empty or meaningless rhetoric. True liberty, however, can never prevail unless justice is assured for all members of the society. The quest for justice is an ongoing process that at times demands that past transgressions, violations, and injustices be eradicated. It is an indelible sign of a truly great society when it acknowledges and attempts to atone for its misdeeds.

That is why on July 15, 2003, California State Senator Joseph Dunn convened a meeting of the Senate Select Committee on Citizen Participation, at the state capital in Sacramento. The purpose of the meeting was to hear testimony concerning the unconstitutional deportation and coerced emigration from the United States of approximately 1,000,000 Mexican Nationals and their American-born children, during the Great Depression of the 1930s. They were expelled under a program commonly, but inappropriately, referred to as "repatriation." Senator Dunn, became aware of the travesty when his field representative Bernardo Enríquez called his attention to the book *Decade of Betrayal*. Subsequently, on a flight to Washington, D.C., he decided to pass the time by reading the book. Like most Americans, Dunn had never heard or read about the expulsion or the inhumane treatment accorded members of the Mexican American community during the 1930s. The more he read, the more intrigued and incensed he became. He was stunned! He could not believe that anything of that magnitude could have possibly escaped the stern scrutiny of history or been omitted from American history textbooks.[1]

In truth, the historical omission is not that surprising. Until recently, for a variety of reasons, much of the background concerning the deportation and repatriation of Mexicans during the 1930s, had not only been omitted from historical and sociological textbooks, it had also remained a "hush, hush" topic in the Mexican community. As former Congressman Esteban Torres, who was only three when his father was deported, revealed, he had to wait more than twenty years before learning the details about the deportation of his father, from his mother and grandmother.[2] As Torres stated sadly, "The deportation of my father was the equivalent of an unconfirmed death."[3] The heartache, trauma, and the shame that gnawed at the repatriates' conscience, relegated the topic of repatriation to the "ashcan" of the mind. Scholars seldom delved into the topic. In fact, most American historians were unaware that such a travesty had ever taken place. The few studies that were done were limited in scope and dealt primarily with a city, state, or a particular region. Prior to *Decade of Betrayal*, no one had fully investigated and assessed the national scope of repatriation and its impact on Mexico and the survivors themselves. Reflecting the lack of knowledge about the topic, a history student from UCSB, University of California at Santa Barbara, remarked, "What's the big deal, there were only 250 or 300 people involved, right?" When informed the number was approximately 1,000,000, he gasped in disbelief. He was not alone in either his lack of knowledge or in his stunned reaction. When an auditorium full of college students at

Concordia University in Irvine, California in 2002 were asked if they had ever heard or read about repatriation, not a single hand was raised.[4]

Lack of knowledge about repatriation means that American society is unaware of its grave consequences for the Mexican community and larger American society, particularly the loss of a generation of potential leaders. As attorney Jesse Araujo surmised regretfully, "Who knows how many teachers, doctors, lawyers, politicians, and other leaders were lost as a result of repatriation."[5] As an example of what occurred and its impact, consider the case of Dr. Julian Nava. His family was on the verge of being repatriated, but on the morning they were supposed to board the train, little Julian became ill. That postponed their departure and the family ended up remaining in the United States. As an adult, Nava earned a doctorate in history at Harvard University, became a history professor, won election to the Los Angeles Unified School Board, authored several books, and eventually was appointed American ambassador to Mexico. Imagine this nation's loss if he had been repatriated. One can only speculate how many potential "Navas" were denied a similar opportunity because, unfortunately, they were unconstitutionally expelled.[6]

Not only was there a loss to the Mexican community as a result of those who were sent to Mexico, but those who remained behind kept a low profile. They feared drawing attention to themselves and being harassed and deported. As a result, Mexican families, who were dirt poor and on the verge of starvation, refused to risk asking for public assistance. They were afraid, and rightly so, that they too would be sent to Mexico. Loss of a generation of established and potential leaders may help to explain why the Chicano Movement on the college campuses did not occur until a generation later, in the mid 1960s. Incipient Chicano Studies courses, were in many instances the first time that the topic of repatriation had ever surfaced in classroom discussions. Like their white counterparts, most Chicano students knew precious little, if anything about the topic. Elena Herrada recalled that she first heard about repatriation while she was a student at Wayne State University. She was shocked to learn about what had taken place. "I rushed home and asked my grandfather if it was true," she stated excitedly.[7]

After hearing about repatriation in her Chicano Studies class and talking with her grandfather, Elena wanted to learn more about what had happened to her family. However, she soon discovered that assessing the extent or impact of repatriation on the Mexican and Mexican American community was impossible to ascertain with any degree of certainty. One major problem is that many grandparents, parents, aunts, uncles, cousins, and other relatives are no longer alive to share their experiences and observations. And as in the cases of Elena Herrada and José López, only within the past few years have the children and heirs of the repatriates undertaken the frustrating and challenging task of exploring the facts and piecing together a patchwork quilt of the tragic episode.

Among the most notable efforts are those of a group in Detroit, Michigan, organized by Elena Herrada, whose grandfather, José Santos Herrada and family were among the more than 15,000 Mexicans repatriated from Detroit. In pursuing the topic she came in contact with others who were seeking similar information. None of them had any idea about the extent of the repatriation program. They believed that the repatriation efforts were concentrated in Detroit as a result of Mexican workers being laid off by the automobile plants. Then, a librarian at the University of Michigan, called their attention to *Decade of Betrayal*. It opened up an entirely new historical vista to them. Just as important, was becoming aware of the fact that the onus of being repatriated was not something peculiar only to Detroit and Michigan. The realization that their parents and grandparents had not failed them and were not to blame for what had happened to them, encouraged them to pursue their research more avidly. Their mutual interest led to the formation of *Fronteras Norteñas* (Northern Frontiers). As a result of their combined research efforts, the group has inspired the writing of the play, "Remembrances of the Repatriated" and produced the documentary video, "Los Repatriados: Exiles from the Promised Land." It relates a gripping, emotional tale of the fate suffered by their parents and grandparents, including, of course, their children. They have also created a web site, www.losrepatriados.org, to enable interested parties to communicate with them and share information.[8]

In their enthusiasm to discover as much as possible about the long forgotten or suppressed saga, members of Fronteras Norteñas made what amounted to a pilgrimage to San Luis Potosí, in Mexico. They chose that particular state because that was where many of their families were from originally. However, much to their dismay, only one of the repatriates was willing to make the trip. All of the others refused to accompany the group. For them, the bitter memories, even seventy years later, were still too painful to face. In addition to learning more about their particular families, those who made the journey were also hopeful about establishing contact with relatives who had not returned to the United States.

While in the city of San Luis Potosí, the group attended a conference on repatriation, hosted by Professor Fernando Saúl Alanis Enciso of El Colegio de San Luis Potosí. Professor Alanis has done extensive research on the topic of repatriation and colonization with an emphasis on the policies and politics that governed them. Due to his expertise, Alanis was invited to share his knowledge and views at the July 15th hearing in Sacramento. Unfortunately, a change in scheduling prevented him from participating. However, he remains vitally interested in the various developments surrounding repatriation and has expressed the hope, "That perhaps we can create an event similar to what was done in Detroit to pay homage to the repatriates."[9]

After the conference in San Luis Potosí, some of the Detroit researchers from Fronteras Norteñas went to Aguas Calientes to seek out long lost relatives. Although disappointed in not being able to establish contact after the passage of so many years, they considered the trip well worthwhile and hope to make it a regular event. Enthused by their experience, the group, Fronteras Norteñas, is formulating plans to establish a Midwest Mexican Museum dedicated to all those who were repatriated. It is a project that will entail a great deal of time and effort, but they are not discouraged. As one of the participants stated resolutely, "We are the descendants of indomitable survivors."[10] The group is buoyed by the fact, that in spite of all the adversities, they have managed to stay focused and are in the process of achieving their goals. Detroit artist, Nora Chapa Mendoza, who made the pilgrimage to San Luis Potosí, produced an impressive and compelling painting appropriately entitled, "Los Repatriados: Exiles from the Promised Land." It vividly depicts the repatriates with their earthly possessions heaped on their overladened vehicles, wearily making their way south. Truly, a caravan of sorrow! It will occupy a prominent spot in the proposed museum. Reprints of the painting were sold to raise money to assist individuals who needed financial assistance in order to make the trip to San Luis Potosí. An acclaimed artist, Mendoza's works have been exhibited not only in the United States but also in Europe.

Also doing research regarding repatriation and the situation of Mexicans in the Midwest is John Ortega, a retired attorney. John's family settled in Des Moines, Iowa, in the 1920s, in an area along the Des Moines River called Box Town. As John recalled wistfully, "Times were hard and everyone had to pitch in and help in order for our family to survive."[11] Although his own family escaped being repatriated, John was aware that other families did not fare as well. Ortega firmly believes his own family escaped being repatriated because they were very fair skinned and had blue-green eyes. Since his retirement several years ago, John has made several trips not only to Iowa but also to neighboring states seeking information about the fate of the Mexican colonias in the Midwest. John has uncovered vital information plus invaluable pictures depicting the life of early Mexican residents. Due to his research, John has developed an ongoing interest as well as a great empathy regarding the fate of repatriates from the Midwest. On his latest trip, he stopped in Silvis, Illinois and discovered that Pedro Terronez, whose grandson Rosendo (Andy) Terronez, Jr. has compiled an award winning exhibit about the soldiers in whose honor Hero Street, USA, was named, had taken his family to Mexico during the depression. He later sent his children back to Silvis, although he was not allowed to reenter the United States. On his deathbed Pedro Terronez confessed that his only regret was having to give up his children.[12] Based on his research and personal recollections, John is currently writing a book about the Mexicans who settled in the Midwest.

An unexpected source of interest regarding the topic of repatriation surfaced when California State Senator Joseph Dunn read *Decade of Betrayal*. In an attempt to ascertain the truth of the matter, Senator Dunn invited the authors to meet with him and members of his staff. In a two hour session, punctuated by insightful and thought provoking questions, Senator Dunn became convinced that the issue of repatriation merited additional study and research. He, therefore, assigned an aide to research the background of repatriation and ascertain how such a travesty could have been allowed to occur. Dunn declared, "This is a part of American history where society through its federal, state, and local officials failed miserably in the justice part of the American ideal."[13] After two years of research, using sources in California, the national archives and talking with survivors, Senator Dunn concluded that something needed to be done to rectify the gross injustice that had been done to the Mexican community. It was inconceivable to him that an action involving a million or more people had been kept under wraps for so long, and that most American history texts made no mention or reference of the tragic saga. While everyone knows about the

Jewish holocaust in Germany and the incarceration of 125,000 Japanese in the United States during W.W. II, it was nearly impossible to find anyone in the general public who had an inkling about the travesty that had occurred in the Mexican community in the 1930s.

Therefore, Senator Dunn decided to initiate legislative action to rectify the situation, at least in California. However, before doing so, the question of proper or legal terminology had to be resolved. The commonly used term "repatriation" did not adequately or legally define the exodus of 1,000,000 Mexicans from the United States during the 1930s, approximately 400,000 of them from California. The term was commonly used by officials because it denoted or conveyed the impression that the exodus was voluntary, although such was not true in the vast majority of cases. Even those individuals who left "voluntarily," did so because of legal coercion and fear generated by the anti-Mexican hysteria prevalent during the period. Others left due to threats of bodily harm if they did not leave, or because they were unable to find jobs due to racial discrimination. Although not legally correct, through common usage, the term "repatriation" was accepted as a convenient means of identifying en masse all of the people who went or were sent to Mexico. The term was used and accepted on both sides of the border by the general public as well as by government officials and public agencies. Nonetheless, legislative language requires legal and precise terminology.

Under Senator Joseph Dunn's leadership, the California State Senate Committee conducted an inquiry about a legal definition or a more appropriate term than "repatriation." Among the terms considered were expatriation, illegal deportation, coerced emigration, coerced relocation, unconstitutional deportation and forced or illegal repatriation. After due deliberation and consultation, it was agreed that "coerced emigration" and "unconstitutional deportation" best described the illegal and forced nature of the repatriation movement engaged in by federal, state, and local government entities as well as civic and private organizations. Those terms were chosen because "coerced emigration" denotes the involuntary aspect of the forced relocation of American citizens to Mexico. Coerced emigration exemplifies the process of an individual leaving one country for another with the intent of never returning. No provision had been made for encouraging or facilitating the return of the repatriates, including children born in the United States. Their expulsion was considered final.

In regards to "unconstitutional deportation," it signifies the illegal nature of the action states, counties, and cities engaged in to accomplish the expulsion of legal or illegal residents. Only the federal government, under its vested authority to regulate commerce, can legally deny entry or expel individuals from its sovereign territory. Once the terminology issue had been settled, Senator Joseph Dunn was ready to proceed with the next vital step. However, before doing so, he conferred with his colleague, State Senator Gloria Romero. Senator Romero supported Dunn's efforts because she believes, "It is an opportunity to understand the type of politics that are applied in difficult economic times and the effect they have on the people." The Senator added, "We also have to think about what our obligation is in the matter, what is it that morally, we must do as a state?"[14]

Critics, however point out that the issue of repatriation is a very difficult one to resolve because the information is scattered among the federal, state, and local governments. This makes it difficult to ascertain who is to blame and to what extent. Concern is also voiced about how the question of financial reparations would be received by the American public. Other critics opposed taking any action because they view it as counterproductive. They claim it punishes today's taxpayer for something that occurred more than seventy years ago. Others purport to see a hidden agenda. Craig Nelson, representing "Friends of Immigration Law Enforcement," declared, "We oppose the whole group—victimhood ethos being perpetrated today, and this seems to be more of the same."[15] His sentiments were echoed by Mark Krikorian, executive director of the Center for Immigration Studies. "As I understand it, most of the U.S. citizens who were . . . removed from the country were U.S. born children of illegal aliens whose parents chose to take them back to Mexico rather than leave them with relatives in the U.S." Krikorian added, "essentially, the proponents of this idea want amnesty for any illegal alien who has a child born in the United States. Of course, this only strengthens the arguments of those who want to change current policy and deny U.S. citizenship to the U.S. born children of illegal aliens."[16] This pronouncement evinces a rather truncated interpretation, for no one associated with the legislative action has proposed any sort of amnesty. Although the proposed legislation had strong bipartisan support, there was also opposition from conservative political elements. Mike Spence, president of the California Republican Assembly, stated, "At some point, we'll run out of taxpayer money to pay for all the problems that happened in America's past."[17]

No doubt, there is cause for concern, but of the estimated 400,000 Californians allegedly expelled from the state, it is believed only about 25,000 would be directly effected by the legislation or have any legal standing.

Nonetheless, the critics notwithstanding, armed with the vast amount of information his staff had accumulated over a period of two years, Senator Dunn, decided to proceed. He drafted and introduced two bills in the California Senate. However, to substantiate and strengthen his position, and to make his colleagues aware of the issue, he convened a hearing of the Senate Select Committee on Citizen Participation on July 15, 2003.[18] First to testify was Dr. Kevin Starr, State Librarian, and noted California historian, who stated and clarified the importance of the issue to the history of California regarding atonement and correction of the injustice. In his opinion, it was a historical event that merited being looked into and acted upon. His presentation was followed by Professors Francisco Balderrama and Raymond Rodríguez, who were invited to give expert testimony regarding the various aspects and effects of repatriation both in the United States and Mexico. They spoke at length about the trauma of repatriation that the survivors, especially their children, had suffered.

Substantive, first hand testimony was given by survivors Emilia Castañeda and José López. Both were less than ten years old when their respective parents were repatriated and forced to leave the United States. Emilia recounted her experiences, including being told by county officials that if she and her brother declared themselves orphans, they would become wards of Los Angeles County and would be placed in an orphanage. That way they could avoid being sent to Mexico. Although her mother had died of tuberculosis, the previous year, Emilia steadfastly declared she was not an orphan because she still had a father. She also recounted a series of heart-rending experiences regarding the deprivations she was forced to endure. She related that on one occasion, lacking drinking water, she and her brother had started digging by hand until water began to seep into the hole. Greedily, they scooped up the dirty water and drank it to quench their thirst. The childhood memories still brought tears to her eyes, seventy years later. To this day, she believes that she was done a grave injustice in being forced to abandon the land of her birth and being sent to live in a foreign country for nine years. During the entire period she was there, she never stopped thinking of herself as an American. She was extremely proud of the fact and proclaimed it for everyone to hear, even if they made fun of her or teased her for being a "rapatriada." To this day, Emilia has never been able to understand or accept the fact that she was exiled and punished for being poor and having a Mexican father. In her eyes, that was not a crime!

José López testified that he and his family had been sent to Mexico by the welfare authorities in Detroit, Michigan. Since he was only five years old at the time, he was not aware that his family had been forcibly relocated to Mexico until he started doing research fifteen years ago, after he retired. He was especially bitter regarding his experiences and holds the government directly responsible for inflicting such a heinous punishment on him. He felt that his whole life has been adversely affected as a result of being forced to spend fourteen years of his life in Mexico. Adding to the tragedy was the fact that his father and mother died while only in their forties. José and his four brothers and sisters were orphaned at a young age. José blamed the trauma and the terrible circumstances they had been forced to endure due to being repatriated, for their early deaths. He was equally perturbed about having missed out on getting a good education. When he returned to Detroit 14 years later, his lack of an education doomed him to laboring in an automobile plant until he retired. He also felt that his health and physical development had been severely impaired as a result of the poor diet and lack of adequate medical care while in Mexico. He attributes the horrible ordeal he had suffered, for his failure to pass the physical and serve in the military during World War II. José López was pleased that the tale of what he and other survivors had been forced to endure was finally coming to the public's attention. And he was thankful that he was able to play a role in seeking justice, in behalf of all those who had suffered a similar fate. José was adamant about not seeking or wanting any financial remuneration.

Immigration law expert, Kevin Johnson, Associate Dean, U.C. Davis School of Law, discussed the unlawful and unconstitutional aspects of the repatriation program instituted by local, state, and federal authorities in order to get rid of the Mexican population. Since only the federal government is empowered to remove or forbid foreigners the right to reside in the United States, and then only for cause and utilizing due process, no other entity has the right or can exercise the authority to do so, he emphasized. In the vast majority of instances, individuals were denied the right to seek legal counsel and were not accorded due process by authorities acting under the guise or color of law. Therefore, the deportation and repatriation programs were inherently illegal and unconstitutional. In compendium, they violated the Fourteenth Amendment's provisions against the denial of due process, the guarantees of the equal protection clause, and the Fourth Amendment's protection against unreasonable search and seizure. The latter was applied not only to those who were actually repatriated but to all who were accosted in public places solely because they "looked Mexican." Mr. Johnson asserted, that it constituted a clear case of racial or ethnic profiling, a practice strictly forbidden by law. As a rule, individuals may be stopped, interrogated and subjected to search only for reasonable cause.

In his testimony, Dale Shimasaki, former executive director of the Federal Civil Liberties Public Education Fund, drew several parallels between the expulsion of Mexican Nationals and their American-born children and the detention and incarceration of the Japanese and their American-born children, commonly referred to as Nisei. Dr. Shimasaki detailed several similarities between the two cases: Violation of constitutional rights, loss of property and income, amenities denied and psychological trauma suffered, young men drafted to serve in the army despite the injustices sustained by them and their families, and incarceration of those who violated the legal dictums. He also pointed out that it took community action by the Japanese themselves to call attention to the injustice, and to the fact that it was based not on any definite need or compelling reason, but on racism, prejudice, hysteria, and a failure of official leadership. In fact, he pointed out that in both instances, the authorities had hyped and skewed the evidence to support their preconceived and racially discriminatory agenda. To assure that such a dastardly misdeed never happens again, Shimasaki recommended that a program modeled after California's Civil Liberties Public Education Program be established. It should undertake to create public consciousness and awareness of the coerced emigration and the unconstitutional deportation of Mexicans. He also recommended that a commission be created and empowered to gather data and assemble a record of the injustices and make them public. Dr. Shimasaki advised that multiple avenues of action should be explored in seeking appropriate remedies. He also suggested that a variety of school curricula and civic projects be undertaken to call attention to the illegal exodus and to commemorate the historical event.

Susan Dunbar, Special Counsel to the Select Committee, gave an overview and documented the "legal" or official aspects of the repatriation process. She began by displaying letters and internal memos commenting on the techniques and rationale to be utilized in the attempt to repatriate as many Mexicans as possible and scare tactics that could be used to induce many of them to leave "voluntarily." Her emphasis was on Los Angeles County because it developed the repatriation methods copied and used by communities throughout the nation. The presentation stressed the fact that not even patients in county hospitals, sanitariums, or asylums escaped the repatriation net. Others were duped into thinking that if they left voluntarily, they could return when the economic climate improved. In actuality, all those who had been public charges were barred from ever reentering the country again. Since some of the repatriates owned property, the county foreclosed on the property and sold it to cover the expense of sending the owner to Mexico or providing relief assistance. If the owner ever returned, which was unlikely, and attempted to recover the property, the county would file a counter suit seeking repayment of funds utilized in providing public assistance. In essence, the county had little to fear from its high-handed tactics.

Attorney Dunbar also introduced evidence to illustrate how the federal, state, and local government entities worked together in support of their repatriation schemes. In California, Governor Culbert Olson, furnished Los Angeles County Supervisor John Anson Ford, letters of introduction so that he could confer with Mexican officials in developing a more effective repatriation program. In essence, the State of California and the County of Los Angeles were conducting their own independent diplomatic dealings with Mexico, in clear violation of federal law. In Detroit, Michigan, the federal government made immigration officials available to accompany repatriation trains to the Mexican border to assure that things went smoothly and no one got off the trains. The federal government was not only aware and abetted repatriation efforts, it was also kept well informed about the results of Mexico's failed attempts at colonization. Yet, it did nothing to protect the rights of individuals who were American citizens. Photographs and press releases covering repatriation were also presented at the hearing in an attempt to give the senators and the audience a better understanding of the magnitude of repatriation and the horrific human suffering and sacrifice to which adults and children were subjected.

The hearing in Sacramento caused quite a media sensation and English as well as Spanish language newspapers throughout California carried the story. In Los Angeles, *La Opinión*, the city's leading Spanish language newspaper gave the hearing and repatriation story an unprecedented four page coverage. In an article entitled "Heridas Que No Cierran," Injuries That Don't Heal, it discussed the background of the repatriation, its causes and the current ongoing situation. Various professors in California and Texas were asked to comment and give their opinions concerning the repatriation issue. Another article, "El tren sin Retorno," The Train of No Return, summarized the experiences of Emilia Castañeda, from East Los Angeles, who was repatriated when she was nine and returned nine years later. In "Vidas Truncadas," Lives Turned Upside Down, it related the memories of Esteban Torres, former United States Congressman, concerning the hardships the family endured when his father was deported. He stated that the experience influenced his entire life and that when he became a congressman, he always stood up for the underdog. Torres later went on to become the American Ambassador to UNESCO. Other articles in *La Opinión* dealt with various aspects of repatriation. In addition, *La Opinión* published an editorial supporting the creation of a commission to investigate the shameful episode. "It is time," the newspaper stated, "to open up the past and let the light illuminate this dark event."[19] The newspaper praised Senator Joseph Dunn for undertaking the challenging and thankless task of seeking justice, long overdue.

Some newspapers, including the *Metrotimes* in Detroit, Michigan and the *Press-Telegram* in Long Beach, California ran feature articles devoting two or more pages highlighting repatriation, its causes and consequences. The *Press-Telegram* quoted Senator Dunn on his involvement as saying, "Why would an Irish guy from Minnesota be vesting some of his capital on this issue? [Because] It is an injustice that needs to be corrected."[20] Dunn also acknowledged, "While there are lots of past injustices, there has been no effort politically or legally to try to rectify this injustice. I don't mean financial, just a simple apology from the government entities that were involved in something that was purely motivated by racial bigotry."[21] Dunn's comments echo those of Emilia Castañeda, "I want the city and county of Los Angeles, the state of California and the federal government to apologize to all those thousands of people, maybe millions, that this happened to. That's all I want."[22] That is a sentiment heard time and again from those who were expelled.

The *Metrotimes*, Detroit, Michigan published a rather extensive history of the repatriation movement and the effect that it had on the people and families involved. Featured was Elena Herrada, who explained why the historic episode had been neglected for so long. In response, she cited a brief passage from John Phillip Santo's book of memoirs, *Places Left Unfinished at the Time of Creation*, "Forgetting is to Mexicans, what remembering is to Jews."[23] The *Metrotimes* also interviewed repatriate José López. He gratefully recalled that he and his little brother and two younger sisters were able to return to Detroit, due to the efforts of one of his aunts. Both his parents and an older brother died while in Mexico. Also interviewed were Marta Ornelas de Manrique and her son Jesús Manrique, who was only three years old when he and his mother were repatriated. As indicated earlier, they chose to remain in Mexico rather than return to the United States.[24]

Other newspapers throughout California also reported or commented on the unfolding story. The *Sacramento Bee*, an influential capital newspaper, related the sordid details of individuals being denied their rights, jailed and then forced to leave despite the fact that more than half were American citizens.[25] The *Los Angeles Times* explained that the attempt to obtain an apology or reparations for the repatriates was inspired by Ronald Reagan's administration's compensation of the Japanese who were unconstitutionally interned during World War II. It also cited Senator Joseph Dunn's statement justifying the action. "It is important for us as a society to recognize the wrong that was committed. The best approach would be for Congress to enact a reparations program similar to that which was done for victims of the Japanese American interment."[26] Dunn also expressed the hope that, "by acknowledging this, we can minimize the likelihood of unjustly treating future immigrants to this great nation."[27] In a separate article, the newspaper quoted Kevin Johnson, associate dean of the UC Davis School of Law, who testified at the hearing in Sacramento, regarding the wanton violation of the constitutional and legal rights of the repatriates. He asserted that, "It is a bedrock principle of U.S. immigration law that U.S. citizens cannot be removed from the United States. This is why this episode is so troubling to me"[28] As Senator Joseph Dunn so aptly stated, "They were deported for just one reason: They happened to be of Mexican descent."[29]

The *San Jose Mercury News* has published several stories since columnist José Rodríguez declared, following the hearing in Sacramento: "Finally! Seventy years later, justice may be done. And many Americans may hear for the first time about one of the worst and least-known chapters in their history."[30] To emphasize his point, Rodríguez cited the experience of Professor Alberto Camarillo of Stanford University who delivered a lecture on Mexican American history to a group of journalists. He had just finished talking about repatriation, when a participant declared angrily. "I can't believe this wasn't in our history books."[31] He was not alone in his sense of frustration. The *Orange County Weekly* reported that after reading *Decade of Betrayal* and learning about repatriation, Senator Dunn stated, "It changed my life forever. It taught me about something I had absolutely, positively never heard about anywhere."[32] If that is indeed the case, the Senator has something in common with the heirs of the repatriates.

Also running a series of articles regarding the repatriation hearing and the reparations being sought for the survivors was the *Orange County Register*. One article told the sad story of Trinidad Rubio from North Orange County who suffered the humiliation of being repatriated and after seven decades still feels betrayed by her country. Like so many other repatriates she is not interested in financial reparation. "All I want is for the government to admit what happened to me was wrong. All I want is an apology," she stated firmly.[33] The repatriation issue and its subsequent developments also received extensive radio and television media coverage, in both Spanish and English. The prestigious *Jim Lehrer News Hour* devoted an eight-minute segment entitled "Painful Past" to the story. María Ofelia Acosta who had been repatriated as a child and later returned home, was interviewed. She was convinced that she and her brothers and sisters could have had a better life if they had not been repatriated. "No money can repay that," she asserted, "years that you wasted of your life."[34] Florida based Spanish language television network Telemundo also featured an interview on the story. José López, Emilia Castañeda, and other survivors suddenly found themselves in demand as media reporters sought more first hand information regarding their ordeal. Although Castañeda and López met for the first time at the hearing in Sacramento, after relating their heart rending stories, they tearfully hugged each other. Strangers before the hearing, there was now a common bond between them. Both of them have been interviewed with the possibility of using their experiences as footage in a full length documentary about repatriation and its survivors. Even if nothing else happens, they are pleased that the repatriation story has at long last seen the light of day and received the media publicity it merits. That assures that the tragic story can never again be ignored or neglected.

To assure that repatriation, will not be forgotten or ignored, in conjunction with the hearing, California State Senator Joseph Dunn introduced two new bills. He had previously introduced SB 933, in an attempt to extend the statute of limitations for filing law suits, but the bill was vetoed by Governor Gray Davis. Davis's rationale for the veto was that he was concerned about the cost of the liability. However, he asserted that in principle, he supported a reparations program. The new bills were intended to overcome objections and concerns. Both bills were passed by the state legislature with overwhelming bipartisan support. SB 37 provided a two year window of opportunity, until December 31, 2006, for any of the aggrieved who wished to file action against the State of California, local government or agencies in seeking redress of their grievances. Governor Arnold Schwarzenegger, who replaced Davis as a result of a recall election, vetoed the measure. While expressing sympathy for individuals who were illegally repatriated, the Governor stated, "these individuals were able to pursue legal action within a fixed period of time."[35] Steven Reyes, MALDEF, Mexican American Legal Defense and Educational Fund, attorney, accused the governor of refusing to extend to the aging repatriates the courtesy they had been denied when they were expelled. [36]

The second bill, SB 427 called for the establishment of an independent, privately financed commission to investigate and gather information regarding the coerced emigration and unconstitutional deportation of Mexicans during the period from 1929 to 1944, inclusive. The commission was to issue a report on its findings and make any appropriate recommendations. However, SB 427 was also vetoed by Governor Schwarzenegger. Basically, there were two reasons for the veto. The governor stated that there was no need or reason to create such a commission because it created another administrative box and he had sworn to do away with bureaucratic boxes, when he took office. He also asserted that the legislature was already empowered to create commissions without executive approval. In researching that assertion, Senator Joseph Dunn's office could find no state statute authorizing such independent action.[37] Latino leaders were dismayed at the Governor's actions. As an immigrant, they had hoped that he would have greater empathy for the plight of the repatriates. Although Senator Joseph Dunn was disappointed, he was not discouraged and stated he planned to introduce new bills during the next legislative session.

Senator Dunn also sponsored SJR21, soliciting Congress to establish a commission to investigate the role that the federal government played in the mass expulsion program. Congresswoman Hilda Solís has expressed support for establishing the commission. She sent a "Dear Colleague Letter" to the members of Congress providing them with informational background on the repatriation topic. This was done in anticipation of pending legislation, which she plans to introduce, calling for the establishment of a national fact finding commission. It will be empowered to review the facts and circumstances regarding the repatriation of legal residents and citizens of Mexican descent from 1929–1939. It will also review federal, state, and local directives that were issued to promote repatriation, and to recommend appropriate remedies. It will be directed to report its findings to Congress within one year after its creation.[38] Congresswoman Solís hosted a congressional staff briefing attended by Senator Dunn's staff. Dr. Francisco Balderrama was invited to brief the participants on the historical background of the coerced repatriation movement and MALDEF attorney Steve Reyes spoke about the lawsuit and pending legislation in California. The briefing sought to develop bipartisan support in Congress for establishing a commission.

Heeding Dale Shimasaki's advice to pursue multiple avenues in seeking acknowledgment and justice, the law firm of Kiesel, Boucher, and Larson and the Mexican American Legal Defense and Educational Fund (MALDEF) jointly filed a class-action lawsuit in the Superior Court of Los Angeles. They did so in behalf of repatriate Emilia Castañeda and 400,000 Mexicans forced to leave the State of California between 1929 and 1944. Named as defendants were the State of California, the County and City of Los Angeles, and the Los Angeles Area Chamber of Commerce. The suit claims that they conspired with federal immigration authorities to carry out a "coordinated, aggressive campaign to remove people of Mexican ancestry from California in large numbers," in violation of their constitutional rights. In addition, the suit also includes as defendants 500 as yet unnamed individuals and entities. Jesse Araujo, an attorney who assisted in preparing the suit, said, "We owe it to the victims and their families to bring this to everyone's attention."[39] The lawsuit seeks both monetary reparations and an apology. Attorney Steve Reyes, MALDEF, who is handling the case vowed, "to fight to see that justice is done and an apology was given to the affected individuals. And the legal action will include victims found in the future."[40] The *Guardian*, in London, also reported on the hearing in Sacramento, the repatriation ordeal and the resultant lawsuit. It quoted attorney Raymond Boucher of the Beverly Hills law firm that is cosponsoring the lawsuit as stating, "This lawsuit goes to the essence of who we are as a state and the dignity of a people. We have to recognize that in the 1930s we used the Mexican population as a scapegoat. Until we take an honest look in the mirror, none of us is truly safe."[41] The action does not preclude the possibility that a similar class-action suit may be filed against the federal government, the Department of Labor and the Immigration and Naturalization Service for their role in the unconstitutional deportation and coerced repatriation program they launched and abetted during the 1930s. However, the lawsuit was withdrawn to avoid an unfavorable ruling when legislation extending the statue of limitations failed. Yet MALDEF remained committed to "seek justice. . . . We intend to refile this lawsuit as new legislation makes its way through the legislature."[42]

At the American GI Forum's annual national convention in Frankenmuth, Michigan, in 2004, a resolution was passed supporting the creation of a commission to investigate the illegal deportation of American citizens of Mexican descent and legal Mexican residents. The convention also supported allowing the victims to sue for proper compensation.[43] Other organizations such as the California Federation of Teachers as well as the LCLAA Labor Council for Latin American Advancement joined the GI Forum in passing resolutions supporting the establishment of a commission "to study unconstitutional deportation."[44] The Hispanic National Bar Association, HNBA, at its annual convention in September 2003, also took cognizance of the illegal expulsion of members of the Mexican community during the 1930s. María Blanco, MALDEF national senior counsel, addressed the HNBA. She called attention to the fact that truth and reconciliation commissions had been established in more than 16 countries during the past 20 years, including Argentina, Chile, Bosnia, and South Africa. Blanco stressed the fact that, "In establishing the commissions, the governments of those countries understood that official recognition of the wrongs committed by government and private individuals is necessary to move beyond the past and into the future as one nation (or in this case one state) reconciled with its own history." She added, "As long as public denial exists and there is no collective truth . . . thousands of individuals are left to heal for themselves. Truth and reconciliation also is about governments asking their citizens for forgiveness for their acts in order to ensure what happened in the past would not be repeated."[45]

In addition, outreach efforts were made through Senator Joseph Dunn's office and other interested groups to call the public's attention to the issue of repatriation and the pending legal action. One particular event that created a great deal of interest was a town hall presentation at La Placita Church, in Los Angeles. It was both a fitting site and an emotional experience, for it was at the little park across the street, where on February 26, 1931, the INS conducted a notorious raid in an attempt to scare Mexicans into leaving "voluntarily." The presentation on September 13, 2003 drew a capacity crowd and was well covered by all phases of the news media. In addition to State Senator Joseph Dunn, Congresswoman Hilda Solís and Steve Reyes of MALDEF were also present. News of the hearing in Sacramento and the filing of a lawsuit were received by cheers from the enthusiastic audience. Their reaction exhibited both a sense of pride and relief that something was at long last being done to correct an injustice after so many years. *Decade of Betrayal* was cited as being the catalyst that provided the impetus for the hearing and the lawsuit, by making people aware of the scope of the tragedy.[46]

Events to publicize and draw public attention to the repatriation issue have also been held in Orange County, adjacent to Los Angeles County. One of them was a meeting with the Orange County Hispanic Chamber of Commerce. They were very supportive of the efforts to obtain justice for the victims of repatriation. An informational meeting was held in the city of Orange, hosted by several Mexican American advocacy groups in cooperation with Senator Dunn's office. Another meeting was held on September 24, 2004 at the *Los Angeles Times* corporate center in Costa Mesa to support the production of a full-length documentary of repatriation headed by Alex Cortes, Alfonso Alvarez, and Gerardo Briceño. The producers have conducted extensive interviews with repatriation survivors both in the United States and Mexico. More than 300 persons attended the meeting to support the making of the documentary. Film clips of repatriation interviews were shown along with displays illustrating the repatriation experience. Another highlight of the evening was the reading of a poem entitled, "A Spirit of Hope." It was written by Madrigal A. Cuauhtlatoatzin in memory of six of his relatives who, in spite of being American citizens, were taken from their home and deported. A former marine, Cuauhtlatoatzin, promised to be faithful and never forget. He ended the poem with the heartfelt words, "Semper Fi."[47]

In Los Angeles, County Supervisor Gloria Molina is pressing for establishing a museum housing the history of the Mexican community. It would be similar in some respects to the National Hispanic Cultural Center in Albuquerque, New Mexico. In any museum dealing with the Mexican experience, the repatriation and deportation programs of the 1930s would have to be appropriately featured. It has also been proposed that a plaque be placed or a monument be erected at the La Placita Park commemorating the historic role it played in the initiation of a tragedy that eventually engulfed one million people. With renewed awareness about what happened to the Mexican community during the 1930s, there is a degree of apprehension of what may lie ahead.

The apprehension is due to the fact that although at the end of the 2004–2005 legislative session, Governor Schwarzenegger signed SB 670, which called for an official acknowledgment and apology, he vetoed SB 645 which would have established a commission to study the repatriation issue and make recommendations regarding pertinent aspects, such as reparations.[48] Failure to sign both bills, introduced by California State Senator Joseph Dunn, prevented a sense of closure which would have helped to heal the traumatic wounds of the long suffering repatriation survivors.

¿Qué Pasó?
DOCUMENTS

■ ■

OPENING REMARKS OF DR. KEVIN STARR, CALIFORNIA STATE
LIBRARIAN, FOR CALIFORNIA SENATE SELECT COMMITTEE ON CITIZEN
PARTICIPATION HEARING, "EXAMINATION OF UNCONSTITUTIONAL
DEPORTATION AND COERCED EMIGRATION OF LEGAL RESIDENTS AND
U.S. CITIZENS OF MEXICAN DESCENT DURING 1930S." 15 JULY 2003.
Source: Transcription of Video Tape, Courtesy of Kevin Starr.

Since the early 19th century, which is to say following the enlightenment,
history has provided us with our most compelling philosophical category.
We live in time. We live in history. This history, moreover, is multidimen-
sional and complex. In one sense, if we take time as an absolute, history
is over and done with. It is the past. What has been done is done including the glories and triumphs of human achievement and also the abysmal
moments of misbehavior on the part of the human race. Even the most
flexible periods of temporal relativity does not allow us to return exactly
to the precise moment in the past and change the course of events.
This happens only in science fiction.

Thus we must relate to history on one level as something that is
not adjustable. It happened and we cannot undo it. On the other hand,
we human beings who study and try to understand history do so for a
present tense perspective. Our history which is the present is not fixed for
all time. We are making that history now by what we do, what we value,
and what we understand. This understanding of the past, moreover not
only feeds into the present but affects the future as well. Once we understand the past and once we internalize its moral meaning we can act
differently in the present and acting differently in the present we shape
a different future. History then is not fixed in terms of its affect on the
present and future. This is an important lesson otherwise we can become
slaves to the past and unable to change it and learn from it as well.

What do we owe history then as past, present, and future activity?
First and foremost we owe it the truth as far as we are able to determine

that truth. That is why historians search the record to establish past events as accurately as possible. Secondly, we need to interpret these events from a variety of perspectives: socially, culturally, politically, and from a moral perspective as well. Events in short, must be put into their proper context. Once these perspectives are understood, once these moral interpretations are achieved, we can deal with the present and future more effectively.

As late, our great and beloved state of California which means all of us together all 35 million of us functioning as individuals as society as a free elected government, this great state of California has been internalizing thanks in great measure to a generation of young scholars increasingly nuanced and complex message regarding the past. Some of these messages have been almost too terrible to bear. In the 1850s and 1860s, for example, we Californians hunted down and virtually extermi-nated our Native American brethren. That was a hard event for us today to assimilate. It does not fit into our concept of ourselves as a humane and liberal people. It is not this history that we wish were ours. But it is the history that we must research and repossess. We have also come to recognize that the State of California pursued a policy of enforced sterilization in the name of eugenics that will not pass muster today in any political or public constituency. Yet we acknowledge that we did this. The record stands clear. As state librarian of California, I have for the past 4 years been responsible for an ongoing program authorized by this legislature dealing with the presumptive and unjustified incarceration of Japanese Americans in 1942. Again, a painful lesson but one that we must face squarely and learn from.

Thanks to the research of scholars like Dr. Francisco Balderrama and Raymond Rodríguez, we are now facing another previously obscured fact of our history, in California and American history alike. The enforced repatriation of millions of Mexican residents of California and the American Southwest during the depression to include native-born American citizens. Like the extermination of Native Americans, sterilization of the unfortunate, and incarceration of Japanese Americans, this is a hard lesson for us to face. And I will leave these two distinguished scholars and your other testimonies to outline for you in further detail.

I would like, however, to just briefly ask the question: Why do we do this? Why do we plow up the past? Why do we establish an historical record through research that in so many ways is so unflattering to us. First of all, there is the basic human instinct to know the truth. We human beings do not like to dwell in ignorance or falsehood. Our minds are constituted to engage with reality. If these terrible things happened and they did, then we must set the record straight. Secondly, that record once it is set straight has meaning for our time. In the year 2003 of our common era the great state of California finds itself once again, as was the case in the 18th and 19th centurys until 1849 blessed with an Hispanic majority to include my own two granddaughters Raquel and Eva. As we move forward as a revitalized world community ecumenapolis, with a Hispanic majority. It is important that we understand everything that the Hispanic peoples of our state and the American Southwest endured during the repatriation program. What was endured—the uprooting of families, violations of citizenship, scenes of train stations where people were forced to board departing railroad cars, so suggestive of similar scenes in Europe at the same time.

It is painful to contemplate but we must do so. We must moreover internalize its moral meaning. We do this not to pick the scabs of our wounds although there is much pain involved. We do this because we must build our future relationship on a foundation of truth. We must face the past honestly and when the past is tragic as in the case of the repatriations we must make the highest form of atonement. What is that highest form of atonement? To determine that nothing like this would ever happen again. The pain of the past has already been suffered by those who endured it. We cannot go back in time and alleviate the pain. But we can assure that the pain was not meaningless. That pain reverberates into the present with its message. Never again, never again. History has given our great state and beloved state of California a most compelling challenge. To build up the world community to achieve ecumenapolis, the foundation of such a community must be the truth which is why these hearings are being held. This sheer acknowledgment of bad behavior begins the healing process. Since we have a grand multicultural California to build, let that healing begin now.

■ ■

10B. "MY FELLOW AMERICANS,"
CALIFORNIA STATE SENATOR JOSEPH DUNN.
Source: Courtesy of Joseph Dunn.

SACRAMENTO OFFICE
STATE CAPITOL
SACRAMENTO, CA 95814
TEL (916) 445-5831
FAX (916) 323-2323

RICK BATTSON
CHIEF OF STAFF

DISTRICT OFFICE
12397 LEWIS STREET, SUITE 103
GARDEN GROVE, CA 92840-4965
TEL (714) 705-1580
FAX (714) 705-1586

NORMA CAMPOS COBB
DISTRICT DIRECTOR

California State Senate

SENATOR
JOSEPH L. DUNN
THIRTY-FOURTH SENATE DISTRICT

STANDING COMMITTEES:
CHAIR, JUDICIARY
CHAIR, BUDGET AND FISCAL REVIEW
  SUBCOMMITTEE #4
ELECTIONS, REAPPORTIONMENT AND
  CONSTITUTIONAL AMENDMENTS
ENERGY, UTILITIES AND
  COMMUNICATIONS
GOVERNMENTAL ORGANIZATION
LABOR & INDUSTRIAL RELATIONS
PUBLIC EMPLOYMENT AND
  RETIREMENT
VETERANS AFFAIRS

SELECT COMMITTEES:
CHAIR, MOBILE AND
  MANUFACTURED HOMES
CHAIR, CITIZEN PARTICIPATION

JOINT COMMITTEE:
JOINT RULES

February 22, 2005

Dear Concerned Friends,

This letter addresses a little know but very tragic chapter in American history. During the 1930s, the United States government executed a systematic program of illegally deporting Americans for one reason and one reason alone: they were of Mexican descent. The program was called "repatriation," a fictitious word that created the illusion of returning to one's homeland. In reality, the deportees arrived in a country that was foreign to them, where they did not understand the culture and were treated like outcasts.

These unconstitutional deportations occurred throughout the country, with the largest number of deportees originating from California, Michigan and Texas. In particular, Los Angeles County was notorious for conducting mass roundups in its Latino neighborhoods, during which people were randomly taken from public areas, such as parks and market places, and herded onto trains bound for Mexico with no regard for their legal status or citizenship. Local authorities went through employee payrolls and hospital patient lists in search of last names that sounded Latino and deported them on the spot. Whether they were deported by force or by intimidation, the deportees all left behind their property and their livelihood. Whether the individuals had been promised that they would receive their belongings once in Mexico or that there would be ample land and opportunity awaiting them there, their fate was the same. The families and young children arrived in the interior of rural Mexico without plumbing or electricity and deprived of educational or economic opportunity.

I, like most Americans, was unaware of this injustice until the summer of 2001 when Bernie Enriquez, a member of my staff, recommended the book, *Decade of Betrayal*. What I read left me awestruck. Not only did the government commit a crime that discriminated against Americans on the basis of the color of their skin, the accent in their voice and the sound of their name, but 70 years later, not one public official had addressed, let alone corrected, this injustice.

I took several steps to bring about corrective measures. I held public hearings and town hall meetings where expert analyses and personal testimonies were presented and entered into public record for future generations to see. In an effort to determine the role California played in the illegal deportations, I organized a state Senate investigation. What we found was uglier than anything we imagined. Public records reveal communications between public officials that clearly demonstrate the mal intent of those who carried out this program. To complete our investigation, I introduced a bill (Senate Bill 427) in the California Legislature that would launch a formal state investigation and lay the groundwork for reparations. In 2004, SB 427 passed out of both houses of the state Legislature, only to be vetoed by Governor Arnold Schwarzenegger, who said, "I am going to blow up boxes; this bill creates new boxes."

To date, I have introduced a half-a-dozen bills that address this injustice and allow survivors to take legal action. Unfortunately, three bills died in the Legislature and, even more disappointing, three more were vetoed by two governors. Thus far, the system has not been able to provide real recourse to those who it has wronged, yet we must remain open to taking the action necessary to correct this injustice. Recently, I introduced a comprehensive bill (SB 645) that launches an investigatory commission, establishes a reparations fund to provide compensation for the survivors and provides victims with the right to take legal action for the damages they suffered.

I also initiated a process that requests a formal apology from the state of California to the victims and the construction of a public memorial near the site of the Olvera Street roundups. I firmly believe an apology is a necessary first step in achieving justice for those who were wronged. Moreover, this important missing piece of our state's history must be entered into public record – and the public's memory – if we are to prevent such an act from ever occurring again.

We will continue in this worthy endeavor until we are successful and this injustice is corrected. I hope that you will join us and support these efforts.

Very truly yours,

Joseph L. Dunn
Senator, 34th District

JLD:lmr

■ ■

10C. VETO MESSAGE BILL 933. CALIFORNIA GOVERNOR GRAY DAVIS
Source: Courtesy of Joseph Dunn.

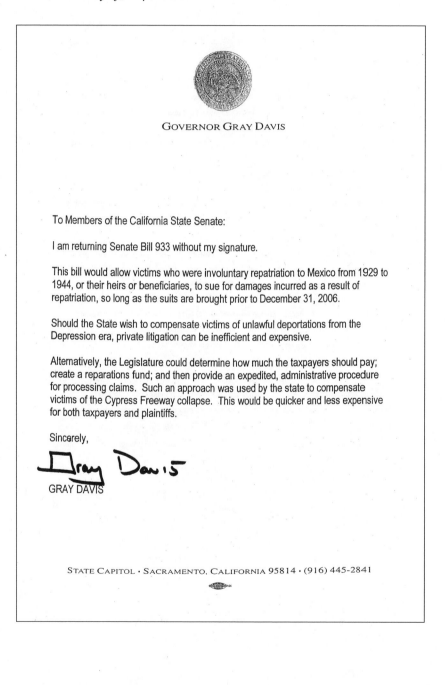

GOVERNOR GRAY DAVIS

To Members of the California State Senate:

I am returning Senate Bill 933 without my signature.

This bill would allow victims who were involuntary repatriation to Mexico from 1929 to 1944, or their heirs or beneficiaries, to sue for damages incurred as a result of repatriation, so long as the suits are brought prior to December 31, 2006.

Should the State wish to compensate victims of unlawful deportations from the Depression era, private litigation can be inefficient and expensive.

Alternatively, the Legislature could determine how much the taxpayers should pay; create a reparations fund; and then provide an expedited, administrative procedure for processing claims. Such an approach was used by the state to compensate victims of the Cypress Freeway collapse. This would be quicker and less expensive for both taxpayers and plaintiffs.

Sincerely,

GRAY DAVIS

STATE CAPITOL · SACRAMENTO, CALIFORNIA 95814 · (916) 445-2841

■ ■

10D. VETO MESSAGE BILL 37. CALIFORNIA GOVERNOR ARNOLD SCHWARZENEGGER

Source: Courtesy of Joseph Dunn.

GOVERNOR ARNOLD SCHWARZENEGGER

To the Members of the California State Senate:

I am returning Senate Bill 37 without my signature.

While I am very sympathetic towards victims who were involuntarily sent to Mexico as a result of repatriation efforts within California between 1929 and 1944, these individuals were able to pursue legal action within a fixed period of time. The purpose of the statute of limitation is to provide protection to defendants from antiquated claims. Such older claims are difficult to litigate against due to a loss of witnesses, evidence, and other factors.

Additionally, private litigation of potentially thousands of claims against the state, could burden the courts, result in increased costs to the state and local governments, and possibly require a settlement account for any successful claim. If the Legislature should decide, as a matter of public policy, to provide compensation, a reparations fund should be created to expedite the processing of these claims. This would be an efficient and less expensive method for both the taxpayers and the plaintiffs.

Once legislation creating this policy is enacted, it can be considered along with all other priorities and in the context of the State's fiscal condition at that time.

For these reasons I am returning this bill without my signature.

Sincerely,

Arnold Schwarzenegger

STATE CAPITOL • SACRAMENTO, CALIFORNIA 95814 • (916) 445-2841

10E. VETO MESSAGE BILL 427. CALIFORNIA GOVERNOR ARNOLD SCHWARZENEGGER

Source: Courtesy of Joseph Dunn.

GOVERNOR ARNOLD SCHWARZENEGGER

To the Members of the California State Senate:

I am returning Senate Bill 427 without my signature.

The establishment of a new commission is not necessary. The Legislature and the Administration can create commissions to advise them without the need for legislation. As I said in my State of the State I am going to "blow up the boxes"; this bill creates new boxes without explaining the need for a new commission. The Legislature and the Administration have many resources to advise them on the issues that this commission is being created for.

For these reasons I am returning Senate Bill 427 without my signature.

Sincerely,

Arnold Schwarzenegger

STATE CAPITOL • SACRAMENTO, CALIFORNIA 95814 • (916) 445-2841

Old Mexican laborer saying: "I have worked all my life and all I have is my broken body." Imperial Valley, California, June 1935. Photograph by Dorothea Lange, courtesy of the Library of Congress, FSA Project.

Epilogue
Fin

No lloro, pero me acuerdo.　　　　*I don't cry, but I remember.*

　　—Dicho Mexicano　　　　　　　Mexican Proverb

The foregoing work chronicles the tragedy of a people who, in spite of being maligned and mistreated by American society, refused to surrender to adversity. Like other immigrant groups, they were proud of the contributions they had made to their adopted country. However, during the Great Depression, American society chose to disregard the significant role that Mexicans had played in creating the nation's wealth in such areas as agriculture, mining, manning assembly and production lines, building and maintaining the railroads, as well as enriching the nation's culture and cuisine. Instead, regardless of their place of birth either in the United States or Mexico, it became fashionable to blame Mexicans for the country's economic ills. A relentless campaign was launched to get rid of the pariahs by shipping them to Mexico. Since many of the Mexicans had been actively recruited to come and work in the United States, their ruthless expulsion was an ironic twist of fate. The vendetta created one of the first major contingent of displaced refugees in the twentieth century.

One of the most tragic aspects of the movement was the wholesale violation of basic human rights. When individuals were caught in INS raids, they were summarily deported without being informed of or accorded their legal rights. The wanton disregard of legal constraints in denying deportees their constitutional rights was so flagrant that groups as diverse as the Los Angeles Bar Association, the Wickersham Commission, industrialists, merchants, bankers, and ranchers felt compelled to condemn the illegal tactics, but to no avail. Protests about the injustice were drowned out by the roar of approval from opportune politicians, labor unions, civic, and patriotic groups. In 1942, another minority group, the Japanese, also learned the bitter lesson that constitutional guarantees are meaningless when mob hysteria is accorded institutional or legal status.

In many instances, the same charges of illegal and unconstitutional action can be made regarding the repatriation and deportation efforts. As in the days of slavery, when families were split asunder by selling members "downriver," Mexican families suffered the same fate. Wives often refused to return to Mexico with their husbands because their children were American-born and were entitled to remain in the United States. American-born spouses who had married Mexican Nationals often refused to go to Mexico. The situation became truly heart wrenching when older children refused to join their parents on the trek south. Younger children who had no choice but to accompany their parents suffered wholesale violations of their citizenship rights. Native-born citizens cannot be legally banished to a foreign country or denied their "inalienable rights" without due process. Children were routinely and callously denied their most basic rights. This accounts for the fact that approximately 60 percent of those summarily expelled were children who had been born in the United States and were legally American citizens.

Lacking concrete or convincing substance were the three facetious claims often used to justify or at least to rationalize banishing the Mexicans: Jobs would be created for "real Americans"; cutting the welfare rolls would save taxpayers huge sums of money; and "those people" would be better off in Mexico with their "own kind!" In every case, the allegations begged or ignored the question. With unemployment rates in the colonias averaging 50 percent or more, due to decrees forbidding their hiring in government or public projects, the Mexicans had been effectively eliminated as a rival working force. Many private employers were also scare headed by mobs into firing their Mexican workers including Mexican Americans. Furthermore, since the Mexicans constituted less than 1 percent of the nation's total population, few jobs would have been made available even if all three and a half million had been shipped to Mexico.

The same false claims were made concerning welfare costs and projected savings. Mexican families with American-born children qualified for welfare assistance if the family could meet residency requirements and prove entitlement. However, even in Los Angeles and Detroit, the cities with the largest number of Mexicans on relief, they constituted 10 percent or less of the total number of welfare recipients. In truth, the anticipated savings were impossible to achieve for the simple reason that 85 percent of the approximately 20 million people on welfare were native-born or naturalized American citizens. Yet politicians and the media adroitly created and nurtured the impression in the public's mind that Mexicans constituted the overwhelming majority of those on the public dole. The baseless and misleading charges were merely a ploy to inflame an overwrought public's anti-Mexican passions.

Equally inane were repeated attempts to justify the expulsion of the Mexicans by claiming that they would be better off in Mexico among relatives and friends. The irony was that Mexican families residing in barrios or colonias were already living among close relatives and friends. Many of them had resided in the United States for such a long time, often their entire adult life, that they did not have close friends or relatives in Mexico. Bearing the traumatic burden of being shipped "back" to Mexico were those least able to cope with their plight: the children. Shipping them to Mexico so they could be with "their own kind" was absolutely absurd. Although of Mexican ancestry, they considered themselves to be Americans and many of them spoke only a limited amount of Spanish. To them, historically and culturally, Mexico was a foreign country.

Nonetheless, welfare authorities reasoned that young children rightfully belonged with their parents and should accompany the family to Mexico. This convenient rationale relieved repatriation authorities of any blame or responsibility for failing to protect the rights of the American-born children. Regretfully, no one seemed to care about what was happening to them. Their personal identity and sense of self-worth were stripped from them without any qualms and hardly a ripple of protest in their behalf. The prevailing attitude was that "a Mexican was a Mexican," regardless of birthright.

The assumption that a Mexican was a Mexican prevailed in both the United States and Mexico, but for different reasons. The Mexican government accorded dual citizenship to children who were born abroad and whose parents were Mexican citizens. This dual citizenship was intended to enable them to move freely between the respective countries. It was also used as an inducement for them to relocate and settle in Mexico, with all the rights and privileges enjoyed by native-born individuals. It was hoped that they would not only augment Mexico's relatively small population, but would also contribute to the nation's socioeconomic stability.

In American society, the attitude of "once a Mexican, always a Mexican" enabled authorities to take collective action against the entire Spanish-speaking population. They were not hampered by the task of having to differentiate between Mexican Nationals and native-born Mexican Americans. As a matter of fact, individuals who "looked Mexican," regardless of their country of origin were subjected to the same abusive treatment. This convenient ploy made racial and anti-Mexican propaganda easier to disseminate and more readily acceptable. In addition, it created a situation in which people blindly condoned illegal and discriminatory acts against a defenseless minority. The public's support dramatically eased the awesome task of expelling, with complete impunity, hundreds of thousands of people whose only crime was poverty and being of Mexican ancestry.

Despite the odds arraigned against them, most Mexicans struggled to maintain their self-respect and independence. Three significant examples attest to their dauntless perseverance and their determination to survive. As has been previously stated, the overwhelming majority disdained applying for welfare and attempted to survive by a variety of innovative means. A resourceful lot, they often managed to cope with the relentless and bruising depression better than did their Anglo counterparts. Families who had lost their breadwinners, experienced prolonged unemployment or were split apart by deportation or repatriation were aided by families, friends, and neighbors. In most barrios and colonias, a common bond evolved in order to help each other survive. Families who had always paid their own way were reluctant to admit defeat and seek any type of government assistance. In many instances, that attitude served as the impetus for families who decided to return to Mexico of their own volition.

Disdaining any sort of government interference, the vast majority of Mexicans who lived adjacent to, or within driving distance of, the border simply loaded their personal belongings into the family sedan and headed south. Individuals who owned a truck and were returning to Mexico often found it convenient to take two or three families with them. This enabled the owner either to charge them a small fee or to share the trip's expenses.

Women traveling alone or with young children welcomed the opportunity to hitch a ride with family or friends. Given the perilous nature of the journey, it was always best to travel with several companions especially on the desolate roads south of the border. The highly individualistic Mexicans found it more to their liking to ignore the bureaucratic red tape on both sides of the border and to make their own arrangements. Many chose to leave the same way they had arrived, unobtrusively.

The individualistic and philosophical attitude of the Mexicans illustrates the third aspect of their struggle to survive. Even during the darkest days of the Great Depression, they persevered in attempts to overcome racial discrimination, social injustice, segregated schooling, and unfair treatment in the workplace. Protests, demonstrations, and strikes were utilized in attempts to achieve their goals. In pursuing their aims, however, they were often set upon by hoodlums, goon squads, and local police and sheriff's deputies. Despite the beatings inflicted, barrio leaders repeatedly exhorted their compatriots not to abandon the struggle to improve the quality of life for themselves and for their children.

Exacerbating their plight and adding to their dilemma were the routine violations of legal rights by the judicial system. Basic procedural rights were commonly ignored as judges, sworn to uphold the law, turned their chambers into nothing more than kangaroo courts. The news media joined in discrediting protestors and their goals by accusing them of being un-American and labeling them as communist agitators. With the willing connivance of the Labor Department and the Immigration Service, and the collaboration of police and the court system, trumped-up charges were used to justify deporting Mexicans who advocated ending discrimination, better working conditions, or desegregated schools.

Plagued by such adverse circumstances and envisioning little change for the better, many destitute and desperate Mexicans viewed returning to Mexico, if not a boon, at least as a chance for a better life. Official releases on both sides of the border emphasized the benefits to be reaped by those who took advantage of the opportunity to return and colonize productive lands awaiting the plow. Using the work habits and skills acquired in El Norte, they would be able to help Mexico achieve new heights in agricultural and industrial production. The newcomers would also enrich the country's social development by augmenting the nucleus of the emerging middle class. Politically, they could infuse the nation with the ideals of a viable democratic system. Optimistic returnees and government officials envisioned Mexico assuming the role of "los yanquis" of Latin America. With the help of the repatriates, Mexico would be propelled into the twentieth century.

In actuality, the results were radically different from what the repatriates had envisioned. The dreams, hopes, and lofty aspirations failed to materialize. The task of resettling and assimilating the horde of people returning to la madre patria overwhelmed the Mexican bureaucracy. The sheer numbers and the enormity and complex nature of the vast undertaking taxed the government's ability to respond effectively. Farmland— vital to successful colonization and the crucial factor on which the nation's prosperity would be based—was not available in sufficient quantities. Despite the government's good intentions and its heroic efforts to build dams and irrigation canals, there were simply too many people who desperately needed help. No one anticipated that one million people would be dumped into a society of fifteen million, still struggling to recover from the aftermath of a revolution that had ended barely a decade ago. No one foresaw or anticipated the duration or extent of the depression. Thinking and planning were geared to the repatriation experience of the limited depression of the early 1920s. Unfortunately, official Mexican edicts or decrees could not change the nation's climate or topography.

Lacking the opportunity to colonize and having no place else to go, most repatriates gradually drifted back into their native villages and ranchitos. Some opted to settle in the larger cities in the hope of earning a decent living. For the majority of the newcomers, the scenario they had foreseen when they made up their minds to go back to Mexico remained an illusion. Instead of being welcomed home with open arms, acquiring good land, and regaining their self-respect, they were trapped in a morass of grinding poverty rivaling or even worse than what they had left behind in the United States.

Compounding their plight and adding to the misery of the repatriates was the fact that their status and well-being often became expedient political footballs. Politicos were aware that efforts to aid the resettlement of repatriates did not set well with rank-and-file Mexicans. Despite official policy, many politicians and their supporters believed that the nation's fiscal and material resources should be used to benefit loyal sons and daughters who had stayed home. Repatriates accused antagonists of conveniently overlooking the financial remuneration consisting of millions of dollars that they had remitted to families and relatives in Mexico during more prosperous times. Each group viewed the other as ingrates.

Many Mexicans felt that the expectations and demands of the repatriates were unwarranted and that they should stop badgering the Mexican government, who could ill afford to grant them the aid they so desperately needed. Mexicanos believed that repatriates should have exhausted all legal means available to them before succumbing to their fate. Instead, they had readily acquiesced in their own expulsion. By doing so, they had completely absolved the United States of any responsibility for their well-being; this was especially true for those with American-born children. The children were deemed to be the responsibility of the American, rather than the Mexican government.

In hindsight, the protestors were undoubtedly correct. The callous attitude of American authorities exposed the repatriated children to a cruel and virtually untenable fate. Ultimately, it was the children who bore the brunt of rejection and discrimination. They were neither Americans nor Mexicans as defined by their respective cultures. In the U.S. they were unilaterally classified as Mexicans, regardless of birthright. In Mexico they were regarded as Americanized Mexicans, and called derogatory names such as *pochos*, *tejanos*, or even *gringos*. Adjustment was especially difficult for teenagers and they constantly badgered their parents to return to the United States.

In covering the repatriation situation objectively, the Mexican media was caught in a tri-cornered dilemma. It had to support the official government policy while cognizant of the problems and resentment generated by the repatriates. It was also aware of the fact that many of them resented living in Mexico and wanted to return home to the United States. The Mexican press reacted with hostility toward "ingrates" who sought to leave. Their departure was viewed as a slap in the face to Mexico's generous hospitality. The media failed to understand the urge that tormented young repatriates and compelled them to return to their rightful homeland. The predictable reaction was an example as already noted, of the perverse dilemma that beset the Mexican press. Failure to support and expound the government's official policy could have dire consequences. In commenting on the problems associated with the repatriates, the press had to be careful to absolve the government of any responsibility for the deplorable situation. While lauding the government's efforts, it unmercifully castigated the United States for its inhumane and racist actions.

Although not faced with the constraints that hindered the Mexican press, few English-language newspapers in the United States protested the injustices perpetrated against Mexican Nationals or American citizens who happened to be of Mexican ancestry. While legal justification could be made for getting rid of unwanted aliens, it was an entirely different matter to deprive American citizens of their constitutional rights solely because of the accident of birth. Instead of protesting the horrendous injustice and wholesale violations of basic human rights, the media acquiesced in the despicable action by commending authorities for their zeal and success in getting rid of as many Mexicans as possible. The failure to speak out in behalf of justice for the Mexican community remains a black, irredeemable blot on the record of the American press.

In assessing the biased coverage accorded repatriation and deportation by the media, it must be borne in mind that neither the American nor the Mexican government was anxious to have its role in the tragedy publicly disclosed. The United States feared that the massive repatriation and deportation efforts could have negative repercussions upon its relations with countries in Latin America. It did not want to exacerbate the situation at a time when it was seeking to curtail immigration from the Western Hemisphere. To counter the adverse publicity, emissaries were sent abroad to convey assurances of America's goodwill. The United States was zealous in its efforts not to be perceived as a heartless society that turned its back on indigent immigrants in their hour of need.

The Mexican government also sought to minimize the repatriation issue in order to not alarm its own people about the magnitude of the problem. It diligently sought to avoid any embarrassment due to its inability to cope with the situation. The official figure of approximately 500,000, for example, fails to acknowledge those repatriates who returned of their own volition for a variety of reasons. Additionally, the Mexican government was caught between the horns of the proverbial dilemma: Since it was pursuing its own policy of expulsion against the Chinese and other unwanted individuals, it was not in a position to protest the expulsion of its Nationals from the United States. Mexico judiciously supported the right of every nation to determine who would be allowed to reside within its borders.

Obviously, authorities in both countries would have been acutely embarrassed if an accurate record of the number of Mexicans shipped to Mexico had been kept. However, a definitive body count is not essential to the essence of the tragic experience. Of greater importance were the consequences suffered by those forced to depart as well as those who remained behind. The loss of approximately one-third of the Mexican population in the United States augured an uncertain future for residents of México de afuera. Barrios and colonias were not only physically gutted; they lost a large cadre of dedicated community leaders. More significantly, they suffered the loss of a generation of young minds.

The loss effectively stifled the socioeconomic development of Mexican colonias in the United States. Seemingly, the community had to await the coming of age of a new generation unencumbered by the stifling experience of a decade of betrayal before recovering from the ordeal. That may help to explain why the "Chicano Movement" did not occur until twenty-five years after the end of the ominous decade. One can only speculate what might have been achieved in the intervening period if the Mexican community had not been devastated by the massive travesty unleashed against it. In truth, that may well constitute the ultimate tragedy of the anti-Mexican movement during the Great Depression.

What may have been accomplished by the Mexican community in the intervening years is perhaps best illustrated by the success of the repatriates who returned and the achievements of their children. In spite of the harrowing ordeal suffered on both sides of the border, the vast majority of them managed to readjust to life in the United States. In addition to their strength of character and perseverance, there are several key aspects that contributed to their successful integration into society. Most of those who returned were in their late teens or in their twenties. Their most ambitious and productive years lay ahead. Just as their forced repatriation was fomented by the Great Depression, their return coincided with the advent of World War II. Anxious to overcome the adversity that had plagued them most of their lives, they enthusiastically seized the opportunity to join the labor force engendered by the booming defense industry. In addition, the transition from a wartime status to a thriving domestic economy enabled them to buy homes, send their children to school, and find their niche in American society.

In most instances, the major adjustment was in establishing relationships with family members and friends who had escaped the deportation and repatriation dragnets and remained in the United States. Inevitably, both groups had become the products of vastly different cultures. The dissimulation of families grown apart, at times caused the returnees to reject the familial association and strike out on their own by moving out of the colonia and by marrying non-Mexicans. It was often an aggravation to their Americanized relatives to tolerate or readily accept back into the family fold, individuals who were "different" and whose lack of proficiency in English proved an embarrassment. Depending on their age when they returned, some ex-repatriates attended school in an effort to overcome their language deficiency in English and it enabled them to proceed successfully with their lives. Without dissension, the returnees were all extremely proud of the success their children had achieved. In a sense, it signified the fruition of their indomitable will and spirit that had sustained them when all hope of ever returning to the land of their birth seemed utterly hopeless. From their point of view, it made all their suffering and despair worthwhile. It also contributed to their reluctance to encumber their children with the details of the shame and abuse they had been forced to endure at a very young and impressionable age. Those who returned home, were forced to undergo a period of readjustment with varying degrees of success.

Perhaps the group of former repatriates, who experienced the most difficult challenge in their quest to return home, were the young men who were called upon to serve in the military. In some instances, there were young repatriates who resented being drafted and forced to fight for a country that had ignored their inherent rights as American citizens and expelled them without any qualms. Understandably, some decided not to return home until a more opportune time. Those who served did so with distinction, because despite everything that had happened to them, the United States was still their country. Upon returning from the war, many Mexican American servicemen bitterly resented the fact that in spite of their sacrifice, American society still regarded and treated them as second class citizens. However, they were resolved not to accept the discriminatory treatment their parents had stoically endured in the past. Emboldened by their unity of purpose, they formed their own American Legion or Veterans of Foreign Wars posts and the GI Forum and they also joined LULAC, League of United Latin American Citizens. The quest for equality and an end to discriminatory practices had begun. Eventually, they would be joined by organizations like MALDEF, Mexican American Legal Defense and Educational Fund and the Southwest Voter Registration. What became known as the GI Generation also led the assault on higher education. Due to the GI Bill, some of them became the first in their family to earn a college degree. They became the vanguard of an emerging professional class.

Once successfully established, the aging repatriates, often prodded by their children and grandchildren, became interested in exploring the role their particular families had played in the repatriation tragedy. In many instances, they believed that repatriation had been a local phenomenon restricted to places like Los Angeles, El Paso, or Detroit that had a large un-employed Mexican population, some of them on welfare. As they began their efforts to delve into the personal and historical aspects of the situa-tion, they were amazed by the lack of information available. They were stunned to learn about the national scope of the operation and the fact that minimally, at least 1,000,000 Mexican Nationals and Mexican Americans had been forcibly expelled or scare headed into going to Mexico. For indi-viduals and groups, such as Fronteras Norteñas in Detroit, *Decade of Betrayal* became a prolific source of information. It became the catalyst for impelling them to continue their research including a pilgrimage to San Luis Potosí and the production of a documentary depicting the repatriation ordeal. Their quest received renewed impetus as a result of the hearing on repatriation in Sacramento.

The hearing was conducted by State Senator Joseph Dunn, who became intrigued with the subject after reading *Decade of Betrayal*. He was dumb-founded to learn about the tragic travesty that had been illegally perpetrated upon the Mexican community, and the fact that it was ignored in our history books. He resolved to undertake the task of attempting to correct the gross injustice. As a result of the hearing, Senator Dunn introduced two bills, one to provide a window of opportunity for repatriates who wished to file for redress of the injustice and the second to create a commission to study the issue and propose recommendations. The governor vetoed both bills. A res-olution was also passed, calling on Congress to create a federal commission to study the issue of coerced or unconstitutional deportation and repatria-tion. A lawsuit was filed in the Los Angeles Superior Court of Los Angeles County seeking acknowledgment of the injustice, an apology and fiscal remu-neration. A series of town hall meetings, including one at Our Lady Queen of the Angels Church on historic Olvera Street, were held. At the events, repatri-ation survivors have adamantly declared that they were not interested in monetary compensation because no amount of money would repay or make up for all they lost and the shame and suffering they were forced to endure.

What they would like is to receive a formal, public apology from the federal, state, and local entities that subjected them to such a cruel and unjust experience. They also want to bring the topic of repatriation "out of the closet" so that the educational system and the general public can become as aware of repatriation as they are of the holocaust and the unconstitutional incarceration of the Japanese during World War II. Of the alleged 400,000 people repatriated from California, it is estimated that only about 25,000 survivors would be eligible for any settlement agreed upon.

The state senate hearing in Sacramento, the lawsuit filed in Los Angeles, and the town hall meetings have attracted a great deal of media attention. Both the English and Spanish language media in the United States and Mexico have given the repatriation topic unprecedented coverage. Suddenly, repatriation survivors found themselves being interviewed not only in the press but also on radio and television. The media reaction was overwhelmingly fair and sympathetic. The sincerity, demeanor, and candor of the survivors created a very positive image of people whose only "crime" was being poor and of Mexican ancestry. That alone was enough to label them as undesirables and subject them to being unlawfully deprived of their American citizenship. Media commentaries invariably called attention to the illegal and unconstitutional measures utilized, under the color of law, to deny their most basic rights, rights all human beings are entitled to in a democratic society. Without doubt, the repatriation nightmare ranks as one of the most horrendous acts ever committed by government authorities and sanctioned by American society. Many repatriation survivors have expressed the hope that by calling attention to their plight as the result of unbridled, anti-Mexican hysteria, it will prevent any future group of immigrants from ever being subjected to denial of their constitutional rights by the same government that is sworn to uphold them.

Such concern is justified because of the rising anti-foreigner, anti-immigration, anti-illegal hysteria that once again seems to be engulfing the country. This is especially true since the 9/11 terrorist attack. Once again, people are being held incognito, without formal charges being levied against them, or being allowed to consult a lawyer. As happened to the Mexicans deported or repatriated during the 1930s, denial of legal counsel constitutes the first step in the breakdown and willful violation of the judicial process. We have seen the treatment accorded to Arab and Muslim individuals suspected of being terrorists. We also have seen evidence, once again of wholesale violations of the rights of immigrants, especially Mexicans and Latinos in sporadic raids in their neighborhoods in the San Bernardino and Riverside County areas in Southern California. Individuals who looked "Mexican" were accosted in the street by immigration officials with the intent of ascertaining their status in the United States even though such racial profiling is forbidden by law. Additionally, the initiative has been utilized in California and Arizona in well orchestrated attempts to deny social services to undocumented residents. Both initiatives were passed by sizable voter majorities but were challenged in the courts. In the interest of national security, sealing our borders and suspending all immigration for an unspecified period of time are alternatives that are also being proposed and seriously considered.

Cooler heads are proposing more moderate and accommodating means of insuring our safety and controlling immigration. Mexico's President Vicente Fox and President George W. Bush had several discussions about controlling the estimated influx of one million undocumented immigrants allegedly crossing the border each year. Approximately, only a third are caught. In an effort to deter or delay their reentry to the United States, flights were instituted to fly detainees to the interior of Mexico, rather than just releasing them back across the border. In many instances, the individuals apprehended were back in the United States within twenty-four hours. It has been proposed that a guest worker program be instituted in cooperation and under the supervision of both nations. One aspect of the proposed program that has engendered a great deal of opposition is the fear that it constitutes an amnesty program in disguise, especially if workers are allowed to earn legal residency. There is also growing opposition to granting any concessions to undocumented immigrants. That includes denying them drivers license or accepting as valid, the ID cards, matrículas, issued to Mexican Nationals by the Mexican consular offices in the United States. The issuance of visitor visas is also drawing stiff opposition because many individuals exceed their authorized stay and disappear into the abyss of undocumented residents. As yet, no one has come up with an equitable solution to the daunting immigration problem. Each proposed solution engenders minute scrutiny by nearly all areas and segments of society.

Due to the recent influx of large numbers of Mexicans and Latinos into the Midwest and Deep South, those areas are struggling to adjust to the invasion. That is why states as diverse as Colorado and Georgia are contemplating action similar to that undertaken by California and Arizona. The local

reaction is mixed. Towns that were dying on the vine due to loss of population, suddenly find themselves being regenerated. However, small, rural communities are struggling with questions about education, housing, and
assimilation, which they are facing for the first time. ESL (English as a Second
Language) classes and books in English and Spanish are in great demand.
Bookstores in California and Texas are being called upon to provide bilingual
materials. A new wave of immigrants is spreading rapidly throughout the
nation. Latinos are the largest and fastest growing segment of society. What
it forebodes for the future of the nation is anyone's guess. To a large degree,
the result will depend upon the attitude and the reaction of the American
people. The bills sponsored by California State Senator Joseph Dunn, would
have provided a sense of closure and helped heal old wounds.

However, as in the 1930s, events beyond our political control may once
again end the controversy regarding Mexican immigration policy. In this
instance, the ravages of old age rather than war will be the deciding factor.
In the United States the population over sixty-five is aging twice as fast as
the general population. That fact, plus the nation's low birthrate, means that
as the twenty-first century progresses, the United States will be forced to
import workers. Once again, Mexico will be a prime source of dependable
labor. As Mexicans are fond of saying about what the fickle and unpre-
dictable fates have in store for us: "Dios sabrá, Qué será, será!" (God's will
be done. What will be, will be).

Sources and Methodology

Decade of Betrayal rests primarily on new and original sources while incorporating appropriate secondary sources such as theses, dissertations, monographs, and articles. The study draws heavily from archival materials in the United States and Mexico, in particular the Archivo de la Secretaría de Relaciones Exteriores in Mexico City and the United States National Archives in Washington, D.C. Particular attention has been given to the extensive documentation prepared by the respective Consular Services. Dispatches from American and Mexican consuls provided a wealth of detailed information. American consuls presented site observations, insightful evaluations, and personal commentaries. Mexican consuls expounded on employment and unemployment forecasts as well as immigration and repatriation trends and statistics. The Mexican consuls also reported the rendering of assistance to Mexican Nationals encountering economic, social, or legal problems while living in the United States. Among the American and Mexican government records are telegrams, letters, and petitions by individuals and various groups. These statements provide a unique personal dimension. The archival materials were supplemented by journals and newspapers in Spanish and English from both sides of the border. These publications chronicled on a daily basis, the immensity and gravity of the repatriation movement. Various primary sources from regional and local collections in Mexico and the United States were also incorporated to strengthen the narration and analysis.

A critical complement to the archival and printed sources was rich oral history testimony. The personal and professional associations of the authors proved especially helpful in arranging interviews. Those interviewed included government and community leaders, but priority was given to repatriates. Among the repatriates interviewed were men and women who had experienced repatriation as children and others whose experience occurred as adults. The interview sessions varied in length from one to three hours and were tape-recorded. Discussions focused not only on the repatriation experience, but also on life during the depression years. Interview transcripts and recordings by other researchers were also utilized to expand the oral history testimony. Analysis of the various interviews confirmed or refined information found in written sources. Oral history contributed significantly to determining the impact of the repatriation movement on the lives of Mexican Nationals, Mexican Americans, and their families in the United States and Mexico.

Notes

Introduction

1. Abraham Hoffman, *Unwanted Mexican Americans in the Great Depression: Repatriation Pressures, 1929–1939* (Tucson: University of Arizona Press, 1974) and Mercedes Carreras de Velasco, *Los Mexicanos que devolvió la crisis, 1929–1932* (México, D.F.: Secretaría de Relaciones Exteriores, 1974).

    The authors first explored aspects of Mexican repatriation in Francisco E. Balderrama, *In Defense of La Raza: The Los Angeles Mexican Consulate and the Mexican Community, 1929–1936* (Tucson: University of Arizona Press, 1982); and Raymond Rodríguez, "Mexicans Go Home," *Southland Sunday Magazine*, in *Independent, Press-Telegram* (14 October 1974), 8–14.

2. See: Richard A. García, *Rise of the Mexican American Middle Class: San Antonio, 1929–1941* (College Station: Texas A & M University Press, 1991); Zaragosa Vargas, *Proletarians of the North: A History of Mexican Industrial Workers in Detroit and the Midwest* (Berkeley: University of California Press, 1993); Vicki L. Ruiz, *Cannery Women/Cannery Lives: Mexican Women, Unionization, and the California Food Processing Industry, 1930–1950* (Albuquerque: University of New Mexico Press, 1987).

3. George Sánchez, *Becoming Mexican American: Ethnicity, Culture, and Identity in Chicano Los Angeles, 1900–1945* (New York: Oxford University Press, 1993); Camille Guerin-Gonzales, *Mexican Workers and the American Dream: Immigration, Repatriation, and California Farm Labor, 1900–1939* (New Brunswick, NJ: Rutgers University Press, 1994); Fernando Saúl Alanis Enciso, *El valle del Río Bravo, Tamaulipas, en la décade de 1930.* (Ciudad Victoria: El Colegio de Tamaulipas-El Colegio de San Luis, 2003).

Immigration

1. See *Los Angeles Times*, 8 October 1991, for an extensive report on immigration movements throughout the world.

2. México, Secretaría de Relaciones Exteriores, *Informe de la Secretaría de Relaciones Exteriores* (México, D.F.: Imprenta Nacional, 1900), 160.

3. Victor S. Clark, "Mexican Labor in the United States," *Bulletin of the Bureau of Labor* 17 (September 1908), 496.

4. Interview: Daniel Torres; Safe-Conduct Pass, Agua Prieta, Mexico, 31 January 1916, courtesy of Daniel Torres.

5. Ibid.

6. México, Secretaría de Relaciones Exteriores, *Memoria de la Secretaría de Relaciones Exteriores de agosto de 1928 ajJulio de 1929 presentada al H. congreso de la Unión por Genaro Estrada* (México, D.F.: Imprenta de la Secretaría de Relaciones Exteriores, 1929), 1549–50.

7. United States Department of Commerce, Bureau of the Census, *Fifteenth Census of the United States, 1930: Population, Special Report of Foreign-Born White Families by Country of Birth of Head* (Washington, D.C.: United States Government Printing Office, 1933), 199.

8. Manuel Gamio, *Mexican Immigration to the United States: A Study of Human Migration and Adjustment* (Chicago: University of Chicago Press, 1930), 3; and Paul S. Taylor, *Mexican Labor in the United States: Migration Statistics* (Berkeley: University of California Press, 1929), 254. Official immigration figures for this historical period and other eras are definitely undercounts, whether based upon American or Mexican sources. Ricardo Romo has shown Mexican figures to be significantly higher than American estimates, in "Responses to Mexican Immigration, 1910–1930," *Aztlán: International Journal of Chicano Studies Research* 6 (Summer 1975), 178.

9. United States Immigration Commission, *Reports of the Immigration Commission, Immigrants in Industries* (Washington, D.C.: Government Printing Office, 1911), pt. 24, 3:449. The report and commission was named Dillingham after its chairman, Senator William P. Dillingham of Vermont.

10. Interviews: Dr. Reynaldo Carreón and Eduardo Negrete.

11. Interviews: Pablo Alcántara; Hicks interview: Jesús Casárez, and Ramón Curiel.

12. Mario T. García, *Desert Immigrants: The Mexicans of El Paso, 1880–1920* (New Haven, Conn.: Yale University Press, 1981), 46–47.

13. Mark Reisler, *By the Sweat of Their Brow: Mexican Immigrant Labor in the United States, 1900–1940* (Westport, Conn.: Greenwood Press, 1976), 12;

Lawrence A. Cardoso, *Mexican Emigration to the United States, 1897–1931: Socio-Economic Patterns* (Tucson: University of Arizona Press, 1980), 34.

14. Reisler, *By the Sweat of Their Brow*, 60–61.

15. Vera L. Sturges, "Mexican Immigrants," *Survey* 46 (July, 1921): 470–71.

16. Gamio, *Mexican Immigration*, 13–17; Gamio was the first to reveal the significance of the Central Plateau as a source of Mexican immigration.

17. Cardoso, *Mexican Emigration*, 9–10.

18. For the most extensive examination of the *Porfiriato* see the classic multiple-volume study of Daniel Cosío Villegas, ed., *Historia moderna de México* (México, D.F.: Editorial Hermes, 1962–72).

19. George McBride, *The Land Systems of Mexico* (New York: American Geographical Society, 1923), 154.

20. Cardoso, *Mexican Emigration*, 10–11.

21. Ibid., 17. An excellent discussion of economic and political tensions in rural Mexico for campesinos is Ann L. Craig, *The First Agraristas: An Oral History of a Mexican Agrarian Reform Movement* (Berkeley: University of California Press, 1983).

22. Ibid.

23. Interviews: Lucas Lucio, José B. Solórzano; Claremont Colleges interviews: Enrique Vásquez.

24. Ricardo Romo, *East Los Angeles: History of a Barrio* (Austin: University of Texas Press, 1983), 42.

25. Gamio, *Mexican Immigration*, 13–17.

26. Interview: Julio Guerrero and José David Orozco; Hicks interviews: Jesús Casárez and Eduardo Rubio. The preceding were leaders and participants in Mexican Catholic organizations.

27. Interview: Torres.

28. Ibid.; Torres Family Letter of Introduction from the Methodist church, Guanajuato, Mexico, courtesy of Daniel Torres.

29. Luis Nicolau d'Olwer, *El Porfiriato, La Vida Económica*, vol. 7 in Cosío Villegas, ed., *Historia moderna de México* (Mexico, D.F.: Editorial Hermes, 1965), 1067, 1103.

30. Naco Consulate to Secretaría de Relaciones Exteriores, 18 October 1908, in ASRE 12–5-79.

31. García, *Desert Immigrants*, 51–59.

32. Interview: Elena Herrada.

33. Discussion regarding Driggs business practices over the years is noted in Mexican Ambassador to Secretary of State, 17 August 1939, in RG 59, 311.1215/137.

34. García, *Desert Immigrants*, 52–53.

35. Mexican Embassy to Department of State, 12 May 1917, and San Francisco Consul General Rafael Millan y Alba to Ambassador Ygnacio Bonillas, undated, circa May 1917, in RG 59 311.1211/6.

36. Trabajadores Mexicanos en Alaska, 17 February 1931, in ASRE IV-341–24; *El Universal Gráfica*, 17 February 1931.

37. Sidney Kansas, *U.S. Immigration, Exclusion, and Deportation* (New York: Matthew Bender Co., 1948); and Charles P. Howland, *Survey of American Foreign Policy, 1929* (New Haven, Conn.: Yale University Press, 1929), for a discussion of immigration restrictions and quota laws.

38. United States Congress, House Committee on Immigration and Naturalization, *Seasonal Agricultural Laborers from Mexico Hearing*, 69th Cong., 1st sess. (1926), 24.

39. Anita Edgar Jones, "Mexican Colonies in Chicago," *Social Service Review* 2 (December 1928), 579–97; United States Bureau of Labor Statistics, "Increase of Mexican Labor in Certain Industries in the U.S.," *Monthly Labor Review* 32 (January 1931), 82.

40. International Institute of the YWCA, "The Mexican Nationality Community in St. Paul: A Study Made in February to May 1936," Immigration History Research Center, St. Paul, Minn.

41. Ibid.

42. United States Department of Commerce, *Statistical Abstract of the United States, 1932* (Washington, D.C.: Government Printing Office, 1932), 62.

43. Dennis Nodín Váldes, *Al Norte: Agricultural Workers in the Great Lakes Region, 1917–1970* (Austin: University of Texas Press, 1991), 33.

44. James W. Byrkit, *Forging the Copper Collar: Arizona's Labor Management War, 1901–1921* (Tucson: University of Arizona Press, 1982).

45. United States Congress, House Committee on Immigration, *Hearings on Restriction of Western Hemisphere Immigration* (70th Cong., 1st sess., 1928), 82.

46. Reisler, *By the Sweat of Their Brow*, 206–8.

47. "The Ebb-Tide in Immigration," *Literary Digest*, 27 August 1927. See also the Mexico City press, in particular, the *Excélsior*, 19 June 1931.

48. "Our Mexican Immigrants," *Foreign Affairs*, 8 (October 1929) 99–107.

49. *Transactions: Commonwealth Club of California* 21 (23 March 1926), 1–34.

50. Charles C. Teague, "A Statement on Mexican Immigration." *Saturday Evening Post*, 200 (10 March 1928), 169–70.

51. Ibid., 126.

52. United States Department of Commerce and Labor, *Annual Report of the Commissioner General of Immigration* (Washington D.C.: United States Government Printing Office, 1911), 121.

53. *Seasonal Agricultural Laborers from Mexico Hearing*, 126.

54. As quoted by Raymond A. Mohl and Neil Batten, "Discrimination and Repatriation: Mexican Life in Gary," in *Forging a Community: Latinos in Northwest Indiana, 1919–1975* Edward Excobar and Henry Lang eds. (Chicago: Cattails Press, 1987), 173.

55. *Seasonal Agricultural Laborers from Mexico Hearing*, 24.

56. Ibid., 6, 62.

57. As quoted in Matt S. Meier and Feliciano Rivera eds., *Readings on La Raza: The Twentieth Century* (New York: Hill and Wang, 1974), 66. Better discussions of the Mexican immigration restriction debate are Reisler, *By the Sweat of Their Brow*, 151–226; and Robert J. Lipshultz, "American Attitudes toward Mexican Immigration, 1924–1952" (Master's thesis, University of Chicago, 1962).

58. George L. Cady, "Report of Commission on International and Interracial Factors on the Problem of Mexicans in the United States," 15, ms. in Bancroft.

59. This observation is drawn from a random analysis of Mexican Consular Service Matrícula records reporting birthplaces and birthdates of Mexican Nationals from various consulates in ASRE.

60. Interviews: Francisco Balderrama Terrazas and Emilio Martínez.

61. Balderrama, *In Defense of La Raza*, 8.

The Family

1. *Press-Telegram*, 30 April 1985.

2. Ruth Ann Krause, "V. F. Garza," *Steel Shavings: Latinos in the Calumet Region*, 13 (1987), 6.

3. George Sánchez, "Becoming Mexican-American: Ethnicity and Acculturation in Chicano Los Angeles, 1900–1940" (Ph.D. diss., Stanford University, 1989), 180–81. The preceding study shows that intermarriage between Mexican and Anglos appeared to occur only occasionally during the early twentieth century.

4. This observation is drawn from an analysis of various *Matrícula* records submitted by Mexican consulates from throughout the United States during the late 1920s and early 1930s in ASRE.

5. Interviews: Angelina Ayala and Rafael Ruiz de Balderrama.

6. *Reports of the Immigration Commission, Immigrants in Industries*, vol. 3, part 1, 11–12.

7. Alejandra de la Torre interview: Cruz Sánchez; Interview: John Ortega.

8. Interviews: Ayala, Francisco Balderrama Terrazas, Ramón Curiel, Catarino Cruz, Lucas Lucio, José B. Solórzano, and Enrique Zaragoza.

9. Interviews: Ayala, Balderrama Terrazas and Raymond Rodríguez; Christine Valenciana interview: Eliseo Martínez; Judith Melgoza interview: Dora Raya.

10. Robert R. Alvarez, Jr., *Familia, Migration and Adaptation in Baja and Alta California, 1800–1975* (Berkeley: University of California Press, 1987).

11. Helen W. Walker, "Mexican Immigrants and American Citizenship," *Sociology and Social Research* 13 (May–June 1929), 466.

12. Latinos & Latinas interview: Lorenza Lujano.

13. Latinos & Latinas interview: Gloria Moraga.

14. Interview: Raymond Rodríguez and Albino Piñeda.

15. Emory S. Bogardus, "The Mexican Immigrant," *Sociology and Social Research* 11 (May–June 1927), 478; Bogardus, *The Mexican in the United States* (Los Angeles: University of Southern California, 1934).

16. García, *Desert Immigrants*, 118. For Mexicans and education in this era, see Gilbert Gonzales, *Chicano Education in the Era of Segregation* (Philadelphia: Balch Institute Press, 1990).

17. Latinos & Latinas interview: Ignacio Guerrero and Antonia Medina.

18. Interview: Ayala.

19. Latinos & Latinas interview: Hermina Cadena.

20. Piedras Negras American Consul Stewart E. McMillan to Secretary of State, 1 June 1934, in RG 59, 311.1215/59.

21. Gilbert C. González, "Racism, Education, and the Mexican Community in Los Angeles, 1920–1930," *Societas* 4 (Fall 1974), 287–301. Interview: Anna Hebel, an Americanization teacher expressed a similar attitude.

22. Ayala and Rodríguez interview.

23. Judith Ann Laird, "Argentine, Kansas: The Evolution of a Mexican American Community, 1905–1940" (Ph.D. diss., University of Kansas, 1975), 87–89.

24. Norman D. Humphrey, "The Migration and Settlement of Detroit Mexicans," *Economic Geography* 19 (October 1943), 358; Paul S. Taylor, *Mexican Labor in the United States: Chicago and the Calumet Region* (Berkeley: University of California Press, 1932), 50–51.

25. Ciro Sepulveda, "La Colonia del Harbor: History of Mexicanos in East Chicago, Indiana, 1919–1932" (Ph.D. diss., University of Notre Dame, 1976), 129; William W. McEuen, "A Survey of Mexicans in Los Angeles" (Master's thesis, University of Southern California, 1914), 67–78.

26. *La Prensa*, 2 February 1918, 2 March 1918, and 8 March 1919.

27. Elizabeth S. Johnson, *Welfare of Families of Sugar-Beet Laborers: A study of Child Labor and Its Relation to Family Work, Income and Living Conditions in 1935* (Washington, D.C.: U.S. Department of Labor, Children's Bureau Publication, 1939).

28. Anita Edgar Jones, "Conditions Surrounding Mexicans in Chicago," (Master's thesis, University of Chicago, 1928), 83–84.

29. Helen Walker, "The Conflict of Cultures in First Generation Mexicans in Santa Ana, California" (Master's thesis, University of Southern California, 1928), 35.

30. Interview: Flavio Valenciana.

31. Ernesto Galarza, "Life in the United States for Mexican People: Out of the Experience of a Mexican," *Proceedings of the National Conference of Social Work*, 56th Annual Session 56 (1929), 64.

32. Ruth Allen, *The Labor of Women in the Production of Cotton* (Austin: University of Texas Publications, 1931), 229.

33. J. H. Winslow to Rex Thomson, "Subject Mexicans," 26 January 1934, in Box 80, Bundle 15, Clements Collection; California, Department of Industrial Relations, Governor's Mexican Fact-Finding Committee *Mexicans in California: Report of Governor C. C. Young's Mexican Fact-Finding Committee* (San Francisco: State Printing Office, 1931), 86.

34. Bromley G. Oxnam, "The Mexican in Los Angeles from the Standpoint of the Religious Forces of the City," *Annals of the American Academy* 93 (1921), 131; Charles A. Thomson, "What of the Bracero? The Forgotten Alternative in Our Immigration Policy," *Survey* 54 (1 June, 1925), 291.

35. Richard A. García, "Class, Consciousness and Ideology—The Mexican American Community of San Antonio, Texas: 1930–1940," *Aztlán: International Journal of Chicano Studies Research* 9 (Fall 1978), 44; Julia Kirk Blackwelder, *Women of the Depression: Caste and Culture in San Antonio, 1929–1939* (College Station: Texas A & M Press, 1984), 112.

36. Richard A. García, "The Making of the Mexican-American Mind, San Antonio, Texas 1929–1941: A Social and Intellectual History of an Ethnic Community" (Ph.D. diss., University of California, Irvine, 1980), 100.

37. Melgoza Interview: Dora Raya; Valenciana interview: Emilia Castañeda de Valenciana.

38. Interviews: Ayala, Rodríguez, and Flavio Valenciana.

39. Interviews: Ayala and Rodríguez.

40. Gamio, *Mexican Immigration*, 76–83; and Manuel Gamio, *The Mexican Immigrant: His Life Story* (Chicago: University of Chicago Press, 1931), 82–83, 161–66.

41. Interviews: Ayala, Balderrama Terrazas, and Rodríguez.

42. Samuel Ortegón, "The Religious Status of the Mexican Population of Los Angeles" (Master's thesis, University of Southern California, 1932); Charles C. Carpenter, "A Study of Segregation versus Non-Segregation of Mexican Children" (Master's thesis, University of Southern California, 1935).

43. Carpenter, "Study of Segregation," 60.

44. Melgoza interview: Vera Godoy.

45. Latinos & Latinas interview: Richard Dominguez

46. Thomas E. Sheridan, *Los Tucsonenses: The Mexican Community in Tucson, 1854–1941* (Tucson: University of Arizona Press, 1986), 212.

47. Interview: Vera Godoy.

48. Melgoza interviews: Alicia Apodaca, Irma Amparano, Margarita Brown, Esperanza Gallardo, Inez Salazar, and Jesusita Solís.

49. Melgoza interviews: Amparano and Raya.

50. For Detroit, see Humphrey, "Migration and Settlement of Detroit Mexicans," *Economic Geography*, 19 (October 1943), 358–61; for Los Angeles, interview: Ruiz de Balderrama.

51. Melgoza interviews: Amparano and Raya.

52. Blackwelder, *Women of the Depression*, 55; Green Peyton, *San Antonio: City in the Sun* (New York: McGraw and Hill, 1946), 166.

53. Frances J. Woods, *Mexican American Ethnic Leadership in San Antonio, Texas* (Washington, D.C.: The Catholic University of America Press, 1949), 114.

54. Interview: María Anaya.

55. *La Opinión*, 22 February 1931.

56. Francisco E. Balderrama and Raymond Rodríguez, "Juan Reyna: Victim of Anti-Mexican Hysteria," Western History Association Conference, Los Angeles, California, 1987.

57. Nellie Foster, "The Corrido: A Mexican Culture Trait Persisting in Southern California" (Master's thesis, University of Southern California, 1929), 121.

58. Interviews: Alejandro Castro and Eduardo Negrete.

59. Interviews: Castro, Lucas Lucio, and Negrete.

60. Balderrama, *In Defense of La Raza*, 37–39, 46–49.

61. Interviews: Ayala and Rodríguez.

62. Melgoza interview: Gallardo.

63. *Mexicans in California: Report of Governor C. C. Young's Mexican Fact-Finding Committee*, 94; see Ruiz, *Cannery Women/Cannery Lives*, for a pathbreaking exploration of cannery life for Mexicana women.

64. Melgoza interviews: Amparano, Raya, and Solís.

65. Douglas Monroy, "La Costura en Los Angeles, 1933–1939: The ILGWU and the Politics of Domination," in *Mexican Women in the United States: Struggles Past and Present*, Magdalena Mora and Adelaida R. Del Castillo, eds. (Los Angeles: University of California Los Angeles Chicano Studies Research Center, 1980), 171–78.

66. Interview: Josefina Chávez Pérez.

67. Melgoza interviews: Amparano, Gallardo, and Raya.

68. Melgoza interview: Gallardo; Rosalinda M. González, "Chicanas and Mexican Immigrant Families, 1920–1940: Women's Subordination and Family Exploitation," in *Decades of Discontent: The Women's Movement, 1920–1940* (Westport, Conn.: Greenwood Press, 1983), 74; Douglas Guy Monroy, "Mexicanos in Los Angeles, 1930–1941, An Ethnic Group in Relation to Class Forces" (Ph.D. diss., University of California Los Angeles, 1978), 77.

69. Sheridan, *Tucsonenses*, 211, for bootlegging in Tucson.

70. Seldon Menefee and C. C. Cassmore, *The Pecan Shellers of San Antonio* (Washington, D.C.: Government Printing Office, 1940), 49.

71. Mexican Consul Armando Amador to G. C. Martin, New Orleans Chief of Police, 14 July 1931, in ASRE IV-186–51.

Deportation

1. Roy L. Garis, *Immigration Restriction: A Study of the Opposition to and Regulation of Immigration in the United States* (New York: MacMillan, 1927), 13.

2. Kansas, *United States Immigration, Exclusion, and Deportation*, 97–109.

3. D. H. Dinwoodie, "Deportation: The Immigration Service and the Chicano Labor Movement in the 1930s," *New Mexico Historical Review* 52, 3 (Summer 1977), 193–203; Los Angeles Consul Joel Quiñones to San Francisco Consul General, 24 March 1932, in ASRE IV-351–1, for a lengthy report on the usual reasons for Mexican deportation during the depression years. Attorney David Marcus confirmed this observation for the Los Angeles consulate and community during the 1930s. Interview: David Marcus.

4. "Lawless Enforcement of the Law: Report of the Subcommittee of Constitutional Rights Committee of the Los Angeles Bar Association on Alleged Illegal Law Enforcement in Connection with the Deportation of Aliens," ms. in Bancroft.

5. Phoenix Consul to El Paso Consul General, 24 March 1931, in ASRE IV-346–3.

6. Del Rio Consul to San Antonio Consul General, 2 June 1932, 13 July 1932, 19 July 1932, and 29 July 1932, in ASRE IV-343–48.

7. Phoenix Consul to El Paso Consul General, 24 March 1931.

8. Winslow to Thomson, "Subject Mexicans," 26 January 1934, in Clements.

9. Subsecretario Oscar Duplan to Secretario de Gobernacíon, 20 July 1932, in ASRE IV-348–4. This file contains personal data regarding ninety prisoners sent from McNeil Federal Penitentiary to Mexico.

10. Oklahoma City Consul to Secretaría de Relaciones Exteriores, 24 November 1930, in ASRE IV-342–75.

11. Los Angeles Consul Rafael de la Colina to Mexican Embassy, 29 January 1931, in ASRE IV-343–19.

12. "Lawless Enforcement of the Law," 1.

13. As cited by John Perry Clark, "Aliens in the Deportation Dragnet," *Current History* 36 (April 1932), 29.

14. Interviews: Dr. José Díaz and Emilio Flores.

15. "U.S. Department of Labor, Immigration and Naturalization Service," June 30, 1930, to June 30, 1939, RG 85, 10a–39.

16. C. P. Visel to Colonel Arthur Woods, 6 January 1931, in Box 62, Bundle 7, in Clements.

17. Bank of America Branch at Seventh and Olive to Arthur Arnoll, 8 May 1931, in Box 62, Bundle 7, in Clements.

18. Mr. Emile Pozzo of the International Branch of the Bank of America expressed these sentiments during the height of the deportation crisis. See Los Angeles Chamber of Commerce Memorandum, 4 June 1931, in Box 62, Bundle 7, in Clements.

19. Bank of America Branch at Seventh and Olive to Arthur Arnoll, 8 May 1931, in Box 62, Bundle 7, in Clements.

20. Interview Elena Herrada. The case of a Mexican American army sergeant, a veteran of World War I, confronting job discrimination is reported in *La Opinión*, 8 February 1931.

21. The anti-Mexican Campaign in 1931–32 was the subject of extensive reports by the Los Angeles Consulate in ASRE IV-185–11, IV-185–30, IV-185–60.

22. "Commissioner Hull, Exporter," *The Saturday Evening Post* 202, (18 January 1930), 24.

23. "Back Where They Came From," *New Masses* (18 April 1939) 12–13; Ruben Klainer, "Deportations of Aliens," *Boston University Law Review* 15 (November 1935), 722.

24. Ibid.

25. Ibid.

26. "Lawless Enforcement of the Law," 6.

27. Interviews: José David Orozco and Díaz.

28. R. Reynolds McKay, "Texas Mexican Repatriation during the Great Depression," (Ph.D. diss., University of Oklahoma, 1982), 98–101.

29. Secretaría de Relaciones Exteriores, *Informe de labores de la Secretaría de Relaciones Exteriores de agosto de 1933 a Julio de 1934, presentado al H. Congreso de la Unión por el Dr. José Manuel Puig Casauranc* (México, D.F.: Imprenta de la Secretaría de Relaciones Exteriores, 1934), 432.

30. *El Universal*, 26 March 1935.

31. Relaciones, *Informe agosto de 1933 a julio de 1934*, 432.

32. Visel to Woods, in Clements.

33. *La Opinión*, 22 February 1931.

34. Ibid.

35. Los Angeles Consul Rafael de la Colina to Mexican Ambassador, 29 January 1931, in ASRE IV-343–19.

36. Ibid.

37. *Los Angeles Times*, 28 January 1931; *Illustrated Daily News*, 28 January 1931.

38. Los Angeles Consulate to Secretaría de Relaciones Exteriores, 27 February 1931, in ASRE IV-343–19; *La Opinión*, 27 February 1931.

39. *La Opinión*, 27 February 1931.

40. *El Universal*, 11 February 1931.

41. *New York Times*, 12 April 1931, 19 April 1931, and 25 April 1931. See also Robert S. Allen, "One of Mr. Hoover's Friends," *American Mercury* 25 (January 1932), 53–62.

42. *San Angelo Times*, 16 June 1931.

43. R. Reynolds Mckay in "The Federal Deportation Campaign in Texas: Mexican Deportation from the Lower Rio Grande Valley during the Great Depression," *The Borderlands Journal* 5, 1 (Fall 1981), 97.

44. H. T. Manuel, "The Mexican Child in Texas," *Southwest Review* 17 (April 1932), 290–302.

45. McKay, "The Federal Deportation Campaign," 95–120.

46. Ibid.

47. *La Opinión*, 13 July 2003; Dinwoodie, "Deportation," 193–203, outlines in general terms the deportation of Mexican labor activists in the American Southwest.

48. Pedro J. González has been the subject of the following documentaries: "Ballad of an Unsung Hero," 30 minutes, San Diego: Cinewest, KPBS, 1983; "Break of Dawn," 100 minutes, San Diego: Cinewest, KPBS, 1989.

49. Robert S. Allen, "Mr. Hoover's Friends," *American Mercury* 25 (January 1932), 57–58.

50. Dinwoodie, "Deportation," 197.

51. "Deportation during the Fiscal Year Ended June 30, 1934," *Interpreter Releases: An Information Service on Immigration, Naturalization, and the Foreign-Born* (New York, 1935), 40.

52. San Antonio Consul to Mexican Embassy, 10 March 1931, in ASRE IV-346–51.

53. Form no. 180 may be found in ASRE IV-343-3.

54. *Chicago Evening Post*, 20 April 1932.

55. Phoenix Consul to El Paso Consul General, 24 March 1931.

56. Ibid.

57. Mexican consuls regularly complained about late or no notice of Mexican deportations. See Los Angeles Consulate correspondence in ASRE IV-345–11.

58. San Antonio Consulate General to Houston Consulate, 13 July 1932, in ASRE IV-344–41.

59. Consul Juan Anchado to Secretaría de Relaciones Exteriores, 10 June 1932, in ASRE IV-314–12.

60. *Continental*, 3 July 1932; *Herald Post*, 3 July 1932; Consul Luis Lupián to Secretaría de Relaciones Exteriores 3 July, 1932 in ASRE IV-314–12.

61. Gladys Harrison, "Enforcement of the Deportation Laws," in *American Bar Association Journal* 18 (February 1932), 100.

62. Consul Rafael de la Colina to Secretaría de Relaciones Exteriores, 31 January 1931, in ASRE IV-343–19.

63. *La Opinión*, 31 January 1931.

64. Kerr Press Release is in Box 80, Bundle 15, in Clements.

65. *El Universal*, 15 June 1931, 20 June 1931; see correspondence regarding the Ariza trip in Clements.

66. Clements to Arnoll, 11 June 1931, in Box 80, Bundle 15, in Clements.

67. George P. Clements to Arnoll and Matson, 4 June 1931, in Box 62, Bundle 7, in Clements.

68. Clements to Arnoll, 11 June 1931, in Clements.

69. "Deportation during the Fiscal Year Ended June 30, 1934," 36.

70. "Aliens from the United States to Mexico: June 30, 1925 to June 30, 1950," RG 85, 10a–34.

Welfare

1. *El Universal*, 11 May 1935.

2. Latinos & Latinas World War II interview: Betty Medina.

3. *Los Angeles Times*, 7 April 1931. See *San Francisco Chronicle*, 29 August 1931, for a discussion of California state law barring aliens from employment by state, county, and municipalities.

4. Latinos & Latinas interview: Concepción Alvarado Escobedo.

5. Interviews: Catarino Cruz, Emilio Martínez, and Celso Medina; Melgoza interviews: Irma Amparano, Alicia Apodaca, Vera Godoy, and Dora Raya.

6. *New York Times*, 25 April 1931.

7. Interview: Herrada.

8. Latinos & Latinas World War II interview: Alvarado.

9. "Concerning the Employment of Aliens on WPA Projects," in *Interpreter Releases: An Information Service on Immigration, Naturalization, and the Foreign-Born* (New York, 1938), 413–14.

10. Earl E. Jensen to Board of Supervisors, 15 February 1934, LAC Board of Supervisors *Minutes* 196:233.

11. Latinos & Latinas World War II interview: Pablo Segura.

12. *New York Times*, 18 February 1937.

13. "Mexicanos sin Trabajo: Datos Estádisticos sobre Mexicanos Residentes," Junio/Julio 1931, in ASRE IV-341–9.

14. Ibid.

15. *Excélsior*, 27 November 1931.

16. "Resolution," 12 March 1940, in LAC Board of Supervisors *Minutes*, 297:379.

17. Consul Joaquín Terrazas to Secretaría de Relaciones Exteriores, 13 June 1932, in ASRE IV-0185–35; Interviews: Ayala and Lucas Lucio.

18. Los Angeles Consul F. A. Pesqueira to Secretaría de Relaciones Exteriores, 24 June 1930, in ASRE IV-100–9. This policy was stated repeatedly.

19. Colonia Mexicana de Rockdale to Chicago Consulate, 30 December 1930, in ASRE IV-354–4.

20. Ruth Frances Norrick, "My Huesita: An Interview with Pilar," *Steel Shavings: Latinos in the Calumet Region* 13 (1987), 2.

21. *Los Angeles Record*, 16, 18, 28, August 1931.

22. Interview: Rex Thomson; Christine Valenciana interview: Rex Thomson.

23. Ibid.

24. *The Nation*, 30 December 1931.

25. Superintendent of Charities Rex Thomson to Board of Supervisors, 25 May 1937, in LACC Minutes 231: 51.

26. *The Nation*, 30 December 1931.

27. *New York Times*, 20 March 1934; "The Repatriation of Destitute Aliens," 23 May 1935, *Interpreter Releases*, 12:201–14; *Illinois, State of Illinois Second Annual Report of the Illinois Emergency Relief Commission* (June 1934).

28. *Excélsior*, 27 November 1931.

29. "American Legion Activity in Behalf of Repatriation in East Chicago," circa 1932, American Legion File, East Chicago Historical Society Collection, Courtesy of John Ortega.

30. *The Nation*, 30 December 1931.

31. *El Informador*, 15 October 1930.

32. *Excélsior*, 6 January 1931.

33. Mexican Embassy to Secretary of State, 24 August 1933, in RG 59, 311.1215/46–47.

34. California State Chamber of Commerce, "Migrants: A National Problem and Its Impact on California," (May 1940), Box 63, Bundle 7, in Clements.

35. R. Reynolds McKay, "Texas Mexican Repatriation during the Great Depression" (Ph.D. diss., University of Oklahoma, 1982), 225.

36. Ibid.

37. California State Relief Administration, Bureau of Statistics, *The Problem of Interstate Migration as It Affects the California Relief Administration* (San Francisco: State Printing Office, 1936), 8.

38. See H. Mark Wild, "If You Ain't Got That Do-Re-Mi: The Los Angeles Border Patrol and White Migrations in Depression-Era California," *Southern California Quarterly* 83, 3 (Fall 2001), 317–334.

39. J. H. O'Connor, County Counsel to Los Angeles County Board of Supervisors, 4 November 1938, in LAC 740.

40. Royal C. Stephens, National Club of America for Americans, to Roger W. Jessup, Los Angeles County Board of Supervisors, 23 October 1939, in LAC Board of Supervisors *Minutes*, 254:398.

41. "Legal Entry Certificate" Motion Los Angeles County Board of Supervisors, 17 January 1939, in LAC Board of Supervisors *Minutes,* 248:2.

42. "Solution Found Difficult," Newspaper clipping of unidentified periodical in Carey McWilliams Collection Folder 2–25.

43. Stephen E. Aguirre of the Mexican Embassy to C. H. Matson, Los Angeles Chamber of Commerce, Box 62, Bundle 7, in Clements.

44. *El Universal Gráfico*, 9 November 1933.

45. L. Clark to Department of State, 17 January 1934, in RG 59, 311.1215/48.

46. George P. Clements to Nela Anderson, undated, Box 64, Bundle 9, in Clements.

47. Clements to Allen, U.S. Farm Placement Service, 17 September 1935, Box 64, Bundle 9, in Clements.

48. Frank Y. McLaughlin to F. J. Palomares, 5 October 1935, Box 64, Bundle 7, in Clements.

49. Los Angeles Chamber of Commerce Labor Committee Meeting, 5 October 1935, Box 64, Bundle 9, in Clements.

50. A. G. Arnoll to Clements, "Interdepartment Memorandum," 8 October 1935, in Box 64, Bundle 9, in Clements.

51. Clements to Frank Persons, Employment Service Department, 16 October 1935, Box 64, Bundle 9, in Clements.

52. "Agriculture Labor Committee Meeting," 22 October 1935, Box 64, Bundle 9, in Clements.

53. *New York Times*, undated, in Folder 2–25, McWilliams.

54. Norman D. Humphrey, "Mexican Repatriation from Michigan: Public Assistance in Historical Perspective," *Social Service Review* 15 (September 1941), 508–9.

55. Ibid.

56. *New York Times*, 4 April 1939.

57. *Los Angeles Times*, 26 March 1940.

58. Union General de Trabajadores Mexicanos to Presidente Ortiz Rubio, 27 January 1931; Union General de Trabajadores to Genaro Estrada, Secretaría de Relaciones Exteriores, 27 January 1931, and other documents in ASRE IV-349–1.

59. Walter E. Barry, Los Angeles Mexican Chamber of Commerce, to C. H. Matson, 2 February 1932, Box 80, Bundle 15, in Clements.

60. Matson to Barry, 8 March 1932, Box 62, Bundle 7, in Clements.

61. Arnoll to Clements, 20 June 1936, Box 64, Bundle 9, in Clements.

62. Arnoll to Clements, 2 December 1936, Box 64, Bundle 9, in Clements.

63. Charles L. Bennett, "Housing for Field Employees," reprint of articles in *San Dimas Press* (Berkeley: University of California, 1936).

64. Virginia E. Newell, "The Social Significance of Padua Hills as a Cultural and Education Center" (Master's thesis, University of Southern California, 1938), 33, 92.

65. W. W. Robinson, *Los Angeles from the Days of the Pueblo: A Brief History and Guide to the Plaza Area* (San Francisco: California Historical Society, 1959), 95–102.

66. *Excélsior*, 3 January 1931.

67. Bank of America (Seventh and Olive Branch) to Arnoll, 8 May 1931, Box 62, Bundle 7, in Clements.

68. J. H. Winslow to Rex Thomson, 26 January 1934, Box 80, Bundle 15, in Clements.

69. Earl E. Jensen, Superintendent of Charities, to Los Angeles Board of Supervisors, 15 February 1934, LAC Board of Supervisors *Minutes*, 196:233.

70. Ibid.

71. Ibid.

72. "Charities Board Acceptance of Mortgage from Francisco and Carmen Esquivel for Transportation Costs," 21 March 1932, LAC Board of Supervisors, *Minutes*, 349.

73. Mexican Community Association Executive Director Siegfried Goetze to Los Angeles County Board of Supervisors, 8 February 1935, in LAC 40.31.

74. Interview: Rubén Jiménez in "Expulsion of U.S. Citizens."

75. Department of State Memorandum, Visa Division, 14 September 1938, RG 59, 311.1215/104. This is a revealing study of Mexican Nationals in the United States drawn from various government agencies.

76. "Memorandum Concerning the Reported Discharge of Mexican Citizens from Works Progress Administration Projects in San Antonio, Texas," RG 59, 311.12/508.

77. "Conversation Memorandum" between Lawrence Duggan and Quintanilla, 19 July 1937, in RG 59, 311.12/504.

78. Ibid.

79. *Excélsior*, 27 July 1939.

80. California Attorney General Earl Warren to Chief Clerk Assembly Jack C. Greenberg, 14 January 1939, LAC Decimal File 40.36/4.

81. Clerk L. E. Lampton to County Counsel H. J. O'Connor, 20 November 1938, LAC Board of Supervisors *Minutes*, 246:250.

82. *Los Angeles Evening Herald Express*, 20 July 1939.

83. Siegfried Goetze to Roger Jessup, Chairman, Board of Supervisors, 25 January 1940, LAC Decimal File 40.36/18.

84. Ibid.

85. Sepulveda, "La Colonia del Harbor," 145.

86. Los Angeles County Board of Supervisors, *Annual Report for Fiscal Year Ending June 30, 1929*, 99.

87. "Deportation of Canadian John McNeil Family," 15 June 1939, in LAC 40.36.

88. L. C. Schreiber to Board of Supervisors, 19 August 1941, LAC *Minutes*, 271:172.

89. Wayne Allen to Board of Supervisors, LAC Board of Supervisors *Minutes*, 273:293.

90. John Anson Ford to Honorable Culbert Olson, 13 November 1941, in Boxes 64 & 75, in John Anson Ford Papers.

91. John Anson Ford, "Repatriation of Mexicans," 18 November 1941, LAC *Minutes*, 273:385.

92. Allen to Supervisors, 1 December 1941, LAC *Minutes*, 274:88.

93. Supervisors, 2 December 1941, LAC *Minutes*, 274:88.

94. Culbert Olson to John Anson Ford, 18 November 1941, in Boxes 64 & 75, in John Anson Ford Papers.

95. Ed C. Iler to Supervisors, 4 December 1941, LAC *Minutes*, 274:247.

96. Mr. and Mrs. Dean Hanson to Supervisors, 8 December 1941, LAC Decimal File 40.36/35.4.

Repatriation

1. Mohl and Batten, "Discrimination and Repatriation," in Escobar and Lang, eds. *Forging a Community*, 176.

2. Vidral Pedrozca to New Orleans Consul Armando C. Amador, 1 January 1931, in ASRE IV-358–14.

3. Luz G. Salas to New Orleans Consul Armando C. Amador, 5 October 1931, in ASRE IV-358–1.

4. *Los Angeles Times*, 10 January 1931.

5. Consul General Luis Lupián to Secretaría de Relaciones Exteriores, 20 May 1931, in ASRE 329–3.

6. "A Caravan of Sorrow," *Living Age* 332 (15 May 1927), 870–72. Also playing a major role in fomenting repatriation pressures and anti-Mexican sentiment was The *Saturday Evening Post*. See: Roy L. Garis, "The Mexican Invasion," 202 (19 April 1930), 43–44, and "The Mexicanization of American Business," 202 (8 February 1930), 46, 51, 178, 181–82.

7. *La Prensa*, 21 May 1931.

8. *El País*, 1 November 1931; Secretaría de Gobernacíon, 28 October 1931, in ASRE IV-359–6. Discussion about the departure of Midwest repatriates from New Orleans is reported in Consul Fernando Alatorre's correspondence in ASRE IV-355–5.

9. New York Consulate General to Secretaría de Relaciones Exteriores, 6 December 1932, in ASRE IV-359–6.

10. San Diego *Union*, 5 March 1932; *Progreso* correspondence between the Mexican consulates and Foreign Relations is in ASRE IV-360–38.

11. Hicks interview: Adolfo Tapia.

12. Judith Melgoza interview: Alicia Apodaca.

13. Claudia Juárez interview: Sebastiana Briones Casas; Interview: Lucas Lucio.

14. Melgoza interview: Apodaca.

15. *New York Times*, 10 July 1933, 28 July 1933, and 30 July 1933.

16. *Excélsior*, 9 March 1931.

17. Chicago Consulate to Secretaría de Relaciones Exteriores, 20 May 1932, Denver Consulate to Secretaría, 22 September 1931, Denver Consulate to Marcelo Ramirez, 6 December 1932, in ASRE IV-354–12; Kansas City Consulate to San Antonio Consul General, 5 December 1932, in ASRE IV-356–23; Oklahoma City Consulate to San Antonio Consulate General, 13 February 1931, in ASRE IV-360–14; San Diego Consulate to Secretaría, 20 May 1932, in ASRE IV-360–38; Detroit Consulate to Secretaría, 14 November 1931, in ASRE IV-355–5.

18. The Kansas City Consulate reported on the repatriation of the Bayard, Nebraska Mexicanos by The Great Western Sugar Company, 13 June 1932, in ASRE IV-356–23. Also see: Consul Ignacio Batiza to Secretaría de Relaciones Exteriores, 20 August 1930, in ASRE IV-76–49. Consul Batiza reported at length on conditions in the sugar-beet industry.

19. *Decatur Wise County Messenger*, 10 December 1931; For a description of the Bridgeport miners see: R. Reynolds McKay, "Texas Mexican Repatriation during the Great Depression" (Ph.D. diss., University of Oklahoma, 1982), 386–392.

20. New York Consul Enrique Ruiz to Mexican Embassy, 31 August 1931, in ASRE IV-359–6; Pittsburgh Consul to Secretaría de Relaciones Exteriores, 17 August 1932, in ASRE IV-360–15.

21. *New York Times*, 20 March 1934.

22. "The Repatriation of Destitute Aliens," 23 May 1935, *Interpreter Releases*, 12:201–14.

23. Melgoza interviews: Dora Raya and Irma Amparano.

24. Interview: Raymond Rodríguez.

25. Cecilia Morales interview: Carmen Martínez.

26. Christine Valenciana interview: Eliseo Martínez.

27. Los Angeles Consulate to San Francisco Consulate General, 29 November 1929, in ASRE IV-71–1.

28. Interview: Lucas Lucio.

29. Robert N. McLean, "Goodbye Vicente," *Survey Graphic* 66 (1 May 1931), 82.

30. American Consul Richard R. Boyce, "Statistical Report on Repatriation Through Nuevo Laredo," 6 Feburary 1930, in RG 59, 311.1215/18. Regarding automobiles also see: Mary Lanigan, "Second Generation Mexicans in Belvedere" (Master's thesis, University of Southern California, 1932), 52.

31. Various documents about Francisco C. Barron and family from Denver Consul Y. M. Vásquez, are in ASRE IV-354–40.

32. Interview: Elena Herrada.

33. Interview: Catarino Cruz.

34. Consul General Luis Medina Barrón to Secretaría de Relaciones Exteriores, 15 December 1930, in ASRE IV-109–55.

35. Interview: Adolfo Martínez.

36. H. A. Payne to W. H. Holland, Superintendent of Charities, 10 February 1931, LAC Decimal File 40.31/340.

37. Memorandums, telegrams, and letters of the Los Angeles Chamber of Commerce reporting on Mexicans in Southern California are available in Clements.

38. Interview: Rubén Jiménez in "Expulsion of U.S. Citizens."

39. Rex Thomson to Wayne Allen, Chief Administrative Officer, 1 July 1940, in LAC 40.36.

40. Valenciana interview: Allan A. Hunter.

41. *Los Angeles Times*, 24 April 1931; Interview: Lucio; Valenciana interview: María Bustos Jefferson.

42. Carey McWilliams with Matt S. Meier, *North from Mexico: The Spanish-Speaking People of the United States* (New York: Greenwood Press, 1990), 193.

43. Balderrama, *In Defense of La Raza*, 28.

44. James B. Lane interview: Abe Morales.

45. Bogardus, *Mexican in the United States*, 94–95.

46. Even the children of the Mexican Consular Service were not exempt, El Paso Consul Luis Medina Barrón declared: "My own children prefer the English language and rarely express themselves in Spanish; all my children speak English even for their most intimate conversations." *La Opinión*, 18 May 1930, 19 May 1930.

47. *Los Angeles Times*, 24 April 1931.

48. Lucio and Martínez interviews; Valenciana interview: Bustos Jefferson.

49. Valenciana interview: Emilia Castañeda de Valenciana.

50. Neil Batten and Raymond A. Mohl, "From Discrimination to Repatriation: Mexican Life in Gary, Indiana during the Great Depression," in Norris C. Hundley, Jr., ed., *The Chicano: Essays from the Pacific Historical Review* (Santa Barbara, Calif.: American Bibliographical Center, 1975), 139.

51. Ernest Besig of Mount Hollywood Church's Goodwill to Mexico Committee to Dear Friend, 8 June 1931, in Box 62, Bundle 7, Clements; Lucio interview; Doty interview: María Bustos Jefferson; Valenciana interview: María Bustos Jefferson.

52. There are various versions of "La Pensilvaña." One appears in Américo Paredes, *A Texas-Mexican Cancionero: Folksongs of the Lower Border* (Urbana: University of Illinois Press, 1976), 56–57.

53. Rex Thomson to Board of Supervisors, 20 March 1940, LAC Board of Supervisors *Minutes*, 258:114.

54. Inspector Harry Yeager to Detroit Immigration Director, 21 November 1932, in RG 85, 55784/585.

55. "Shipping of the García Family," 15 September 1931, in ASRE, IV-348–70.

56. "Report of Repatriation" by Gordon L. McDonough to Los Angeles Board of Supervisors, 21 November 1938, in LAC Board of Supervisors *Minutes*, 246:109.

57. Thomson to Board, 16 May 1938, LAC Board of Supervisors *Minutes*, 244:33.

58. "Report of Repatriation," 246:109.

59. Rex Thomson to Los Angeles County Board of Supervisors, 13 October 1939, in LAC *Minutes*, 255:28.

60. Marjorie Walker Saint, "Woven within My Grandmother's Braid: The Biography of a Mexican Immigrant Woman" (Senior thesis, University of California, Santa Cruz, 1991), 57–58.

61. Ibid.

62. *Laredo Times*, 19 October 1931.

63. "Instructions about Repatriation to Avoid Problems" by Denver Consul Y. M. Vázquez, 5 October 1932, in ASRE IV-354–40.

64. Rex Thomson to Los Angeles Board of Supervisors, 7 March 1939, in LAC *Minutes*, 249:159.

65. San Diego Consulate to Secretaría de Relaciones Exteriores, undated, in ASRE IV-648–28.

66. Rex Thomson to Los Angeles Board of Supervisors, 22 September 1937, in LAC *Minutes*, 234:270.

67. Secretaría de Relaciones Exteriores, *Memoria de la Secretaría de Relaciones Exteriores de agosto de 1932 a julio de 1933, presentada al H. Congreso de la Unión por José Manual Puig Casauranc, Subsecretario del Ramo* (México, D.F.: Imprenta de la Secretaría de Relaciones Exteriores, 1933); *Weekly News Sheet*, 27 November 1936.

68. Los Angeles Consul Rafael de la Colina to Secretaría de Relaciones Exteriores, 20 October 1930, in ASRE IV-357–5.

69. Department of Public Welfare, Globe, Arizona to Phoenix Consul, 27 May 1930, in ASRE IV-110–74.

70. *Redlands Daily Facts*, 22 June 1931.

71. *San Bernardino Sun*, 24 February 1932.

72. Jones, "Mexican Colonies in Chicago," 579–597.

73. Morales interview: Martínez.

74. *El Demócrata Sinaloense*, 4 April 1931; *El Universal*, 2 February 1930.

75. Correspondence between Department of State and Governor of Texas, December 1920, in RG, 311.125.

76. An especially revealing analysis is "The Distribution of Communal Lands in Mexico," *Pan American Union* (18 May 1933).

77. The Mexican Constitution as well as the Mexican Nationality and Naturalization Act of 1934 granted citizenship *jus sanguinis*—that is, the nationality of the children was that of the parents regardless of the children's birthplace. See *Ley de nacionalidad y naturalización*, 5 January 1934, Art. 1 in Diario Oficial, 20 January 1934.

78. "A Demographic Analysis of First and Second Generation Mexican Population in the United States 1930," *Social Science Quarterly* 24 (September 1943): 138–49.

79. Instructions for the issuance of Certificates of Residence were explained in detail in Circular No. 202, 14 December 1926, in ASRE IV-68–42.

80. *El Heraldo de México*, 24 June 1931; "Animal Inspection Fees at the Border, Ciudad Juárez," 17 May 1932, in ASRE IV-348–78.

81. San Antonio Consul General Enrique Santibañez lobbied his Mexico City superiors for greater franquicias for repatriates. See correspondence between Santibañez and Secretaría de Relaciones Exteriores, 29 January 1930 to 17 March 1930, in ASRE IV-111–12.

82. New Orleans Consul Armando C. Amador to Comisión Honorífica Mexicana, 29 September 1931, in ASRE IV-358–14.

83. Secretaría de Relaciones Exteriores Circular IV-12–25, 10 February 1933, in ASRE IV-666–12.

84. Valenciana interview: Castañeda de Valenciana; for details on Juan Rodríguez, see Secretaría de Relaciones Exteriores, *Boletín* 56:1 (January 1931), 57–58.

85. *Excélsior*, 1 March 1931.

86. *Excélsior*, 17 January 1931, 11 November 1931.

87. *Excélsior*, 4 April 1938.

88. El Paso Consul General Luis Lupián to Presidio Texas Consulate, 17 May 1932, in ASRE IV-348–78.

89. Consul Rafael Aveleyra to Miss Mary Grace Wells, 13 May 1931, in ASRE IV-354–12.

90. As quoted by Mohl and Batten, "Discrimination and Repatriation," 176.

91. Interview: Lucio.

92. Thomson interview: it appeared that Mexican immigrants definitely favored Mexican-style food. A study discovered that 95 percent of Mexicano families made tortillas while 72 percent served beans. See: Heller Committee for Research in Social Economics of the University of California and Constantine Panunzio, *How Mexicans Earn and Live: A Study of the Incomes and Expenditures of One Hundred Mexican Families in San Diego, California, Cost of Living Studies*, 5 (Berkeley: University of California Press, 1933), 28–29.

93. Immigration Inspector Harry G. Yeager to District Director of Immigration, Detroit, Michigan, 21 November 1932, in RG 85, 55784/585.

94. Saint, "Woven within My Grandmother's Braid," 58.

95. Valenciana interview: Bustos Jefferson; Interviews: Lucio and Martínez.

96. Interview: Lucio.

97. District Director of Immigration Detroit District John L. Zurbrick to Inspector in Charge, Laredo, Texas, 28 November 1932, in RG 85, 55784/585.

98. "Testimony of Emilia Castañeda," for California State Senate Select Committee on Citizen Participation, "Examination of the Unconstitutional Deportation and Coerced Emigration of Legal Residents and U.S. Citizens of Mexican Descent during the 1930s," July 14, 2003.

99. John L. Zurbrick to Inspector in Charge, U.S. Immigration Bureau, Laredo, 23 November 1932, in RG. 85 55784/585.

100. *La Prensa*, 21 October 1931.

101. McLean, "Goodbye Vicente," 182.

102. "Repatriates from Des Moines, Iowa," 5 August, 1932 in ASRE IV-549–1.

103. U.S. Immigrant Inspector R. W. Gangewere to District Director of Immigration, Detroit, Michigan, 29 November 1932, RG 85, 7017/2463.

104. For example, see authorizations for transportation: A. C. Price to Board of Supervisors, 29 March 1932, in LACC 40:31.

105. Lane interview: Morales.

106. *La Opinión*, 14 June 1931.

107. Saint, "Woven within My Grandmother's Braid," 58.

108. Interview: Hortensia Nieto.

109. "Report of the Mexican Chamber of Commerce," 13 May 1931, in Box 62, Bundle 7, in Clements.

110. George P. Clements to Arnoll and Martin, 4 June 1931, in Box 62, Bundle 7, in Clements; see also Los Angeles Consulate to Secretaría de Relaciones Exteriores 27 January 1932 in ASRE IV-343–19.

111. Los Angeles Consulate to Maritime Building Loan Association, 22 September 1932, in ASRE IV-329–1.

112. *El Universal*, 15 February 1930.

113. Ernest Besig to Dear Friend, 12 August 1931, in Box 62, Bundle 7, Clements.

114. Balderrama, *In Defense of La Raza*, 22–23; *La Opinión*, 2 May 1931.

115. *Ideal Liberal*, 23 November 1931.

116. *Excélsior*, 2 June 1932.

117. *La Opinión*, 23 October 1932.

118. The activities of the Los Angeles Mexican consulate and consuls are probably the best known. See Balderrama, *In Defense of La Raza*.

119. American Consul Richard F. Boyce to Secretary of State, 26 November 1930, RG 59, 311.1215/17; also see Boyce to State, 8 January 1931, RG 59, 311.1215/18.

120. Bryce to State, 16 February 1931, RG 59, 311.1215/20.

121. "The Repatriation of Mexican Nationals, 1930–1935," American Consulate General Report, Mexico City, 18 September 1936, RG 59, 311.1215/90.

122. *El Universal*, 22 August 1932; *Excélsior*, 16 December 1932; Secretaría de Relaciones Exteriores, *Memoria de la Secretaría de Relaciones Exteriores de agosto de 1931 a julio de 1932 presentada al H. Congreso de la Unión por Manuel C. Téllez* (México, D.F.: Imprenta de la Secretaría de Relaciones Exteriores, 1932), 314.

123. "Entrada y Salida de Nacionales y Extranjeras Registradas," DAPP, *Revista de Estadística* (Enero–Diciembre 1940).

Revolutionary Mexico

1. The historiography of the Mexican Revolution is extensive. Essential reading is Ramón Eduardo Ruiz, *The Great Rebellion: Mexico, 1905–1924* (New York: W. W. Norton, 1980), a prize-winning account. Additional readings include the important works by Alan Knight, *The Mexican Revolution* (Cambridge, Great Britain: Cambridge University Press, 1986); and John Mason Hart, *Revolutionary Mexico: The Coming and Process of the Mexican Revolution* (Berkeley: University of California Press, 1987).

2. Interviews: Lucas Lucio and Celso Medina.

3. Interview: Elena Herrada.

4. Ruiz, *Great Rebellion*, ix; Also see his biography: Ruiz, *Memories of a Hyphenated Man* (Tucson: University of Arizona Press, 2003).

5. Interviews: Pablo Alcántara, Nicolás Avila, Evelyn Velarde Benson; Medina and Lucio interviews.

6. For the muralists in the United States see: Anthony W. Lee, *Painting on the Left: Diego Rivera, Radical Politics, and San Francisco Public Murals* (Berkeley: University of California Press, 1999).

7. Interview: Herrada.

8. *El Universal*, 3 March 1921, 5 March 1921, 26 April 1921, and 11 May 1921. Secondary accounts are John Martínez, *Mexican Emigration to the United States, 1910–1930* (San Francisco: R and E Research Associates, 1972), 52–57; and Lawrence A. Cardoso, *Mexican Emigration to the United States, 1897–1931: Socio-Economic Patterns* (Tucson: University of Arizona Press, 1980), 96–103.

9. Internal memorandum by the Secretaría de Relaciones Exteriores, undated, in ASRE 18–5-168. See also Cardoso, *Mexican Emigration*, 96–103.

10. Secretaría de Relaciones Exteriores Telegram to Washington Embassy, 24 February 1921, in ASRE 1349–6; Consejo Directivo de Denver to President Alvaro Obregón, 27 February 1922, in ASRE unclassified; Internal Memorandum Denver Consulate, 16 March 1922, in ASRE unclassified; *El Universal*, 24 October 1921.

11. Andrés Landa y Piña, *El servicio de migración en México* (México, D.F.: Talleres Gráficos de la Nación, 1930).

12. Alfonso Fabila, *El problema de la emigración de obreros y campesinos mexicanos* (México, D.F.: Talleres Gráficos de la Nación, 1929).

13. Gilberto Loyo, *Emigración de mexicanos a los Estados Unidos* (Roma: Instituto Poigráfico dello stato, 1931), and Loyo, *La política geografico de México* (México, D.F.: Talleres Tipográficos de S. Turanzas del Valle, 1935).

14. Roderic A. Camp, *Mexican Political Biographies, 1935–1975* (Tucson: University of Arizona Press, 1978), 191–92.

15. *El Universal*, 11 December 1928.

16. Gamio, *Mexican Immigration*, 184; For information about Gamio's relationship with the Mexican government, see Thomson interview and Ramón Eduardo Ruiz, *Mexico: The Challenge of Poverty and Illiteracy* (San Marino, Calif.: The Huntington Library, 1963), 139.

17. Enrique Santibañez, *Ensayo acerca de la inmigración mexicana en los Estados Unidos* (San Antonio: The Clegg Company, 1930).

18. Carreras de Velasco, *Los Mexicanos*, 88.

19. *Excélsior*, 17 April 1929, 25 March 1929, and 20 October 1929.

20. San Antonio Consul General Luis Lupián to Consuls of the Jurisdiction, 19 January 1932, in ASRE IV-671–47; Presidential Decree by Abelardo L. Rodríguez, 11 March 1933 in ASRE IV-671–47.

21. "Repatriation of Mexicans" by American Vice Consul Thomas J. Maleady to Secretary of State, 12 May 1932, in Rg. 59, 311.1215/33.

22. The authors found the collections of the Hemeroteca in Mexico City consisting of Mexico City's *El Universal* and *Excélsior* as well as Guadalajara's *El Informador* and Monterrey's *Porvenir* useful. Frequently, México de Afuera press coverage from San Antonio's *La Prensa* and Los Angeles's *La Opinión* complemented the Mexican treatment.

23. Abraham Hoffman, "The Repatriation of Mexican Nationals from the United States during the Great Depression" (Ph.D. diss., University of California, Los Angeles, 1970), 193–97.

24. Luis N. Vera to President Pascual Ortiz Rubio, 15 May 1931, in ASRE IV-353–38.

25. Santiago L. Gómez to President Pascual Ortiz Rubio, 21 February 1931, in ASRE IV-360–4.

26. Comisión Honorifica Mexicana of Wiley to Ministro Manuel C. Téllez, 16 May 1932, in ASRE IV-350–48.

27. Balderrama, *In Defense of La Raza*, 30–31.

28. El Paso Consul Luis Medina Barrón to Secretaría de Relaciones Exteriores, undated circa 1931, in ASRE IV-355–20.

29. New Orleans Consul Armando C. Amador to Secretaría de Relaciones Exteriores, undated circa 1931 in ASRE IV-358–14; Salt Lake City Consul Raúl Domínguez to Secretaría de Relaciones Exteriores, undated circa, in ASRE IV-358–14.

30. *La Prensa*, 27 September 1931, 6 October 1931, 18 October 1931, and 20 October 1931; *El Universal*, 6 October 1931, 15 October 1931, and 18 October 1931. Secondary accounts appear in Carreras de Velasco, *Los Mexicanos*, 101–3; and McKay, "Texas Mexican Repatriation during the Great Depression," 365–86.

31. Ibid.

32. *La Prensa*, 4 September 1930.

33. Woods, *Mexican Ethnic Leadership in San Antonio, Texas*, 20–21.

34. García, "Making of the Mexican-American Mind," 508–66.

35. Texas and Mexican newspapers provided press coverage of the Karnes City caravan. See San Antonio's Spanish-language *La Prensa*, for September and October of 1931, for the most extensive treatment.

36. Camp, *Mexican Political Biographies*, 28.

37. Balderrama, *In Defense of La Raza*, 23–24.

38. Ibid.; see also interview: Rafael de la Colina.

39. Interview: Roberto Galvan and Adolfo Martínez.

40. Quote from Dennis Nodín Váldes, "Mexican Revolutionary Nationalism and Repatriation during the Great Depression," *Mexican Studies/Estudios Mexicanos* 4, 1 (Winter 1988), 8–9; Váldes, *El Pueblo Mexicano en Detroit y Michigan: A Social History* (Detroit: McNaughton-Gunn, 1982), 24–44.

41. Consul Rafael Aveleyra to Mary Grace Wells, 9 June 1932, in ASRE IV-354–12. Case is also mentioned in Balderrama, *In Defense of La Raza*, 24.

42. Denver Consul S. J. Treviño to Secretaría de Relaciones Exteriores, undated circa 1931, in ASRE IV-354–40.

43. V. E. Roque, "Despedida de Karnes City, Texas, Octubre 18, De 1931," in ASRE IV-360–28; and Jesús Osorio, "Good-bye Countrymen," in Foster, "Corrido," 189–94.

44. *Excélsior*, 3 December 1932.

45. *Excélsior*, 14 December 1932.

46. Mexico City's *Excélsior*, 3 December 1932, 10 December 1932, and 11 December 1932; and *El Universal*, 3 March 1932; Guadalajara's *Porvenir*, 18 March 1932 and 1 April 1932; and *El Informador*, 24 January 1933, 25 January 1933, and 31 January 1933; secondary accounts: Hoffman, *Unwanted Mexican Americans*, 137–38; and Carreras de Velasco, *Los Mexicanos*, 95–97.

47. *El Universal*, 30 May 1934; see also *El Universal*, 2, 3, 6, and 15 June 1934.

48. Mexico City Vice Consul John S. Littell to Department of State, 27 July 1934, RG 59, 311.1215/71; Secretaría de Relaciones Exteriores, *Informe de labores de la Secretaría de Relaciones Exteriores de agosto de 1933 a julio de 1934, presentado al H. Congreso de la Unión por el Dr. José Manuel Puig Casauranc* (México, D.F.: Imprenta de la Secretaría de Relaciones Exteriores, 1934), 415–21.

49. For Mexican citizenship, see Cecilia Molina, *prática consular mexicano* (México, D.F.: Editorial Porrúa, 1970), and S. A. Bayitch and José Luis Siqueiros, *Conflict of Laws: Mexico and the United States, A Bilateral Study* (Coral Gables, Fla.: University of Miami Press, 1968), 31–34. The proposal for changing conditions of Mexican citizenship is presented in Secretaría de Relaciones Exteriores, *Memoria de la Secretaría de Relaciones Exteriores: agosto de 1938 a julio de 1939* (México, D.F.: Secretaría de Relaciones Exteriores, 1939), 154–55.

50. James W. Wilkie, *The Mexican Revolution: Federal Expenditure and Social Change since 1910* (Berkeley: University of California Press, 1970), 76.

51. *Excélsior*, 7 January 1931.

52. *Excélsior*, 14 December 1932.

53. Chihuahua Consul Lee R. Blohm to Department of State, 12 March 1939, in RG 59, 311.1215/129.

54. Ibid.

55. Ibid.

56. Ibid.

57. *Weekly News Sheet*, 5 June 1936.

58. *Weekly News Sheet*, 6 March 1936.

59. For understanding the repatriation and colonization policy of the Cárdenas government, see the Cárdenas campaign platform: Partido Nacional Revolucionario, *Memoria de la segunda convención ordinaria del Partido Nacional Revolucionario efectuada en la cuidad de Querétaro del 3 al 6 de diciembre de 1933* (México, D.F.: Partido Nacional Revolucionario, 1934).

60. For Spanish exiles in Mexico, see Patricia W. Fagen, *Exiles and Citizens: Spanish Republicans in Mexico* (Austin: University of Texas Press, 1973), 48. For Mexico's involvement with the Spanish Civil War, see T. G. Powell, *Mexico and the Spanish Civil War* (Albuquerque: University of New Mexico Press, 1981).

61. James W. Wilkie and Edna Monzón de Wilkie, *México Visto en el Siglo XX: Entrevistas de historia oral* (México, D.F.: Instituto de Investigaciones Económicas, 1969), 23–71; Camp, *Mexican Political Biographies*, 36–37. For Ramón Beteta's own views, see Ramón Beteta, *Pensamiento y Dinamica de la Revolución Mexicana: Antologia de documentos politicosociales* (México, D.F.: Editorial México Nuevo, 1950). Beteta's brother was General Ignacio Beteta Quintana, Director of Military Industry and Chief of Staff for President Cárdenas. The sub-secretary was also a close friend of Moisés Saénz, a respected government minister in various presidential administrations during the 1920s and 1930s.

62. Powell, *Mexico and the Spanish Civil War*, 187.

63. Betty Kirk, *Covering the Mexican Front: The Battle of Europe versus America* (Norman: University of Oklahoma Press, 1942), 187.

64. *Ultimas* Noticias, 5 April 1934. Lengthy correspondence regarding the Beteta trip between Mexico City Embassy and the State Department are in RG 59, 311.1215/122.

65. Ciudad Juárez Consul William P. Blocker to State, 13 April 1939, in RG 59 311.1215/118.

66. Nuevo Laredo Consul Romeyn Wormuth to State, 19 April 1939, in RG 59, 311.1215/121.

67. Stewart to State, 23 June 1939, in RG 59, 311.1215.132; interviews: Eduardo Negrete and Medina. According to oral history interviews, many colonia residents vividly recall the proposal but frequently think mistakenly that the proposal became law.

68. Stewart to State, 9 May 1939, in RG 59, 311.1215/124.

69. *El Universal*, 25 April 1939.

70. *El Universal*, 25 April 1939, 22 June 1939; "Mexican Exodus," *Newsweek* 14 (31 July 1939), 11.

71. Fernando Saúl Alanis Enciso, *El valle del Río Bravo, Tamaulipas, en la décade de 1930* (Ciudad Victoria, Tamaulipasi: El Colegio de Tamaulipas-El Colegio de San Luis, 2003), 47, 55.

72. Stewart to State Department, 23 June 1939, in RG 59, 311.1215/132.

Colonization

1. A classic example is *Excélsior*, 28 January 1931.

2. *Ideal Liberal*, 2 November 1931.

3. Secretaría de Agricultura y Fomento to Secretaría de Relaciones Exteriores, undated, in ASRE IV-108–61.

4. Departamento Consular to Secretario de Agricultura y Fomento, 6 November 1929, in ASRE IV-108–61.

5. *Excélsior*, 18 October 1929.

6. New York Consul General Manuel Cruz to Secretaría de Relaciones Exteriores, undated, in ASRE IV-341–39.

7. *Excélsior*, 6 April 1930.

8. Antonio Villarreal Muñoz to President Herbert Hoover of the United States, 10 December 1930, in RG 85, 39–1254.

9. Comité Pro-Repatriación to President Pascual Ortiz Rubio, 20 July 1931, in ASRE IV-341–9.

10. "Cuestionario Que Deben Llenar: Quienes Deseen Ser Admitidos Como Colonos en los Sistemas Nacionales de Riego," Comisión Nacional de Irrigación, undated, in ASRE IV-354–40.

11. "Acuerdo de la Secretaría de Hacienda y Crédito Público y El Secretario de Agricultura y Fomento," 20 March 1930, in ASRE IV-354–40.

12. "Acuerdo de la Secretaría de Hacienda y Crédito Público y El Secretario de Agricultura y Fomento," 4 September 1930, in ASRE IV-354–40.

13. "Circular Q," Comisión Nacional de Irrigación, September 1930, in ASRE IV-354–40.

14. Consul Maurice W. Altaffer to Department of State, 7 March 1930, in RG 59, 812.5511/03. For the Manzo uprising or the Plan of Hermosillo, see John W. F. Dulles, *Yesterday in Mexico: A Chronicle of the Revolution, 1919–1936* (Austin: University of Texas Press, 1961), 438–39.

15. Ibid.

16. Denver Consulate to Secretaría de Relaciones Exteriores, 30 November 1930, in ASRE IV-69–45.

17. Interview: Rubén Jiménez in "Expulsion of U.S. Citizens."

18. Secretaría de Agricultura y Fomento to Secretaría de Relaciones Exteriores, 14 December 1931, in ASRE IV-444–31.

19. *Excélsior,* 17 March 1931; see also Phoenix Consul E. Cota to Secretaría de Agricultura y Fomento, 16 August 1932, in ASRE IV-554–2.

20. A classic example is the editorial in *El Universal,* 4 April 1933.

21. *El Universal,* 13 October 1934.

22. *El Universal,* 12 August 1932.

23. *El Universal,* 13 August 1932.

24. *El Universal,* 4 April 1933.

25. American Consulate General Montreal to Department of State, 23 March 1936, in RG 59, 812.56/18.

26. *El Universal,* 25 August 1932.

27. Ibid.

28. *El Universal,* 22 August 1932.

29. An excellent example of correspondence emphasizing the limits of consular assistance is Secretaría de Relaciones Exteriores to San Bernardino Consulate, 5 January 1932, in ASRE IV-547–7.

30. Consul J. M. Vásquez to Secretaría de Relaciones Exteriores, 20 February 1931, in ASRE IV-354–1.

31. San Bernardino Consul Hermolao Torres to Los Angeles Consulate, 26 May 1932, in ASRE IV-547–7.

32. Consul Torres to R. H. Dunn and Company, 17 December 1930, in ASRE IV-73–1.

33. San Bernardino Consul Fernando Alatorre to Secretaría de Relaciones Exteriores, 17 December 1931, in ASRE IV-547–7.

34. Consul Fernando Alatorre to Isaac López, 14 April 1932, in ASRE IV-547–7.

35. Los Angeles Consulate to San Bernardino Consulate, 16 May 1932, in ASRE IV-547–7.

36. Isaac López to Secretaría de Relaciones Exteriores, 19 May 1932, in ASRE IV-547–7.

37. Los Angeles Consul Joaquín Terrazas to Fresno Consulate, 29 June 1932, in ASRE IV-547–7.

38. Torres to Secretaría de Relaciones Exteriores, 10 April 1934, in ASRE IV-547–7.

39. Torres to Los Angeles Consulate, 14 June 1934, in ASRE IV-547–7.

40. Departmento Consular, Secretaría de Relaciones Exteriores to Fresno Consulate, 24 May 1932, in ASRE IV-444–39.

41. Mexico City Vice Consul John S. Littell to Department of State, 20 April 1933, in RG 59, 311.1215/43.

42. *Ibid.*

43. Littell to State, 26 February 1934, in RG 59, 311.1215/50.

44. Littell to State, 9 March 1934, RG 59, 311.1215/51.

45. Littell to State, 28 May 1934, RG 59, 311.1215/61.

46. James C. Gilbert, "A Field Study in Mexico of the Mexican Repatriation Movement," (Master's thesis, University of Southern California, 1934), 108–10.

47. Littell to State, 26 May 1934, in RG 59 311.1215/61.

48. American Consul J. B. Stewart to State, 4 August 1938, in RG 59, 311.1215/102.

49. William R. Harriman to Board of Supervisors, 26 September 1932, in LAC Decimal File 40.31/340.20.

50. Thomson to Supervisors, 20 October 1932, in LAC Decimal File 40.31/340.20.

51. Ibid.

52. *El Universal*, 2 March 1933; Harriman to Board, 22 May 1933, in LAC Decimal File 40.31/340.261; interview with Rex Thomson.

53. *El Universal*, 13 October 1934.

54. *El Universal*, 18 September 1934.

55. Littell to State, 12 March 1935, RG 59, 311.1215/76.

56. *Weekly News Sheet*, 5 June 1936; *El Universal*, 29 September 1936, 8 March 1937.

57. *El Universal*, 3 March 1937.

58. Stewart to State, 4 August 1938, in RG 59, 311.1215/102.

59. Departmento Consular to Secretaría de Gobernación, 24 May 1932, in ASRE IV-444–39.

60. *Excélsior*, 28 January 1931.

61. *Excélsior*, 22 October 1937.

62. *El Universal*, 11 March 1931.

63. *Excélsior*, 5 April 1934.

64. *Ultimas Noticias*, 5 April 1934.

65. DAPP, *Revista de Estadística* 5 April 1939.

66. *El Universal*, 15 April 1939.

67. *El Universal*, 12 August 1939.

68. Christine Valenciana interview with Francisco E. Balderrama: Ramona Ríos de Castro.

69. Stewart to State, 9 May 1939, in RG 59, 311.1215/124.

70. *El Universal*, 22 June 1939.

71. Ibid.

72. *La Prensa*, 19 June 1939.

73. Fernando Saúl Alanis Enciso, *El valle del Río Bravo, Tamaulipas, en la década de 1930* (Ciudad Victoria Tamaulipas: El Colegio de Tamaulipas-El Colegio de San Luis, 2003), 63–64, 86–87.

74. Ciudad Juárez Vice Consul Leon L. Cowles to State, 10 June 1939, RG 59, 311.1215/129.

75. Ciudad Juárez Consul Blocker to State, 27 June 1939, in RG 59, 311.1215/131.

76. Stewart to State, 23 June 1939, in RG 59, 311.1215/132.

77. Ibid.

78. "Entrada y Salida de Nacionales y Extranjeras Registradas," DAPP, *Revista de Estadística* (Enero–Diciembre 1934).

Adjustment

1. Lanigan, "Second Generation Mexicans in Belvedere," 34.

2. Judith Melgoza interviews: Irma Amparano and Dora Raya; Christine Valenciana interview: Emilia Castañeda de Valenciana.

3. Helen W. Douglas, "The Conflict of Cultures in First Generation Mexicans in Santa Ana, California" (Master's thesis, University of Southern California, 1928), 19.

4. Cecilia Morales interview: Carmen Martínez.

5. Paul J. Crawford, "Movie Habits and Attitudes of the Under-Privileged Boys of the All Nations Area in Los Angeles" (Master's thesis, University of Southern California, 1934), 19, 61–73; Rena Blanche Peek, "The Religious and Social Attitudes of Mexican Girls of the Constituency of the All Nations Foundation in Los Angeles" (Master's thesis, University of Southern California, 1929), 44–48.

6. "Lista de Mexicanos/Repatriados," 16 August 1932, in ASRE IV-360–15.

7. Mexico City American Consul James B. Stewart to Department of State, RG 59, 311.1215/124.

8. *Porvenir*, 19 March 1931.

9. *El Universal*, 16 April 1933.

10. Gilbert, "Field Study in Mexico," 68.

11. Stewart to State, RG 59, 311.1215/124.

12. *Excélsior*, 25 April 1939.

13. *El Universal*, 28 April 1932.

14. Valenciana interviews: Castañeda de Valenciana, Teresa Martínez Southard, Hortensia Martínez de Benitez.

15. Valenciana interview: Martínez Southard.

16. Interview: Castañeda in "Expulsion of U.S. Citizens"; Valenciana interview: Castañeda de Valenciana.

17. Valenciana: Castañeda Valenciana and Martínez Southard.

18. Interview: Josefina Pérez.

19. Valenciana interview: Francisco Castañeda and Castañeda de Valenciana.

20. Interview: Hortensia Nieto.

21. Valenciana interview with Balderrama: Ignacio Piña.

22. Interview: Albino Piñeda; Albino Piñeda, "The Repatriated: Autobiography of a Mexican-American," unpublished manuscript.

23. Interview: Rubén Jiménez in "Expulsion of U.S. Citizens."

24. Valenciana interview: Martínez de Benitez.

25. Valenciana interview: Castañeda.

26. Ibid.

27. Valenciana interview: Martínez Southard.

28. Valenciana interview: Enrique Vega.

29. Interviews: Lucas Lucio and Celso Medina; Valenciana interview: Martínez de Benitez. Also see Saint, "Woven within My Grandmother's Braid," for death among children.

30. Interview: Arturo Herrada.

31. *Excélsior*, 2 June 1932.

32. *Ideal Liberal*, 2 November 1931.

33. Piedras Negras Consul Foster to Department of State, 27 January 1931, in RG 59, 812.5511/105.

34. *Porvenir*, 15 November 1931.

35. Gilbert, "Field Study in Mexico," 37.

36. *El Universal*, 17 March 1931.

37. Ernesto Martínez de Alva, *Vida Rural* (México, D.F.: Talleres Gráficos, 1933).

38. Valenciana interview: María Ofelia Acosta.

39. *Proposiciones del Trabajo a la Primera Convención Nacional de Población* (México, D.F.: Imprenta de la Nación, 1938), 12.

40. *La Prensa*, 9 September 1930.

41. *El Universal*, 11 March 1931.

42. *Excélsior*, 4 November 1931.

43. *El Universal*, 11 March 1931.

44. Mexico City Vice Consul John S. Littell to Department of State, RG 59, 311.1211/39. Also see *El Universal*, 19, 20, 31 January and 4, 9 February 1933.

45. Ibid.

46. *Excélsior*, 14 December 1932.

47. *Excélsior*, 6 October 1939.

48. Enrique González Flores to Secretaría de Relaciones Exteriores, 2 September 1932, in ASRE IV-354–40.

49. Valenciana interview: Antonio Méndez Lomelí.

50. Valenciana interview: Castañeda de Valenciana.

51. Clara Gertrude Smith, "The Development of the Mexican People in the Community of Watts" (Master's thesis, University of Southern California, 1933), 120.

52. Gilbert, "Field Study in Mexico," 42.

53. Interview: Herrada; José López Testimony for California Senate Select Committee on Citizen Participation Hearing, "Examination of Unconstitutional Deportation and Coerced Emigration of Legal Residents and U.S. Citizens of Mexican Descent During 1930s," 15 July 2003.

54. Interview: Piñeda; Piñeda, "The Repatriated," unpublished manuscript.

55. Valenciana interview: Castañeda.

56. Valenciana interview: Martínez Southard.

57. Valenciana interview: Vega.

58. Pablo Guerrero to Los Angeles County, 28 May 1934, in LAC Decimal File 40.31:340.39.

59. Ibid.

60. Saint, "Woven within My Grandmother's Braid," 68; Interviews: Ramón Curiel, Lucio, and Medina provide further testimony of returning repatriates.

61. *National Catholic Welfare Conference, Annual Reports* 1933–1934, 33.

62. Valenciana interview with Balderrama: Piña.

Accommodation

1. *El Universal*, 22 August 1932; *Excélsior*, 16 December 1932; Secretaría de Relaciones Exteriores, *Memoria de la Secretaría de Relaciones Exteriores de agosto de 1931 a julio de 1932* (México, D.F.: Imprenta de la Secretaría de Relaciones Exteriores, 1932), 314; "Entrada y Salida de Nacionales y Extranjeras Registradas," DAPP, *Revista de Estadística* (Enero–Diciembre 1934).

2. Interview: Raymond Rodríguez.

3. Ibid.

4. *Metrotimes*, 28 July–3 August 2004.

5. José López, Testimony for California Senate Select Committee on Citizen Participation Hearing, "Examination of Unconstitutional Deportation and Coerced Emigration of Legal Residents and U.S. Citizens of Mexican Descent During 1930s," 15 July 2003; interview José López, "Los Repatriados: Exiles from the Promised Land"

6. Ibid.

7. Ibid.

8. Ibid.

9. Emilia Castañeda de Valenciana, Testimony for California Senate Select Committee on Citizen Participation Hearing, "Examination of Unconstitutional Deportation and Coerced Emigration of Legal Residents and U.S. Citizens of Mexican Descent During 1930s," 15 July 2003; Christine Valenciana interview: Emilia Castañeda de Valenciana.

10. Interview: Arturo Herrada.

11. Interview: María Ofelia Acosta, "Public Broadcasting News Hour With Jim Lehrer," 8 minutes, PBS 27 November 2003; Christine Valenciana interview: María Ofelia Acosta.

12. Interview: Albino Piñeda; López Testimony, Hearing.

13. Interview Arturo Herrada.

14. Interview: Hortensia Nieto.

15. Interview: Rubén Jiménez, "Public Broadcasting News Hour With Jim Lehrer," 8 minutes, PBS 27 November 2003.

16. Interview: Elena Herrada; *Metrotimes*, 28 July–3 August 2004.

17. Ibid.

18. Interview: Nieto.

19. Valenciana interview with Balderrama: Ramona Ríos de Castro.

20. *Metrotimes*, 28 July–3 August 2004.

21. *La Opinión*, 13 July 2004; Christine Valenciana interview: Francisco Castañeda.

22. Castañeda Testimony Hearing; Valenciana interview: Castañeda de Valenciana.

23. Christine Valenciana interview: María Ofelia Acosta.

24. Interview: Carmen Martínez Monroe.

25. *San Bernardino Sun*, 24 February 1932.

26. Valenciana interview: Castañeda; López Testimony, Hearing; Valenciana interview with Balderrama: Ignacio Piña.

27. Interview: Nieto.

28. *Press-Telegram*, 5 September 2004; Interview: Piña; Valenciana interview with Balderrama: Ignacio Piña.

29. Interview: Nieto

30. Interview: Arturo Herrada.

31. Ibid.

32. Ibid.

33. Interview: Josefina Pérez.

34. Interview: Fernando Pérez.

35. Ibid.

36. Latinos & Latinas World War II interview: Isabel Solís Thomas.

37. Valenciana Interview with Teresa Martínez Southard.

38. *Press-Telegram*, 5 September 2004.

39. Interview: Fernando Pérez.

40. *Metrotimes*, 28 July–3 August 2004.

41. Francisco E. Balderrama, "Unconstitutional Deportation and Coerced Emigration of Legal Residents and U.S. Citizens of Mexican Descent During the 1930s," Hispanic National Bar Association, San Jose, Calif., 6 September 2003.

42. Interview: Piñeda.

43. Ibid.

44. Ibid.

45. Ibid.

46. Interview: Arturo Herrada; Raul Morin, *Among the Valiant: Mexican Americans in World War II and Korea* (Alhambra Calif.: Borden Publishing Company, 1966), 232–33.

47. López Testimony, Hearing; Interview: Pérez.

48. Morín, *Among the Valiant*.

49. Interview: Jiménez in "Expulsion of U.S. Citizens," 15 minutes. Los Angeles, 2004.

50. Ibid.

51. Raymond Rodriguez interview.

52. "Hero Street USA" Silvis, Illinois, 28 Minutes, Innervision Studies, 1984.

53. Robert Jones, "Mexican War Workers in the U.S." in *Mexican Manpower: Recruiting Program and Operation* (Washington: D.C.: Pan American Union, Division of Labor and Social Information, 1945), 24–25.

54. Valenciana interview with Balderrama: Piña.

Retrospect

1. *La Opinión*, 13 July 2003; Introduction for California Senate Select Committee on Citizen Participation Hearing, "Examination of Unconstitutional Deportation and Coerced Emigration of Legal Residents and U.S. Citizens of Mexican Descent During 1930s," 15 July 2003.

2. *La Opinión*, 13 July 2004.

3. *Press-Telegram*, 5 September 2004.

4. "Decade of Betrayal Forum." 60 minutes. Concordia University, Irvine, Calif., 13 November 2002.

5. "This Week in Garden Grove" Television Program "Community Forum: Mexican Deportations," Channel 3, Orange, California, Channel 3 22 July 2003.

6. Julian Nava, *My Mexican-American Journey* (Houston: Arte Público Press, 2002), 8. Also see "Foreword" for Abraham Hoffman, *Unwanted Mexican Americans in the Great Depression: Repatriation Pressures, 1929–1939* (Tucson: University of Arizona Press, 1974), ix.

7. Interview: Elena Herrada; *Metrotimes*, 28 July–3 August 2004.

8. *Metrotimes*, 28 July–3 August 2004; *El Central: Hispanic News*, 1 April 2004.

9. "Los Repatriados: Exiles from the Promised Land;" Elena Herrada E-Mail Message, 29 September 2004; *Metrotimes*, 28 July–3 August 2004; *El Central: Hispanic News*, 1 April 2004. Also see "Coloquio Mexicanos en diáspora: los repatriados de 1930," *La gaceta de El Colegio de San Luis* 6:12 (Mayo-Agosto 2004), 1–5.

10. Interview: Elena Herrada; Also interviews: Roberto Galvan and Adolfo Martinez.

11. Interview: John Ortega.

12. *Santa Ana Register*, 30 October 1985.

13. *Orange County Register*, 19 July 2003.

14. *La Opinión*, 13 July 2003.

15. *World Net Daily*, 14 July 2003.

16. Ibid.

17. *Los Angeles Times*, 15 August 2004.

18. The Hearings of the Senate Select Committee on Citizen Participation were videotaped. There are also printed copies of testimony in "Examination of Unconstitutional Deportation and Coerced Emigration of Legal Residents and U.S. Citizens of Mexican Descent During 1930s," 15 July 2003.

19. *La Opinión*, 13 July 2003.

20. *Press-Telegram*, 28 September 2004.

21. Ibid.

22. Ibid; Castañeda Testimony, Hearings.

23. *Metrotimes*, 28 July–3 August 2004.

24. Ibid.

25. *Sacramento Bee*, 16 July 2003.

26. *Los Angeles Times*, 15 July 2003.

27. Ibid.

28. *Los Angeles Times*, 16 July 2003.

29. Ibid.

30. *San Jose Mercury News*, 19 July 2003.

31. Ibid.

32. *Orange County Weekly*, 25 July 2003.

33. *Orange County Register*, 31 August 2003.

34. Interview: María Ofelia Acosta, "Public Broadcasting News Hour With Jim Lehrer," 8 minutes, 27 November 2003.

35. *La Opinión*, 29 September 2004.

36. Ibid.

37. Telephone Conversation with Norma Cobb, District Coordinator for California State Senator Joseph Dunn.

38. Congresswoman Hilda Solís, "Dear Colleague Letter," Undated. Courtesy of Emilia Castañeda.

39. *La Opinión*, 14 September 2003.

40. Ibid.

41. *Guardian*, 17 July 2003.

42. Steve Reyes to Emilia Castañeda, 13 April 2004. MALDEF Correspondence, courtesy of Emilia Castañeda. Also see *Los Angeles Times*, 15 August 2004.

43. Resolutions at National Convention of American GI Forum, Frankenmuth, Michigan, 2004.

44. Resolutions at California Federation of Teachers, AFT, AFL-CIO, Universal City, 19–21 March 2004 and Resolutions at LCLAA: Labor Council for Latin American Advancement, AFL-CIO, Santa Pueblo, New Mexico, 25–29 August 2004.

45. "Unconstitutional Deportation and Coerced Emigration of Legal Residents and U.S. Citizens of Mexican Descent During the 1930s," Hispanic National Bar Association, San Jose, California, 6 September 2003.

46. Francisco E. Balderrama"Unconstitutional Deportation and Coerced Emigration" Town Hall Meeting, Our Lady Queen of the Angels Church, La Placita, Los Angeles, California, Channel 34/ Channel 52, 13 September 2003.

47. Program for "Betrayal and Violations: Mexican Repatriation of the 1930s" Los Angeles Times Center, Costa Mesa, California, 24 September 2004; Madrigal A. Cuauhtlatoatzin "A Spirit of Hope: In Honor of La Familia Madrigal, Los Repatriados."

48. *Los Angeles Times*, 8 October 2005; *La Opinión*, 5 April 2005 and 9 April 2005; Emilia Castañeda to First Lady of California, Maria Shriver, 3 September 2005, and First Lady of California, Maria Shriver, to Emilia Castañeda, 21 September 2005. Courtesy of Emilia Castañeda.

Bibliography

Archival Sources

American Legion File, East Chicago Historical Society Collection, East Chicago, Indiana.

Archivo de la Secretaría de Relaciones Exteriores, México, D.F.

Cady, George L. "Report of Commission on International and Interracial Factors on the Problem of Mexicans in the United States," MS. Bancroft Library. University of California Berkeley (p. 395).

Castañeda Unconstitutional Deportation Papers. Courtesy of Emilia Castañeda.

California State Archives, Sacramento, California.

Clements, George P. Special Collections, Research Library, University of California, Los Angeles.

Columbus Library, Organization of American States, Washington, D.C.

Dunn Papers, Joseph. Courtesy of Joseph Dunn.

Ford Papers, John Anson. Huntington Library, Pasadena, California.

Gamio Papers, Manuel. Bancroft Library, University of California Berkeley.

Hemeroteca Nacional de México, México, D.F.

International Institute of the YWCA, Immigration History Institute, University of Minnesota, St. Paul, Minnesota.

Los Angeles County Board of Supervisors. Minute Books, 1930–1941.

Los Angeles County Board of Supervisors. Supervisors' Decimal File, Hall of Administration, Los Angeles County, California.

McWilliams Papers, Carey. Special Collections, Research Library, University of California, Los Angeles.

Taylor Collection, Paul S. Bancroft Library, University of California Berkeley.

Torres Immigration Documents, courtesy of Daniel Torres.

United States Bureau of Immigration, General Records, Record Group 85, National Archives and Record Service, Washington, D.C.

United States Department of State, General Records, Record Group 59, National Archives and Record Service, Washington, D.C.

Oral History Interviews

Group I

Alcántara, Pablo. Yorba Linda, California, 25 March 1976.

Alvarez, Roberto. San Diego, California, 1 November 1976.

Anaya, María. Long Beach, California, 14 March 1991.

Avila, Nicolás. Los Angeles, California, 8 April 1976.

Ayala, Angelina. Long Beach, California, 15 June 1994.

Balderrama Terrazas, Francisco. Capistrano Beach, California, 25 December 1975.

Benson, Evelyn Velarde. Los Angeles, California, 8 April 1976.

Carreón, Dr. Reynaldo. Los Angeles, California, 9 March 1976.

Castro, Alejandro. El Monte, California, 21 December 1976.

Colina, Rafael de la. Washington, D.C., 23 May 1974.

Corona, Jesús. El Monte, California, 21 December 1976.

Cruz, Catarino. Orange, California, 23 March 1976.

Curiel, Ramón. El Modena, California, 25 March 1976.

Díaz, Dr. José. Los Angeles, California, 11 March 1976.

Flores, Emilio. Los Angeles, California, 17 March 1976.

Galvan, Roberto. Detroit, Michigan, 7 May 2004.

Guerrero, Julio C. Los Angeles, California, 6 March 1976.

Hebel, Anna. Carpinteria, California, 27 October 1976.

Herrada, Arturo. Detroit, Michigan, 8 May 2004.

Herrada, Elena. Detroit, Michigan, 8 May 2004.

Jiménez, Alfonso. El Monte, California, 21 December 1976.

Licero, Nicolás. Tustin, California, 30 March 1976.

Lucio, Lucas. Santa Ana, California, 16 March 1976, 23 March 1976.

Macías, José. Carpinteria, California, 27 October 1976.

Marcus, David. Los Angeles, California, 25 November 1976.

Martínez, Emilio. Stanton, California, 23 March 1976.

Martinez, Adolfo. Detroit, Michigan, 7 May 2004.

Medina, Celso. El Modena, California, 12 April 1976.

Negrete, Eduardo. Fullerton, California, 26 March 1976.

Nieto, Hortensia. Long Beach, California, 19 August 2004.

Núñez, Plutarco. El Monte, California, 21 December 1976.

Orozco, José David. Los Angeles, California, 13 March 1976.

Ortega, John. Long Beach, California, December 13, 2004.

Pérez, Fernando. Long Beach, California, 18 September 2003.

Pérez, Josefina. Long Beach, California, 18 September 2003.

Piñeda, Albino. Santa Paula, California, 19 October 2004.

Rivas, Pascual. Tustin, California, 30 March 1976.

Rodríguez, Raymond. Long Beach, California, 3 September 1990.

Rodríguez, Raymond, Long Beach, California, 9 September 2004.

Ruiz de Balderrama, Rafael. Capistrano Beach, California, 25 December 1975.

Santana, Gabriel. Long Beach, California, 15 March 1991.

Servín, Dr. Camilo. Los Angeles, California, 5 March 1976.

Solórzano, José. Montebello, California, 11 March 1976.

Thomson, Rex. Rancho Bernardo, California, 8 March 1976.

Torres, Daniel. Long Beach, California, 17 June 1994.

Valenciana, Flavio. Riverside, California, 26 December 1989.

Zaragoza, Enrique. Carpinteria, California, 27 October 1976.

(The authors conducted and tape-recorded all of the above interviews.
Tapes, notes, and transcripts are in the possession of the authors.)

Group II

de la Torre, Alejandra. Interview with Cruz Sánchez, Los Angeles, California,
    1 December 1990.

Doty, Judith. Interview with María Bustos Jefferson, Los Angeles, California,
    1 June 1976.

Hicks, Matilde E. Interview with Jesús Casárez, San Bernardino, California,
    2 June 1976.

———. Interview with Eduardo Rubio, San Bernardino, California, 2 June 1976.

———. Interview with José B. Solórzano, San Pedro, California, 24 April 1976.

———. Interview with Adolfo Tapia, San Pedro, California, 24 April 1976.

Juárez, Claudia. Interview with Sebastiana Briones Casas, 1 December 1991.

Melgoza, Judith. Interview with Alicia Apodaca, Montebello, California,
    1 August 1984.

———. Interview with Irma Amparano, Montebello, California, 5 August 1984.

———. Interview with Margarita Brown, Los Angeles, California, 8 August 1984.

———. Interview with Esperanza Gallardo, Montebello, California, 31 July 1984.

———. Interview with Vera Godoy, Monterey Park, California, 15 August 1984.

———. Interview with Dora Raya, Montebello, California, 5 August 1984.

———. Interview with Inez Salazar, Montebello, California, 13 August 1984.

———. Interview with Jesusita Solís, Montebello, California, 10 August 1984.

Morales, Cecilia. Interview with Carmen Martínez, Los Angeles, California, August 1984.

Valenciana de Balderrama, Christine. Interview with María Ofelia Acosta, Rowland Heights, California, 27 September 2003.

_____. Interview with Carmen Martínez Monroe, Redlands, California, 28 July 2003.

Valenciana de Balderrama, Christine with Francisco E. Balderrama

_____. Interview with Ramona Ríos de Castro, Ejido Erienda, San Isidro, Baja California, 17 July 2004.

_____. Interview with Ignacio Piña, Bakersfield, California, 27 November 2003 and 27 December 2003.

(All of the above interviews were tape-recorded and are in the possession of the authors.)

Group III

Lane, James B. Interview with Abe Morales, 4 February 1994. Transcript, Courtesy of John Ortega, Indiana University Northwest Library, Gary Indiana.

Valenciana de Balderrama, Christine. Interview with Emilia Castañeda de Valenciana, O.H. 700.

———. Interview with Francisco Castañeda, O.H. 1301.

———. Interview with John Anson Ford, O.H. 759.

———. Interview with Allan A. Hunter, O.H. 744.

———. Interview with María Bustos Jefferson, O.H. 1300.

———. Interview with Carmen Landeros, O.H. 745.

———. Interview with José Landeros, O.H. 746.

———. Interview with Antonio Méndez Lomelí, O.H. 1297.

———. Interview with Eliseo Martínez, O.H. 747.

———. Interview with Teresa Martínez Southard, O.H. 753.

———. Interview with Hortensia Martínez de Benitez, O.H. 1298.

———. Interview with Antonia Muñatones, O.H. 748.

———. Interview with Carlos Muñatones, O.H. 749.

———. Interview with Lupe Navares, O.H. 751.

———. Interview with Herbert Sánchez, O.H. 752.

———. Interview with Rex Thomson, O.H. 1299.

———. Interview with William A. de Uriarte, O.H. 1296.

———. Interview with Enrique Vega, O.H. 1295.

Oral History Collection, California State University, Fullerton.

Enrique Vásquez interview, Mexican American Oral History Collection, the Claremont Colleges.

Group IV

Stories of U.S. Latinos and Latinas and World War II Narratives, School of Journalism, University of Texas. Interview with Concepción Alvarado Escobedo.

_____. Interview with Hermina Cadena.

_____. Interview with Richard Dominguez.

_____. Interview with Ignacio Guerrero and Antonia Medina.

_____. Interview with Lorenza Lujano.

_____. Interview with Betty Medina.

_____. Interview with Gloria Moraga.

_____. Interview with Pablo Segura.

_____. Interview with Isabel Solís Thomas.

Group V

Interviews on Video Tape.

California Senate Select Committee on Citizen Participation Hearing, "Examination of Unconstitutional Deportation and Coerced Emigration of Legal Residents and U.S. Citizens of Mexican Descent During 1930s," 240 Minutes, California Channel, 15 July 2003.

"Expulsion of U.S. Citizens," 15 minutes, Los Angeles, 2004.

Public Broadcasting News Hour With Jim Lehrer, 8 Minutes, PBS, 27 November 2003.

Newspapers

Anaheim Bulletin

Carpinteria, *The Morning Express*

Chicago Evening Post

Decatur Wise County Messenger

Detroit *El Central: Hispanic News*

Detroit *Metrotimes*

Edinberg (Texas) *El Defensor*

El Demócrata Sinaloense

El Paso *Continental*

El Paso *Herald Post*

Guadalajara *El Informador*

Guadalajara *Porvenir*

Hidalgo County (Texas) *Independent*

Laredo Times

London *Guardian*

Long Beach *Independent Press-Telegram*

Los Angeles *El Heraldo de México*

Los Angeles Evening Herald Express

Los Angeles Examiner

Los Angeles *Illustrated Daily News*

Los Angeles *La Opinión*

Los Angeles Record

Los Angeles Times

México, D.F., *El Nacional*

México, D.F., *El País*

México, D.F., *El Universal*

México, D.F., *El Universal Gráfico*

México, D.F., *Excélsior*

México, D.F., *Ideal Liberal*

México, D.F., *Ultimas Noticias*

México, D.F., *Weekly News Sheet*

National Catholic Welfare Conference. *Annual Reports*

Monterrey, *Porvenir*

New York Times

Orange County Register

Orange County Weekly

Redlands Daily Facts

Sacramento Bee

San Angelo Times

San Antonio Express

San Antonio *La Prensa*

Santa Ana Register

San Angelo Times

San Bernadino Sun

San Diego *El Heraldo*

San Diego *Hispano-Americano*

San Diego *Union*

San Francisco Chronicle

San Francisco *Western Worker*

San Jose Mercury News

South Texas Citizen

World Net Daily

U.S. Government and State Publications

United States Congress. *Congressional Record: Proceedings and Debates of the First Session of the Seventy-Fourth Congress of the United States of America.* Washington, D.C.: United States Government Printing Office, 1935.

——. Bureau of Labor Statistics. "Increase of Mexican Labor in Certain Industries in the U.S." *Monthly Labor Review* 32 (January 1931), 82.

——. United States Department of Commerce and Labor. *Annual Report of the Commissioner General of Immigration.* Washington, D.C.: United States Government Printing Office, 1911.

——. Department of Commerce. *Statistical Abstract of the United States, 1932.* Washington D.C.: United States Government Printing Office, 1932.

——. Department of Commerce, Bureau of the Census. *Fifteenth Census of the United States, 1930: Population, Special Report of Foreign-Born White Families by Country of Birth of Head.* Washington, D.C.: United States Government Printing Office, 1933.

——. Department of Commerce, Bureau of the Census. *Sixteenth Census of the United States, 1940: Population, Nativity, and Parentage of the White Population.* Washington, D.C.: United States Government Printing Office, 1943.

——. House Committee on Immigration. *Hearings on Restriction of Western Hemisphere Immigration.* 70th Congress, 1st Session. Washington, D.C.: United States Government Printing Office, 1928.

——. House Committee on Immigration and Naturalization. *Seasonal Agricultural Laborers from Mexico Heaving.* 69th Congress, 1st Session. Washington D.C.: United States Government Printing Office, 1926.

——. Immigration Commission. *Reports of the Immigration Commission, Immigrants in Industries.* Washington, D.C.: Government Printing Office, 1911.

California. Department of Industrial Relations, Governor's Mexican Fact-Finding Committee. *Mexicans in California: Report of Governor C. C. Young's Mexican Fact-Finding Committee.* San Francisco: State Printing Office, 1931.

——. *Review of the Activities of the State Relief Administration of California, 1933–1935.* San Francisco: State Printing Office, 1932.

——. State Relief Administration. Bureau of Statistics. *The Problem of Interstate Migration as It Affects the California Relief Administration.* San Francisco: State Printing Office, 1936.

——. State Unemployment Commission. *Report and Recommendations.* Sacramento: State Printing Office, 1932.

Heller Committee for Research in Social Economics of the University of California and Constantine Panunzio, "How Mexicans Earn and Live: A Study of the Incomes and Expenditure of One Hundred Mexican Families in San Diego, California" *Cost of Living Studies*, 5 Berkeley, Calif.: University of California Press, 1933.

Illinois. *State of Illinois Second Annual Report of the Illinois Emergency Relief Commission.* June 1934.

LAC Board of Supervisors. *Annual Report for Fiscal Year Ending June 30, 1929.*

Mexican Government Publications

DAPP. *Revista de Estadística.* (Enero–Diciembre 1934). México, D.F.: Talleres de la Nación, 1934.

Departamento del Trabajo. *Proposiciones del Trabajo a la Primera Convención Nacional de Población.* México, D.F.: Imprenta de la Nación, 1938.

Diario Oficial. *Organo del gobierno constitucional de los Estados Unidos Mexicanos.*

Secretaría de Gobernación. *Constitución política de los Estados Unidos Mexicanos.* México, D.F.: Imprenta de la Secretaría de Gobernación, 1975.

Secretaría de Relaciones Exteriores. *Boletin.* México, D.F.: Secretaría de Relaciones, 1931.

Secretaría de Relaciones Exteriores. *Cincuenta años de la revolución: algunos aspectos de la política internacional de la revolución mexicana.* México, D.F.: Secretaría de Relaciones Exteriores, 1960.

———. *Escalafón del cuerpo diplomático mexicano.* México, D.F.: Secretaría de Relaciones Exteriores, 1932.

———. *Funcionarios de la Secretaría de Relaciones Exteriores desde el año 1821 a 1940.* México, D.F.: Imprenta de la Secretaría de Relaciones Exteriores, 1940.

———. *Guía diplomático y consular.* México, D.F.: Imprenta de Francisco Díaz de León, 1902.

———. *Informe de labores de la Secretaría de Relaciones Exteriores de agosto de 1933 a julio de 1934, presentado al H. Congreso de la Unión por el Dr. José Manuel Puig Casauranc.* México, D.F.: Imprenta de la Secretaría de Relaciones Exteriores, 1934.

———. *Informe de la Secretaría de Relaciones Exteriores.* México, D.F.: Imprenta National, 1900.

———. *Ley orgánica del cuerpo consular mexicano y reglamento de la ley orgánica del servicio consular mexicano, 1923.* México, D.F.: Imprenta de la Secretaría de Relaciones Exteriores, 1923.

———. *Ley orgánica del cuerpo consular mexicano y reglamento de la ley orgánica del servicio consular mexicano, 1934*. México, D.F.: Imprenta de la Secretaría de Relaciones Exteriores, 1934.

———. *Memoria de la Secretaría de Relaciones Exteriores de agosto de 1923 a julio de 1926, presentada al H. Congreso de la Unión por Genaro Estrada, Subsecretario del Ramo*. México, D.F.: Imprenta de la Secretaría de Relaciones Exteriores, 1928.

———. *Memoria de la Secretaría de Relaciones Exteriores de agosto de 1927 a julio de 1928, presentada al H. Congreso de la Unión por Genaro Estrada, Subsecretario del Ramo*. México, D.F.: Imprenta de la Secretaría de Relaciones Exteriores, 1928.

———. *Memoria de la Secretaría de Relaciones Exteriores de agosto de 1928 a julio de 1929, presentada al H. Congreso de la Unión por Genaro Estrada, Subsecretario del Ramo*. México, D.F.: Imprenta de la Secretaría de Relaciones Exteriores, 1929.

———. *Memoria de la Secretaría de Relaciones Exteriores de agosto de 1929 a julio de 1930, presentada al H. Congreso de la Unión por Genaro Estrada, Subsecretario del Ramo*. México, D.F.: Imprenta de la Secretaría de Relaciones Exteriores, 1930.

———. *Memoria de la Secretaría de Relaciones Exteriores de agosto de 1930 a julio de 1931, presentada al H. Congreso de la Unión por Manuel C. Téllez*. México, D.F.: Imprenta de la Secretaría de Relaciones Exteriores, 1932.

———. *Memoria de la Secretaría de Relaciones Exteriores de agosto de 1931 a julio de 1932, presentada al H. Congreso de la Unión por Manuel C. Téllez*. México, D.F.: Imprenta de la Secretaría de Relaciones Exteriores, 1932.

———. *Memoria de la Secretaría de Relaciones Exteriores de agosto de 1932 a julio de 1933, presentada al H. Congreso de la Unión por José Manuel Puig Casauranc, Subsecretario del Ramo*. México, D.F.: Imprenta de la Secretaría de Relaciones Exteriores, 1933.

———. *Memoria de la Secretaría de Relaciones Exteriores de agosto de 1936 a julio de 1937, presentada al H. Congreso de la Unión por Eduardo Hay, Secretario del Ramo*. México, D.F.: Imprenta de la Secretaría de Relaciones Exteriores, 1937.

———. *Memoria de la Secretaría de Relaciones Exteriores de agosto de 1938 a julio de 1939, presentada al H. Congreso de la Unión por Eduardo Hay, Secretario del Ramo*. México, D.F.: Imprenta de la Secretaría de Relaciones Exteriores, 1939.

———. *Migración y naturalización: información para los servicios diplomáticos y consular*. México, D.F.: Imprenta de la Secretaría de Relaciones Exteriores, 1932.

———. *Migración y la protección de mexicanos en el extranjero: labor de la Secretaría de Relaciones Exteriores en Estados Unidos y Guatemala*. México, D.F.: Imprenta de la Secretaría de Relaciones Exteriores, 1928.

———. *Requisitos para ingresar en la carrera consular y cuistionarios de examenes*. México, D.F.: Imprenta de la Secretaría de Relaciones Exteriores, 1925.

Primary Sources

Books

Allen, Ruth. *The Labor of Women in the Production of Cotton*. Austin: University of Texas Publications, 1931.

Bogardus, Emory. *The Mexican in the United States*. Los Angeles: University of Southern California Press, 1934.

Fabila, Alfonso. *El problema de la emigración de obreros y campesinos mexicanos*. México, D.F.: Talleres Gráficos de la Nación, 1929.

Gamio, Manuel. *The Mexican Immigrant: His Life Story*. Chicago: University of Chicago Press, 1931.

———. *Mexican Immigration to the United States: A Study of Human Migration and Adjustment*. Chicago: University of Chicago Press, 1930.

———. *Número, procedencia y distribución geográfica de los inmigrantes mexicanos en los Estados Unidos*. México, D.F.: Talleres Gráficos, 1930.

Garis, Roy L. *Immigration Restriction: A Study of the Opposition to and Regulation of Immigration in the United States*. New York: MacMillan, 1927.

Hidalgo, Ernesto. *La protección de mexicanos in los Estados Unidos: defensorías de oficio anexas a los consulados—un proyecto*. México, D.F.: Secretaría de Relaciones Exteriores, 1940.

Howland, Charles P. *Survey of American Foreign Policy, 1929*. New Haven, Conn.: Yale University Press, 1929.

Johnson, Elizabeth S. *Welfare of Families of Sugar-Beet Laborers: A Study of Child Labor and Its Relation to Family Work, Income and Living Conditions in 1935*. Washington, D.C.: United States Department of Labor, Children's Bureau Publication, 1939.

Jones, Anita. *Conditions Surrounding Mexicans in Chicago*. San Francisco: R and E Research Associates, [1928].

Jones, Robert. "Mexican War Workers in the U.S.," *Mexican Manpower: Recruiting Program and Operation*. Washington, D.C.: Pan American Union, Division of Labor and Social Information, 1945, 24–25.

Kirk, Betty. *Covering the Mexican Front: The Battle of Europe versus America.* Norman: University of Oklahoma Press, 1942.

Landa y Piña, Andrés. *El servicio de migración en México.* México, D.F.: Talleres Gráficos de la Nación, 1930.

Loyo, Gilberto. *Emigración de mexicanos a los Estados Unidos.* Roma: Instituto Poigráfico dello stato, 1931.

———. *La Política geográfico de México.* México, D.F.: Talleres Tipográficos de S. Turanzas del Valle, 1935.

Martínez de Alva, Ernesto. *Vida Rural.* México, D.F.: Talleres Gráficos, 1933.

Partido Nacional Revolucionario. *Memoria de la segunda convención ordinaria del Partido Nacional Revolucionario efectuada en la cuidad de Querétaro del 3 al 6 de diciembre de 1933.* México, D.F.: Partido Nacional Revolucionario, 1934.

Perales, Alonso S. *En defensa de mi raza.* San Antonio: Artes Gráficas, 1937.

Pesotta, Rose. *Bread on the Waters.* New York: Dodd, Mead, and Company, 1944.

Santibañez, Enrique. *Ensayo acerca de la inmigración mexicana en los Estados Unidos.* San Antonio: The Clegg Company, 1930.

Taylor, Paul S. *A Mexican-American Frontier, Nueces County, Texas.* Chapel Hill: University of North Carolina Press, 1934.

———. *Mexican Labor in the United States: Chicago and the Calumet Region.* Berkeley: University of California Press, 1932.

———. *Mexican Labor in the United States: Dimmit County, Winter Garden District, South Texas.* Berkeley: University of California Press, 1930.

———. *Mexican Labor in the United States: Imperial Valley, California.* Berkeley: University of California Press, 1930.

———. *Mexican Labor in the United States: Migration Statistics.* Berkeley: University of California Press, 1929.

———. *Mexican Labor in the United States: Migration Statistics II.* Berkeley: University of California Press, 1934.

———. *Mexican Labor in the United States: Valley of the South Platte, Colorado.* Berkeley: University of California Press, 1929.

———. *A Spanish-American Peasant Community: Arandas in Jalisco, Mexico.* Berkeley: University of California Press, 1933.

Articles

Allen, Robert S. "One of Mr. Hoover's Friends." *American Mercury* 25 (January 1932), 53–62.

"Back Where They Came From." *New Masses* (18 April 1939), 12–13.

Bogardus, Emory S. "The Mexican Immigrant." *Sociology and Social Research* 11
     (May–June 1927), 470–88.

———. "The Mexican Immigrant and Segregation." *American Journal of Sociology*
     36 (July 1930), 74–80.

———. "The Mexican Immigrant and the Quota." *Sociology and Social Research* 12,
     4 (March–April 1928), 371–78.

———. "Mexican Repatriates." *Sociology and Social Research* 18
     (November–December 1933), 169–76.

———. "Second Generation Mexicans." *Sociology and Social Research* 13
     (January 1929), 276–83.

Bennett, Charles L. "Housing for Field Employees," reprint of articles in *San
     Dimas Press*, Berkeley: University of California Press, 1936.

"A Caravan of Sorrow." *Living Age* 332 (15 May 1927), 870–72.

Carroll, Raymond G. "The Alien on Relief." *Saturday Evening Post* 208
     (11 January 1936), 17.

———. "Aliens in Subversive Activities." *Saturday Evening Post* 208
     (22 February 1936), 10.

———. "Alien Workers in America." *Saturday Evening Post* 208 (25 January
     1936), 86, 89.

Clark, John Perry. "Aliens in the Deportation Dragnet." *Current History* 36
     (April 1932), 27–31.

Clark, Victor S. "Mexican Labor in the United States." *Bulletin of the Bureau
     of Labor* 17 (September 1908), 466–522.

"Commissioner Hull, Exporter," *Saturday Evening Post*, 202 (18 January 1930), 24.

"Concerning the Employment of Aliens on WPA Projects." *Interpreter Releases:
     An Information Service on Immigration, Naturalization, and the Foreign-
     Born* (New York, 1938), 413–14.

Crawford, Ramsen. "The Menace of Mexican Immigration." *Current History* 31
     (February 1931), 902–7.

"Deportation during the Fiscal Year Ended June 30, 1934." *Interpreter Releases:
     An Information Service on Immigration, Naturalization, and the Foreign-
     Born* (New York, 1935), 36–41.

"A Demographic Analysis of First and Second Generation Mexican Population in
     the United States 1930," *Social Science Quarterly* 24 (September 1943), 138–49.

Dies, Martin. "The Immigration Crisis," *Saturday Evening Post* 207 (20
     April 1035), 11.

"The Distribution of Communal Lands in Mexico." *Pan American Union*
     (18 May 1933), 3.

"Doakery and Deportations." *Literary Digest* (22 August 1931), 6.

"The Ebb-Tide in Immigration." *Literary Digest* (27 August 1931), 8–9.

Editorial. *The Nation*, 133 (30 December 1931), 712.

Galarza, Ernesto. "Life in the United States for Mexican People: Out of the Experience of a Mexican." *Proceedings of the National Conference of Social Work*. 56th Annual Session, 56 (1929), 64–74.

———. "Without the Benefit of Lobby." *Survey* 66, 3 (1 May 1931), 181.

Garis, Roy L. "It is Time to Clean House." *Saturday Evening Post* 199 (25 September 1926), 33.

———. "Lest Immigration Restriction Fail." *Saturday Evening Post* 198 (10 October 1925), 41.

———. "The Mexican Invasion." *Saturday Evening Post* 202 (19 April 1930), 43–44.

———. "The Mexicanization of American Business." *Saturday Evening Post* 202 (8 February 1930), 46, 51, 178, 181–82.

———. "We Must Be On Our Guard." *Saturday Evening Post* 201 (5 January 1929), 29, 197–98, 201.

Garrett, Garet. "Government by Tumult." *Saturday Evening Post* 201 (16 March 1929), 14–15, 43–50.

Goethe, C. M. "Peons Need Not Apply." *World's Work* 59 (November 1930), 47–48.

Harrison, Gladys. "Enforcement of the Deportation Laws." *American Bar Association Journal* 18 (February 1932), 97–100.

Holmes, S. J. "Perils of Mexican Immigration." *North American Review* 227 (May 1929), 615–23.

Humphrey, Norman D. "Mexican Repatriation from Michigan: Public Assistance in Historical Perspective." *Social Service Review* 15 (September 1941), 497–513.

———. "The Migration and Settlement of Detroit Mexicans." *Economic Geography* 19 (October 1943), 358–61.

"Immigration and Unemployment." *Saturday Evening Post* 202 (19 April 1930), 32.

Jones, Anita Edgar. "Mexican Colonies in Chicago." *Social Service Review* 2 (December 1928), 579–97.

Klainer, Ruben. "Deportations of Aliens." *Boston University Law Review* 15 (November 1935), 722.

Lott, Virgil N. "Life in a Rugged Land Where Dame Nature Is Providing Dwellers with Their Necessity." *Lower Rio Grande Valley* (December 1924), 12–14.

Oxnam, Bromley G. "The Mexican in Los Angeles from the Standpoint of the Religious Forces of the City." *Annals of the American Academy* 93 (1921), 130–33.

Manuel, H. T. "The Mexican Child in Texas." *Southwest Review* 17 (April 1932), 290–302.

McLean, Robert N. "Goodbye Vicente." *Survey* 66 (1 May 1931), 182–83.

———. "Mexican Laborers in the United States." *Proceedings of the National Conference of Social Work* 56 (1929), 531–38.

———. "The Mexican Returns." *The Nation* 135 (24 August 1932), 165–66, 170–175.

"Mexican Exodus." *Newsweek* 14 (31 July 1939), 11.

"New Immigration Programs." *Saturday Evening Post* 202 (22 February 1930), 24.

"Present and Future." *Saturday Evening Post* 202 (15 March 1930), 28.

"The Repatriation of Destitute Aliens," *Interpretor Releases* 12 (23 May 1935), 1–14.

———. "The Docile Mexican." *Saturday Evening Post* 200 (10 March 1928), 39–41.

———. "Mexicans or Ruin." *Saturday Evening Post* 200 (18 February 1929), 14–15, 142, 145–46.

Roberts, Kenneth L. "Wet and Other Mexicans." *Saturday Evening Post* 200 (4 February 1928), 10–11, 137–38, 141–42, 146.

Sturges, Vera. "The Progress of Adjustment in Mexican and United States Life." *Proceedings of the National Conference of Social Welfare* (1920), 481–86.

———. "Mexican Immigrants." *Survey* 46 (2 July 1921), 470–71.

Taylor, Paul S. "Mexican Women in Los Angeles Industry in 1928." *Aztlán: International Journal of Chicano Studies Research* 11 (Spring 1980), 99–131.

Teague, Charles C. "A Statement on Mexican Immigration." *Saturday Evening Post* 200 (10 March 1928), 169–70.

Thomson, Charles A. "What of the Bracero? The Forgotten Alternative in Our Immigration Policy." *Survey* 54 (1 June 1925), 290–93.

Walker, Helen W. "Mexican Immigrants and American Citizenship." *Sociology and Social Research* 13 (May–June 1929), 466.

Doctoral Dissertations, Master's Theses, Pamphlets, and Unpublished Papers

Alanis Enciso, Fernando Saúl. *El gobierno de México y la repatriación de mexicanos de Estados Unidos, 1934–1940.* México D.F., Tesis para obtener el grado de Doctor en Historia, El Colegio de México, 2000.

Balderrama, Francisco E. "Unconstitutional Deportation and Coerced Emigration of U.S. Citizens of Mexican Descent During 1930s," Hispanic Bar Association, San Jose, California, 6 September 2003.

——— and Raymond Rodríguez. "Juan Reyna: Victim of Anti-Mexican Hysteria." Western History Association Conference, Los Angeles, California, 1987.

California Senate Select Committee on Citizen Participation Hearing, "Examination of Unconstitutional Deportation and Coerced Emigration of Legal Residents and U.S. Citizens of Mexican Descent During 1930s, Sacramento, California, 15 July 2003.

Carpenter, Charles C. "A Study of Segregation versus Non-Segregation of Mexican Children." Master's thesis, University of Southern California, 1935.

Castillo, Pedro J. "The Making of a Mexican Barrio: Los Angeles, 1890–1920." Ph.D. diss., University of California Santa Barbara, 1979.

"Coloquio Mexicanos en diáspora: los repatriados de 1939," *La gaceta de El Colegio de San Luis*, 6:12 (May–August), 1–5.

Crawford, Paul J. "Movie Habits and Attitudes of the Under-Privileged Boys of the All Nations Area in Los Angeles." Master's thesis, University of Southern California, 1934.

Cuauhtlatoatzin, Madrigal A. "A Spirit of Hope: In Honor of La Familia Madrigal, Los Repatriados."

Douglas, Helen W. "The Conflict of Cultures in First Generation Mexicans in Santa Ana, California." Master's thesis, University of Southern California, 1928.

Foster, Nellie. "The Corrido: A Mexican Culture Trait Persisting in Southern California." Master's thesis, University of Southern California, 1929.

García, Richard A. "The Making of the Mexican-American Mind, San Antonio, Texas, 1929–1941: A Social and Intellectual History of an Ethnic Community." Ph.D. diss., University of California, Irvine, 1980.

Gilbert, James C. "A Field Study in Mexico of the Mexican Repatriation Movement." Master's thesis, University of Southern California, 1934.

Guerin-Gonzales, Camille. "Cycles of Immigration and Repatriation: Mexican Farm Workers in California Industrial Agriculture, 1900–1940." Ph.D. diss., University of California, Riverside, 1985.

Hoffman, Abraham. "The Repatriation of Mexican Nationals from the United States during the Great Depression." Ph.D. diss., University of California, Los Angeles, 1970.

Jones, Anita Edgar. "Conditions Surrounding Mexicans in Chicago." Master's thesis, University of Chicago, 1928.

Kerr, Louise Año Nuevo. "The Chicano Experience in Chicago." Ph.D. diss., University of Illinois at Chicago Circle, 1976.

Laird, Judith Ann. "Argentine, Kansas: The Evolution of a Mexican American Community, 1905–1940." Ph.D. diss., University of Kansas, 1975.

Lanigan, Mary. "Second Generation Mexicans in Belvedere." Master's thesis, University of Southern California, 1932.

"Los Repatriados: Exiles from the Promised Land," Elena Herrada E-mail Message. 29 September 2004.

Lipshultz, Robert J. "American Attitudes toward Mexican Immigration, 1924–1952." Master's thesis, University of Chicago, 1962.

Martínez, Camilo Amado, Jr. "The Mexican and Mexican-American Laborers
    in the Lower Rio Grande Valley of Texas, 1870–1930." Ph.D. diss.,
    Texas A & M University, 1987.

McEuen, William W. "A Survey of Mexicans in Los Angeles." Master's thesis,
    University of Southern California, 1914.

McKay, Reynolds R. "Texas Mexican Repatriation during the Great Depression."
    Ph.D. diss., University of Oklahoma, 1982.

Miranda, Porfirio J. "Perceptions of Locus of Control Among Multigeneration
    Chicano/Mexican Families." Ph.D. diss., University of California, Los
    Angeles, 1978.

Monroy, Douglas Guy. "Mexicanos in Los Angeles, 1930–1941: An Ethnic
    Group in Relation to Class Forces." Ph.D. diss., University of California
    Los Angeles, 1978.

Newell, Virginia E. "The Social Significance of Padua Hills as a Cultural and
    Education Center." Master's thesis, University of Southern California, 1938.

Ortegón, Samuel. "The Religious Status of the Mexican Population of Los Angeles."
    Master's thesis, University of Southern California, 1932.

Peek, Rena Blanche. "The Religious and Social Attitudes of Mexican Girls of
    the Constituency of the All Nations Foundation in Los Angeles."
    Master's thesis, University of Southern California, 1929.

Piñeda, Albino R. "The Repatriated: Autobiography of a Mexican-American."
    Unpublished Manuscript, Courtesy of Albino R. Piñeda.

Program for "Betrayal and Violations: Mexican Repatriation of the 1930s"
    Los Angeles Times Center, Costa Mesa, California, 24 September 2004.

Reccow, Louis. "The Orange County Citrus Strikes of 1935–1936: The 'Forgotten
    People' in Revolt." Ph.D. diss., University of Southern California, 1975.

Resolutions at California Federation of Teachers, AFT, AFL-CIO, Universal City,
    19–21 March 2004.

Resolutions at LCLAA: Labor Council for Latin American Advancement,
    AFL-CIO, Santa Pueblo, New Mexico, 25–29 August 2004.

Resolutions at National Convention of American GI Forum, Frankenmuth,
    Michigan, 2004.

Rutter, Larry G. "Mexican Americans in Kansas: A Survey and Social Mobility
    Study, 1900–1970." Master's thesis, Kansas State University, 1972.

Saint, Marjorie Walker. "Woven within My Grandmother's Braid: The Biography
    of a Mexican Immigrant Woman." Senior thesis, University of California,
    Santa Cruz, 1991.

Sánchez, George. "Becoming Mexican-American: Ethnicity and Acculturation in
    Chicano Los Angeles, 1900–1940." Ph.D. diss., Stanford University, 1989.

Sepulveda, Ciro. "La Colonia del Harbor: History of Mexicanos in East Chicago, Indiana, 1919–1932." Ph.D. diss., University of Notre Dame, 1976.

Smith, Clara Gertrude. "The Development of the Mexican People in the Community of Watts." Master's thesis, University of Southern California, 1933.

Walker, Helen. "The Conflict of Cultures in First Generation Mexicans in Santa Ana, California." Master's thesis, University of Southern California, 1928.

Secondary Sources

Films and Television

"America Tropical." 30 minutes, Los Angeles, Jesus Trevino Film, 1971.

"Ballad of an Unsung Hero." 30 Minutes, San Diego: Cinewest, KPBS, 1983.

"Break of Dawn." 100 minutes, San Diego: Cinewest, KPBS, 1989.

"Decade of Betrayal Forum." 60 minutes. Concordia University, Irvine, California, 13 November 2002.

"Hero Street USA" Silvus, Illinois, 28 Minutes, Innervision Studies, 1984.

"The Lemon Grove Incident." 60 minutes, San Diego, KPBS, 1987.

"This Week in Garden Grove" Television Program "Community Forum: Mexican Deportations," Orange, California, Channel 3, 22 July 2003.

"Unconstitutional Deportation and Coerced Emigration" Town Hall Meeting, Our Lady Queen of the Angels Church, La Placita, Los Angeles, California, Channel 34/ Channel 52, 13 September 2003.

Books

Acuña, Rudolfo. *Occupied America: A History of Chicanos*. Fifth Edition. New York: Pearsons & Longman, 2004.

Alanis Enciso, Fernando Saúl. *El valle del Río Bravo, Tamaulipas, en la décade de 1930*. Ciudad Victoria, Tamaulipas: El Colegio de Tamaulipas-El Colegio de San Luis, 2003.

Alvarez, Robert R., Jr. *Familia: Migration and Adaptation in Baja and Alta California, 1800–1975*. Berkeley: University of California Press, 1987.

Bailey, David C. *Viva Cristo Rey: The Cristero Rebellion and the Church-State Conflict in Mexico*. Austin: University of Texas Press, 1978.

Balderrama, Francisco E. *In Defense of La Raza: The Los Angeles Mexican Consulate and the Mexican Community, 1929–1936*. Tucson: University of Arizona Press, 1982.

Bayitch, S. A., and José Luis Siqueiros. *Conflict of Laws: Mexico and the United States, A Bilateral Study*. Coral Gables, Fla.: University of Miami Press, 1968.

Beteta, Ramón. *Pensamiento y Dinamica de la Revolución Mexicana: Antologia de Documentos Politicosociales*. México, D.F.: Editorial México Nuevo, 1950.

Blackwelder, Julia Kirk. *Women of the Depression: Caste and Culture in San Antonio, 1929–1939*. College Station: Texas A & M Press, 1984.

Byrkit, James W. *Forging the Copper Collar: Arizona's Labor Management War, 1901–1921*. Tucson: University of Arizona Press, 1982.

Camarillo, Albert. *Chicanos in California: A History of Mexican Americans in California*. San Francisco: Boyd and Fraser, 1984.

———. *Chicanos in a Changing Society: From Mexican Pueblos to American Barrios in Santa Barbara and Southern California, 1848–1930*. Cambridge, Mass.: Harvard University Press, 1979.

Camp, Roderic A. *Mexican Political Biographies, 1935–1975*. Tucson: University of Arizona Press, 1978.

Cardoso, Lawrence A. *Mexican Emigration to the United States, 1897–1931: Socio-Economic Patterns*. Tucson: University of Arizona Press, 1980.

Carreras de Velasco, Mercedes. *Los Mexicanos que devolvió la crisis, 1929–1932*. México, D.F.: Secretaría de Relaciones Exteriores, 1974.

Cockcroft, James D. *Intellectual Precursors of the Mexican Revolution, 1900–1913*. Austin: University of Texas Press, 1968.

Corwin, Arthur F. *Immigrants—and Immigrants: Perspectives on Mexican Labor Migration to the United States*. Westport, Conn.: Greenwood Press, 1978.

Cosío Villegas, Daniel, ed. *Historia moderna de México*. México, D.F.: Editorial Hermes, ed. 1962–1972.

Craig, Ann L. *The First Agraristas: An Oral History of a Mexican Agrarian Reform Movement*. Berkeley: University of California Press, 1983.

d'Olwer, Luis Nicolau. *El Porfiriato: La Vida Económica*. Vol. 7 of Cosío Villegas, ed. *Historia moderna de México*. México, D.F.: Editorial Hermes, 1965.

Dulles, John W. F. *Yesterday in Mexico: A Chronicle of the Revolution, 1919–1936*. Austin: University of Texas Press, 1961.

Fagen, Patricia W. *Exiles and Citizens: Spanish Republicans in Mexico*. Austin: University of Texas Press, 1973.

Galarza, Ernesto. *Barrio Boy: The Story of a Boy's Acculturation*. Notre Dame, Ind.: University of Notre Dame Press, 1971.

García, Mario T. *Desert Immigrants: The Mexicans of El Paso, 1880–1920*. New Haven, Conn.: Yale University Press, 1981.

Garcia, Matt. *A World of Its Own: Race, Labor, and Citrus in the Making of Greater Los Angeles, 1900–1970*. Chapel Hill: University of North Carolina Press, 2001.

García, Richard A. *Rise of the Mexican American Middle Class: San Antonio, 1929–1941*. College Station, Texas: Texas A&M University Press, 1991.

Gómez-Quiñones, Juan. *Sembradores: Ricardo Flores Magón y El Partido Liberal Mexicano, A Eulogy and Critique*. Los Angeles: Aztlán Publications, University of California Press, 1971.

Gonzales, Gilbert. *Chicano Education in the Era of Segregation*. Philadelphia: Balch Institute Press, 1990.

_____. *Labor and Community: Mexican Citrus Worker Villages in a Southern California Country, 1900–1950*. Urbana: University of Illinois Press, 1994.

———. *La Familia: Chicano Families in the Urban Southwest, 1848 to the Present*. Notre Dame, Ind.: University of Notre Dame Press, 1984.

Griswold del Castillo, Richard. *The Los Angeles Barrio, 1850–1890: A Social History*. Berkeley: University of California Press, 1979.

Guerin-Gonzales, Camille. *Mexican Workers and the American Dream: Immigration, Repatriation, and California Farm Labor, 1900–1939*. New Brunswick, N.J.: Rutgers University Press, 1994.

Hall, Linda B. *Alvaro Obregón: Power and Revolution in Mexico, 1911–1920*. College Station: Texas A & M University Press, 1981.

Hart, John Mason. *Revolutionary Mexico: The Coming and Process of the Mexican Revolution*. Berkeley: University of California Press, 1987.

———. *An Oklahoma Tragedy: The Shooting of the Mexican Students, 1931*. El Paso: Texas Western Press, 1987.

Hoffman, Abraham. *Unwanted Mexican Americans in the Great Depression: Repatriation Pressures, 1929–1939*. Tucson: University of Arizona Press, 1974.

Kansas, Sidney. *United States Immigration, Exclusion, and Deportation*. New York: Matthew Bender Co., 1948.

Knight, Alan. *The Mexican Revolution*. Cambridge, Great Britain: Cambridge University Press, 1986.

Lee, Anthony W. *Painting on the Left: Diego Rivera, Radical Politics, and San Francisco Public Murals*. Berkeley: University of California Press, 1999.

Lister, Florence C. and Robert H. Lister. *Chihuahua: Storehouse of Storms*. Albuquerque: University of New Mexico Press, 1960.

Martínez, John A. *Mexican Emigration to the United States, 1910–1930*. San Francisco: R and E Research Associates, 1972.

MacLachlan, Colin M. and William H. Beezley. *El Gran Pueblo: A History of Greater Mexico.* Englewood Cliffs, N.J.: Prentice Hall, 1994.

McBride, George. *The Land Systems of Mexico.* New York: American Geographical Society, 1923.

McWilliams, Carey. *Factories in the Field: The Story of Migratory Farm Labor in California.* Boston: Little, Brown, and Company, 1939.

———. with Matt S. Meier. *North from Mexico: The Spanish-Speaking People of the United States.* New York: Greenwood Press, 1948; repr. 1990.

Meier, Matt S., and Feliciano Rivera, eds. *Readings on La Raza: The Twentieth Century.* New York: Hill and Wang, 1974.

Menefee, Seldon, and C. C. Cassmore. *The Pecan Shellers of San Antonio.* Washington, D.C.: Government Printing Office, 1940.

Meyer, Jean A. *The Cristero Rebellion,* trans. Richard Southern. New York and London: Cambridge University Press, 1976.

Meyer, Michael C., and William L. Sherman. *The Course of Mexican History.* New York: Oxford University Press, 1987.

Mirandé, Alfredo, and Evangelina Enríquez. *La Chicana: The Mexican-American Women.* Chicago: University of Chicago Press, 1979.

Molina, Cecilia. *Prática consular mexicano.* México, D.F.: Editorial Porrúa, 1970.

Monroy, Douglas. *Rebirth: Mexican Los Angeles From the Great Migration to the Great Depression.* Berkeley: University of California Press, 1999.

Morín, Raul. *Among the Valiant: Mexican Americans in World War II and Korea.* Alhambra, Calif.: Borden Publishing Company, 1966.

Nava, Julian. *My Mexican-American Journey.* Houston: Arte Público Press, 2002.

Paredes, Américo. *A Texas-Mexican Cancionero: Folksongs of the Lower Border.* Urbana: University of Illinois Press, 1976.

Peyton, Green. *San Antonio: City in the Sun.* New York: McGraw and Hill, 1946.

Powell, T. G. *Mexico and the Spanish Civil War.* Albuquerque: University of New Mexico Press, 1981.

Reisler, Mark. *By the Sweat of Their Brow: Mexican Immigrant Labor in the United States, 1900–1940.* Westport, Conn: Greenwood Press, 1976.

Robinson, W. W. *Los Angeles from the Days of the Pueblo: A Brief History and Guide to the Plaza Area.* San Francisco: California Historical Society, 1959.

Romo, Ricardo. *East Los Angeles: History of a Barrio.* Austin: University of Texas Press, 1983.

Rosales, F. Arturo. *Pobre Raza!: Violence, Justice, and Mobilization Among México Lindo Immigrants, 1900–1936.* Austin: University of Texas Press, 1999.

Ruiz, Ramón Eduardo. *The Great Rebellion: Mexico, 1905–1924*. New York: W. W. Norton, 1980.

_____. *Memories of a Hyphenated Man*. Tucson: University of Arizona Press, 2003.

———. *Mexico: The Challenge of Poverty and Illiteracy*. San Marino, Calif.: The Huntington Library, 1963.

Ruiz, Vicki L. *Cannery Women/Cannery Lives: Mexican Women, Unionization, and the California Food Processing Industry, 1930–1950*. Albuquerque: University of New Mexico Press, 1987.

_____. *From Out of the Shadows: Mexican Women in Twentieth Century America*. New York: Oxford University Press, 1998.

Sánchez, George. *Becoming Mexican American: Ethnicity, Culture, and Identity in Chicano Los Angeles, 1900–1945*. New York: Oxford University Press, 1993.

Sheridan, Thomas E. *Los Tucsonenses: The Mexican Community in Tucson, 1854–1941*. Tucson: University of Arizona Press, 1986.

Tamayo, Jorge. *Geografía de México*. México, D.F.: Talleres Gráficos de la Nación, 1949.

Váldes, Dennis Nodín. *Al Norte: Agricultural Workers in the Great Lakes Region, 1917–1970*. Austin: University of Texas Press, 1991.

———. *El Pueblo Mexicano en Detroit y Michigan: A Social History*. Detroit: McNaughton-Gunn, 1982.

Vargas, Zaragosa. *Proletarians of the North: A History of Mexican Industrial Workers in Detroit and the Midwest*. Berkeley: University of California Press, 1993.

Wasserman, Mark. *Capitalists, Caciques, and Revolution: The Native Elite and Foreign Enterprise in Chihuahua, Mexico, 1854–1911*. Chapel Hill: University of North Carolina Press, 1984.

Wilkie, James W. *The Mexican Revolution: Federal Expenditure and Social Change since 1910*. Berkeley: University of California, 1970.

———, and Edna Monzón de Wilkie. *México Visto en el Siglo XX: Entrevistas de historia oral*. México, D.F.: Instituto de Investigaciones Económicas, 1969.

Wollenberg, Charles P. *All Deliberate Speed: School Segregation and Exclusion In California Schools, 1855–1975*. Berkeley: University of California Press, 1976.

Woods, Frances J. *Mexican American Ethnic Leadership in San Antonio, Texas*. Washington, D.C.: The Catholic University of America Press, 1949.

Zorrilla, Luis G. *Historia de las relaciones entre México y los Estados Unidos Americanos, 1800–1958*. México, D.F.: Editorial Porrúa, S.A., 1966.

Articles

Batten, Neil and Raymond A. Mohl. "From Discrimination to Repatriation: Mexican Life in Gary, Indiana during the Great Depression." In Norris C. Hundley, Jr., ed., *The Chicano: Essays from the Pacific Historical Review.* Santa Barbara, Calif.: American Bibliographical Center, 1975.

Chacón, Ramón D. "The Chicano Immigrant Press in Los Angeles: The Case of El Heraldo de México, 1916–1920." *Journalism History* 4 (Summer 1977), 48–50, 62–64.

Cortés, Enrique. "Mexican Colonies during the Porfiriato." *Aztlán: International Journal of Chicano Studies Research* 10 (Summer–Fall 1979), 1–14.

Daronatsy, Art. "Forced Exodus." In James B. Lane, ed., *Steel Shavings: Latinos in the Calumet Region.* 13, 1987, 6.

Dinwoodie, D. H. "Deportation: The Immigration Service and the Chicano Labor Movement in the 1930s." *New Mexico Historical Review* 52, 3 (Summer 1977), 193–203.

Durón, Clementina. "Mexican Women and Labor Conflict in Los Angeles: The ILGWU Dressmakers Strike of 1933." *Aztlán: International Journal of Chicano Studies Research* 15, 1 (Spring 1984), 161.

García, Juan R. "Midwest Mexicanos in the 1920s: Issues, Questions, and Directions." *Social Science Journal* 19, 2 (1982), 89–99.

García, Mario T. "Americanization and the Mexican Immigrant, 1880–1930." *Journal of Ethnic Studies* 6, 2 (1978), 19–34.

———. "Mexican Americans and the Politics of Citizenship: the Case of El Paso, 1936." *New Mexico Historical Review* 5, 2 (1984), 187–204.

———. "On Mexican Immigration, the United States and Chicano History." *Journal of Ethnic Studies* 7, 1 (1979), 80–88.

García, Richard A. "Class, Consciousness and Ideology–The Mexican American Community of San Antonio, Texas: 1930–1940." *Aztlán: International Journal of Chicano Studies Research* 9 (Fall 1978), 23–69.

González, Gilbert. "Racism, Education, and the Mexican Community in Los Angeles, 1920–1930." *Societas* 4 (Fall 1974), 287–301.

González, Rosalinda M. "Chicanas and Mexican Immigrant Families, 1920–1940: Women's Subordination and Family Exploitation." In *Decades of Discontent: The Women's Movement, 1920–1940.* Westport, Conn.: Greenwood Press, 1983.

González Navarro, Moises. "Efectos sociales de la crisis de 1929." *Historia Mexicana* (April–June 1970), 536–58.

Griswold del Castillo, Richard. "The Mexican Problem: A Critical View of the Alliance of Academics and Politicians during the Debate over Mexican Immigration in the 1920's." *The Borderlands Journal* 4, 2 (Spring 1981), 241–51.

Guzmán, Ralph. "La repatriación forzosa como solucíon política concluyente al problema de la inmigración ilegal: una perspectiva histórica." *Foro Internacional* 18, 3 (1978), 494–513.

Hendrick, Irving G. "Early Schooling for Children of Migrant Farmworkers in California: The 1920s." *Aztlán: International Journal of Chicano Studies Research* 8 (Spring–Summer 1977), 11–26.

Hoffman, Abraham. "El cierre de la puerta trasera norteamericana: restricción de la inmigración Mexicana." *Historia Mexicana* 25, 3 (1976), 302–422.

———. "The Federal Bureaucracy Meets a Superior Spokesman for Alien Deportation." *Journal of the West* 14, 4 (October 1975), 91–106.

———. "A Note on the Field Research Interviews of Paul S. Taylor." *Pacific Historian* 20:2 (1976), 123–31.

———. "Mexican Repatriation Statistics: Some Suggested Alternatives to Carey McWilliams." *Western Historical Quarterly* 3, 4 (October 1972), 391–404.

———. "Stimulus to Repatriation: The 1931 Federal Deportation Drive and the Los Angeles Mexican Community." *Pacific Historical Review* 42, 2 (May 1973), 205–19.

———. "The El Monte Berry Strike: International Involvement in a Local Labor Dispute." *Journal of the West* 12 (January 1973), 71–84.

Kerr, Louise A. "Chicano Settlements in Chicago: A Brief History." *Journal Of Ethnic Studies* 2, 4 (1975), 22–32.

Kiser, George, and David Silverman. "Mexican Repatriation during the Great Depression." *Journal of Mexican American History* 3, 1 (1973), 139–64.

Krause, Ruth Ann. "V. F. Garza,". In James B. Lane, ed., *Steel Shavings: Latinos in the Calumet Region* 13, 1987.

Levenstein, Harvey A. "The AFL and Mexican Immigration in the 1920s: An Experiment in Labor Diplomacy." *Hispanic American Historical Review* 48 (May 1968), 206–20.

López, Ron W. "The El Monte Berry Strike of 1933." *Aztlán–Chicano Journal of the Social Sciences and Arts* 1 (Spring 1970), 101–14.

Medeiros, Francine. "La Opinión, A Mexican Exile Newspaper: A Content Analysis of its First Years, 1926–1929." *Aztlán: International Journal of Chicano Studies Research* 11 (Spring 1980), 65–87.

McKay, Reynolds R. "The Federal Deportation Campaign in Texas: Mexican Deportation from the Lower Rio Grande Valley during the Great Depression." *The Borderlands Journal* 5, 1 (Fall 1981), 90–120.

Miranda, Gloria E. "The Mexican Immigrant Family: Economic and Cultural Survival in Los Angeles, 1900–1945" in Norman M. Klein and Martin J. Schiesl, eds., *Twentieth Century Los Angeles: Power, Promotion, and Social Conflict.* 39–60 Claremont, Calif.: Regina Books, 1990.

Mohl, Raymond A. "The Saturday Evening Post and the 'Mexican Invasion.'" *Journal of Mexican American History* 3, 1 (1973), 131–38.

Mohl, Raymond A., and Neil Batten. "Discrimination and Repatriation: Mexican Life in Gary" in Edward Escobar and Henry Lang, eds., *Forging a Community: Latinos in Northwest Indiana, 1919–1975.* 161–83 Chicago: Cattails Press, 1987.

Monroy, Douglas. "La Costura en Los Angeles, 1933–1939: The ILGWU and the Politics of Domination" in Magdalena Mora and Adelaida R. Del Castillo, eds., *Mexican Women in the United States: Struggles Past and Present,* 171–78. Los Angeles: University of California Los Angeles Chicano Studies Research Center, 1980.

Norrick, Ruth Frances. "My Huesta: An Interview with Pilar," in James B. Lane, ed., *Steel Shavings: Latinos in the Calumet Region,* 1–5. 13, 1987.

Oppenheimer, Robert. "Acculturation or Assimilation: Mexican Immigrants in Kansas, 1900 to World War II." *Western Historical Quarterly* 16 (October 1985), 429–48.

Pintó, Alfonso. "When Hollywood Spoke Spanish." *Américas* 32, 10 (1980), 3–8.

Redwine, Augustín. "Lovell's Mexican Colony." *Annals of Wyoming* 51, 2 (1979), 26–35.

Reisler, Mark. "Always the Laborer, Never the Citizen: Anglo Perceptions of the Mexican Immigrant during the 1920s." *Pacific Historical Review* 45, 2 (1976), 231–54.

———. "The Mexican Immigrant in the Chicago Area during the 1920s." *Journal of the Illinois State Historical Society* 66, 2 (1973), 144–58.

Rodríguez, Raymond. "Mexicans Go Home." *Southland Sunday Magazine,* in *Independent, Press-Telegram* (14 October 1974), 8–14.

Romo, Ricardo. "Responses to Mexican Immigration, 1910–1930." *Aztlán: International Journal of Chicano Studies Research* 6 (Summer 1975), 173–94.

———. "Work and Restlessness: Occupational and Spatial Mobility among Mexicanos in Los Angeles, 1918–1928." *Pacific Historical Review* 46 (May 1977), 157–80.

———. "The Urbanization of Southwestern Chicanos in the Early 20th Century." *New Scholar* 6 (1977), 183–207.

Rosales, Francisco A., and Daniel T. Simon. "Chicano Steel Workers and Unionism in the Midwest, 1919–1945." *Aztlán: International Journal of Chicano Studies* 6, 2 (1976), 267–75.

———. "The Regional Origins of Mexicano Immigrants to Chicago during the 1920s." *Aztlán: International Journal of Chicano Studies* 7, 2 (1976), 187–201.

———. "Shifting Self Perceptions and Ethnic Consciousness among Mexicans in Houston, 1908–1946." *Aztlán: International Journal of Chicano Studies Research* 16:1–2 (1985), 71–94.

Ruiz, Vicki L. "'Star Struck': Acculturation, Adolescence, and the Mexican American Woman, 1920–1950." In Adela de La Torre and Beatríz M. Pesquera, eds., *Building with Our Own Hands: New Directions in Chicana Studies.* Berkeley: University of California Press, 1993.

San Miguel, Guadalupe, Jr. "The Struggle against Separate and Unequal Schools: Middle Class Mexican Americans and the Desegregation Campaign in Texas, 1929–1957." *History of Education Quarterly* 23, 3 (1983), 343–59.

Sepulveda, Ciro. "Una Colonia de Obreros: East Chicago, Indiana." *Aztlán: International Journal of Chicano Studies Research* 7, 2 (1976), 327–36.

Servín, Manuel P. "The Pre-World War II Mexican-American: An Interpretation." *California Historical Society Quarterly* 45 (1955), 325–38.

Shankman, Arnold. "The Image of Mexico and the Mexican American in the Black Press, 1890–1935." *Journal of Ethnic Studies* 3. 2 (1975), 43–56.

Sifuentes, Roberto. "Aproximaciones al Corrido de los hermanos Hernández ejecutados en la cámara de gas de la penitenciaria de Florence, Arizona el día 6 de Julio de 1934." *Aztlán: International Journal of Chicano Studies* 13, 1–2 (1982), 95–109.

Simon, Daniel T. "Mexican Repatriation in East Chicago." *Journal of Ethnic Studies* 2, 2 (1974), 11–23.

Skirus, John. "Vasconcelos and México de Afuera (1928)." *Aztlán: International Journal of Chicano Studies Research* 7, 3 (Fall 1976), 479–97.

Smith, Michael. "Beyond the Borderlands: Mexican Labor in the Central Plains, 1900–1930." *Great Plains Quarterly* 1, 4 (1981), 239–51.

———. "The Mexican Immigrant Press beyond the Borderlands: The Case of *El Cosmopolita,* 1914–1919." *Great Plains Quarterly* 10, 2 (Spring 1990), 71–85.

———. "Mexicans in Kansas City: The First Generation." *Perspectives in Mexican American Studies* 2 (1989), 29–57.

Stefano, Onofre di. "'Venimos a Luchar': A Brief History of La Prensa's Founding." *Aztlán: International Journal of Chicano Studies* 16, 1–2 (1985), 55–118.

Valdés, Dennis Nodín. "Perspiring Capitalists: Latinos and the Henry Ford Service School, 1918–1928." *Aztlán: International Journal of Chicano Studies Research* 12, 2 (Fall 1981), 227–39.

———. "Mexican Revolutionary Nationalism and Repatriation during the Great Depression." *Mexican Studies/Estudios Mexicanos* 4, 1 (Winter 1988), 1–23.

———. "Settlers, Sojourners, and Proletarians: Social Formation in the Great
Plains Sugar Beet Industry, 1890–1940." *Great Plains Quarterly* 10, 2
(Spring 1990), 110–23.

Weber, Devra Anne. "The Organizing of Mexicano Agricultural Workers in the
Imperial Valley and Los Angeles, 1928–1934, An Oral History Approach."
Aztlán: Chicano Journal of the Social Sciences and Arts 3 (Fall 1972), 307–43.

———. "Raíz Fuerte: Oral History and Mexicana Farmworkers." In Vicki L. Ruiz
and Ellen Carol Dubois, eds., *Unequal Sisters: A Multicultural Reader in
U.S. Women's History*, 2nd ed. New York: Routledge Press, 1994.

Wild, H. Mark. "If You Ain't Got That Do-Re-Mi: The Los Angeles Border Patrol
and White Migrations in Depression-Era California," *Southern California
Quarterly* 83, 3 (Fall 2001), 317–34.

Wilkie, James W. "The Meaning of the Cristero Religious War against the Mexican
Revolution." *Journal of Church and State* 8 (Spring 1966), 214–33.

Wollenberg, Charles. "Race and Class in Rural California: The El Monte Berry
Strike of 1933." *California Historical Quarterly* 51 (Summer 1972), 155–64.

Index

Page numbers in **bold type** indicate photographs.